Maarten Maartens

My Lady Nobody

A Novel

Maarten Maartens

My Lady Nobody
A Novel

ISBN/EAN: 9783337029548

Printed in Europe, USA, Canada, Australia, Japan

Cover: Foto ©Thomas Meinert / pixelio.de

More available books at **www.hansebooks.com**

MY LADY NOBODY

A Novel

BY

MAARTEN MAARTENS

ILLUSTRATED

NEW YORK

HARPER & BROTHERS PUBLISHERS

1895

Dedication

GOD'S Angel of Human Love sat alone in the garden of lilies. Her arms hung listless among the blooms she had gathered into her lap. For her eyes— sole mirrors of the Inapproachable Presence—were gazing steadfastly down upon the darkness, deep down where the black bar of sorrow strikes across the wide radiance of eternity, down on the sin-laden star that still hastens athwart the shadow. A single teardrop stole out upon her cheek, and, falling, crept away into a milk-white chalice. Suddenly, with a movement of ineffable pity, she flung forth all the flowers upon her lap, into the world below.

Into my bosom, O Beloved, is fallen the flower with the tear at its heart. Unto thee, O fair among God's flowers, white among his angels, strong among his saints, unto thee, with the thorn in thy side, and the star on thy forehead, unto thee do I dedicate this ray from a life of which thou art the light.

CONTENTS

Part I

Part II

Part III

ILLUSTRATIONS

MY LADY NOBODY

URSULA

It was a white-hot July morning. Long ago the impatient
earth had cast aside her thin veil of summer twilight; already
she lay, a Danae, in exultant swoon beneath the golden sun.
Yet the bridegroom had barely leaped forth to the conquest;
his rath kisses were still drinking the pearly freshness from the
dawn, while the loud birds filled the resonant heavens with the
tumult of their bridal song.

It was still so early, and already so .immovably warm; all
wide earth and deep sky agasp in the naked blaze. Ursula
drew forward her broad-brimmed straw hat, where she stood
picking pease among the tall lines of pale-green, blossom-speck-
led tangle.

"Oof!" she said. Not as your burly farmer says it, but with
the prettiest little high-pitched echo of the louder note. And
she buried her soft brown cheeks in the cool moisture of her
half-filled basket. Then she gravely resumed her work, and a
great, big, booming bumblebee, which had thought to play hide
and seek with Ursula's nose, sailed away in disgust that on
such a sun-soaked morning any of God's creatures should bend
to toil in his sight.

Ursula Rovers was not one of those who serve their Maker
with dancing and a shout. Yet she sang to herself, very sedate-
ly, as she broke off each bursting pod, amid the fiercer jubilation of the passion-drunk blackbirds and finches,

1

"Stand then with girded loins, and see your lamps be burning;
   What though the sun lie fair upon your paths to-day,
Who reads the evening sky? Who knows if winds be turning?
   The night comes surely. Watch and pray!"

The prim vegetable garden, with its ranks of gay salads
and pompous cabbages, lay serenely roasting, as vegetable gardens delight to do, in unabated verdure. About Ursula's corner
the lattice-work of creepers put forth some faint attempt at a
stunted shadow. Dominé Rovers came down the walk, his
coat-flaps brushing the currant-bushes.

"Who reads the evening sky? Who knows if winds be turning?"

"Ursula!"

"Yes, Captain."

"Come in and shell your pease, while I recite you my sermon."

"But I must pick them first, father!"

"True. What I love best in you, Ursula, is that you are as
logical as if you were not a woman."

The pastor drew nearer to the scaffolding of greenery, and
strove vainly to shelter his tall figure in its shade. He was a
spare, soldierly-looking man, with an honest complexion and
silvery hair. You knew he had a very gentle countenance until
you gave him cause to turn a wrathful look upon you.

"I might as well begin at once," he said, and, proud though
she was of her father's preaching, the girl's soul rose in momentary protest on behalf of the birds and flowers. "I have
chosen a text for to-morrow, Ursula, which has troubled my
thoughts all through the week. All through the week, I
couldn't understand it. And when I came to look it out, it
wasn't there at all."

Ursula's dutiful lips said, "I see."

"I imagined the verse to be as follows: "Flee from youthful lusts that war against the soul." But I see the word used
is 'Abstain.' I could not believe it of St. Peter that he
would have instructed any man to run away in battle. You
will find the 'flee' in Timothy, my dear, but the connection is
not the same."

Dominé Rovers paused and stood tenderly watching his natty daughter in her cool print dress. Suddenly he burst out quite impetuously, "Resist! Resist! That is the true Bible language. Resist the devil. Resist temptation. And so I shall tell them to-morrow morning. 'Dearly beloved,' I shall say, ' life is a—' "

" War," cried Ursula, facing round. A bold blackbird had alighted on one of the stakes, and sang loudly of peace and good-will.

" Don't interrupt me, child "—the Dominé's eyes grew vexed —" I know I have said it before ; they cannot hear the truth too often. Life is a battle, dearly beloved. Against the city of Mansoul all the powers of evil band themselves together. But in the vanguard march ever the lusts of the flesh. You cannot escape the conflict. And therefore "—the speaker lifted an energetic arm—" remember what said the Corinthians —the grandsires of St. Paul's Corinthians—to the Spartans, their allies, ' He that, for love of pleasure, shrinks from battle, will most swiftly be deprived of those very delights which caused him to abstain.' My subject divides itself—Ursula, you are not attending—into seven natural parts : the enemy, the weapons, the—"

Nobody listened. All God's creation, busy with its individual loves and pleasures, luxuriously lapped in the sensuous sunlight and rejoicing in universal allreument, was twittering and fluttering and blushing and blooming in clouds of perfume and pollen. The great All-father smiled down upon his manifold children—and shrivelled them up.

Ursula was not listening. Her father was a dear, dear man, but she had heard it all so often before ! And fortune had pity upon her and upon the sleepily staring marigolds, and created a diversion ere the sermon was ten sentences old.

Shrill shrieks of childish protest under punishment arose from beyond the garden-wall. The pastor of an unruly flock immediately ran to peer over the bushes. And Ursula followed more slowly, flitting into the full morning glow.

Out on the gleaming high-road a peasant-woman was belaboring an eight-year-old urchin in a whirlwind of dust. " I'll teach you to use bad words," she was screaming. "Damn me, I can't make out, for the life o' me, what taught the child to swear!"

Ursula, leaning one round arm on the top of the garden-wall, turned spontaneously to her father, all her serious young face a swift ripple of fun; but the Dominé counted not a pennyworth of humor among his many militant virtues. He pressed his thin lips tight, under his Wellington nose. He was not going to reprove a mother in the presence of her son.

"Discipline first," said the Dominé. "One thing I note gratefully, Ursula, that the wretched habit of swearing is now confined to the lower classes in this country. In my time even gentlemen would swear—"

A dog-cart had turned the sharp angle at the back, where the road breaks off to the Manor-house. In the dust and the skirmish it pulled up with a jerk, and a clear voice was heard crying,

"Confound you! Get out of the way, can't you? Scuffling in the middle of the road!"

The dog-cart was a very smart dog-cart, and the mare was a high-stepping mare. She fretted under the sudden restraint, amid an appetizing jingle and smell and glitter of harness. There was not so much promiscuous dust but that the speaker could instantaneously perceive the two heads over the low brown wall.

He lifted his cap. "Good-morning, Dominé! Good-morning, Ursula!" he said, with nonchalance. "Awfully hot already, isn't it?"

The Dominé raised a flashing eye. The woman and boy had slipped away. "Gerard," said the Dominé, "why do you swear at our people? How often must I remind you of our joint responsibility? We must lead them to what is right; I by my precept, you by your example."

"Oh, Dominé, I'll exchange, if you're agreeable," retorted the young man, with a quick smile. The Dominé looked away.

"You are going to the station to fetch your brother, Gerard?" interposed Ursula, carelessly cracking the pods in her basket.

" ' CONFOUND YOU ! GET OUT OF THE WAY, CAN'T YOU ?' "

" Yes, at your service," replied the young man, as he loosened the reins.

" How strange it will be for you to meet Mynheer Otto again after all these years!"

Gerard turned quickly from his prancing steed. " Are you going to call Otto ' Mynheer ' ?" he asked.

She blushed with annoyance, in an overflow of innocent confusion.

" Oh, very well," he went on. " Only, of course, you will have to call me Mynheer Gerard."

He raced off, laughing. " I *know* you," she stammered ; but the words were lost in the dog-cart's departing rattle. She appealed to her father in dismay. " Why, father," she cried, " I have known Gerard all my life !"

Together they stood watching the dust-enfolded vehicle disappear into the far blue sunshine. Its occupant was young, light-hearted, and handsome. Evidently a cavalry officer : you could see that by the way in which his tweeds and he conjoined without combining.

"LET us go in to breakfast," said the Dominé. Father and daughter passed up between the stiff stalks of the gooseberry-bushes, among the sallow, swollen fruit. Both of them walked with a straight step, the figure erect, and a little self-reliant.

The pastor fell back a few paces with meditative gaze. He was wont to rejoice tremulously in Ursula's physical health, in the easy carriage of the head, the light swing of the hips. He rejoiced in the clear brown of her complexion and the calm depth of her brave brown eyes. No weak woman in blood or brain, this stately, strong-limbed maiden. He thanked God mournfully, ever reminiscent of the pervading sorrow of his life, the loss of the frail young creature who had dropped by the road-side wellnigh twenty years ago.

It was that affliction which had made a cleric of Captain Roderick Rovers. By nature he was a soldier, recklessly brave and almost devil-may-care. A man who thought straight, if not far, and struck straight in the front. He had escaped from the inertia of the long Batavian peace to the red-hot tumult of Algerian desert war, and had come back, early bronzed and silvered, *plus* the Legion of Honor and *minus* an arm. He had married a pure white clinging thing, like a lily, that twined every tendril round his sturdy support, and then dropped from the stem. She was a good woman. To him she had come as a revelation. "I have fought the good fight," she had whispered in dying. He, with the medals on his breast and the memory of not a few killed and wounded—could he have said as much face to face with death?

He began to comprehend something of that battle which is

not to the strong. On their wedding-day the bride had given her soldier-husband Bunyan's *Holy War* — a Dutch translation—substituting it on his table for the weather-beaten little Thucydides which had been his companion in all his campaigns. He had demanded back the Greek historian. He now took up the spiritual conflict, and fought the powers of darkness, as he had ever met an enemy, at arm's-length.

His mutilation having incapacitated him from active service, he took orders, henceforth to do battle with his country's inmost foes in the heart of every parishioner. The old militant spirit flamed in him still, and he led his slow flock like a regiment under the banner of the great Captain. On the high days of the Church he wore his Cross of the Legion in the pulpit. His clerical superiors had objected : he dared them to object. It was gained, he said, like their reverend titles, in honorable war.

He had cherished the solitary treasure of his heart, but his care had been free from coddling ; he had even combated the enervating influence of his sister-in-law, who kept house for him. " Coolness and cold water " was one of his maxims in any sudden emergency ; late into the autumn you could have seen the gaunt father and the little solemn-featured girl wending their way towards the river for a swim. The bathless villagers watched and wondered. They judged the good man to be a little daft, no doubt, but they loved his cheery helpfulness. Dozing on the battle-field, they caught, between two yawns, the stir of his *réveillé*, and its clarion note passed like a breeze through the foulness of their sleeping-ditch.

Then they turned in the trenches and fell asleep again.

Ursula learned early that life was no dream-garden. " Duty, like a stern preceptor," often pushed himself unpleasantly to the fore in her young existence and extinguished the sunlight, provoking thunder-storms. Not that these were by any means the rule ; her father loved her too tenderly for that ; he kissed her leisurely upon the forehead. " Be sober," he said, " be vigilant." Her aunt gave her sweets.

Yet Ursula, from a two-year-old baby, loved her father best. Even when, once, he chastised her because she had told a lie.

"Gerard will be late for the train," said the pastor. "Headlong, as usual. Either he will get there too late or he will drive
too fast."

"He will drive too fast," replied Ursula, quietly. "Tell me,
father, about this elder brother of his. How strange it will
seem! A new son at the house whom nobody knows. I wish
he were not coming."

"I have told you before, Ursula, but women are so resolutely curious. A man's curiosity is impulse, a woman's is
method. Besides, you remember him yourself; he was here
twelve years ago."

"I don't remember much, only a quiet, kind-looking gentleman who seemed afraid of children. What had he been doing
in Germany, Captain?"

"Earning his daily bread, no more and no less."

"And what has he been doing these twelve years in Java?"

"Earning his daily bread, not less, but no more."

"I know," mused Ursula, with feminine inconsistency. "It
seems so ridiculous, a Van Helmont earning his living."

But this was a red rag to a bull. "It is never ridiculous!"
cried the pastor. "Give us this day our daily bread;" that
means: we would accept it, Lord, from no other hands than
Thine!"

"As manna?" queried Ursula.

"No, child, as the harvest of toil. By-the-bye"— the old
man stood still on the veranda steps, his limp sleeve hanging
against his long black coat—"it is a strange coincidence, my
preaching to-morrow's sermon, and Otto coming home to-day.
The Sabbath before he first started for Germany I preached on
resisting the devil."

Ursula smiled, a harmless little smile, all to herself.

"I remember it as if it were yesterday," continued the Dominé, thoughtfully watching a wheeling swallow. "Do you know,
Ursula, why Otto van Helmont went away?"

"No," she responded, quickly inquisitive. "Tell me why."

"I suppose you think it was some love-story?"

"No," she said again. "Why should I think? I don't
know."

" You are not like other girls, Ursula. Most women think
everything is a love-story. Come, let us go in."

" But he is quite old now ?" she persisted, with her hand on
his arm.

" He is what children call old. I believe he is seventeen
years older than Gerard. I have always liked Otto exceedingly,
little as I know of him. He is a true, simple-hearted gentleman, is Otto."

" I don't doubt it," replied the girl, with a shade of petulance ;
" but it will be so awkward, a stranger at the house !"

" I wish you would close the veranda door, Roderigue," said
a querulous voice from inside. " You are letting in all the
heat."

The occupant of the room came forward, a little yellow lady,
with red ringlets, in a red wrapper. This was Miss Mopius, the
Dominé's sister-in-law, and an invalid.

" I had kept down the temperature so beautifully," she complained, during the performance of the usual perfunctory pecks.
" What's the use of my scolding the servant if she sees that *you*
don't care ! Look at the thermometer, Ursula ; it was under
65°."

Ursula obediently reported that it was now nearing 67°.

" You see," said Miss Mopius. She said nothing else, but the
words dragged down upon the little room a fearful weight of
guilty silence, from which Ursula fled to wash her hands.

As the girl was coming down-stairs again, she heard the rumble of returning wheels. She could not resist a swift run to the
veranda, where she had abandoned her basket. As she caught
it up the dog-cart came flying past. The two brothers were in
it now. The elder turned sideways, started, hesitated, took off
his hat. Ursula remained watching them, a symphony in yellow and brown, with the marigolds at her feet in a lake of
golden orange, and the pink-tipped honeysuckle all around her,
against the staring sunflowers loud and bold.

CHAPTER III

" Who is that yellow-frock among the yellow flowers?" asked Otto van Helmont. " But, of course, I can guess," he added, immediately. " That was the parsonage we just passed. The ' nut-brown maid ' must be Ursula Rovers."

" Ursula? Was she there still?" replied Gerard, flicking a fly from the horse's flank. " She seems to live in the garden. Doesn't care tuppence about her complexion."

" She is very remarkably beautiful."

" Do you think so? I never noticed. You see, I have known her all my life. She is just the parson's daughter. I suppose she reminds you of your own Javanese."

Otto flushed, and the two drove on, side by side, in silence. They were very unlike to look at; there must have been, as Dominé Rovers had said, from fifteen to twenty years' interval between them. The young man was spruce and slender, carelessly elegant in appearance and attitude, the elder brother, the planter, sat square and stalwart, with ruddy skin and tawny beard. He was coming home for rest, weary of the jaded splendor of the tropics. As they drove on, he turned right and left, with eager, misty eyes. The salute of the passing peasants delighted him ; he watched, in quiet ecstasy, their long-drawn glances of inquiry or semi-acknowledgment. This was better than the humbly crouching savages under the cocoa-trees. This was recognition ; this was home.

The avenue was home, the white house behind the trees was home, and the clasp of his mother's arms—no, *that* was home. Never mind, for one moment, the rest.

" You have gray hairs here and there, Otto," said the Baroness van Helmont, fondly. "I never knew I was an old woman before."

Otto's father bent down quickly and kissed her slender hand. "My dear, you will never grow old," he said. "You belong to the things of beauty, and you remember what the English poet said of *them*."

The little porcelain lady laughed among the laces of her morning-gown.

"Yes, but the French poet said just the reverse, and in matters of beauty the Frenchman is the better judge."

"Well, let Otto be umpire. He is best able to decide. Otto, do you find that your mother has grown a day older since you left?"

The old Baron looked towards his big son with what, on his easy features, was almost an anxious expression.

"Yes, she is older," said Otto.

The Baroness laughed again.

"My dear," she said, "he is as impossible as ever. Leave him. He, at least, has not changed."

Mynheer van Helmont dropped his eyelids with a quick movement of vexation, and walked from the room.

Mother and son were left together. They went into the Baroness's little turret-chamber, a rounded *bonbonnière*, all pale flowered silk and Dresden china, with a long window overlooking the park.

"Sit down, child," said the Baroness. "Are you glad to be home again?"

A lump in the strong man's throat prevented immediate reply. Presently he took his mother's jewelled fingers in his own. "And what have you been doing all this time?" he said.

"Doing? But, my dear, we have been living. What else should we do? It is you who have shot the tigers. Nothing has happened here."

"Grandpa is dead," said Otto, meditatively.

"Ah, yes, grandpapa is dead. That is very sad, but he had been childish for years. He lived up-stairs in the blue-room and never came out of it. He did not know us. He used to mistake me for some horrid recollection of his youth, and call me Niniche. It was very embarrassing."

They were both silent.

"Your father said it was a great compliment," added the Baroness, gravely.

"And his pension? What has become of that? How did you manage? I have often wanted to ask.

"Well, of course, his pension went. Your father had always said it would make a tremendous difference. I cannot say I find it has."

"But it must," persisted Otto.

"Of course. My dear boy, have you still your old liking for business? I beg of you, do not begin talking of it just yet."

Otto smiled.

"Come, lean your head on my lap as you used to do. Wait a minute; you will spoil my dress."

She spread out a flimsy piece of cambric which could have protected nothing, and sat softly stroking the dark hair from his face, as he lay on the rug.

"You have come back heart-whole?" she said, presently, but there was not much interrogation in her voice.

"Yes, mother." The tone excluded doubt; not that any one ever thought of doubting Otto.

"Gerard was always prophesying that you would bring back a 'nut-brown' wife."

The words seemed to strike home strangely to Otto, like an echo. "Gerard appears very lively," he said. "He always had exceedingly high spirits as a boy. But, of course, I hardly know him."

"He is brightness itself," said the Baroness. "He is like a constant sunbeam. Dear boy, I hope he will make an advantageous settlement. And you too, dear Otto, I wish you would marry and"—her voice grew tremulous—"stay at home."

"But, mother, I must first find a wife." He spread out his fingers contemplatively on the white plush beneath him, among the gold-embroidered lilies.

"That is a woman's work, not a man's. It is a mother's, and

I could easily manage it. A man should find all his loves for himself, except the one he marries in the end."

"But would you look for a consort, mother, or merely for a mule with money-bags?"

"Otto, how rudely you put things! Contact with black people has not improved you. I should look for an angel, worthy of my boy—an angel with golden wings." She paused, and played shyly with the velvet at her wrist. "Indeed, I hope you will marry a little money," she added, looking away. "You father expects it. And, besides, you must."

He did not answer. "Gerard is going to," she added, blushing over the pink-and-white tints of her delicate cheek. "He quite understands it is necessary. He is doing his best."

"How commendable!" cried Otto, sitting up. "He deserves, indeed, that his gilt-feathered seraph should bear him to a matrimonial heaven."

The Baroness looked placidly alarmed. "My dear," she said, "don't, I beg of you, go spoiling your brother. He takes a much simpler view of duty than you. You have always complicated existence, poor child. You were a steel-clanging knight, Otto, in search of ogres; he is a troubadour under Fortune's window. And he never plays out of tune."

And then again there was silence between them, while she drew down his head once more. But their thoughts were conversing still.

"Marrying for money," he continued at last, and his voice was black with scorn.

"Marrying money and marrying for money are two very different things," rejoined the Baroness, patiently, "as you know. I should not like Gerard to marry for money, nor you. You never will. But you can do as your father did."

The turret-chamber was cool, yet the glowing sun from outside seemed to penetrate to the cheeks of both mother and son.

"My father is a lucky man," said Otto. "But supposing you had not turned out to be *you*?"

"Then there would not have been money enough. As it is, we had a little love and a little money; that is the best blend .

on the whole, to commence housekeeping with. Both, I suppose, should go on increasing; with us, only one has done that."

"Nobody has ever missed the money," interposed Otto, smiling pitifully down on the costly rug at his feet."

"Ah, you say that! But I have often regretted that mamma's
fortune was not larger. Papa, you remember, had squandered
his share. Your poor father might have got many things he
had set his heart upon, and which now he is compelled to go
without."

"Yes," said Otto, "the house would have been twice as full
again."

"Exactly. For instance, he has always longed, passionately, to possess a 'Corot.' He has never been able to procure
one. There is a very good 'Daubigny' in the small drawing-
room. By-the-bye, it is new; you must go and have a look
at it presently. But the poor man has never ventured to buy a
'Corot.' I cannot help feeling it is almost my fault. Certainly
grandpapa's. Yet he was always so considerate to grandpapa
after we took him to live with us, never reproaching him with
word."

Otto did *not* ask, What is a 'Corot'? He lay stroking his
mother's hand. Presently he started to his feet and walked
towards the window.

"How beautiful it is!" he cried; "how lovely! Oh, mother,
the sun-heat across the park!"

The little lady came dancing after him. "Yes, is it not exquisite?" she cried, standing close beside him. "Look at the
patch of yellow color there, in the break between the beeches.
Why, Otto, since when do you notice the merely beautiful?
Do you see that far line of white roof with the sun full upon
it? That is the gallery round the new Italian garden. Well,
not exactly new, only you have been away such a very long
time!"

She pressed his arm. "Now go down to your father," she
added, softly. "Ask him to show you the 'Daubigny.' And
don't talk to him of business. You know he doesn't like it."

"A fortune for a picture," said Otto to himself as he closed
his mother's door, "while I was out in Java growing tea!"

He passed along a corridor which was hung with arms of all times and nations, into the large entrance hall, a museum of old oak and heraldry among the masses of summer flowers.

There he found his father pacing impatiently to and fro. The old Baron, whose life motto had been "Tout s'arrange," was only impatient about things of no importance. He was now eager to show his son the acquisitions of the last twelve years. He knew that the display would be productive of pleasure neither to himself nor to his heir, but he remained eager all the same.

The returned exile—his heart soft with the morning's impressions—resolved at once to take an interest in everything. "Mother was speaking of a new picture, he began, "a daub—daub-something. She said I must be sure and ask to see it."

The Baron smiled. "The Daubigny," he replied. "I suppose the name has not penetrated to India yet. With us, you know, he has made himself a little reputation." He led the way into a small drawing-room, but stopped before pointing to his treasure. "Do you notice any change here?" he asked. "Anything new in the arrangement of the whole?"

Otto hesitated. He was horribly ill at ease, and afraid of making a fool of himself. It was the old sensation of twelve years ago. He felt like a shy man that doesn't know a cob from a charger suddenly called upon to judge of a horse.

"Oh, it's nothing," said the Baron. "Only the ceiling's been painted. It was done by Guicciardi, the same who decorated the last Loggia in the Prelli Palace just before the poor prince went smash. That was a magnificent finale, Otto. Poor old Prince Luigi knew that he couldn't possibly hold out much longer—not a hundred thousand francs to the good, I am told. And he gave a commission to Guicciardi to paint the place with that last hundred thousand, just finished the thing and left an immortal whole to his country, and then —pwhit!" The Baron snapped his fingers lightly. "Pooh," he said, "I know you don't care for that kind of thing. I beg your pardon. I didn't mean to give you offence. That is the 'Daubigny.'"

Otto stood staring at the little golden landscape. He was

seeking hard for something sensible to say. He could not talk
of art as his brother Gerard did, while knowing nothing about it,
trustful to Fate to make his talk no greater nonsense than that
of those who do know.

"It didn't cost me very much," said the Baron, a little
shamefacedly. "It is not, of course, a first-rate specimen,
though I flatter myself it is by no means bad."

"It is very pretty," said Otto. "The sky is something like a
Javanese sunrise."

"Really? That reminds me, I have some beautiful ivories
in the west room, if you care to see them. Japanese, but they
were bought at Batavia. What wonderful opportunities you
must have had, had you only known!" He looked wistfully at
his son. "Dirt cheap, I dare say."

"I don't think anything's dirt cheap anywhere," replied Otto.
"And dirt seems the most expensive of all—in the end."

He shrank back, with a sudden misgiving of his own meaning; but, if the speech were discourteous, the Baron quite misunderstood it. "I hope you have got into no entanglements,"
said the Baron, sharply. "Although, true, it is not the expensive ones that are the most dangerous. We expect you to
marry now, Otto, and settle down. Your mother is very
anxious you should marry a little money. I sincerely hope you
will."

"There is time still, father," said Otto; "I'm only just
back."

"Well, I don't know. You are nearly forty. And you have
wasted a great many years, after all. Here have you been toil-
ing in Java, working hard the whole time, and with what
result? The same as in Germany before. You might just as
well have lived leisurely at home, and better. Your cheeks
would have been less brown, and your manners no worse."

He faced his son; he had been bracing himself for this, and
he was astonished to find it came so easily. "After all, I think
you must admit, Otto, that we easy-going people understand
life better than you."

"I have no wish to deny it, sir."

"Well?"

" Well? I have tried to do my duty—the nearest duty."

" Java! It seems to me your duty was a very far one. Well, well, we are heartily glad to have you back. Come into the smoking-room, and we will smoke a really good cigar."

CHAPTER IV

BARON VAN HELMONT could have dug out no better epithet to apply to himself and his race than the word which rose naturally to the top, "easy-going." He knew he was "easy-going." The Van Helmonts had always been that. "Stream with the stream." "Tout s'arrange." He could hear his grandfather saying these things in a far-away mist of Louis XV. powder and ruffles ; he remembered how he had brought home his Watteau-faced bride, and how the old gentleman, bent double over his gold-headed cane, had blessed the pair, with a sceptical grimace, at the top of the moss-grown steps.

"My children," he had said, "you have launched your boat on the current. However you steer, the river flows to the sea. Take an old man's advice. Let it flow. Laissez couler."

Said the young wife to her husband, as soon as they were alone, "But 'laissez couler' means 'let the boat *sink*,'" and she laughed the prettiest protest into his face. She had plenty of brains.

He stopped her mouth with a kiss. "You are too young a married woman," he replied, "to study 'équivoques.'" He, also, had plenty of brains, but neither had the art of using them.

The old gentleman, his grandfather, had made a tranquil ending ; he had lain on his death-bed unruffled except at the wrists. His was surely a bright civilization with its "What does it signify?" Our self-clouded century repeats the words, but with passionate inquiry. And, after all, so many things that torment us signify so exceedingly little. Yet, perhaps, none the less, we are wiser than our grandfathers, for "it," in their case, signified the French Revolution.

The present Baron van Helmont could not, of course, be "pure Louis XV." None of us can, not even our clocks. You are unable—it is a stale truth—to push back the hand on the dial. The Baron, for instance, could not contemplate dissolution with the composure of his grandsire. He tried hard not to contemplate it at all. "Live and let live" was one of his favorite sayings. One day, long ago, he had used it to close the discussion with regard to a case which had recently occurred in his village of what he would have labelled "unavoidable distress." His hobbledehoy of a son—the only one then— had suddenly joined in the conversation. "But that means," the boy Otto had said, "live well yourself, and let the poor live badly." It was the first symptom. The father shrugged his shoulders. Otto must have been, if we use the scientific jargon of our day, a reversion to an anterior type. To judge by the discrepancy of any half a dozen brothers, most families must possess a good many types to revert to.

The Baron van Helmont was a good man, lovable, and universally respected. In his youth he had enjoyed himself and spent freely as a young gentleman should do. He had been gay, but no irretrievable scandal had ever been mixed up with his name. He had married a charming wife, who had brought him a little more money. They had spent that together, and had quietly enjoyed the spending; but their friends and connections had been permitted to enjoy it too. The Baron had one of the finest collections of curios in the Netherlands, and also some very good pictures. He was a gentleman to his fingertips, and thoroughly cultivated. No one could possibly be a better judge of bric-à-brac.

"Bric-à-brac," said the Baroness to the pastor, "is in itself a vocation ; and the best judge of bric-à-brac in Holland is better than a taker of cities." She spoke under strong provocation. At intervals the Dominé would make himself superfluous by speaking in the Manor-house drawing-room of "righteousness, temperance, and judgment to come." "As if we got drunk," said the Baroness.

Undeniably, the Baron was a gentleman, courteous and comely. There is a story about him which he loved to tell in the privacy of his after-dinner circle. It happened in Paris, at the court of the Citizen King. The Baron, passing through that promiscuous capital, had received a card for a monster reception. He went, and somehow got astray in the crush at the entrance, so that when he tried to pass in at a side door he found himself stopped by a gentleman-at-arms.

"Excuse me, monsieur; but this door is reserved for the members of reigning families."

The Baron hesitated. To withdraw was absurd. He straightened himself in his small but serene hauteur.

"And who am I, then?" he said.

"Entrez, mon prince."

But that was long ago, unfortunately. Even while the Baron said "Stream," he regretted that his life could not lie stagnant in a bay, among water-lilies. And yet he hurried on each individual day to its close. He was always wanting to pick other flowers a little farther down the bank.

Two sons were left him at the close of his life, and one of these was already annoyingly old. Between the two lay a couple of hillocks in the village church-yard. The Baroness had begged to rescue the small relics therein contained from the musty family vault. "The vault is so cold," she said. Her husband proved quite willing to adopt the suggestion; he availed himself of the opportunity it gave him to put up a charming Italian marble of a cherub gathering flowers. The "Devil's Doll," the Calvinist villagers called it. Occasionally, when her husband was not attending, the Baroness would go and weep a few quiet tears upon the hillocks. There was a chamber in her heart which she occasionally liked to enter, but she never had much objection to coming out again.

"I met Ursula this afternoon, Otto," said Gerard at dinner. "I told her she had aroused your enthusiastic admiration. I fancy she was very much pleased." He laughed; the others laughed.

Otto's bent face sank lower beneath a sudden thunder-cloud. "That was an ungentlemanly thing to do," he said.

"Ungentlemanly!" The younger brother's voice had en-

tirely changed its key. "What on earth do you mean? How
dare you say such a thing as that?"

A man-servant was in the room. The remarks had been made
in Dutch. The man would have understood them in French,
but that would not have mattered.

"I mean," responded Otto, rather awkwardly, floundering
into the foreign language to which his plantation life had
somewhat choked the inlets, "that it is a shabby thing to do,
to go and tell a lady what a man has said of her in confidence."

"My dear, not if it be a compliment," interposed the Baroness, mildly ignoring, as her sex was bound to do, the all-impor-
tant concluding words. "Every woman likes a harmless compliment."

"Not sensible women. Sensible women despise them,"
edged in the Freule* van Borck. Nobody heeded her.

"Confidence! Confidence!" echoed Gerard, hotly. "Who
talked of confidence?" He lapsed, purposely, into Dutch. "I
decline to be told," he said, "whether at my father's table or
anywhere else, that I behave in an 'ungentlemanly' manner."

The old Baron waved a conciliatory hand. "The word was
unfortunate," he admitted, "but, Gerard, you press too heavily
upon it. *Glissez, n'appuyez pas.* Otto meant to say you had
stolen an unfair advantage. He had doubtless been wanting to
tell Ursula himself. Fie, what an ado about nothing. To me
it is most remarkable that, after so long an absence, Otto should
still speak Dutch so well."

The obvious retort that Dutch is spoken in Java sprang
straight to Gerard's lips, but he bit it down again.

"I consider Ursula Rovers distinctly plain," remarked the
Freule van Borck. The Freule was the Baroness van Helmont's only sister; she had lived at the Manor-house for years.
She was what humdrum people call "a character," as if all of
us were not that when you shift the lights.

"She is common-looking," said the Baroness, "but I think
she is pretty."

---

* Title of unmarried ladies of rank.

"All women are pretty," smiled the Baron, "even those whom the pretty ones think plain."

"My dear," his wife nodded across at him, "it is a fallacy, old as Adam, that Eve, in her Paradise, is jealous of all the Liliths outside."

"Stuff and nonsense!" cried the sharp-faced Freule van Borck, "there are women enough yet—thank Heaven—and to spare, that don't care a cent about looks."

Her sister puckered up a small mouth into a most innocent expression. "If it be so," she said, suavely, "it is a merciful dispensation. God tempers the wind to the shorn lamb."

The two brothers sat in silence, not so much sullen as constrained. Presently the father proposed the health of the one who had that day returned to them. "We celebrate," he said, with good-natured banter, "*le retour du fils prodigue, trop prodigue—de lui-même.*"

After the toast had been honored, he turned to his Benjamin. "You, sir," he said, "prefer the fruits of other people's labors. You take after your father. And, when the time comes, precious little you will find to take." They both laughed heartily enough this time, and the whole family rose from table.

Otto came out to Gerard on the terrace. "I am sorry I offended you," he said; "I meant to be angry, but not to be insulting."

Gerard's face cleared like a pool when the sun comes out. He gave his brother's hand a hearty grasp. "Don't speak of it again," he said. "I dare say I was wrong, though Heaven knows I didn't mean to annoy you. You will find me, sometimes, a little thoughtless, I fear. You mustn't always take things quite as seriously as to-day, though. I·wish you would come down to the stables with me, Otto; you haven't even seen my saddle-horses yet."

Mynheer van Helmont, standing cigar in mouth before the great bay window, turned and nodded to his wife.

"They are friends again," he said. "Isn't it dreadful? That is the worst thing that can happen to brothers."

"What is?" queried the Freule van Borck.

"Why, to be friends again."

"I like Otto very much," said the Freule, irrelevantly, not comprehending.

Mevrouw van Helmont laid down her bit of fluffy fancy-work. "Of course you like Otto very much, Louisa," she said. "I should be exceedingly vexed did you not."

The Baron walked out into the after-glow. "It is most irritating," he mused, "to have to say all one's good things to an audience one-half of which is deaf to all meanings, and the other half of which is one's wife."

He stood looking at the white pile which lay softly imbosomed in its dark green half-circle, like a pearl set in emeralds, beneath the amber sky. He was deeply proud of its possession. "These Havanas," he reflected, "are as excellent as if they were genuine," and he wreathed a faint blue whorl on the tranquil air. Then another thought struck a sudden chill to his heart. "To die and leave it all!" He shivered, and returned to the window. "Louisa," he said, "how about our piquet?"

A couple of hours later Otto stood on the same terrace, also cigar in mouth. He had come out for a last smoke before turning in. He was an inveterate and uninterrupted smoker. It was his one weakness, and he indulged it to the full.

The night was perfectly still, and translucent. A soft flutter, that was not wind, but the very restlessness of dreaming nature, weighted the balmy air with wandering gusts of incense. All creation seemed lapped in luxury, asleep on the breast of love.

Otto, alone in the dusk, looked up at the silent windows. The rest were gone to their rooms; a light glimmered here and there. The great stable-clock boomed heavily eleven long trembling strokes. "It is home," said Otto, under his breath. But he said it aloud. He rejoiced with tumultuous delight for a moment in being able to speak to that home from a spot where the bricks and mortar could hear him. His memory strayed away to the low house with the long verandas among the spreading palms. How often had he lain back in there in his wicker lounge, his cigar a deep red spot of attraction among the insect whirl of the Indian night, while he said the word out vainly to the bats and moths and butterflies. Home. He stood and looked—looked at the mere walls till his eyes were burning with physical exhaustion. He was back again at last. He loved his mother very faithfully. He loved his father. He felt kindly towards his brother. Yet, somehow, he could not control an impression of loneliness as he turned to go upstairs.

CHAPTER V

"GIRD up your loins!" cried the Dominé, striking his only hand into the pulpit-cushion. The peasant congregation, with bodies huddled awry in wondrously diversified angles of drowsiness, nodded lower under the accustomed storm. One red-faced yawner, opening misty eyes, stared vaguely through the heat-cloud, and with some far perception of the preacher's meaning, hitched up his trousers before sinking back into his seat.

"For the city of Mansoul is taken, is taken while the garrison slept!" In the Manor-house pew, under the glitter of armorial gaudery against sombre oak, sat their Baronial Highnesses, all except Gerard, who, coming down too late, had found himself compelled to elect between breakfast and church. Their Highnesses preserved an exemplary attitude of erect attention. It is even quite possible that the Freule Louisa was listening.

To Otto the little barn-like building, in its white unchangedness, had brought that sudden quietude of soul which comes upon us when the rush of life has briefly cast us back into a long-remembered harbor. It was good to be here. It was good to find nothing altered, neither the gaunt externals of the service, nor the inharmonious music, nor even the long discourse. It was good to breathe the atmosphere of dutiful curiosity which played about the heir until at last it also sank, half-sated, beneath the all-oppressive heat. The crimson farm-wives sat perspiring under their great Sunday towers of gold-hung embroidery. There was not a cool spot in the building, except Ursula's muslin frock.

As his eye rested there, Otto felt that one change at least

made itself manifest. Where a little lonely child had formerly faced the Manor-house pew, a maiden now sat, calm and self-possessed, her gaze neither seeking nor avoiding his own. And suddenly he realized that he was growing old.

He realized it all the more when, presently, he found himself walking back by the side of the parson's daughter, through wide stretches of sun-soaked corn. The older people had passed ahead, unconsciously hurried forward by the sweeping stride of the Dominé. In that opening search for words which always disturbs the meeting of long-acquainted strangers, Otto's soul swelled anew with wrath against the brother whose indiscretion had doubly tied either tongue.

"Yes, everything is exactly as it used to be," he replied to Ursula's perfunctory question, when it ultimately blossomed forth from the marsh of their embarrassment. "That struck me more especially this morning in church. The people are pretty much the same, of course; at least, they look it. And so is the whole appearance of the place, and the odor of the fustian and the service."

"And the sermon?" she laughed, lamely, thinking also of Gerard's banter, and annoyed by her annoyance.

But his face clouded over. She noticed this, and it put her still less at her ease. She hurriedly added something about her father's "coincidence," thereby causing her companion to write her down insincere.

"Nevertheless," she continued, desperately, feeling all the while that she might just as well, and far better, keep silence, "twelve years seems to me a most tremendous time."

"That is because you are young."

"Young or not, people change in twelve years."

Gerard would have availed himself of this palpable opportunity to suggest something pretty; clumsy Otto merely made answer, "My grandfather is dead." The most tragic words can somehow sound funny, and Ursula, in her nervousness, very nearly laughed.

"I miss him," continued Otto, quite unconsciously. "He wasn't—childish, you know, when I went away. How the poor old man would have enjoyed some talks about my tiger-hunts. He was such a splendid shot."

"'GIRD UP YOUR LOINS!' CRIED THE DOMINÉ"

" Have you really shot tigers ?"

" Yes." A man always feels foolish under such a question as that.

" Many ?"

" That depends on your ideas of proportion. Tigers must not be confounded with rabbits. I have shot enough to be able to beg your father's acceptance of a skin when my boxes come."

They walked on for some minutes in silence, awkward silence, she flicking at the corn-ears with her white parasol. Then she said, " I feel sorry for the tiger."

He answered, dryly, " The parents of his final supper did not take that view."

" But," he added, " I dare say you don't quite understand about wild beasts, or heathen countries. I shouldn't wonder, Juffrouw Rovers, if you had never even crossed the frontier."

" No, I haven't," she answered, shortly, much put out by his innocent patronage, " and I am glad I haven't. I should hate to come back as people do, finding all things small at home. And, above all, I should hate to go to India—a horrible place with spiders as big as my sunshade, and a python curled up, perhaps, under one's pillow of nights. You needn't laugh ; I may have forgotten the dreadful creatures' names, but I know they're there, for my Uncle Mopius told me."

" Ah, yes, your Uncle Mopius. He was out in Java, wasn't he ?"

" Yes, he was notary there, and he tells the most awful stories."

" Then don't believe them. So you would never go to India ?"

" Never."

" Well, it's a good thing there's no necessity. I had to, you see. People even face pythons, when they *must*. And there's always the fun of killing them."

She shuddered. " The fun of killing," she repeated, " I cannot understand at all. We are speaking different languages, Mynheer van Helmont. I hate the idea of killing anything. And do you know what I hate still more ? It is what you call 'a splendid shot.' Gerard is a splendid shot, like his grand-father; the finest, they say, in the province. Yes, I can't help it; I've often told him." She plunged headlong. "I dare say you're a splendid shot. But it's just my hobby. To go creep, creeping through God's creation, a gun in one's hand, seeking some innocent life you may slay for the pleasure of slaying! Or, still worse, to sit in a chair and have the poor fluttering wretches driven in quantities on to one's barrels! It's the one thing that spoils the country for me, and only in the autumn I long to get away from Horstwyk. There's no shooting in towns."

"I was thinking of real sport," he answered, with provoking meekness, "but I dare say you are right."

"Oh, I know what real sport means!" she cried, and her eyes flashed. "Hallooing after some little palpitating victim with beagles or harriers or hounds! You may think me very stupid—I dare say you do—but I wouldn't shake hands, if I could help it, with a man whom I knew to have voluntarily 'hunted' anything. As for women, I can't believe they do it." She broke off, in that nervous "unstrungness" which only comes to the gentler sex, hardly knowing, after her sudden burst of eloquence, whether to laugh or to cry.

"You are quite right, quite right," he said again; but in his grave regard she only read approval of her callow softness. They had reached a little well-known wicket, and he stopped. The path went twisting away at this spot from the yellow fields into the deep recesses of the park.

"I think we separate here?" he said, and to her amazement she caught a touch of regret in his tone.

"Yes, as a rule. But papa has gone on—in honor of you, I suppose."

"Then you cannot do better than follow." He held open the gate for her to pass. "I think you must forgive me," he said, with downcast eyes. "It was only once. In Ireland. And we didn't kill the fox."

"Because you couldn't," she answered, fiercely. "Or do people keep foxes, like stags, to uncart?"

Her hand, in its long "Suède" glove, closed almost viciously

on the filmy folds of her frock. Not another word was exchanged between them as they threaded the shady mazes of
suddenly delicious green, but she felt that he was watching her
all the time out of the corners of his eyes. A good man enjoys
the arousing a womanly woman's righteous indignation. Her
heart beat till he saw it. He liked that.

"Ah, Dominé, there was sense in your sermon!" cried the
Freule van Borck, haranguing everybody in a group on the
lawn. "What I enjoy in your preaching is the protest against
latter-day flabbiness"—the Freule van Borck had read and misunderstood Carlyle. "Where are the heroes of old?" she cried,
pointing her "church-book" at the imperturbable Gerard, who
had come strolling out, cool in the coolest of flannels, to greet
the clergyman. "Where, as you asked them, are Gideon and
Moses and Joshua the son of Nun, that was never afraid?"

"We give it up," said Gerard, gravely. "Did the congregation know?"

"Be silent, Gerard. Your conduct is bad enough already.
Instead of remaining to scoff, you should have gone to pray."
It was the Baron who spoke, looking up from his great St.
Bernard.

"I bow to your command, sir, especially on a Sunday. But
Aunt Louisa should not propound conundrums when the answers appear to have got beyond her control."

"I was not speaking to you; I was speaking seriously," replied the Freule, with lofty scorn. "And I thoroughly agree
with the Dominé, that the age of troubadours is dead."

The Dominé writhed. "Yes, yes," he said—"undoubtedly.
Though I should hardly, myself, have employed the names you
mentioned as examples of fearlessness"— He stopped in despair. The Freule was grabbing, with her handkerchief in front
of her, at a wasp which serenely buzzed behind. Mevrouw van
Helmont, on a garden seat, against a great flare of MacMahons
that looked, among their gold-rimmed leaves, like a mayonnaise
of lobster—Mevrouw van Helmont seemed entirely engrossed
by the interest of sticking her parasol into a fat bundle before
her which wriggled and kicked. The Dominé sighed. This

was "the Family." These were the temporal lords of his spiritual domain. He turned, wistfully, to watch his daughter coming across the sward, by Otto's side, between gay patches of color.

"You two have been renewing your acquaintance," he said. "Or was there none left to renew?"

"Indeed, we are already old friends," replied Otto, "for Juffrouw Rovers has been scolding me vigorously; and ladies, I believe, never scold mere acquaintances?" Ursula bit her under-lip. "I understand that Juffrouw Rovers objects to the killing of animals—all animals?" His heavy mustache hung unmoved as he looked across.

"Oh, that is a fad of Ursula's," broke in Gerard. "You should teach her her Bible better, Dominé. She admits that Nimrod may have been a mighty hunter, but never 'before the Lord.'"

"Gerard," said the Dominé, with a grave flash of his eyes on the prodigal, "the Bible is a holy book. Some day, perhaps, you will learn, with regard to holiness, that 'Fools rush in where angels fear to tread.'" The rebuke was almost a fierce one, from gentle lips. In the painful silence Gerard, flushing, took it like a man.

The Baron's mild voice intervened. "The daughter of a hero," said the Baron, smiling and bowing, "can afford to appear soft-hearted. Ursula preaches peace, and her father preaches war. But *I*, were I Otto, should be most afraid of Ursula."

"Mynheer van Helmont," answered that young lady, goaded almost beyond endurance, "I am going next Wednesday to my Uncle Mopius, to stay with him for a week or two."

"Coming to Drum!" cried Gerard, whose regiment was quartered in the small provincial town. He checked himself. "I beg your pardon, sir," he said. "You were about to speak?"

"Oh, it's nothing!" cried the Baroness across from her seat. "Your father was only going to observe something about eclipses of the sun. You know you were, Theodore. It has done duty a dozen times before."

"My dear, do I deny it?" replied the Baron, sadly. "We

have lived too long together. You know all my little jokes, Cécile. You are tired of my compliments. And yet, after more than forty years of marriage, I still address ninety per cent. to yourself."

"But none of the new ones," replied the Baroness, pouting before the whole circle like a girl.

"The new ones are an old man's compliments, and, therefore, insincere." He went across to her, followed by the dog, and the gray couple sat laughing and flirting, like any pair of lovers.

"Ah, Dominé, you needn't look sour," said the Freule, her own angular face like skim-milk. "Surely, by this time, you no longer expect *sobriety* at the Manor-house of Horst."

"I was only thinking," replied the Dominé, softly, and his eyes seemed to pierce beyond the couple on the seat.

The Freule gave a smart snap—meant not unkindly—to her "church-book" clasp.

"But your wife is in heaven," she rejoined, "and much better off, unless sermons mean nothing, than anybody here below."

The Dominé started, and an old scar came out across his cheeks, as if a whip-lash had struck him. "Yes, yes," he said, hurriedly. "Thank God. Ursula, I think it is time we were going."

But the spinster laid a detaining hand upon her pastor's arm. "Surely you must admit," she persisted, "that you Christians are strangely illogical. What, to a Christian, is the King of Terrors? We should speak, not of Mors, but of Morphia!"

This sentence was taken from the Freule's favorite periodical, the *Victory*, in which, however, the concluding word had been printed "Morpheus."

"Yes, yes, exactly," replied the Dominé, pulling away. "You remember what Thucydides said, Freule Louisa? I mean, Thucydides says it's no use discussing a subject unless men are agreed on the meaning of the terms they employ. Ursula, we must really be going. Your aunt has such a dislike to irregular hours."

"Juffrouw Mopius?" exclaimed Otto. "I didn't see her in church. I hope she is well?"

Gerard burst out laughing. "Have you been away so long," he said, "that you have forgotten Miss Mopius's Sunday headache?"

The Dominé, who could fight *men*, looked as if he would have liked to answer something about Gerard's Sunday ailments, but he refrained, evidently feeling that he had already said enough.

The two young men stood watching father and daughter as they swung away into the woodland shadows. "It will be rather a bore," yawned Gerard. "Ursula's coming to Drum. I shall have to show the poor creature all over the place. I don't think she ever spent a night outside Horstwyk before." He lounged away to the Baroness. "Mother, Otto is very much smitten with Ursula, in spite of her lamentable lack of style. I suppose he doesn't notice that, after India. Has he been making any terrible confessions yet about other brown damsels out there?"

The Freule van Borck shot a keen glance at her elder nephew's solemn face. "Yes, Otto," she said, "it can't be helped. Gerard's humor is part of your home-coming."

Meanwhile the Dominé went scudding through the corn as if the very wind of panic were after him. Presently his daughter ventured to hint that the day was rather warm.

"Ursula"—the Dominé's cowardice had put him out of temper with all around him—"Ursula, I heard you remark to the Jonkers that you were exceedingly fond of your uncle Mopius. Now, Ursula, surely that was untrue."

"It was irony, father," the girl made answer rather testily, screening her tormented face.

"Irony? I do not understand irony. There is no room for irony in the Christian warfare. It is a sort of unchivalric guerilla. I'm afraid you are not always quite honest and straightforward. Always, in everything, be quite honest and straightforward, my dear."

When Ursula was safe in her own room she sat down to cry. She had never, from her earliest recollections upward, enjoyed the luxury of rational grief; an altogether causeless outpouring, such as this, could, therefore, but increase her irritation against herself. What did it matter, after all, if she made a good impression on people? She was self-conscious. With angry energy she dabbed her blazing cheeks and went down to luncheon.

"Ursula, my dear child, your face is all blotchy," said Miss Mopius. "I make no doubt you are going to have the measles; they are very prevalent in the village. Did you sneeze during service? Roderigue, did you notice if Ursula sneezed during service? No, you are no good in church; you only think of your sermon. Well, Ursula, I must give you some Sympathetico Lob. You may be thankful you have an aunt whose own health is so bad that she doesn't care at all about infection."

The Dominé looked up uneasily. His coffee tasted bitter, like remorse.

"Or is it hay-fever," said Miss Mopius, "that begins with sneezing? I must get my little Manual and see."

CHAPTER VI

THREE days later Ursula started for Drum. Looking down the straight vista of her shaded past, she could not have discovered, within measurable distance, an event to compare with this departure from home. Hitherto her world had been Horstwyk, and mundane greatness had been the Horst.

In those three days of delicious preparation she had nevertheless seen a good deal of the new arrival. His affection for the Dominé was palpable to all men, and he seemed to slip away, almost gladly, down the long road from the Manor to the Parsonage. All Monday evening they had sat over their teacups in the green veranda, and the Dominé, roused thereto by the guest's brief descriptions of daring, had leisurely recalled his own stories of Algerine lion-hunts. Ursula, looking up from her work at Otto's earnest attention, wondered if twelve years of absence could really suffice to efface the ofttold tale.

On Tuesday a great dinner at "The House" had fêted the return of the first-born. The Dominé had made a speech, and enjoyed himself notwithstanding. But Ursula considered the entertainment had been rather a failure, for amid the due honoring of dowagers and heiresses, nobody but the Baron had found time to say a civil word to herself. Helena van Trossart, the Helmonts' wealthy cousin, had looked lovely, though bored, in the seat next to Otto, assigned her by the Baroness; she had brightened up visibly when the younger son joined her for an endless flirtation in the drawing-room.

Ursula now stood waiting and mildly reviewing last night's disappointments, on this, to her, eventful Wednesday morning. Gerard, who was returning to his regiment, had promised to call for her on his way to the station.

"Ten minutes too soon!" she said in surprise, running to the door as the sound of wheels became audible. But it was Otto who called to her from the box.

"Oh, I'm so sorry," she cried, half-way down the garden path. "But Gerard—I thought you would know?"

"I know nothing of Gerard's arrangements," answered Otto with cold annoyance. "Never mind; I have brought your father's tiger-skin. Is there any one here could hold the horse?"

"Why, of course," she said, springing forward.

"You? I fancied you would be afraid of horses." Otto began tugging at a brown-paper parcel wedged under the seat. As the carriage swayed forward the animal, grown restless, plunged.

"Naturally," replied Ursula, one firm hand at its mouth. She flushed. "Hatred of cruelty stands, with an average man, for cowardice."

"Don't. You hurt one," cried Otto, turning, with altered voice. She calmed down immediately.

"As a matter of fact," she said, "Hector knows me longer and better than you. Your father often lets me drive him."

"This is it," replied Otto, tearing back a strip of covering. A tawny mass of fur, broken suddenly loose, poured down into the dusty road.

"Oh, what a beauty!" exclaimed Josine, who had ventured out in a wrap beneath the laughing sky.

And, "Oh, what a beauty!" echoed Ursula.

"These are for you," he continued, in the eager delight of giving, as he bundled out two gorgeous Indian shawls. "I thought you would like to wear them to church on Sundays"— he stopped, before the ripple on Ursula's face. "You like them, don't you?" he asked, dismayed. "You like them, don't you, Miss Mopius?"

"They are exquisite," replied the latter lady, affectedly, with a scowl at her niece. "My dear Mynheer van Helmont, you have inherited all your father's charming taste." Ursula murmured something about "a beautiful drapery."

"All modern girls are alike," thought Otto, "everything for ornament." He was almost relieved to see Gerard's trap come rattling up.

"You here !" cried the younger brother, looking down from his height. "Oh, I see ! What a hurry you're in to bestow your gifts !"

"I came here to conduct Juffrouw Rovers to the station," answered Otto. "The message I sent appears not to have reached her."

"Oh, I'm so sorry !" Ursula stood distressful, by the little green gate, in her dust-ulster, the rainbow cloth over one arm. At her feet lay the white-fanged brute with gleaming eyes and distended maw. Otto climbed slowly back into his old-fashioned wagonette. By his side the smart dog-cart jingled and creaked. "Hurry, Ursula !" cried its driver. "We haven't any time to spare !" Otto whipped up Hector almost savagely. "It's of no account," he said, "of no account at all."

"Gerard, I'm afraid we shall miss the train," said Ursula, as the trees went flying past them.

"Possibly," answered Gerard. "You don't mind my ciga-rette ?"

"Gerard, my uncle will never forgive me."

"Oh yes, he will. Dozens of damned people have said they would never forgive me, but they always did. You would have missed the train with Hector, anyway."

"But if I had started with your brother, you would have taken me on."

"No, indeed," replied Gerard, with deep conviction. "Once with Otto, always with Otto." He looked down into her face through half-closed eyelids. "Once with Otto, always with Otto," he repeated, "and so you would have missed your train."

She laughed. "Well, I'd much rather go with you," she answered, gayly. He made her a mock little bow of acknowl-edgment.

"For, you see, you take me all the way to Drum."

"Thank you. *If.* Gently, Beauty, gently ; it's only a bit of paper in the middle of the road. I like you for not being

"'OH, I'M SO SORRY,' SHE CRIED"

nervous, Ursula. My mother wouldn't sit behind a horse that shied."

" I want to catch my train," responded Ursula.

" Don't be so peevish. Is this all the reward I get for allowing your box to scratch the paint off my dog-cart?"

" Oh, Gerard, will it do that?"

" Of course it will. But make yourself easy. I'm going to have the cart repainted, anyway. The green spikes were well enough two years ago, but I've seen another shade I like better."

" Gerard, you are horribly extravagant."

" So my father says each time he gets himself some new plaything. By George! I believe we really *are* too late."

With a shout to the groom he leaped from his seat, and was lost in the interior of the station; as Ursula hurriedly followed, a whistle of departure pierced straight through her heart.

" Quick, you stupid," she heard Gerard's voice saying to somebody. The train had stopped again. She was bustled in. They were off !

" Now that never happened to me before," said Gerard. " The man is an ass. But, in fact, it is all your fault."

Ursula sat staring at her hero in unmixed awe. Her infrequent railway journeys had always been occasions of flurry and alarm. Never had she realized that any son of man could influence a station-master.

" Yes," she answered, meekly.

" Of course it is. I should just have jumped in. But they had to stop the train for you. And now they will make us pay a monstrous fine for travelling without a ticket."

" Is that also my fault?" asked Ursula, more meekly still.

" No, it was Beauty's. I've a great mind to deduct the money from her oats. Only that would make her do it over again." He laughed once more, a jolly, self-satisfied laugh.

" But, oh, what *should* we have done," said Ursula, presently, " if the station-master hadn't listened to you?"

" Stopped the train myself, of course ; and Santa Claus would have forgotten to send that man cigars."

" Gerard, you wouldn't have dared !"

Her innocent amazement drove him on.

" You have a poor idea of my desire to oblige you," he made answer. " It would have cost me a pair of gloves, I suppose, and a lot of depositions at the end, and a fine. It would have been a great bore ; I do not pretend to deny that."

She relapsed into silence, reflecting. She thought Gerard was youthfully overbearing. But she also saw he was in earnest. To her it had always seemed in the village of Horstwyk that the powers in authority—the Beadle, the Squire—were made to be implicitly obeyed. Submission, in the Dominé's system, stood forth as an article of faith. In the great world outside she felt it must be the same, only still more resistlessly. Order and Law, however erroneous, were always ex officio infallible.

But for great people, evidently, the world was otherwise. The Irrevocable possessed no barriers which rank and insolence could not laughingly push aside. The railways in their courses obeyed these rulers of men. For the first time in her recollection she envied—perhaps with last night's discomfiture rising uppermost—she envied " the Great."

She sat furtively watching her companion behind his newspaper. He was handsome, with his light mustache and strong complexion, well-dressed, well-groomed, completely at his ease. She felt that the world belonged to him. She felt exceeding small.

At the little town of Drum she was able to continue her studies. Porters naturally selected Gerard to hover round ; every one seemed anxious to please him. Whatever he desired was immediately " Yes, my lord " ed. He gave double the usual number and double the necessary quantity of tips. He insisted upon personally seeing Ursula to her uncle's door and overpaying the cabman. " I have a reputation," he said, merrily, " to keep up in Drum." He turned back as she stood on the door-step.

" And your uncle has a reputation, too," he called, waving his hat.

Ursula knew her uncle by more than reputation, and her courage began to ooze after Gerard's retreating figure. Immediately she pressed a resolute finger on the leak ; she was come to enjoy herself, and Gerard had promised to help her.

Villa Blanda, the residence of Mynheer Jacóbus Mopius, stood in a good-sized garden, some way back from the street. The garden was very brilliant, very brilliant indeed. The first impression it used to make was that of the hideous conglomeration of colors which children saw in former days through so-called kaleidoscopes; after a time you perceived that its complex disharmony was principally produced by a mal - assortment of flowers. These received some assistance, it must be confessed, from a glittering " Magenta " ball, two terra-cotta statuettes of fat children with baskets, and other pleasing trifles of similar origin.

The whole house had manifestly cost a great deal of money; it was its single duty to proclaim this fact, and it did its duty well. A hundred flourishes of superfluous ornament showed upon the face of it that the terra-cotta man and the gilder, and the encaustic-tile people, and the modeller of stucco monstrosities, had all sent in lengthy bills. The bills had been paid.

Yes, Mynheer Jacóbus Mopius owed no man anything—not even courtesy, not even disregard. He button-holed you to inform you how much more important a personage he was than yourself. If you tried to escape him you were lost.

Inside, the house was, as outside, a record of wealth misspent. Money, they say, buys everything; it is certainly wonderful to consider what hideous things money will buy.

Ursula was shown into the drawing - room, where her aunt came forward to greet her. " How are you, my dear?" said Mevrouw Mopius, in a tone whose indifference precluded reply. Mevrouw Mopius was a washed-out-looking lady in a too-stiff black silk. She immediately returned to her low chair and her Berlin woolwork frame. For Mevrouw Mopius still worked on canvas. She preferred figures—Biblical scenes. She was now busy on a meeting between Jacob and Laban, in which none of the gorgeously robed figures were like anything that has ever been seen on earth.

Ursula seated herself, unasked, on a purple plush settee. The room was large and copiously gilded. From the farther end of it a girl approached—a pale girl in a plain dark gown.

"Oh, I forgot," said Mevrouw Mopius, pausing with uplifted needle. "My step-niece Harriet. Harriet, this is Ursula Rovers."

"Will you come and take off your things?" said the dark girl. "Shall I show you your room?" Ursula rose, with a spring of relief, and began hastily to explain about the loss of her luggage as she moved towards the door. Just before she reached it her aunt spoke again.

"Harriet has come to live with us, you remember, since her father died." Mevrouw Mopius always conversed in afterthoughts, when she troubled herself to converse at all.

"You won't be able to change your clothes," said the pale girl, as the two went up-stairs together.

"No. Does it matter?"

"Matter? No. What does matter? Certainly not Uncle Mopius."

"What a fine house this is, is it not? I was never on the second floor before, though I've sometimes been to lunch."

"Oh yes, it is charming, charming in every way," said the pale girl, with a sneer. "This is your room, the second best guest-chamber. I'm afraid I can't lend you much for the night. I've three night-gowns; one's in the wash, and one's torn. Uncle Mopius gave me them."

She went and stood at the window while Ursula hurriedly washed her hands. "Are you ready?" she asked, presently. "Then come down-stairs again. Better tell Uncle Mopius you admired your room. The washing-things, for instance, they are English. Cost thirty-six florins. Come along." Ursula shuddered under the continuous sneer of the girl's impassive tones.

As soon as they opened the drawing-room door Mevrouw Mopius's voice was heard exclaiming, "Harriet, get me my Bible immediately, Harriet." She sat up quite awake and alert, her needle unused beside her. "I've been waiting," she continued. "What a long time you've been. Ursula, I hope you're not vain. It's a bad thing in a pastor's daughter to be vain of her appearance." After a minute's silence she became aware of the proximity of her other niece, who stood waiting beside her, Bible in hand. "And in all other girls," she added, "for the matter of that;" but Harriet, having missed the discourse, lost the application as well.

" It was on the table in the next room," said Harriet.

" I know. Did you expect *me* to get it ?"

The lady took the sacred volume, which immediately fell open at the story of Jacob and Rebecca, much bethumbed. In the midst of her search she paused, to cast a sharp look at Ursula. " And not much to be vain of, anyway," she said. She could not possibly have authenticated this remark, but she chose to consider it " judicious."

" Here is the place," she continued. " You see, it says Leah had ' tender eyes.' Now, what, I wonder, is the color of tender eyes ?"

" I always thought it meant ' watery,' " hazarded Ursula.

" Do you really think so ?" Mevrouw Mopius reflected, sitting critically back from her screen, and surveying her cherry-colored Orientals. " Really, *watery*. Ursula, I wonder if that view is correct ?"

" Like a perpetual cold in her head," volunteered the dark girl, listlessly. " I know such people."

Mevrouw Mopius sniffed unconsciously.

" In that case I should have to make them red," she said. " I had just decided on dove color."

" You couldn't make red show against the cheeks," said Harriet. " Hadn't you better send round and ask Mevrouw Pock's opinion ?"

Mevrouw Mopius smiled immediate approval.

" A very sensible suggestion," she said. Mevrouw Pock was the wife of her favorite parson. " You have plenty of sense if only you were always good - tempered. Get me my escritoire from the table over there. No ; writing letters fatigues me "— she couldn't spell — " you must run across after dinner, and get Mevrouw to consult her husband as to what it says in the Greek."

" But I shall have to change my dress again," protested Harriet.

" Well, and what of that? So much the better. There's few things a girl likes more than changing dresses. I'm sure you ought to be thankful you've dresses to change."

Without further reply the girl dropped away into her corner and resumed her interrupted reading. Ursula sat with her hands in her lap. Mevrouw began sorting wools, but presently remembered the guest.

"Harriet," she called, "why don't you come and amuse Ursula? You waste all your time over novels. I can't imagine what you find in them. What's this you're reading now? A novel, of course?"

The girl came forward, lazily. "Yes, aunt," she said.

"What is it? What's it about?"

"It's a historical romance called *Numa Pompilius*, translated from the German. Everybody's reading it just now."

"I can't understand what you find in them. And they're all alike. It always ends in Pompilius marrying Numa."

Before Ursula had stopped laughing behind Mevrouw Mopius's back her uncle came in. Harriet did not laugh.

Mynheer Mopius, though a very secondary personage in this story of the Van Helmonts, would be mortally offended did we not give him a chapter to himself.

CHAPTER VII

"AMUSING yourselves?" said Mynheer Mopius. "That's right. That's what you've come for, Ursula. I'm glad your aunt's been amusing you."

Translated, this meant that Mynheer Mopius considered his wife had been taking a liberty. For, although Mynheer Mopius despised wit or humor of any kind, and but rarely condescended to utter what he considered a joke, yet he somehow believed his conversation to be a source of constant refreshment to his family. And he felt annoyed at their making merry without him.

"I'm sure, if Ursula's laughing it's no fault of mine," said Mevrouw. "I was merely telling Harriet—where's Harriet?"

"Gone up to dress. You had better follow her example, Ursula. Dinner at 6.30. We dress for it here, at least the women do. So do I when there's company. It's a custom I brought with me from Batavia. Must show the natives here what's what."

"I've nothing but this," said Ursula, in some confusion. "My box hasn't come, and I haven't got much in the way of evening frocks anyhow."

"I'll give you one. I gave Harriet hers. That girl's fallen nose foremost into fat* if ever girl did. Hasn't she, wife?"

"She doesn't know it," replied Mevrouw Mopius, picking at Laban's goggle eyes.

"Then she's a greater fool than I take her for. She'd have been a nurse-maid, sure as fate. And now she's as good as a rich man's daughter."

* Vulgar Dutch idiom.

"And I'm a mother to her that was motherless," grunted Mevrouw complacently, "and because she's poor and no real relation I allow her to call me 'aunt.'"

"Besides which, if she behaves herself, who knows what may happen to her!" Mynheer Mopius jingled the loose cash in his trousers-pockets and looked askance at Ursula.

Ursula looked back at him, peacefully unconscious.

"I might leave her my money," said Mynheer Mopius.

"Oh, that would be splendid!" cried Ursula.

Her uncle looked at her again. "Sly little thing!" he thought, but he said nothing. Only Jacóbus Mopius could have called Ursula little. His greatness caused him to see all things small.

He was a stunted, pompous man, with a big head and yellow checks. He had made his money in the Dutch Indies, as a notary.

Harriet came back in a fawn-colored frock with a pink rosebud pattern, made of some kind of nun's veiling, high in the throat. Mynheer Mopius gazed at it in admiration.

"Looks well, doesn't she?" he said to Ursula in a loud *sotto voce*. "You shall have just such another; but Harriet's a devilish good-looking girl."

The subject of this comment did not appear to hear it, but Ursula fancied she saw her aunt wince. Harriet was helping the faded woman to put things together. In the hall a gong was sounding a hideous bellow at the door.

"Late as usual," remonstrated Mynheer Mopius. "Hurry up, my dear. Gracious goodness, how awkward you are getting!" The frail little creature in the stiff silk caught hold of Harriet's arm with one skinny hand, and Ursula, as she watched her movements, understood something of her unwillingness to exert herself.

For his own use Mynheer Mopius never bought anything cheap, and all the appointments of the dinner-table were excellent. Of course he communicated prices to the new arrival, and Ursula, soon discovering that she was expected constantly to admire, entered into the spirit of the thing, and asked the cost of the silver candlesticks. Her uncle ascended into regions of unusual good humor, and ordered up a bottle of sweet Spanish wine for her, "such as you ignorant females enjoy," he said. He grew very angry with his wife for refusing to have any. "But the doctor forbids it." "Oh, damn your doctor. Never have a doctor till you're dead; that's my advice. Then he can't do any harm."

Mevrouw Mopius meekly swallowed a little of the liquid, her long nose drooping over the glass. Her husband sat tyrannically watching her. "Drink it all," he said; "you want a tonic. You shall have some every day." And she drank it, although she implicitly believed in the doctor, and the doctor, a teetotaler, had told her it meant death.

"Doctors are all scoundrels," said Mynheer Mopius. "Hey, Harriet?"

The girl's dead father had been a medical man.

"Yes, I know," she said. "Only lawyers are honest. That's why doctors die poor."

Mynheer Mopius laughed heartily. "I like your cheek," he said. "Make hay while your sun shines, Harriet. A man can't stand it from an old woman."

Mevrouw Mopius sniffed.

"We must have some fun, hey, wife, while Ursula's here? We might give a dinner-party, and show the grandees what's what."

"But the grandees don't come to our dinner-parties," objected Mevrouw Mopius.

"No, they don't, hang 'em. But they'd hear from the people who do. Your Dominé Pock knows 'em all. We'll have Pock to dinner. He's always asking for money for something or other, but he's a good judge of victuals. Trust a parson to be that, and a poor judge of wine. At least the Evangelicals. And he'll tell every one I've the best venison in the city. I get my venison from Brussels, Ursula, and it's better, they'll all say, than the Baron van Trossart's, who shoots his himself."

"The Baron van Trossart!" said Ursula. "That is the guardian of the Van Helmonts' cousin, Helen, the heiress. I am to go to a party there. Gerard promised me an invitation."

Mynheer Mopius's face grew very dark.

"Look here," he said, "are you staying with me or in barracks? If with me, you must allow *me* to amuse you. I won't hear anything about your Barons Gerard. And I won't have nothing to say to them."

"Gerard isn't the Baron," replied Ursula, hotly. "That's his father. Not that it matters."

"No, I shouldn't think it did. I won't hear anything about them. What did you say the father's name was?"

"Theodore, Baron van Helmont van Horstwyk en de Horst," rolled forth Ursula, proudly.

"Yes, poor Roderick likes that sort of thing. Is "the Horst" the name of the house? Is it grander than .this?"

Ursula laughed. "It's quite different," she said.

"Well, I dare say. But I won't hear another word about them. That kind of people are all a mistake."

Harriet lifted her indolent eyes, and fixed them on Ursula's face.

"Do you like your wine?" she said. "Mind you deserve it."

For the rest of the meal Mynheer Mopius talked of the entertainments he would organize for Ursula. He refused to let her accompany Harriet on the theological errand concerning Leah's eyes.

"No, no," he said, "come into the drawing-room and amuse us. Do you play? Do you sing? Harriet does neither. We do both."

Ursula played well. She gave them a Concert of Liszt, and Mynheer did not talk till Mevrouw dropped her scissors and asked him, after a wait, to pick them up for her. As soon as he could, he got hold of the piano himself, and called out to his wife to join him. He had been possessed of a fine bass twenty years ago, and had enjoyed much admiration in Batavian society. It now stopped somewhere down in his stomach, and only a rumble came out. His wife rose wearily to play his accompaniments, and he kept her chained to the piano for the rest of the evening, though Ursula could not help seeing that the playing seemed to cause her physical pain.

He sang only love-songs of the ultra-sentimental kind, all

about broken hearts and lovely death and willing sacrifice. Many of them were of a by-gone period when everybody pretended—at least in verse—to be absolutely ill with affection.

Harriet came back and poured out tea. When her uncle said it was bad she shrugged her shoulders.

"It always is," she replied.

"Yes, Harriet, it is, though I get it direct from the East," he rejoined. His whole attitude betokened reproof.

"The East," interposed Mevrouw, from her tambour-frame.

"Quite so. I wonder, when Laban welcomed Jacob, do you think he gave him tea?"

"Coffee, rather, I should fancy," replied Mopius.

"Do you really believe they drank coffee, Jacóbus?* I wish I was sure"—for the fiftieth time that day (as every day) she fell to contemplating her work with arrested needle. "I could so well fill up this corner with a little table, and put on the rolls and cups and things."

"And work an 'L' in the napkin corner," suggested Harriet.

Mevrouw Mopius gazed suspiciously into her niece's face, but Harriet's expression was perfectly serious.

"And—work—an—'L'—into—the—napkin—corner," repeated Mevrouw Mopius, very slowly. "Well, I think that might be nice."

Ursula had just extinguished her light, and was dozing off into a dream-land of Mopiuses and Jonkers, when the door opened and Harriet entered hurriedly, candle in hand, a white   . wrap flung loosely about her.

"I didn't knock," she said. "Knocks are heard all over a house at night."

She threw herself into an easy chair by the bed. "Finished already!" she said. "*You* don't make much work of your beauty."

"It's so little, I should be afraid of killing it with over-care," replied Ursula, smiling.

* To "drink coffee" is old-fashioned Dutch for "lunch."

But Harriet frowned. "Don't tell lies," she said. "You must know you're lovely. You are. Am I lovely too?"

"I think you look very nice," replied Ursula, hesitatingly.

"Thank you. I understand." She tossed back her black locks from her sallow cheeks, and her sad eyes flashed. "But see here, I didn't come to talk about looks." She pushed forward the candle so that its light fell full on Ursula's sleepy face. "Wake up for a minute, can't you? You and I may as well understand each other at once." She leaned back, and folded her bare white arms, from which the loose sleeves fell away.

"Uncle Mopius is always telling me that you are his natural heir," she said. "He tells me whenever he wants to make himself disagreeable, which is not infrequently. I dare say you know."

Ursula sat up. "No, indeed I don't," she said, "and I don't want to. Once my Aunt Josine said something about it, a couple of years ago, and father called me into his study and said he didn't think I should ever get a penny of Uncle Jacóbus's money, and he earnestly hoped not. I've never thought of it since."

Harriet jerked up her chin. "Your father must be a peculiar sort of man," she said, "if sincere. Did he mean it?"

Ursula blew out the candle. "I'm going to sleep," she said. "Good-night. I don't want to be rude to you."

But Harriet quietly drew a box of matches from her pocket. "I like that," she said, leisurely. "I wish I had somebody to stick up for. But I came to say this—Uncle Mopius is sure to bring up the subject constantly in your presence. He'll taunt me, as is his habit, especially now you're here, with your good-luck in being his own sister's child. Now, I want you fully to understand"—she leaned forward her big dark face till Ursula struggled not to shrink back—"that I—don't—care. I don't care a bit. I'm not like men. And if you think you're enjoying a cheap triumph, you're mistaken, that's all. And if you imagine it's bravado on my part, because I can't help myself, you're mistaken too. I don't want his dirty money. I'm sick of it. I want something better. I'm not going to hate you

for nothing. In fact, I rather like you. So he can go on as
much as ever he chooses, and if you enjoy it you're free to do so."
"But I don't," cried Ursula, with hot cheeks. "I don't a
bit. You know I don't. And, in fact, uncle talked quite differently this afternoon. I thought you—"

The other girl stopped her with a gesture.
"Don't," she said, "I won't hear it. I'm sick of the whole
business. Be sure that, whatever he said, it was a lie." She
got up and began pacing the room, her limbs quivering under
the light folds of her gown. Suddenly she stood still, looking
down at Ursula. "Shall I tell you what will really happen?
Do you care to know? It's easy enough." Ursula did not answer, but Harriet went on, unheeding, "Aunt will die, and he
will marry again as soon as he can. That's all. There." Ursula's continuous silence seemed to goad her companion. "You
think he may die before aunt? He may; but when a chimney
falls down into the street, it usually manages to hit a better
man. You watch aunt. Good-night." She was departing, but
again reflected, and came back to the bed. "You poor thing,"
she said, "I believe you really would have liked me to get the
money. Why?"

"Oh, I should indeed," replied Ursula, earnestly, "though it
looks a long way off. You seem so lonely and—will you mind
my saying it?—so unhappy, Harriet." To her amazement her
visitor fell forward on the bed and hugged her. A moment
afterwards, however, Harriet again sat in the big chair. "You
are quite mistaken," she said, arranging her draperies with
downcast eyes, "I am not at all unhappy." There followed a
moment's agitated silence, and then:

"Ursula, I like you. I want to tell you something. You'll
listen for a moment, won't you? I've nobody else to tell it to."
Without further consideration the girl pushed one hand between the loose folds about her throat, and from the snowy
recesses of her bosom drew forth a paper which she hurriedly
thrust in front of Ursula. "There, read that," she said, excitedly. "It never leaves me lest *they* should find out." Still
sitting up, with one elbow on the little table beside her, Ursula
read a printed advertisement, a scrap from a newspaper:

4

"H. V. Meet me on Thursday next at eight o'clock in the Long Walk outside the West Gate. Wear a white feather and, if possible, a red shawl. Carry your parasol open, *in any case.* Dearest, I am dying to see yóu, but can't come before then. Your own Romeo."

"Well?" queried Ursula, but immediately her voice changed. "Harriet, you don't mean to tell me that this is an entanglement of yours?"

"You choose a strange word," replied Harriet, loftily. "There is no entanglement. But I hope there is going to be. As yet there is merely an answer to an advertisement. Yes, the advertisement was mine. Oh, Ursula, isn't it delightful? He says he is dying to see me. Imagine that. And he doesn't even know me yet."

"That surely makes his eagerness less delightful," replied Ursula, dryly.

"Oh, but I gave him a very accurate description, tall, luminous eyes, dark locks, ivory skin. I told him I was of distinctly prepossessing appearance. Yes, in spite of your opinion, I ventured to tell him that. Uncle informs me so frequently that I am very good-looking, and aunt repeats so consistently that I am exceedingly plain, I feel I have a double right to be satisfied with my beauty. Besides, every woman's glass declares to her that her appearance is prepossessing; it is the one reason why I fancy, on the whole, women's lives must be happier than men's."

"Did you put all that in the advertisement?" asked Ursula, still staring stupidly at the scrap of paper on the bed.

"I—I wrote him a letter, just one."

"Addressed to ' Romeo '?"

"To ' Romeo ˌde Lieven.' * Isn't it a charming name?"

"It's an assumed name. Imagine a Dutchman called Romeo!"

"Of course, it's a pseudonym, like Carmen Sylva. I wasn't clever enough to think of one ; besides, I hate subterfuges. So I just put my own name, H. V.—Harriet Verveen."

***

* To love.

" Harriet, you don't mean to say that you wrote a signed love-letter you don't in the least know to whom ?"

" Love-letter, no. I told him who I was and what I wanted. Besides, I shall know him to-morrow."

" You're not going."

Once more Harriet assumed her almost defiant attitude.

" Yes, I'm going," she said. " So there !"

" What do you think ?" she suddenly burst out. " It's all very well for you comfortable, sheltered girls, at home. What's to become of the likes of me if we don't look out for ourselves ? Nobody 'll help to find me a husband or a hiding-place. Nobody 'll ever do anything for me except abuse me because I do things for myself."

" But *I* haven't had a lover found for me," interposed Ursula. " It seems so unwomanly—"

" Womanly ! There we have the word—womanly !"

Harriet's words came stumbling and tossing ; she thrust out her limbs and the muslin fell away from them. " It's womanly to live on day by day in bitterness, with every womanly feeling hourly insulted and estranged ; after a year more, perhaps, of this, to go to some fresh situation and look after other people's children, and when you are worn out at last, to die, soured and in want. That's honest independence, that's womanly modesty. Well, then, I'm immodest. Do you understand me ?" She threw herself wildly forward. " I'm immodest. I want love. I told you just now I didn't want the old scoundrel's money. I don't. But I want love. I want love. And I mean to have it. A woman has a right to love and be loved. I won't be some lazy rich woman's substitute, with brats I don't care for. I want to love children of my own. Children that love me when I kiss them. I love my own body." She fell back again, and her eager voice died into a pensive murmur ; while speaking, she softly stroked her rounded arm. " I love it, and I want others to love it also. I want it to belong to some one besides my lonely self. Great Heaven, don't you understand ?"—her tone grew shrill again—" one's youth goes—goes. But you don't understand." She stopped abruptly, just in time, and hid her face in her hand.

Ursula knew not how to speak or act. There was only one thing she wanted to do; so she did it. She put an arm round Harriet's neck and kissed her. But the girl shook herself free, and, without another word, hurried away.

The next day passed in an atmosphere of sombre expectation. Ursula and Harriet barely spoke to one another; the latter seemed to be holding aloof. Mynheer Mopius took his niece the round of the house amid a steady flow of self-laudation, and Ursula put in pleasing adjectives as full-stops. He showed her everything, even to the water-supply and the wine-cellar. There was but one exception, his wife's store-cupboard ; Mevrouw Mopius, to his annoyance, actually held out in refusing the key. But he found a compensation in unmitigated china and glass.

After a morning thus profitably spent, the afternoon brought a long drive and a visit to a flower show. The drive was merely an opportunity for parading Mynheer Mopius's equipage among the beauties of nature, but that gentleman was made happy, after prolonged anxiety and craning, by meeting the very people he was desirous should see it. The visit to the exhibition, however, must be regarded as an act of kindness to his guest, for the committee had had the manifest stupidity to award Mynheer Mopius's double dahlias a third prize.

In the gardens Ursula espied Gerard with his cousin Helena among a crowd of stylish-looking people, whom Jacóbus described as " swells." She had received, that morning, the promised card for the Baroness van Trossart's party, and she would gladly have sought an occasion of thanking the sender, but to this proposal her uncle, in a sudden fit of shyness, opposed resolute and almost rampant refusal.

" I don't want to know the people," he repeated, excitedly, his eyes fixed on the distinguished group by the central lake.

"I don't want to have anything to say to them. Ursula, you belong to my party. I desire you to stay where you are."

"Oh, very well," replied Ursula, offended; "though, of course, I should not have gone up to him as long as he was conversing with that violet-nosed old woman in blue."

"That lady is the wife of the Governor, and I will thank you to speak of her with more respect."

Ursula listened in amazement. She was not enough a student of human nature to explain her uncle's change of front. She went and sat down on the bench beside her aunt, with a few kind words about the weather.

"Oh, beautiful!" gasped Mevrouw Mopius. "Jacóbus, don't you think it is time we went home?"

Jacóbus assented, and in the midst of plans for to-morrow sought to impress upon Ursula the number and importance of his acquaintances as instanced by frequent salutes.

Ursula came upon her aunt alone in the drawing-room half an hour before dinner. The vast apartment was darkened to a mellow glow behind its yellow venetians. Mevrouw Mopius sat with closed eyes and cavernous cheeks before her unused frame. She stirred as the door opened, and beckoned her niece to her side.

"My dear," she said in a faint voice, "come and sit by me for a minute. I have something to ask you." Ursula obeyed. "Your uncle was speaking of the opera for to-morrow night. I want you to tell him you don't care to go."

"But I do care," objected the girl. "I think it's simply glorious. I've never been to the opera before."

"My dear, I can assure you it's not worth seeing. The singers make such a noise you can't hear a word they say. Not that that matters, for they always say the same thing."

"Oh, but I should like it," repeated Ursula.

"Say, for my sake, that you don't care to go." Mevrouw Mopius's manner became very nervous. "Ursula, I can't go out at night. Have you set your heart on this performance?"

"Yes, aunt," said the girl, frankly; "but, even if I hadn't, I shouldn't know of any valid excuse. However, I can very well go with Harriet and uncle. I'll tell him you'd rather not."

Mevrouw Mopius clutched her arm. "Hold your tongue," she said, quite roughly. "I didn't want to have you here. I tell you so honestly. I knew it would be like this. It was Jacóbus. Poor fellow, I suppose he felt how dull the house was getting." She paused meditatively. "He'd never go without me; he wouldn't enjoy himself."

"I'm sure I didn't ask to come," protested Ursula, "but now I'm here, I can't begin inventing a parcel of lies. You must tell uncle yourself, aunt, please."

Mevrouw Mopius tightened her grip till the nails dug into the flesh. She turned her dull eyes full on Ursula. "Girl," she gasped, "what are you, with your little pleasures or prejudices to come athwart such a sorrow as mine? I'll tell you my secret, if it must be. Swear, first, that you'll not breathe it to a living soul."

Ursula was alarmed by her aunt's earnest manner. "I can't swear," she said in a flurry, "but I'll promise. I never swore in my life."

"Swear," repeated the other woman under her breath; unconsciously she tightened her grasp till Ursula shrieked aloud. "Hush! Are you mad? He'll hear. Oh, is that it?" She relaxed her hold. "Fool, did you never feel pain?"

"I—I don't know," gasped Ursula, now thoroughly frightened, convinced that her aunt must have mad fits of which no one had spoken.

"Swear, I tell you. Say, so help me, God Almighty. Louder. Let me hear it. Now, listen. I'm ill, incurably ill. Never mind what the doctor calls the illness. Enough that he says I can't live beyond two months. Perhaps he's mistaken. They often are. Not that I want to live. Not in this agony, my God! Not except for *him*. Ursula, your uncle knows nothing. I don't want him to know. I'd bear twice as much, if I could, so that he shouldn't know. Poor fellow, he has his faults, perhaps, but he's so soft-hearted, he can't bear to see suffering, not even to hear of it. There, now, I have told you. I've never told a living soul, as I said. I can hide it from him, Ursula, if things go on as usual. But I can't go taking long drives, or to flower-shows, and oh, Ursula, dear, I *can't* go out at night."

Ursula was dumb-struck with horror and pity. Still, she
could not help feeling, even at that moment, that her visit to
her uncle was becoming hopelessly perplexed. She had expected a round of gayeties, all the delights of a début.

"I'll do whatever you wish me to," she said, helplessly.
"Oh, aunt, I'm so sorry, but I hope you'll get better. Father
says doctors never know."

"Not about curing, they don't," replied her aunt, grimly.
"Now, Ursula, remember, not a word. It's a secret between
you and me. I don't think it 'll be for very long. Move away;
I hear some one coming!"

Harriet entered the room with her novel under her arm.
Presently she looked up at Mevrouw Mopius's deathly countenance lying back as if asleep, and nodded meaningly to Ursula.
Mynheer Mopius came in, and his wife sat up. "Jacóbus," she
said, "you were laughing at the blueness of my sky yesterday. I saw one in the exhibition aviary that was every bit
as blue."

"But did you look at the real article up above us?" questioned Jacóbus.

"No," admitted Mevrouw Mopius, "I didn't think of that."

Harriet rose hurriedly from dessert. "Aunt is tired," she
said. "You must excuse us, uncle," and she offered Mevrouw
her arm. At the door she turned. "You don't want me just
now, I suppose?" she continued. "I am going out to get a
breath of fresh air."

"Yes," added Ursula quickly, "Harriet and I are going for
a walk."

A moment later the two girls met on the bedroom-landing.
Both were dressed to go out. Harriet had a white feather on
her hat, and a red shawl over one arm. "Leave me alone, can't
you?" said Harriet. She spoke fiercely, and a gesture escaped
her which was almost a menace.

"No, I'm going with you," replied Ursula, quietly.

"Indeed you sha'n't. What a fool I was to tell you. Women
always are fools to ask sympathy from each other."

"I shall not be in your way," persisted Ursula, with coaxing decision. "Let me wait with you till he comes, if he comes, and then I can step aside."

"Of course he will come," said Harriet. Perhaps it was the thought of this certain triumph which induced her to forbear all further opposition to Ursula's accompanying her.

"I bought this shawl," began Harriet, as they walked through the shadowed streets. "I had to pawn my only brooch to get it."

"Does uncle allow you no pocket-money?" asked Ursula.

"Ten florins a month," replied Harriet, bitterly. "I spend most of it in scents and chocolate-creams. They are my one consolation. I adore chocolate-creams. Do you? We might get some now. I've got a florin left from the brooch-money."

"Let me buy them this time," suggested Ursula, sympathetically.

"Very well. I like the pink kind best."

It was still light, but a veil had already fallen over the low-sinking sun. The hot, sleepy streets were waking up in the red glow of the fading day. People in the town, now that the glare had died from their eyes, were telling each other that the air was cool, and trying to believe it.

Outside, however, the assertion had more truth in it. A ripple of refreshment was slowly spreading up from the distant river. The shadows of the straight-lined trees lay across the brick road in great black stripes. The fields looked as if their dusty grass was turning green again beneath the darkening sky; in the dull ditches stood the cattle, dreamily content.

The girls walked on in silence till they reached a point where the road swerved off into a little thicket. This was the spot which Romeo must have had in his mind. It was very quiet and sequestered. They stood looking at each other, still in silence. Harriet's pale cheeks were flushed.

Evening was now rapidly closing in; great folds of gray shadow seemed to come broadening over the landscape; not a sound was heard but the faint whiz of some tiny gnats.

Suddenly the clear chimes began to play from the slender ball-topped tower, which stood out black, like a monstrous ninepin, against the yellow western sky. The eyes of the watchers met. Eight slow strokes came trembling heavily across the hush of sunset. At the other end of the long, straight road a figure appeared, as yet quite indistinct. They watched. They could hear each other's hearts beat.

When it drew nearer they saw that it was a woman. Harriet gave a great gasp of relief. A moment later it had come quite close to them. And both saw simultaneously that the woman wore a white feather and a scarlet shawl.

She passed them suspiciously; she was an independent-looking, weather-beaten female of some forty wintry winters—all angles and frost. After a moment she halted, and hesitatingly retraced her steps.

The last glow paled away from the horizon. In the ashen grayness it even seemed to Ursula that the little breeze from the marshes blew cold. The long road lay motionless, gradually shortening into night.

"A fine evening, young ladies," said the red-shawled female, stopping abruptly near them, and suddenly opening an enormous parasol; "but it's getting late."

"It's not much beyond eight," replied Ursula, for want of an answer.

"Nine minutes," said the female, with precision. "Nine full minutes past 8 P.M. Perhaps I may remark to you, ladies, that this spot is unhealthy after sunset—very particularly unhealthy. The back-sillies, as modern science calls them, come up from the water and produce injurious smells. If I were you I should be careful—very particularly careful." She turned on one heel, but suddenly bethought herself.

"I," she said, nodding her head—the white feather waved— "am compelled by the call of duty to remain. I am waiting for some one—an engagement." She spoke the last word with triumphant pomposity. Its double meaning evidently furnished her extreme satisfaction. She repeated it twice, and jingled a small reticule depending from a cotton-gloved wrist.

"I know of a case," she went on immediately, seeing that neither girl moved or spake, "when a young person (much of your age) spent an evening out here in this wood. Her reasons for doing so I distinctly decline to enter into. They were not

"THE GIRLS WALKED ON IN SILENCE"

laudable, you may be sure; no young girl's would be. Well, she caught the myasthma and died. She *died*."

All the time she was holding forth the speaker peered anxiously to right and left in the darkness.

"Duty," she added, "as I told you, compels me to remain. But I do so at the risk of my health."

"You lying old humbug!" said a deep voice behind her in the darkness. "Then what have you got that red shawl on for, eh?"

The victim to duty spun round as if shot.

"Oh, it's you, is it, Maria?" she said. "I know what *you're* here for. Spying, spying; that's your errand, you nasty, envious thing."

"Then you're wrong, that's all. I'm here on a fool's errand of my own, like yourself."

A short, fat woman stepped into the faint reflection of a distant lantern, and they saw that she also wore a red shawl! Not even courtesy could describe this lady as of "uncertain age."

"Seems to me," she continued, "you and I needn't have been so mighty close with each other. Nor you needn't have crowed over me as you did, Isabella. I don't see that your lover was so much smarter than mine."

"Oh, Harriet, come away," whispered Ursula, breaking a long silence.

Harriet laughed hoarsely. "No," she said, "I'm going to see this comedy out."

"And as for those young ladies there," Maria went on, "they've as much right to be here as we have—at least, the one with the red shawl over her arm has. Yes, my dear, you needn't try to smuggle it away behind your neighbor. You're here from a sense of duty, as much as ever my friend Isabella is. I wonder how many more of us have answered this advertisement?"

"One more has," said a young voice, and a pretty, fair little creature, looking like a dress-maker's assistant, stole from behind a tree into the ring.

"That makes five of us," announced the fat woman, with a

nod to Ursula. "It was mean of you yonder to be ashamed of
your colors. Well, men were deceivers ever, and, girls, we've
been once more deceived."

"It was I advertised first, not he," said the pretty girl,
defiantly.

"So did I," Harriet admitted. "We may as well be fair."

"Well, so did I, if it comes to that," declared the fat woman.
"And so did you, Isabella; we needn't ask you. And so did
that featherless girl, I dare say. I don't see that it makes
much difference. And it was Romeo de Lieven, was it, as
told you all to come here?"

"All," said the whole chorus. They had gradually drawn
nearer to one of the rare street lamps which make a dismal
haze at far intervals along the dark road. They stood in a
circle, with unconsciously uplifted parasols, and all around
them was the soft night, and the little wind, and the damp
smell of the water.

"Then the best thing you can do is to go home again.
Come along, Isabella, you can sing me the praises of your lover
as we go."

"I solemnly swear," said the sour spinster, in sepulchral tones,
"never to trust a man again. Ah, I could tell you a story—"

"There's no time for that now," interrupted her friend,
briskly. "As for solemnly swearing, I don't object. Ladies,
you see what they are, these men. Imagine what would have
happened to you if this Romeo had come, and any of you'd
married him. No, Romeo, we will not marry. Let us promise,
each one of us, after to-night's experience, to turn our backs on
them forever."

All of them, except Ursula, lifted their arms on high. In
chorus they sang out, "We promise," and even as they did
so a vehicle suddenly loomed through the darkness, a high trap,
devoid of carriage lights, occupied by three or four officers in
uniform.

"Way there, please," said a voice which Ursula recognized.
The women scattered on one side, all looking up involuntarily.
The dim light of the lantern fell full on their faces, and, for one
instant, Gerard saw Ursula's features quite plainly. She shrank

back; how she hoped that he had not recognized her! She thought not.

The dog-cart passed down the road, and presently the young men were heard laughing heartily. This masculine hilarity seemed to exasperate the buxom Maria.

"Let us bind ourselves," she said, "to meet together next year, at this spot and this hour, and to prove to each other that each has kept her word."

"We promise," said the others, in taking leave.

But, when the anniversary came round, be it noted here, Maria marched to her solitary vigil. The two younger women had broken their vow, and the weather-beaten spinster much wanted them to believe that she had broken hers.

Not a word was exchanged between the two girls on their homeward way. Ursula felt heartily relieved when she found herself once more safe in the drawing-room. Harriet had a headache, and Ursula poured out tea. Mynheer Mopius took an opportunity of praising her concoction as a set-off against Harriet's.

"Of course it's her fault," he argued, "not that of the tea. How could it be?—best Java imported."

"Uncle Jacóbus," began Ursula, emboldened by this approval, "I don't care about the opera to-morrow. I'd as lief stay at home." Her hand trembled, and she blushed crimson.

Mynheer Mopius set down his teacup cautiously, for it was best Japan. "Well, of all the deceiving minxes!" he said. "And to hear her go on this afternoon in the carriage! Ursula, you *are* insincere."

Mevrouw Mopius sat quite motionless. Her niece did not venture to glance her way.

"Well, of course," said Mynheer, in the silence, "*you* must know. I'm not such a fool as to waste my money, and no thanks for my pains. After I'd sent round to the stationer's, too, for the book of words you said you would like to have. I'm very much disappointed in you, Ursula. I can't make it out."

"Operas aren't really good," piped Mevrouw Mopius's tremulous voice. "They're not a bit like real life. I never had anything happen to me like an opera."

Mynheer Mopius slapped his knee. "I have it," he cried; "it's some religious nonsense of your father's. Well, if it don't rise to the surface quicker, there can't be much of it. Come along, wife, I can't bear to think of her. Come along; let's play and sing."

Mevrouw Mopius staggered to her feet. Ursula remained in the half-light of the front room. Husband and wife spent the rest of the evening at the piano.

> "Dear love, for thee I would lay down my li-i-ife,
> For without thee what would that life avail?
> If thy hand but lift the fatal kni-i-ife,
> I smile, I faint, and bid sweet death all hail,"

sang Mynheer Mopius. And Ursula listened. And Mevrouw Mopius played.

"PLUSH," said the Baroness van Helmont, addressing her silken favorite, "it is a terrible thing to have an incompatible child."

Plush made no answer, but from the other end of the room came Otto's reply: "I can't help it, mother. I suppose you made me what I am."

"I? Never in my life. I could not have produced anything so strong. Plush and I, we are in harmony; we take the same view of existence."

She languidly entangled her fingers in the meshes of her darling's soft white hair. The lapdog, on her crimson cushion, laid two delicate little slender-wristed paws, that looked as if encased in a perfect fit of *peau de Suède*, over a bright black button of a nose. The pair of them, lady and lapdog, looked born to undulate.

"You are resolved, then," continued the Baroness, "to return to Java as soon as you again get tired of us."

"Tired of you! Mother!" His emotion made him both unable and unwilling to say more.

"Tired or not, in a few months you will once more leave us. Otto, it will break your father's heart."

This prophecy Otto considered a decidedly doubtful one.

"I never understood why you first went," continued the Baroness. "Gerard stays. Everybody I know stays. Fifteen years ago you must suddenly resolve to learn gentleman-farming in Germany. It sounds so silly, 'gentleman-farming.' They call it 'economy' over there — I suppose the name pleased you—and after a year or two you came back and said

it couldn't be done without plenty of money. A charming
economy. It is as good as a farce !"

"That is true, Otto, is it not ?" she added, petulantly, after a
pause.

"Quite true," he replied, helplessly, sitting forward on a little
boudoir chair, his brown hands hanging joined between his
heavy legs.

"Well, then, after that you must hurry away to plant tea in
the Indies, as if there were not enough common people to do
that! And doing it, too. I never heard of a break-down in
the tea-supply. And now you have been busied there for a
dozen years, and what's the profit to you or to any one ? You're
no richer, and tea's not even cheaper. So you've benefited neither your neighbor nor yourself." The Baroness sighed. Plush
sighed also, her whole little pink-tinted body a sob of lethargic
content.

"But I've been earning an honest living," burst out Otto,
desperately. It was all so useless ; he had said it so often before ! "At least I've not been droning through my whole life,
spending father's money, and knowing all the time that in fact
there was no money to spend. Of course, I'd hoped to come
back richer from India, but you can't understand about the
crisis in the tea-trade, mother."

"No, indeed," said the Baroness.

"At any rate, however, I've paid my way. I've not lived, as
Gerard does, in a constant entanglement of bills and loans. I
don't depend for my daily bread on the mercy of the Jews."

"Nor does Gerard, thank Heaven ! though he may for his ·
daily champagne!" cried the Baroness, her irrepressible sprightliness bubbling uppermost. "And the Jews, as your father always says, are a dispensation of Providence for the survival of
the fittest. He doesn't mean themselves. They keep the old
families above water till smoother times work round again.
Look at the Van Utrechts, for instance ; the only son tried to
commit suicide for want of a friendly Jew ! And four months
later he married a Rotterdam oil-merchant's daughter. That's
what Gerard will do; only, in his case, I do hope and pray that
the man who made the money will be a generation farther off.

And on the mother's side." The Baroness sank back reflectively, and, for the hundredth time, a procession of ticketed young ladies passed before her pale blue eyes.

"Otto," she said, "you know the desire of our hearts. It is that you marry Helena van Trossart. Then we should say, 'Lord, now lettest Thou Thy servant depart in peace.'"

"Catch my father saying that," cried Otto, roughly, with holy horror in his honest eyes.

The Baroness stopped him by an imperious gesture.

"I don't know what you mean, Otto," she said. "Please don't be profane. Yes, I desire above all things to see this marriage consummated. Gerard will do well in any case. And, after all, it is you who will one day be Baron Helmont of the Horst. You, our first, our eldest." She checked herself, holding out her thin white hand, and her eyes were full of love.

Otto took the hand in his own and kissed it.

"You might *try*, Otto," continued the Baroness. "You don't know her; she was a child when you went away. There is no sense in your refusing to find out whether you could like her or not. The marriage would end all difficulties for good, and you could remain with us."

"What do you want me to do?" asked Otto, heavily.

"Supposing you were to go to Drum to-day, and see them. You might stay over their dance, which is to-morrow night. It would be a pretty attention. I feel sure the coast is clear, and she thinks you interesting. She told me so herself, when they dined here; she considers your life one long romance."

"Romance is the word," said Otto. "Well, mother, I'm willing to go." He took up the *Graphic* from a side-table, and silence brooded over the trio till the Baron came in.

"My dear," said the Baron, eagerly, his eyes alight, "I must just show you this; the carrier brought it. It's Feuillet's *Jeune Homme Pauvre*, with the original drawings by Mouchot. Isn't it charming? I had it over from Fontaine."

The Baroness took the volume, disturbing Plush.

"Yes," she replied, as she turned over the pages. "It's very nice. But I can't help preferring my old friend, Johannot."

"How unkind!" said the Baron, plaintively, "Johannot

6

couldn't be expected to illustrate everything, especially not the books that were written after he died."

He turned to his son.

"I sha'n't show it to you, Otto, for you'd only ask how much it cost."

"Oh, don't," interposed the Baroness.

"And yet this is quite a bargain. Only 625 francs, and the binding by David."

"My dear, I don't care. Besides, I have forgotten already."

"Lucky woman," the Baron laughed. "I, at least, must re-member till it's paid. What's the matter, Jan?"—this to a ser-vant who appeared in the open door. "You can clear away the papers on the library floor."

"There's a poor woman at the kitchen entrance asking to see you, sir," said the man. "She says you know all about her. Her name is Vrouw Klop, from the cottages by Horstwyk Mill."

"I never heard of the creature in my life!" cried the Baron.

"I know her," remarked Mevrouw, quietly. "Her husband drinks."

"Saving your presence, Mevrouw," said Jan, without moving a muscle, "she says her husband's been dead these seven years."

"Well, if he had lived, he'd have drunk," replied the Baron-ess, indifferently. "And, besides, if she's been a widow so long she must have children earning something."

Otto got up and walked towards the window.

"Send her away," exclaimed the Baron. "It's like her in-solence, asking for me!"

"She says she has a letter from the Burgomaster, mynheer," gently persisted the servant. Menials are always pamperedly insolent to mendicants or aggressively sympathetic regarding them. They are never indifferent.

"Then why didn't you bring it up? Why doesn't she go to the relieving officer? I can't be bothered. There, give her a twopenny bit, and let her go."

Otto stood at the window, looking out.

"The people are unendurable," said the Baron, as the servant

departed. "Always wanting something, and always asking for
it. As if it were our duty to supply unlimited gin !"

"Yes," replied the Baroness, "and the respectable poor never
beg. This illustration is charming, Theodore ; I think it is the
best of all. What a sweet face the girl has !"

She held up the beautiful blue morocco volume to the light.
Otto stood at the window, looking out.

Helena van Trossart belonged to one of the most influential
families in Holland. Her mother had been a sister of the Baron
van Helmont ; both mother and father were long since dead.
She lived with an uncle and aunt on the other side, Trossarts,
like herself, and rich, like herself, with Trossart money. The
uncle and aunt were childless, and affectionately interested in
their beautiful heiress, of whom they felt proud to think as the
greatest *parti* in the province. The Baroness was portly and
comfortable ; she had never known any but comfortable people
all her life. The Baron, a fine old gentleman with silver-striped
hair, was concerned in the government of the country, which
means that he occupied his time in procuring lucrative posts for
his wife's poor relations, of whose poverty he lived in monotonous dread.

The fine old double mansion which the Van Trossarts inhabited stood on a green canal behind a sombre row of chestnuts.
Grass grew between the paving-stones, and iron chains swung
heavily from post to post. Not a street boy passed but pulled
those chains. The street boy of Holland is unparalleled in Europe, a pestilence that walketh in darkness, and a destruction
that wasteth at noonday, but here you could hardly take offence
at him, for he imparted an element of liveliness to as dead a
corner as dull respectability could desire to dwell in. The outside of the house wore that aspect of dignified dilapidation
which is characteristic of hereditary wealth. Inside nothing
was new, except in Helena's apartments, nor was anything worn
out.

"Mamma," said the Freule Helena — she called her foster-
mother "mamma "—" I have a note from Gerard. He asks
whether he may bring Otto round to lunch in half an hour's

time. Otto, it appears, has turned up for the day. The orderly
is waiting. I suppose I had better say yes."

"Stop a moment while I ring and ask how many pigeons
there are," replied the Baroness, who was eminently practical.

"You wouldn't keep them away because of that!" cried Helena,
laughing.

"Indeed I should. Gerard detests cold meat. And there's
nothing a man resents like getting what he doesn't eat in a
house where his tastes are known. You've asked people enough
unexpectedly already."

"Only Georgetta van Troyen and her brother. That was to
escape a tête-à-tête with Mechteld van Weylert. We shall be
quite a small party."

"I don't mind large parties, like to-morrow's," replied Mevrouw van Trossart, turning from a confabulation with her confidential maid. "Well, tell them to come. Ann, just say to
the man, 'My compliments, and the Jonkers * are welcome.'
You are terribly gay, child; you can't bear a moment of
quiet."

"Dear mamma, did you want me to sit all the afternoon opposite Maggie van Weylert? Confess though she is your niece,
you would not do it yourself. With some women conversation
is just contradiction. And there are few people outside this
house, except Gerard, I care to be alone with. No guest, or a
number, that is my view."

"Gerard would feel flattered," replied the Baroness, smiling
over her plump hands. "You had better not tell him, or he will
ask you to afford him the opportunity of being alone together
for life."

"How terrible! Mamma, you are perfectly ruthless. There
is not a creature in the world, not even myself, I am fond
enough of for that. Besides, surely one should never marry a
man one likes to be alone with; it is the most fatal way of dying to society at once." She laughed, and threw back the yellow curls from her blue-veined forehead; she was all pink and
gold, like a bunch of wild rose and laburnum. "What I should

* Title for unmarried sons of noblemen, pronounced "Yonker."

like to do," she went on, " would be to marry Otto, and flirt with
Gerard and other people. But, of course, it would be horribly
improper, and it couldn't be done."

" Don't be silly," remonstrated the Baroness van Trossart,
trying to frown. " You are getting too old, Nellie, for saying things you ought to be ashamed of. Now go and get
ready."

" I am half Otto's age," replied the girl, rising.

" That may be. But an *ingénue* should die at nineteen. We
women, my dear, are inverted butterflies, and marriage is our
chrysalis, as your future mother-in-law said the other night. I
can't imagine where she gets her sayings from, I suppose she
reads them somewhere. But neither she nor I would like to see
a Baroness van Helmont who was *ingénue*."

Helena paused in the doorway. " Would you like me," she
asked, " some day, to be Baroness van Helmont ?"

" My dear, you might be a worse thing. Personally, if you
ask me, I should certainly prefer Otto, little as I know of him,
to Gerard. Of Gerard I should say, ' Pour le badinage, bon.
Pour le mariage, non.' And then, Otto is the better match, the
future Baron. You two could restore, together, the glories of the
Horst."

Helena had stood listening, thoughtfully. Thought did not
suit her soft-featured, facile face.

" But you must do what you like, and decide for yourself," added her aunt, " as, with your character, you certainly
will."

" I thought I was so yielding," protested Helena.

" You are, my dear, except when you care."

" Then it's you that have spoiled me," answered Helena, trip-
ping off.

The Baroness looked after her. " Dear girl," she said to herself. " It will end in her marrying Gerard, I fancy. The book-
writers may say what they like, but the woman who can, always
marries for love."

A few minutes later her husband came in. " My dear," he
said, " some of my papers are missing. I wish you would tell
Mary to mind what she's about."

"Yes, my dear," she replied, without looking up. Some of his papers were always missing. He always grumbled. It had come with his appointment to the high government post. For the first month or two she had fretted; then she had understood that it was part of his new importance, and she had returned to her old comfortable life. "Both the Helmonts are coming to lunch," she said, "and one or two other people."

"I don't care who's coming to lunch. I wish you minded more about my papers. They're of very particular moment."

"I do mind. I shall tell some one to find them at once on your table, for I've no doubt that they're there. Mademoiselle"—this in French to a swarthy little lady who came gliding in—"would you mind looking for some papers Monsieur has left on his table—official papers—a dirty yellow, you know."

"But how on earth"— began the state functionary.

"Oh, she'll find them. She knows what your papers are like. How do you do, Georgette? Where is Willie?"

"On the stairs, I believe," replied the young lady thus addressed, "flirting with the Freule van Weylert."

"We should all have said 'of course,' Freule," declared Gerard's voice behind her, "had you omitted the name of the lady. Even Willie could not teach the Freule van Weylert to flirt."

Otto was bowing silently beside his brother, with a specially deep bow for Mademoiselle Papotier, Helena's quondam governess, who had returned, bearing the lost papers, to be welcomed by their owner with a grunt. As a rule, nobody but Helena took any notice of Mademoiselle Papotier.

They all went in to luncheon, a medley of exceptionally noisy and exceptionally silent elements. The old Baron took his seat at the head of the table, and immediately fixed his keen eyes on his food. Opposite him sat the French lady, coquettish in movements and apparel, pouring out coffee, of which no one partook. The mistress of the house strove vainly to converse with her niece Van Weylert, an angular and awkward young girl, or to draw out her other neighbor, Otto, who sat with his attention glumly concentrated on the fair object of his visit. The rest of the company were uproariously merry, led on by Gerard and his pink brother-officer, young Willie van Troyen.

Otto was wondering whatever had induced him to come. Yet, at the bottom of his heart, he knew very well. It was not so much his mother's affectionate expostulation as the thought, ever present within him, never expressed: What will become of the Horst when my father dies? What, indeed? He had never loved the old home as he loved it since his return.

"You are coming to my dance to-morrow, I hope, Mynheer van Helmont?" said his hostess. He awoke as from a reverie. "Oh yes," he said, "I hope so. I intend to stay at Drum for a day or two." He was still watching his cousin; the Baroness followed his gaze, and then their eyes met.

A shout of laughter went up from the opposite side of the table. The old Baron lifted his brows.

"In my time," he said to the shaking mass of pink muslin beside him, "we weren't half as funny as you young people seem to be."

"Weren't you?" retorted Georgette van Troyen. "How slow you must have been! Too bad, not even to have had a good time in your youth! But isn't this too amusing, this story that Willie is telling?"

The Baron returned hastily to his omelet.

"Isn't it too amusing?" cried the young girl, appealing to Otto.

"I haven't heard it," said the latter; at which they all roared again. Willie was in high spirits, though Gerard was endeavoring to arrest his narration.

"Do shut up, Troy; we've had quite enough of it," growled Gerard.

"No, indeed, I am mistress here!" cried Helena, her eyes sparkling with merriment. "Go on, Mynheer van Troyen; you and the Captain had agreed on the wager. And you answered the advertisements; and what happened then? The advertisements," she called across to Otto in explanation, "were from young ladies in search of a husband."

"From ladies," corrected the little officer, who looked like a bibulous cherub. "Well, we got replies to our letters, and we wrote again, arranging a meeting. We convened all the aspirants—there were four of them—at the same spot, and, of course, the same hour, and we bade them dress up in red shawls and white feathers. And when we drove past, taking Gerard and another man as umpires, there they were, the whole four of them ; I think there were even more !"

Renewed shrieks of laughter greeted the final sally.

" It's too killing !" cried Helena, the tears on her checks. " And what were they doing ? Tearing each other's eyes out ?"

" I don't know. I didn't wait to see. They were making a great noise, screaming at each other. I had won my champagne, and I went and drank it. I always knew these advertisements were perfectly genuine."

" But the letters," interposed Georgette. " You must show Helena the letters, Willie."

" No, no, he mustn't," cried Gerard, energetically. " I'm sick of the whole business. Do let's talk of something else."

" But I'm not," protested Helena. " It's new to me. How selfish you are, Gerard. Don't you think it's awfully amusing, Otto ? I'm sure you want to hear more."

" I only want to hear one thing," said Otto, gravely, bending forward, " and that is what Mynheer van Troyen is going to do with those letters ?"

" Why, keep them, of course," replied Willie.

" It is no business of mine, Mynheer; I have not the honor, like my brother, of being your friend. But if I were umpire, I should insist on those letters being given up and burned."

" I suppose you don't approve of the whole joke ?" cried Gerard, hotly, forcing back his own better misgivings, swift in defence of his chum."

" It is not my province to express an opinion. Certainly not here. It is not a thing I should have done myself."

" And the girls who advertised ?" continued Gerard. " We only answered advertisements. What of them ?"

" Poor things !" said Otto, softly.

" What nonsense !" exclaimed Helena. " I think it's great fun ; and for the girls, too. I should like to try the plan. Some day we must do it, Georgette. It's a capital way of getting a husband. What freedom it leaves in the choice !"

"Surely you are not restricted, Freule," said Willie. "You have but to fling your handkerchief wheresoever you will."

"Oh, but I am restricted," she replied; "for instance, I could never marry you."

"Alas, I am sure of it," he answered; "but why not?"

"Imagine what a combination! Helen of Troy!* Who could live up to such an appellation?"

"You could," he replied, fatuously. But she was not listening to him; she was looking across the table at Otto. "What a reputation!" she said. "Who could live up to it? But why was she called Hélène de Trois? There was Menelaus"—she counted on her fingers—"and Paris. But I forget who the third lover was."

That evening Otto appeared again in the drawing-room at the Manor-house. His mother gave a cry of surprise. For a moment her heart stood still.

"I don't care for Helena Trossart," said Otto. "Her conversation is a perpetual dance on the tight-rope of propriety."

"My dear boy," replied his father, "how natural! Consider the continuous pleasure of keeping your balance."

"Well," said Otto, "it seems to me she came some very positive croppers. However, I'm no judge."

He left the room; his mother ran after him.

"You haven't asked her, Otto?" she gasped. "She hasn't rejected you?"

"Oh no," he said, and shut the door.

* Literally, in the Dutch.

CHAPTER X

THE next day dawned for Ursula in unclouded brightness. Those few of us who remember a youth no longer ours will forgive her the excess of an expectancy she was unable to curb by experience. She was going to an entertainment at one of the great houses of Drum. She had never been to anything so magnificent before. And Gerard, whom she had known all her life, was to be there to make things smooth for her. A slight difficulty about a chaperon had been most pleasantly removed. The Freule van Trossart had on the preceding afternoon left a card for Juffrouw Rovers, with a note saying that if she cared to come and dine before the party, she could be present at it afterwards as a house guest, under the Baroness's wing. Ursula had accepted gladly, by no means impervious to so much condescension, and, altogether, she felt very well satisfied indeed. The night before she had written a glorious letter to her father; she had said nothing of her aunt's ill health.

At 9 A.M. there was tranquil jubilation, at 10 A.M. there was sudden dismay. "I can't wear it like this," Ursula was saying to Harriet, with whom she had come to terms on a basis of mutual oblivion. She sat on the floor, a brown heap of perplexity. Her simple evening dress lay on the bed, with a round stain, as of grease, distressingly displayed upon its breast. It was a frock of crushed-strawberry crepon, with ripe-strawberry silk ribbons.

"No, you can't," asserted Harriet, full of interest and sympathy. Harriet was in her element. "You must manage to get some more of that crimson lace for the front. How can it have happened, Ursula? Something must have oozed out in your trunk."

" But colored lace is so difficult to match," wailed Ursula.

" So it is. Never mind. We must try." And the two girls sallied forth on that most hopeless of errands, the only form of shopping no woman enjoys, " the matching " of colors. In every shop they entered their little scrap was held up against an incongruous variety of tints, and they were informed by the assistant that it was " exactly the shade." One especially truthful person qualified her recommendation of a moderate scarlet by the statement that " really it was as near as you could get." But all, without exception, were pertly offended when the girls crept hopelessly, though resolutely, away.

" It's no use," said Harriet at last, as they retraced their steps. But even while she spoke a sudden inspiration struck her. " Do you know what you'll have to do, Ursula? It's V-shaped now; well, you'll have to make it into a low-neck."

" Oh, I don't like that," cried the pastor's daughter, reddening.

" There's no choice left to you. How stupid of me not to think of it before. It 'll look much nicer, too."

" But supposing we matched the ribbons?" suggested Ursula, holding out.

" You never could in this primitive place. They're a very peculiar color. Besides, if you covered up all that space with ribbon, you'd look like a prize cow. No, the top 'll have to come off, and we must see about a dress-maker at once. There's no time to lose."

They turned down a by-street.

" Let us cross to the square," said Harriet. " It's no use taking the little woman that works for me; we must get the best help we can."

A few moments later they entered—not without a feeling of awe, especially on Harriet's part—the largest establishment of its kind in Drum.

" Call Miss Adeline," said the smart personage who had listened to their piteous tale. " We don't usually alter garments not made by ourselves. Still—"

Both of the girls gave a sudden gasp, for in the person of Miss Adeline, who came forward at this moment from far-back recesses, both simultaneously recognized the fair little maiden of the tryst.

"Mynheer Mopius, Villa Blanda," said the black-silk manager. "Very well. Perhaps Miss Adeline had better accompany you at once. There certainly is no time to be lost."

With feelings utterly indescribable the three walked off together.

A few moments later, Harriet having fled, Ursula sat helping the dress-maker in the oppressive silence of the "second best spare room." The click of the scissors was becoming insupportable. Even the occasional rustle of the pendent frock seemed a relief.

"I think we have met before," said Ursula, at last, very gently.

"Really, Juffrouw? A great many ladies come to our place," replied the girl, bending over her work.

For a moment Ursula felt nonplussed, but her pity rose paramount.

"You know what I mean," she said, rather sternly. And then she went on to talk about the folly and wickedness of female initiative in matters matrimonial, and her little lecture broadened into its third well-rounded sentence—

"And you," burst in the girl, fiercely, "a rich young lady in a fine house, well looked after. You!"

So Ursula had to incriminate her absent friend, lest her moral go awry. She found a politely incredulous listener, and began to realize that, with her, it was a case of "caught together, hung together," as the Germans say. If only Gerard had not observed her!

"I can assure you," she said, continuing her homily, though rather disconcerted by the sudden change of front, "that I should never lift a finger to get married for the sake of being married. Every woman may rejoice if God sends her an honest lover and enables her to love that lover. But merely to be able to say 'I am somebody's wife!' I cannot understand any woman wanting that"—this under the stress of her own inculpation—"I cannot understand what for."

She opened her big dark eyes, and looked innocently inter-
rogative.

" Can't you, Juffrouw ?" said the kneeling dress-maker, taking
the pins from between her lips. " Well, I can. There's reasons
would make a girl willing to be *any* man's wife as long as she
was only married. And one of them's mine." She spoke bitterly, and shut her lips with a snap, as she rose from fitting on
the frock.

Suddenly Ursula understood.

She was not given to emotion, still less to showing it ; perhaps her nerves had been wrought on by the previous strain ;
now, quite unexpectedly to herself, she burst into tears.

The girl quivered, stared, and, sinking on to a cane-bottomed
chair, began crying too, but in a soft, self-pitying way, while
speaking all the time.

" You think me a bad, wicked creature," she sobbed, " but
I'm not, I'm not. I didn't know, and he promised to marry me.
There was never any doubt of his marrying me. I'm not as
bad as you think, and I was certain he loved me. And I was
desperate, and I put in the advertisement. I wish I were
married or dead." She stopped crying for a moment. " When
the time comes," she said, earnestly, " I shall be one or the
other." And then she fell to sobbing afresh.

Ursula had dried her eyes.

" My dear," she said, " if he promised to marry you, perhaps he will."

" Oh no, he won't. I know now, and understand things
different. He's a gentleman. He'd marry me if he was not."

" For I'm sure he loved me," she added, softly.

Ursula was trembling from head to foot. Shielded and sheltered through all her simple girlhood, she had never come into
contact, whether by actual experience or in literature, with
any such vision of shame as this. She compared her own happy, unshadowed life with the struggle of the girl before her.
And, full of compassion, she thanked God for the difference.
For, to the very backbone which held her erect, she was womanly and pure.

She had forgotten all about the pressing needs of her toilet,

but the dress-maker had not. Adeline caught up the frock, and
began silently, sullenly sewing.

"If I could but do anything for you," said Ursula, meditatively.

"You can't. Only don't gibe at me. Gibe at the men of
your own class. This one, they tell me, is going to be married.
I dare say *you'd* marry him if you could."

"Never! never!" said Ursula, with quiet passion.

"Well, I don't care whom he marries. It won't be me. I'll
tell you how I know for certain. You seem to be good, you do,
and you mean well. It's not me alone he's ruined. Do you
know"—she laid down her work on her lap—"I believe it was
he who brought us all together the other night. I believe he is
Romeo de Lieven."

"But why?" asked Ursula, incredulously. "Certainly, the
young lady down-stairs—"

"Oh, don't tell me, Juffrouw. We all deny. Women always do. But you remember a carriage passing along the
road? There were officers in it. It flashed across me at once
that they had come to see their handiwork. And he was driving."

The room swam round before Ursula's eyes. She closed
them hastily, and leaned back in her easy-chair. She could think
of nothing distinctly; but she could hear the clock ticking
solemnly on. She longed for some one to stop it. As for herself, she knew that she was incapable of moving, body or
soul. In a lightning flash she had realized two facts undreamed
before — the first, that she was very fond of Gerard van Helmont; the second, that she scorned him forth from her heart
forever.

When at last she opened her eyes she saw the other girl in-
tently watching her. There was a quiet sneer in the dress-
maker's gaze before which Ursula shrank affrighted. She
understood immediately how her elaborate self-exoneration had
crumbled away. This creature had perceived that Gerard was
personally known to her. In the wretched girl's estimation she
was doubtless one rival out of many. She shuddered.

"Yes," said Mademoiselle Adeline, "we all deny. I think,

Miss, if you left me to myself, I could finish this dress a great deal better."

Ursula dragged herself together and crept from the room.

While this uncomfortable interview was in progress, the chief subject of its interest was complacently installed among the thousand elegances of his cousin's sitting-room, on a low stool almost at her feet. He looked a little more extensively red than usual, and his blue eyes were restless; but otherwise he showed no signs of trepidation. Yet he had resolved that this day should decide his fate. His mother's by-play about Otto was becoming a nuisance.

That morning he had risen, after tranquil sleep, and carelessly studied himself in the glass. Of course, he was good-looking—very good-looking. Experience had taught him that quite as much as ocular demonstration. It was the perfect grace of his gracelessness which made women adore him.

He had eaten a hearty breakfast as usual, but he had drunk two more cups of tea and a glass of brandy. That is a man's way of realizing that the crisis has come.

" My dear Gerard," said Helena, " you are dull, while the rest of the family are flurried. People talk about the day after the festival ; *my* ' Katzenjammers' come ten hours before. I shall ring for Mademoiselle Papotier ; she always amuses me."

" Do," said Gerard, surlily, glad of any postponement.

" That is charming. You could not have said that ' do ' more naturally had we been husband and wife. " Do I bore you? Then amuse yourself elsewhere. But don't even expect me to ring the bell." She jumped up lightly as she spoke and ran past him to the bell-pull.

" I don't like Mademoiselle Papotier," said Gerard. " She has taught you a number of things you needn't have known. If you read books like that "— he pointed to *Une Vie* upon the table—" it's her doing. I wish you wouldn't, Helena. Men don't like it."

She came back to her seat : " Oh, but that is still more charming," she said, " especially from your lips. You would have me restrict my reading so that I might the better enjoy your

conversation. I won't hear a word against my dear Papotier.
She brightened my youth with eighteenth-century romances,
and she cheers my old age by nineteenth-century novels. She
is a dear."

Undeniably, the heiress's education had been a peculiar one.
Her governess's tissue-paper rosette of a soul had never given
forth more natural odors than patchouly. The Baroness van
Trossart could have told you how, when Helena was an eight-
year-old little girl, she had come upon the child slapping her
ball up and down in the court-yard, and occasionally muttering
the same words over and over again.

"What on earth are you saying, my dear?" the Baroness
had inquired.

And Helena had looked up with sparkling eyes: "And his
beautiful head," she had spouted, without stopping her ball-
bumping, "went bounding three times across the marble, while
repeating three times the sweet name of 'Zaïre'! Isn't it lovely?
He was dead, you know; they had just cut it off." And she
had run away.

The Baroness had shaken her head. "It sounds like Scudéry,"
she had said. But she was comfortable. She was not going
to object to Mademoiselle Papotier.

"I shall read what I like," repeated the heiress, provokingly.
"And when I am married, I shall go to what plays I choose.
I like impropriety on paper. Paper or boards. And so do
you, Gerard, et plus que çà. You, of all people! I believe you
are laughing at me."

"No, by thunder, I'm not," he cried, violently. "I don't
pretend to be a saint—far from it; but there's not a lover in
the world would like to remember that the girl he's engaged to
has read Maupassant."

She looked at him for a moment with that sweet mixture of
mocking tenderness which a man's eyes can never assume; then
she said to her maid, who had answered the bell,

"No, thank you; I want nothing. I rang by mistake."

"But you are not"— she began, and checked herself. "So
Otto is coming to my party to-night," she said.

She enjoyed his responsive scowl.

"No, Otto is not coming," he answered. "His Highness has gone off in a huff. About that hoax of Willie's, I imagine, but his huffs are not easy to classify. Mind you, I don't defend the trick. I think it was rather a low thing to do."

"To Van Troyen it merely represented so much champagne," she replied. "I like Otto; he is eminently estimable and— and worthy. He, at least, would never have told me not to read Maupassant."

"No," sneered Gerard, "he would never have heard of him."

"Just so. There is nothing more delightful than a husband who is absolutely ignorant of everything. With him, at least, one runs a chance, even in this age, of unreasoning jealousy. And unreasoning jealousy must be delightful. Like mustard. What is the use of a man who keeps saying, 'The vices are my share; the virtues are yours. And each of us has got what he ought to have'? Gerard, rather than a husband who said to me, 'Of course, I am faithless; let us talk of something else,' I would have a husband who said, 'You are faithless. I am going to kill you,' and did it."

"It could only be done once," replied Gerard, languidly. "My dear child, you have been to Verdi's 'Othello.' Evidently you want to be worshipped not wisely but too well. I don't think Otto would tell you that you are faithless. I fancy you'd have to jog him a bit."

"Otto! I wasn't thinking of Otto. I believe you are jealous of Otto."

"Yes, I am. I'll tell you why, if you like, immediately. I have a note here from my mother, received this morning; shall I read it to you?"

"If it concerns me," she said, negligently.

"It concerns you very nearly. My mother tells me to ask whether you would care to come down to the house with me to-morrow, and stay for a few days. You understand what that means, Helen, as well as I do!"

"Yes, I understand," she answered, and with a sudden impulse she caught up the "Maupassant" at her elbow and flung it into a corner of the room.

"So that, knowing the comedy you are expected to take part

6

in, you can foresee and forego the conclusion. I should say, if it is to be only farce, why act it at all?"

She popped out the tips of her little feet and looked down at them.

"The best way to avoid all complications," he went on, "would be to arrive at the Manor-house—engaged."

She lifted her eyes from the ground and fixed them steadily on his face.

"Let me telegraph to my mother that you are coming engaged." His voice broke down.

"But how will you know?" she asked, laughing.

"Let me know *first*." He bent forward. "Oh, my darling, my beauty." He caught her two hands, and, like the passionate young fool he was, covered them with kisses. "My darling, how happy they will all be at home."

Even at that moment the naïve selfishness of this last exclamation amused her. She said nothing, however, prolonging the sweetest silence a woman ever knows.

"Gerard, she said, some minutes later, looking up at him as he bent over her. "You have forgotten that the girl you are engaged to has read Maupassant."

"Yes," he answered, "I have forgotten. I shall never remember."

He went back to his rooms to dress for dinner, highly delighted. He was very much attached to his cousin. And she was the greatest heiress in the province.

CHAPTER XI

URSULA descended from a cab in the full light of the early summer evening, and hurried away into the Van Trossarts' gloomy hall. Her shoulders blushed as the footman took her wrap. It felt like undressing.

"Juffrouw Rovers," said the Baroness, beaming like a crimson sun, "I am glad you have come. My niece is—is occupied. Take off your gloves, my dear, and help me to arrange these flowers."

Ursula had looked round in terror for Gerard. She must dine with him *en famille*, perhaps sit next to him. There was no help for it. Yet she trembled to think of him. To her simple maidenhood, familiar with sermons on sin in the abstract, he was a sudden incarnation of infamy.

The Baroness buzzed and bubbled over her flower-trays, her fat arms all dimples, her fat cheeks all smiles. She chattered about this evening's party, which was Helena's party—" as if anybody in Drum would give a dance in July!—but Helena was so gay she could never sit still for an hour: a nice dance she would lead her husband if only the husband himself was addicted to pleasure. Well, old people were apt to get dull. No wonder Helena fared farther in search of diversion." And she laughed to herself, and winked to herself (a difficult, but by no means impossible, proceeding) while talking to Ursula in the pragmatical cackle with which hens of all ages surround a new-laid matrimonial egg.

Ursula, who was barely acquainted with the Freule van Trossart, could only display a perfunctory interest in that young lady's possible prospects. Harriet had told her that, according to rumor, the Freule was "as good as engaged" to a young politician.

"It is a living romance," the Freule's clear voice was heard saying on the landing, "and a thousand times more amusing, ma vieille, than all your dressed-up dead ones together."

She came into the room with her arm through that of her shrivelled governess, Gerard bringing up the rear. The little Frenchwoman looked depressed as she slid away into a corner. The fat Baroness rustled across to her in a perfect crackle of crimson. "My dear Papotier, is it not delightful?" she said, with tears in her eyes.

"Mon Dieu, madame, yes," replied the governess, "it is the first chapter." And, to herself, she added, "For me it is the last."

Ursula shook hands with Gerard, but a thick curtain had fallen between them; she was surprised by the aloofness of his manner, even while she herself stiffened to a cold "good-day."

How contented and complacent he looked! She watched him as he sat opposite her at table, between the Baroness and the Freule. How prosperous and pleasing! Yes, truly, there was a law for the humble and a license for the high! It was a gloriously simple thing to be born to impurity, like the old Greek gods. What nonsense her good father went preaching about "sin"! The world knew no such thing. It knew only a small hub of pleasure reserved for the rich, and a wide zone all round it of hunger and crime. She felt very bitter; she glanced down with a sensation of physical disgust on the fingers which had touched his, unwilling to break her bread with them.

Her French was rusty, and out of repair; she did not feel up to much conversation with the prim little portrait of the past on her right; the master of the house, on her other side, was sufficiently, but not amply, polite. There is no human insolence such as that indifferent politeness which barely fits—like a glove one size too small.

There were only the six of them; but the fascinating little heiress was a host in herself. Ursula had heard much of her vivacity; she concluded, notwithstanding, that the prospect of the evening's pleasure must be abnormally augmenting it.

Lovely the girl undeniably was, frail, and golden-haired, in a cloud of white over blue, like the sky, and a treble row of pearls. Ursula's grave brown face looked very quiet compared with the other's delicate, clear-veined features ; you might have said a Madonna of the Annunciation, and an immature Venus Anadyomene.

"Ursula," thought Gerard, "is just a nice-looking rustic." As for him, she wondered how he dared to sit beside, and speak to, this white-robed virgin. It seemed as if toads must drop from his full red lips. Well, it was no business of hers. And perhaps—perhaps she was wronging him all the time, this good-natured friend of her childhood ! Perhaps he intended to marry Mademoiselle Adeline, if only his parents would let him. He was waiting, perhaps, for an opportunity—who knows ?—perhaps—

The thought gave her great comfort. Of the truth of the story she could not harbor a doubt, for the girl before leaving had shown her a photograph, worn by a ribbon round the neck.

She noticed that the atmosphere seemed full of a ripple of merriment : asides, which courtesy only kept just above whispers, innuendos, sudden glances, *mots à double entente.* She felt even more awkward than she would have done under ordinary circumstances. And soon she felt exceedingly miserable. Perhaps her kind-hearted hostess noticed it.

"Helena, we must drink to your health," cried the Baroness, her ample bosom swelling under its laces, like a crested wave. "Yes, my dear Gerard, you needn't look at me like that; see how your neighbor is laughing. As Juffrouw Rovers does us the favor of dining here to-day, she will increase that favor, I feel certain, by keeping a secret—an absolute secret —for forty-eight hours. I cannot let this meal pass as if nothing had happened. You must know, Juffrouw Rovers, that it is my dear niece's birthday—her first birthday into a new life. In other words, she is engaged to her cousin Gerard, who is an old friend of yours, so I need not praise him. And we are going to drink their healths, and wish them long life and prosperity."

Afterwards Ursula had a faint recollection of having spilled some champagne on the table-cloth. For the moment her whole strength was concentrated in a wild prayer for outward calm. These people would imagine she cared for Gerard. It was not that—my God, not that !

Fortunately the others were busy lifting their glasses ; all during dinner Gerard had scarcely looked her way. She stared round the table in a dazed manner. She felt sick.

" The strawberries are not good this year," she heard Baron Trossart's grumpy voice saying. " I am not surprised Miss Rovers doesn't care to eat them." She hastily returned to her dessert. " No, I must beg of you. Joris, bring this lady a clean plate."

It was the strawberries, then, that interested her ? So much the better.

" How I envy your father, Gerard," continued the Baron. " It is two years now since we have been at Trossartshage. The fruit cannot bear the transport ; we have tried both water and rail. But the cares of state, you know, the cares of state ! A man sacrifices himself for his country, and his country repays him with ingratitude."

This last sentence was an allusion to a recent article in a small paper which reproached the authorities — in this case Baron Trossart—with not having cleared out a canal before the warm weather came. Nobody ever complained of the ceaseless flow of nephews and brothers-in-law. That, as we all know, is a part of the constitution. Were it not so, the " eminent politician " would be a thing of the past.

" Papa," interrupted Helena, wilfully, " please don't ' be gloomy. I'm engaged."

" Well, there's cause enough for gloom in that," he replied. " I'm as jealous of Gerard as "—he looked round—" as Mademoiselle Papotier."

" Ah ! do not speak of it to me !" cried the Frenchwoman. " I could slaughter Monsieur Gerard if I met him in war."

" That's the last place where you'll meet me," exclaimed Gerard, laughing. Helena had suddenly blanched.

" War !" she said. " How horrible ! No, we will have no

fighting. Juffrouw Rovers, would you have the courage to marry a soldier?"

Across Ursula's brain flashed a vision of a dog-cart filled with uproarious malevolence.

" No, I should not like to marry an officer," she replied.

Her words—perhaps, still more, her unconscious manner—seemed to sting Gerard. He flushed.

" Juffrouw Rovers is never particularly brave," he said. " She is too soft-hearted. The last time I saw her, she was showing the *white feather*, as now."

The words were a challenge. And, unconsciously, his manner betrayed as much ; it was too significant.

Helena looked from one to the other : " What is it?" she asked. " What does it mean, Juffrouw Rovers? Gerard, what is the joke?"

" Joke? None. Ask Juffrouw Rovers."

" So I have, but she doesn't tell me."

" Then you may be sure it is a little secret between Ursula and me, which *I* shall keep. I am not responsible for what she may do."

She had the good taste not to press the subject, but she reverted to it as soon as she found herself alone with her lover.

" Gerard, what is this silly secret between you and Miss Rovers ?"

" My dear child, how inquisitive you are! I thought you liked secrets."

" Yes, when one is in them. I told you I should be jealous."

" Of Ursula! How ridiculous! Utterly absurd! Ursula !"

" Well, I dare say I shall often be absurd. At any rate, Gerard, you would please me by not calling her ' Ursula.' She is not a relation of yours."

" But I have known her all my life. I used to drag her in a go-cart."

" I know. And it seems to me you behave very strangely for people who have always been intimate. You seem suddenly afraid of each other since this afternoon."

" I am afraid of—that is, bored by—every girl but one since

this afternoon.   I am exceedingly bored by the prospect before
me to-night.   Don't let's spoil the one hour of happiness left us."

"The one hour!   How tragic that sounds!" she laughed.

"To-morrow we will go down to the Manor - house; there
will be more hours there in the moonlight on the terrace.   Say
again that you love me, Nellie."

"Yes, I love you," she replied; and her voice was some soul-
voice, quite different from her usual high - pitched tones.   "I
have loved you for a long time," she added; and then, suddenly, with the old every-day ring: "There, I had made up my
mind not to tell you that before our golden wedding.   Papotier
says a girl should never tell it at all, because the confession is
ill-advised; and mamma says she certainly shouldn't, because
the feeling, if there, was a thing to be ashamed of."   ·

"Ashamed of love?   But, my dearest?"

"No, I should never be ashamed of loving any one.   Not
even a footman."

"Thank you," *sotto voce*, from Gerard.

"We must bear the consequences of our virtues.   I can't understand any one's being ashamed of 'love.'   Can you?"

"I can't understand any man's keeping quiet his love for
you.   I want to shout out mine on the house-tops!   Now that
Ursula knows — I mean Juffrouw Rovers — why not proclaim
the engagement to-night?"

"And your mother?"

So they whiled away the time on the veranda, looking down
into the garden, where a large marquee had been put up for the
dancers, with a music - tent and strings of Chinese lanterns.
Meanwhile the Baroness lay back dozing in little audible gasps,
and Ursula sat looking at photographs of Italy with Mademoiselle Papotier, who had forgotten all the names.

"Yes, that is Pavia," said Mademoiselle Papotier.   "Or perhaps it's Pisa.   I think it must be Pisa, because of the crooked
tower."

"Oh, that's only the photograph," replied Ursula, listlessly;
"the angle's wrong."

"Do you think so?   Look at the turtle-doves billing and coo-
ing.   Isn't it sweet?"

Mademoiselle nodded towards the veranda, with keen scrutiny of her companion's face. Ursula blushed again, that terrible tell-tale blush.

"And this place with all the boats," she said, "I suppose is Venice?"

The guests began to arrive, and Mevrouw van Trossart pushed her cap across from the right to the left. It was quite a young people's entertainment, more or less impromptu, and Ursula, already so greatly distressed by her toilet, noticed that many of the girls were more simply dressed than she. The acuteness of annoyance about this deadened, for a time, the sick anxiety at her heart.

She went out into the garden; she had fancied the fête would mean music and refreshments and fireworks; she now suddenly saw that the marquee was prepared for dancing. There had been no intimation, that she knew, on her card. She had never learned the art.

"May I have the first valse?" asked Willie van Troyen, who had just been introduced, for that purpose, by the Baroness.

"I don't dance," she said, pulling at her gloves. "I didn't know people were going to."

"They often do," said Willie, "don't they, at a dance?" He laughed heartily; he thought that was rather witty. And he betook himself to some one else.

So Ursula sat in a corner of the tent, or out on a bench, and was a bore.

The Baroness "made" talk with her from time to time in laborious sentences, and one or two other elderly people tried the same experiment. All the time, as she sat there disconsolate, one question was burning at her brain: How must I act regarding Gerard? Must I save this innocent girl or must I not? Sometimes the girl was Adeline, more often Helena, but the question remained the same.

"And this is your first party?" said a good-natured man. "I don't think you seem to be enjoying yourself."

"Oh, don't let Mevrouw hear you say that!" she cried, in alarm. The Baroness happened to be passing. Yes, undoubtedly, Ursula was a drag.

"Come out into the garden," said Gerard, stopping before
her, "it's tremendously hot here. I've kept this dance free for
you; we'll sit it out." She rose and obeyed him.

Helena came out of the room where her uncle and his cronies
were playing whist, with closed windows. Her whole figure
was a-sparkle with happiness. "Isn't it beautiful?" she asked
of her own Papotier. "The weather is perfect, the garden is
perfect, the music is perfect. I don't think we ever had such
a pleasant party before."

"It is your own joy, *ma chérie*," said the governess, drawing
her pupil to the dark staircase window, where she, Mademoiselle,
stood watching the dancers. She pointed to a corner, half-hidden by a willow, in which Gerard and Ursula could be dimly
descried. "That is the prologue, my child, to your romance,"
she said. "Make haste to get on to the story."

"Mademoiselle!"

"Hush! I watched her at dinner, when Madame the Baroness spoke. I have watched them since. It is nothing, my
dear; it is even delightful — a compliment. But your lover
must put a full-stop to the prologue. Perhaps he is doing it
now. Creep behind, if you will, and hear what they say."

"No, indeed!" cried the young Freule, with warmth.

A little later Ursula was again alone on the garden seat. She
had exchanged but a few distressful sentences with Gerard. He
had reproached her with behavior he hardly cared or dared to
analyze, and she had answered hastily, eager to vindicate herself, but still more firmly resolved to screen Harriet's reputation.
Even while she was explaining, lamely, she had understood the
incredulous smile on his face. He had come out of the brief
conflict as a champion of female modesty, leaving her helplessly, guiltily crushed.

A white figure glided through the dusk and sank down by her
side. The evening was gentle as velvet, caressingly warm and
soft. Over yonder shone the great yellow glare of the music
and the moving shadows; on all sides gay, ghastly paper lanterns went breaking the solemn silence of the trees. This spot
of Ursula's choosing was dark and willow-sheltered, alone beneath the calm blue height of heaven.

"Juffrouw Rovers," said the Freule, "what is this joke between you and Gerard? You see, I am curious. You must
forgive a spoiled child. What did he mean about your showing
the white feather?

"Don't ask me, Freule, please," replied Ursula, shortly.
"For I can't tell you."

"So Gerard says. It must be a very dreadful secret!"
This was said laughingly.

Silence. From the tent came the strains of the "Liebchen
Adé" gallop.

"Great Heaven, it must be a very dreadful secret!" The
Freule half rose from her seat; her voice trembled. She caught
Ursula's arm.

"It can only be," she said, steadying herself, "that Gerard
made love to you formerly. That is rather like him. I am
sorry. It was wrong. But you have made up your mind to
forget him, have you not? He is so charming; no wonder
women love him. Poor child, it was cruel of us, in our ignorance, to invite you to behold our happiness." In a sudden impulse of womanly pity she put an arm round Ursula's bare
neck.

"It isn't that," gasped Ursula. "Don't, please, say I love
Gerard. Oh, Freule, it's a great deal worse."

She hardly knew what she was saying. She covered her face
with her hands.

"A great deal worse!" repeated Helena, drawing away. Ursula started at the hardness which had come into the Freule's
voice. "That can only mean"— Helena got up and stood at
the farther end of the seat. "I refuse to say it," she continued.
"I refuse to believe it. You two are mad."

The dance-music came faster from the lawn. Ursula, her
head bowed low upon her lap, felt that in her cup of unmerited
bitterness not a drop was left undrunk.

"I want to know the truth," Helena went on after a moment.
"I have a right to know it to-night. If you still feel any love
for Gerard, do him a good turn now. We are girls together.
No one will hear you but I. Tell me exactly what there is to
tell, and I will forgive him."

" I have nothing to tell," murmured Ursula.

The Freule stamped her foot.

" You are ruining his life," she said. " I will never marry him till I know how much you have been to each other. What happens after marriage must be settled after marriage ; but what happened before I will know now."

" We have never been anything to each other," whispered Ursula. " Oh, Freule, have pity, and let me alone !" But even as she spoke her mood changed. Why should she agonize to save this girl's selfish happiness at the cost of her own honor, of an innocent victim's peace? She lifted herself up. " Ask no confessions of me," she said. " Ask them of your future husband. He is nothing to me. · You have no right to assume that he ever was."

Even in the shade she saw Helena change color. A long silence deepened between them. Somebody in another nook not far distant laughed shrilly. There was a clatter of glasses.

" What happened before I must know," said Helena, at last. " I will never marry him until I do."

" You do not mean that," said Ursula, but the other took no notice.

" I understand," she continued, " it is some other woman." She tossed up her head. " I knew I wasn't marrying a saint," she said. " He warned me about that himself. But, of course, all you speak of is past." Then she broke into sudden passion. " How dare you come and talk of such things to me ?" she cried, advancing on Ursula. " How dare you do it ?"

" But I have talked of nothing !" exclaimed the pastor's daughter. " It is you who torment me—"

" I know. Never mind," said the Freule, interrupting ; " tell me one thing. This girl that you and Gerard are thinking of was—was—infamous ?"

Again the silence which is dissent. The Freule broke into a cry. Fortunately the music drowned it. The " Liebchen Adé " gallop was finishing up fast and furious.

" Don't tell me she was good like—like you and me ! Don't tell me ; I don't want to hear it. I don't care. I know how the whole story runs; it's in so many novels. All men do such things. And the girl goes on the stage !"

The music had stopped. The bright dancers were flowing out into the cooler grounds.

"You needn't tell me anything," said the Freule, hurriedly but quietly. "I have guessed it all. This girl is good and honest, and she hoped that Gerard would marry her. She hopes so still. *You hope it.* Of course there is a child—there always is. It is the stalest form of pathetic *feuilleton*, and, therefore, it comes true in my life. Good-bye, Juffrouw Rovers."

She sank down on the seat again and waved away her companion, hiding her golden head on her arms against the back. It was very still now in this forgotten corner. Ursula stole off to the house without taking leave of any one, and, having recovered her cloak, went out into the desolate street, alone and on foot, amid the stupefied stares of the domestics.

Several minutes elapsed before Helena lifted her head. She stared from her bench into the night.

"Why not ?" she said, half aloud; "I love him. All women do it. There was that creature at the church gate, with her brats, when Henri van Troyen was married."

She gathered her white laces about her and shivered, as she rose to walk towards the house. On the stairs, at the same post by her dark window, like a spy, still stood the French governess.

"Ma vieille," began Helena, "will you please tell mamma I have gone to my room with a very bad headache, and want nobody to disturb me—not even her or yourself."

"But, my dear—"

"The romance is changing to a tragedy," said Helena. "Good-night."

"YES, uncle, I should like to go back to Horstwyk to-day," Ursula was saying at breakfast. "I have had a letter from father, and Aunt Josine seems far from well."

She had found the letter on her return from last night's dissipation. It was a long and affectionate letter, full of praises of Otto, who came frequently to the Parsonage, enjoying the quiet strength of the minister's talk. The letter certainly stated that Miss Mopius had been laid up with a feverish cold.

"Nonsense, Ursula," cried Mynheer Mopius loudly. "Of course, Josine has been ill; it's her solitary pastime. Why, your visit has hardly begun."

"We want to hear all about last night," interposed Harriet, in her sleepy tones. "You look quite worn out this morning; you must have enjoyed yourself immensely."

"Oh, bother last night," said Mopius. "We don't care to know about the grandees. Were there many of them there?"

"Yes, there were a good many people," replied Ursula, wearily, "most of them young. I didn't enjoy myself so very much, because, you see, I don't dance."

"Was the Governor there, or his wife," asked Mopius, "or the Burgomaster? I suppose you saw the Van Troyens?"

"And the Governor's daughter?" added Harriet. "The pretty girl with the hazel eyes?"

"I remember a Mr. Van Troyen, an officer," said Ursula, vaguely. "Uncle, may I send a telegram for this afternoon. I could always come back on Monday, you know."

"Can't you miss one of your father's discourses? I should have thought Sunday was the one day you'd like to stay away.

But I don't see what you go out into society for, Ursula. At Batavia I danced with the Governor-General's lady."

"Always?" asked Harriet — her invariable question at this stage of the story.

"No, not always. I remember, just as I led her up, I saw there was a huge snake coiled round her arm."

"How dreadful!" said Ursula, stolidly. She had heard the *dénouement* on former occasions, but forgotten it.

"A gold snake! Ha!—ha!—ha! Somebody snatched it off a few months afterwards. A brave man. Ha!—ha!—ha! And your aunt used to dance too. Do you remember, wife? You were really quite pretty in those days. We'll dance to-night," he added, "and teach Ursula. You dance, Harriet, don't you?"

"Oh yes, to any one's pipes," * replied Harriet.

Nevertheless, it was decided, after some wrangling, that Ursula should return to Horstwyk, as she wished, for the present. Mynheer Mopius chose to be offended.

The girl was consumed by a feverish longing to get away out of this hot-house atmosphere into the pure repose of her country home. All morning she hid away in her room, afraid to look out on the little town, over which, to her excited fancy, an ominous thunder-cloud seemed to hang. What would happen next? How would Helena act? How Gerard? In her heart she hoped that justice would be done to the injured shop-girl, and yet dared not measure the result.

Just before luncheon a note was brought her. She sat down before opening it. Harriet laughed. "With due preparation," said Harriet. "What is it? Another invitation to a dance?"

The letter contained only these words written by Helena:

"Keep my secret: I would have kept yours."

They left her no wiser.

"My dear, come into my room for a moment," said Mevrouw Mopius, with timid voice. The feeble little creature sniffed nervously. "Forget what I told you, Ursula," she went on, as

---

* Idiom.

soon as they were alone. "And remember you are bound by oath. If Mopius ever hears, it *must* be through you." She peered sternly at her niece.

"Yes, dear, I will remember," replied Ursula. "But you are feeling better, aunt, are you not? You are not as bad as when I came."

Mevrouw Mopius smiled. "I shall be better soon," she said. Then she went to her particular old-fashioned mahogany "secretary," and, after a good deal of fumbling and searching, extracted from one of many receptacles a small tissue-paper parcel, which she brought back to Ursula. "This is for you," she said, thrusting it into the girl's hand. "I've made it since you came, sitting up in bed these summer mornings." Ursula opened the parcel, her aunt watching meanwhile with a certain pride.

It contained a small square bit of red wool-work, with the bead-embroidered device, "No cross, no crown," the two substantives being presented pictorially.

"I could have taken more time to it," pleaded Mevrouw Mopius, "but I had to wait for the daylight: a candle wakes your uncle; and, once up, I have to work at 'Laban and Jacob.' I am exceedingly anxious to get them ready before"— She stopped. "Good-bye, my dear," she said. "I hope you like my work. You might use it under a lamp, or for the fire-irons, unless you disapprove of that on account of the words. I don't think I should."

So Ursula returned very quietly and humbly. There was no marshalling of porters, and she travelled second class. At the little market-town station her father met her; together they trudged the two miles side by side almost silently, for the girl's few answers had soon convinced the Dominó that conversation had become for the moment, what he most detested, an ambuscade.

In the half-light of the calm, cool study, amid the well-known, stilly sympathetic books, she sat with her two hands in his one, on a footstool by the faded leather arm-chair, and, lifting those big brown eyes of hers to his steadfast response, she told him how the city is full of wickedness incredible, and that Apollyon rules the world.

He listened to her very quietly, and yet he was greatly shocked. True, evil had few secrets for him; he had seen more of the world's corruption than most men, in the red glare of the Algerian night, amid the devil's dance of shrieking drunkenness and bare-breasted debauch. He had seen too much. He was one of those happy mortals who always think the world is better than it used to be. "In my day"—he would begin, and sigh cheerfully—"but we have greatly improved since then." It was doubly sad, therefore, to hear that Gerard, the warrior, despite the weekly bugle-call to resistance, should have sur¹ rendered at discretion to so pitiful a cutthroat as Lustings. The Dominé had an ineradicable weakness for a brave soldier. Havelock and Hedley Vicars hung large against his peaceful wall, and between them a very different hero, Bugeaud.

"Well, my dear," said the Dominé, while Ursula, having finished, sat heavy with sorrowful wrath— "Well, my dear, the farther we go the more we see of the battle-field. I am not sorry you should have reconnoitred a little. And I rejoice all the more now to think how mistaken I was about you and Gerard. You must know, my dear, that at one time, though I never mentioned it to you, I fancied you might be setting your affections on the Jonker. I spoke of it unwillingly to your aunt, for I had no other woman to confide in"—the Dominé's voice grew reflective—"but she said it was all stuff and nonsense, at once, and you weren't such a piece of vanity as that. Your aunt is not a woman of exceptional discrimination; still, I am glad to see she was right. It would have been a great mistake on your part, Ursula, and a cause of much useless regret."

"I shall never love any man but you," said Ursula, vehemently. "They're all alike. No woman ought to marry."

The pastor smiled, and passed his hand over her smooth head.

"I hope," he said, "that you will never know a worthless love. A hopeless love, even a dead love, these may ennoble man or woman. But a love of the undeserving can only lure into an *impasse*."

7

She smiled confidently.

"No; the Jonker van Helmont is not for such as us, Ursula," continued the old man. "So much the better. My child, you will marry if God pleases and whom he pleases; but I hope it will be in your own station of life. Not that we must judge any class as such. There is Otto, for instance. *He* is not a pleasure-seeker. We have seen much of him, my dear, in your absence. He most kindly came to comfort me. He has returned from the Indies as he went, the same pure lover of all that is good. Even in our day the Almighty leads some men untainted through the furnace." And the simple-hearted pastor launched into praises of his favorite, unwittingly digging pitfalls on paths as yet untrod.

"And as for most men," he said, "human nature is still much what it was in the days of Thucydides. What says Diodorus, the son of Eucrates, the Athenian? 'All men are naturally disposed to do wrong; and no law will ever keep them from it.' And that was the historian's own view; he repeats it some chapters later. As for women, you remember what he makes Pericles say of *them*. It holds true, in spite of emancipation. 'Great is the glory of her who is least talked of among the men, either for good or for evil.' You remember that, Ursula?"

"Yes, indeed, Captain," said Ursula, into whose whole life this maxim had been constantly woven.

"You might read the history through once more with the greatest advantage. No writer that I know will reveal to you more of the conflict of human passions, excepting, of course, John Bunyan."

The good pastor did not know many writers. He was not by any means a literary man.

Miss Mopius sailed into the room unannounced, and interrupted their quiet conversation. Two little peculiarities of this lady's—trifles, light as air—were a source of unending irritation to her brother-in-law. The one was her tacit refusal to prelude her invasions of his sanctum, the other was her persistent drawl of his soldierly name into a sound which was neither French nor English, nor anything but absurd. The Dominé was a brave man; he was exceedingly afraid of his dead wife's sister, not so much on account of himself as on account of the use to which Diabolus put her in the great siege of the Dominé's Mansoul.

By sheer force of will Miss Mopius had taught herself to admit that she was thirty-two years old, but she would never see forty again. She was endowed with a sallow complexion, to which she had added auburn ringlets and rainbow-colored raiment. To describe her as an entirely imaginary invalid would have been malevolent; nature had provided her with a tendency to nervous headaches which kindly fostering had developed into a vocation.

She had come to the widower as a thorn in the flesh. Limp and listless, absolutely unable to " resist" anything that attracted her, she devoted herself day and night to the harassing service of her own caprices. Being not entirely destitute of means, she might easily have enjoyed her nerves to the full in some boarding-house, but she knew her duty to her motherless niece.

" I should not stay with *you*, Roderigue," she was wont to say, " though Ursula, of course, will not marry for many years yet. When she does, I shall consider my mission is ended. I should not be wanted *then*."

She paused, expectant. But the Dominé never answered, for he held that, in the spiritual warfare, a falsehood is the easiest and most cowardly method of running away.

" Ursula, my dear," began Miss Mopius, in a flow of sugared vinegar, " I have been suffering the greatest anxiety. I thought you had not returned. I suppose, however, the train was late."

Ursula, rising hastily, confessed that the train had been punctual.

" Really ! Well, I'm afraid I interrupted you. This conversation must have been of the greatest importance, or you would hardly have so entirely forgotten your poor old aunt." Miss Mopius constantly used that appellation ; of late she had sometimes wondered whether it was becoming unwise. She spoke in almost continuous italics ; these, however, were mostly independent of sense.

" I suppose your father informed you," she continued, settling herself in the Dominé's chair, " that I have been exceedingly unwell since you left. Day after day I have dragged myself down-stairs, so as not to let him sit down to his dinner alone, but my nights were too terrible to speak of." She paused, that Ursula might speak of them.

"I'm so sorry," said Ursula, without any accent at all.

"Last night, for instance, I was in agony from twelve to three—in agony. I don't know what I should have done without my vegetable electricity. I took it at three, and the pain vanished immediately."

"Why didn't you take it at once?" asked Ursula.

"Ursula, you have not the slightest comprehension of medicines. Fortunate child, it is your lack of experience. Medicines never act if taken at once."

The Dominé had basely deserted his own fortress.

"Ursula, my dear," said Miss Mopius, sitting up with quite unusual energy, "no wonder my health has suffered. Something very important has happened since you went away."

"Really?" asked Ursula, wondering what the maid-of-all-work had broken.

"Yes, but it's no use speaking of it to your father. Ursula, Otto van Helmont comes here every evening. Since you left, mind you. Now, I ask, what can that mean?"

"He had only four evenings before I left," replied Ursula, with some spirit, "one of them was free, and he came."

"*One* doesn't count. That was a formal call," replied Miss Mopius, loftily. "I ask, what does it mean? He sits and talks and talks. Nominally to your father. Ursula, I have watched him; he never speaks to me." She sank back in her chair and began to count on her lanky fingers, without taking further note of her companion. "He never speaks to me—one. He never looks at me—two. But he brought me a nosegay—three. He said it was from his mother—four." She roused herself from her reverie. "Ursula, my child," she asked, "why does he bring me a nosegay, and say it is from his mother?"

"Because it is," replied Ursula.

Miss Mopius scornfully shook her curls. "Does the Baroness send me roses in midsummer?" she inquired. "Dear girl, you are too young; I should have considered that. But there

arc moments in a woman's existence when she craves for the
sympathy of her sex. If only my dear elder sister were alive—
she was so much my elder!—to help me now. Go, dear child,
go; at some distant day your own turn will come, and then
you will understand."

" Yes, aunt," said Ursula, gladly moving towards the door.

" Stay one instant," cried the spinster. " Child, are you so
eager to return to your diversions? He is good-looking, Ursula.
I have watched him, as I said. His face is careworn and earnest; he is no mere beardless boy just dipping into life, but a
man who has swum against the current. He has experience
and judgment, and he *knows*. Ursula, I would not marry a
beardless boy."

" Aunt," said Ursula, suddenly coming back into the room,
" do you mean to say you want to marry Mynheer Otto van
Helmont ?"

" Silly child, does a woman say such things? Of course, I
know, Ursula, as well as you do, that he is much older than I
am. That is a matter I must seriously consider before I
reply."

" Do you mean to say he has actually asked you?" cried
Ursula, clasping her hands in wonderment.

" Not directly. Child, how raw you are, and how rawly you
put things. But I have my reasons for believing that he will
do so to-night. That is why I was unwillingly compelled to
speak to you on the subject. Be sure that otherwise I should
never have done so."

" But what have I to do with it?" queried Ursula, stupefied.

" Not to give your consent, you may be sure," retorted Miss
Mopius, snappishly. " When Otto comes to-night, as he certainly will, I want you, during ten minutes, to draw off your
father. The poor fellow never gets a chance. He said as much
yesterday, in departing. ' The Dominé and I have so much to
say to each other,' he remarked, ' that I never seem to have an
opportunity of chatting with you, Miss Mopius.' And with
that he gave me a look. Ursula, I believe you take me for a
fool. Do you ?"

" Oh no, dear aunt," exclaimed Ursula, hastily.

"One would say so, if you imagine I suck these things out of my thumb.* I assure you I have very good reason to know what I know. I am not a chit, like you, to fancy a man is in love because he looks at me."

"There, there, go away," she added. "The whole thing has greatly exhausted me. I am not strong; that is the worst. But so I shall honestly tell him."

"You will accept him," cried Ursula, preparing to vanish.

"That will depend upon various considerations," replied Miss Mopius. "What is it, Drika? Ursula, hold your tongue, and let the servant pass."

Ursula turned hastily in the open doorway.

"The Jonker Otto is in the drawing-room," said the red-cheeked maid.

Miss Mopius turned pale, then red. "Go to him, child," she said, pleadingly. "Amuse him till I come. And remember—"

Ursula did not go in to Otto. A sudden shyness was upon her; besides she felt no desire to meet any member just now of the Van Helmont family. So the Jonker paced up and down the little parlor till the Dominé was attracted in to him through the windows.

Juffrouw Josine spent twenty minutes over the secrets of her toilet. Her poor old heart beat wildly. "He cannot even wait till the evening," she thought. "The densest fool would understand." When at last she descended, arrayed in her best Sunday green-silk dress with the poppies, she was surrounded by odors of ess. bouquet and sal volatile.

She had to pause before the drawing-room door and steady herself. She entered. There was Otto, a great bunch of apricot-colored roses in one hand, bending over a map of Java with the Dominé. "That is my part," he was saying. "One of the healthiest, I assure you, Dominé. All the men take their wives out there."

"Ah!" thought Miss Mopius. She shook hands, and the Jonker rather awkwardly presented his flowers.

"From my mother," he stammered, "to welcome Miss Rovers."

* Idiom.

"How kind of you to bring them," replied Miss Mopius, sitting down on the sofa and sniffing. "I hope Ursula will be grateful. *I* consider it most exceedingly kind."

She squinted across at the Dominé, who still bent over the map. There was a long wait, and Otto returned to the table.

"Roderigue," said Miss Mopius, in desperation. "Ursula wants you. She wants you at once!"

The minister lifted a countenance of mild astonishment.

"Very well," he said, remembering his daughter's painful experiences of the last days, "I'll be back in a moment, Otto. I want to ask you about that mission station you were telling me of."

Otto seated himself near to the lady.

"Miss Rovers, I hear," said Otto, "has safely returned."

The lady bowed over her flowers.

"She came back earlier than she had intended," continued the Jonker. "I suppose that she felt being away from what is doubtless a most happy home."

"I try to make it happy," murmured Miss Mopius.

"Could you do otherwise?" said Otto, fervently. And he added, in a tone that was almost sad, "It seems cruel to disturb your trefoil even for a day."

And he looked at her meditatively.

Miss Mopius gasped for breath. She muttered something about "leaving and cleaving."

Otto stared at her.

"Yes; it's very hot," he hazarded. "Shall I open the window?"

Miss Mopius somewhat recovered herself.

"Oh!" she replied, "but not as hot as Java, I suppose? Not nearly as hot as Java. I should enjoy Java. I like heat. I'm not strong, Mynheer van Helmont, but the hot weather always does me good. I'm sure I should feel much better in Java."

"Yes," he said, vaguely. "Would you prefer me, then, to shut the window again?"

"The window? Perhaps it would be better under the circumstances. The question you asked me just now is so mo-

mentous, Mynheer van Helmont, I do not know how to answer
it. Oh, that my dear elder sister were with me still! She was
very much my elder, very much so. I miss her guidance, her
motherly advice."

She hesitated, and her eyelids fluttered.

"Juffrouw Rovers's mother?" said Otto. "I suppose she was
very beautiful?"

"Well, I hardly know if *you* would have called her beautiful.
She was not at all like me."

"Just so," said Otto. "I suppose Juffrouw Rovers is like
her?"

"Oh no; Ursula takes after her father's family. The
Mopiuses were always famous for their delicate skins."

"Ah!" said Otto, shifting on his chair. "Well, I am a
plain man; perhaps not much a judge of beauty—"

"Oh, don't say that," interposed the lady, smiling.

"But I know when I like a face, Miss Mopius. I think
an honest face is of more importance than mere good looks."

"Oh, of course," assented the lady, reddening.

"I mean in a man. I trust, Miss Mopius, that you have no
aversion to my face—or me."

The lady tittered, and buried her nose in her bouquet.

"I wish I could flatter myself you even liked me. But that's
nonsense. I'm a conceited fool."

"I do," whispered the spinster, with downcast eyes—"a
little."

Otto got up and warmly clasped her disengaged hand.

"How good it is of you to say that," he cried, heartily.
"Then you will, won't you? How awfully good of you." And,
with another energetic shake of those skinny fingers, he walked
from the room.

Miss Mopius opened her eyes wide, very wide. Presently,
however, she nodded her curls.

"Of course," she murmured, "he has gone to speak with
Roderigue."

A soft flush spread over her pale cheeks, and she waited.

CHAPTER XIII

URSULA sat by herself in the veranda through the sweetly
fading silence of the summer Sabbath evening. She had now
been back in her tranquil home for more than four-and-twenty
hours. It was good for her that her return had heralded the
holy calm of that long, sunlight-flooded day of rest. She had
slept as young twenty sleeps when worn out, whether from work
or weeping ; she had risen as young twenty rises, to a world
that is bright again. The peace of the familiar village-round
was upon her : the drowsy morning service, the droning Sunday-school, the empty afternoon "catechism." Had her father's text, she wondered, been inspired by the thought of his
absent child at Drum ! He had preached on " Keep yourself
unspotted from the world." She desired nothing more ardent-
ly. Here was she returned in time to point the moral.

Her hands lay idle in her lap, an emblem of the day's repose.
The whole village had folded its hands to watch the lengthen-
ing shadows. A few conspicuous white shirt-sleeves lolled
against the church-yard wall. And somewhere a bullfinch was
carolling, breaking the Sabbath in his own divinely appointed
way.

"How hushed it all is," thought Ursula, looking up to the
far plumes of the motionless poplars. And the lull sank around
her own soul. Why break our hearts over the scuffling and
splashing of one or two swimmers ? The river of God's glory
flows steadily on. She laid a tired head on its current ; for a
moment the waters were stilled.

She did not even care to penetrate the mystery concerning
her Aunt Josine. The confidences of the preceding afternoon

had been succeeded by an extreme reserve which the lady's two companions almost provokingly respected. The pastor knew of nothing. At dinner, on the Saturday, he had been mildly-astonished by an atmosphere of constraint, in the midst of which his sister-in-law had suddenly ejaculated,

" Well, Roderigue?" with the vehemence of a bomb-shell.

He had answered,

" Well, Josine? It certainly is much better than the last joint, though she *will* over-roast it," a reply which did not seem to give full satisfaction to its recipient.

" He has gone, first of all, to obtain his father's permission," thought Miss Mopius. " I might have known. With the aristocracy a father is a very important personage."

She retired early with a headache which not even the vegetable electricity could combat. It extended over the Sunday, as Miss Mopius's headaches naturally would. She lay on her sofa and sighed at intervals. People would not be suprised at her lying on the sofa. Had she not sighed at intervals, Ursula would have risen to see what was wrong.

The church-clock had just struck seven; in the ensuing pause of expectancy its last note was still trembling away into nothing, when Ursula's closed eyes became conscious that somebody was watching them. She started to her feet in confusion, a little ruffled and rumpled, before the admiring gaze of the Jonker Otto van Helmont.

" I must have been dozing off," she said.

" You were asleep. I am sorry I woke you," replied honest Otto, " but I came with a message from my mother. She is very anxious to speak to you. She—she wants you to come up to-night. If you would?"

Ursula hesitated. She saw the dog-cart standing by the gate, a village lad erect at the horse's head. Continental Sabbaths are not like English; still, the Dominé's daughter was not accustomed to Sunday driving.

" She made me come," continued Otto, apologetically; " but if you'd rather stay—"

" I will ask papa, and be ready in five minutes," she answered, promptly. Her pulse quickened. Doubtless there was some fresh trouble about Gerard. If so, it was her duty to "go through."

Presently Otto saw her coming down the garden path with her strong, brisk step, in straw hat and woolley wrap, all light and bright, among the thick gayety of the wall-flowers and the pink flare of the hollyhocks.

"Why, it's Beauty!" she cried, as she drew near, recognizing the mare.

"Yes, none of the other horses were available, and none of the men were about, so I harnessed her myself and came away. I hope Gerard won't object, for once. It couldn't be helped."

No one but Gerard, and Gerard's particular groom, was allowed to touch Gerard's particular mare. She was his prime favorite, and deservedly so, for neither of the saddle-horses could stand in her shadow. But most horses, unlike men, have one or two faults, and Beauty's was nervousness.

"You know we expected Gerard this morning," began Otto, as the dog-cart bowled along. "He was to have brought my cousin with him, you know. But in their stead comes a telegram this afternoon to say that Helena is ill. Mother worries to know what is really the matter, and she has sent for you to give her the latest news of them all."

Ursula did not answer. She had expected further embroilment. And, somehow, she was growing to feel awkward in Otto's presence despite, or perhaps partly on account of, her father's praise. That morning during church she had been sensible of his quiet admiration, and had experienced, for the first time in her existence, not the blush of being stared at, but the glow of being discreetly observed.

Now, again, as she sat watching the horse's head, she perceived, without seeing them, some long-drawn side glances. Her nostrils tingled, and she wished there had been a groom on the back seat.

"Well, and did you enjoy your uncle's Indian stories?" queried Otto, breaking a silence that was becoming acute. "Did he tell you anything very dreadful this time? How often did he find a tiger under his pillow at Batavia?"

She laughed, and they talked lightly of Uncle Jacóbus, and of the life out yonder in the Indies, where everything is gigantic compared to little Holland, even the money-making, and also the mortality.

"So your mind is made up more firmly than ever," he concluded. "You would never go out to Java on any account?"

"No," she answered, flushing. "And, besides, remember my father! What would become of him if I were to leave him alone with "—she pulled up—" himself!" she said.

"True," he replied, exceedingly gravely. Both were occupied with their thoughts for a minute or two, and then they began to talk of something else.

They had reached a spot along the lonely country road where it suddenly curved among a solitary cluster of cottages. On both sides it stretches away, very narrow and smooth, and almost treeless, between parallel ditches and far-extending fields. Two landaus could not pass each other with safety, but it is largely used in summer-time by overloaded hay-wains. For those who know Holland it is unnecessary to add that a tram-line occupies two-thirds of it.

This tram-line, which runs largely through desolation, has to twist round the curve of the cottages. Where it does so it has just emerged from a thicket; and the whole is so arranged by nature and science that the locomotive can flatten the cottage-children without their being alarmed by seeing its approach.

On this slumbrous Sunday evening the women were enjoying a brief period of repose. The smaller children were in bed; the bigger ones had gone plum-stealing. Fathers and mothers sat stolidly by the door with slow pipe or slower speech. As the dog-cart came racing along, the men raised their caps. One of them, however, shouted something.

"The tram!" exclaimed Ursula, half-rising. Otto had already set his teeth tight; both knew it was too late. Even as the cry went up, the great engine, silent and deadly, loomed in front of them like a hideous, falling rock. There was just room enough between the rails and the cottage-walls for it to graze their lateral splash-board in rushing by. But a carelessly projecting shutter rendered this escape impossible. As the mare sprang

"'THE TRAM!' EXCLAIMED URSULA, HALF RISING"

aside, the off-wheel caught the obstacle, and sent it clattering
back against the wall. For an instant—the hundredth part of a
second—the double crash all around seemed to stun her; then
up went her ears, down went her neck; she was off.

The villagers ran round the corner, emptily shouting. The
tram sailed serenely on.

"Sit still," said the Jonker between his closed teeth. The
advice was superfluous, for the girl had immediately sunk back
again, clutching the hand-rail beside and behind her, frozen to
calm. She did not answer, and the vehicle went rushing on.

Forward the naked road stretched, white and thin, between
two dark lines of water; forward the horse flew, drinking, as it
were, that road before it with pendent head—crashing onward
in a cloud of dust and stones and sparks. There was nothing
to confront or pass them as they tore through yielding infinity,
except here and there a sleepy calf that tried to race them as
children would a train. There was nothing but the wide lilac
heaven all around, with the boundlessness of a horizon that
ever recedes and a highway that ever lengthens out. It was the
very delirium and terror of motion, such as few mortals can experience, the irresisted, irresistible forward rush of the whole
being—the concentration of all thought into that one idea of a
sweep through immensity. For one moment the laws of time
and space were annulled; there was no distance, no limit, no
measurement, nothing but an infinite impression of velocity.
The high carriage sailed through the summer warmth like a
bird. On—on—on! For ever and ever. Why, indeed, should
it stop?

And then the conviction that stoppage is inevitable, is imminent, and that it may well mean—death.

All that, not in a succession of impressions, but in one long-
drawn lightning flash, like the flash of the flying brute, only
faster.

Ursula looked up once at Van Helmont. His face was carved
in bronze; his arms were straining back; his feet had bent out
the splash-board. In another moment it burst away from them
in a wide crash of splinters, and threw him forward, silent still.
He righted himself with a jerk, but it seemed as if the horse

had received a new impetus from the slackening even of that illusory hold. She swept the ground from under her as the tall wheels appeared to stop revolving, in a constant blaze of starlight. Ursula fancied, from the height where she clung, that their progress carried with it a crimson glow through the swiftly receding dust. But it was all so short, though it seemed eternity, and yet she remembers, this very day, each sensation that rose and sank across her brain. Her hat was gone ; her hair was flying. One minute of that wild, mad stress, and then—

"I must save you," said Otto. "Don't mind how."

Even as he spoke, she suddenly remembered that the canal lay straight athwart their course. The canal, not level with the road, not clear, but fifteen feet lower, at the bottom of a stone embankment and landing-place for barges. The blood grew cold in her veins. During the brief frenzy of her alarm, the thought of the canal had not as much as occurred to her. It had been with Otto from the first.

And—even as he spoke—the violet line of the horizon deepened upon her eyes, where the white road struck dead against fields on the farther side. It turned at a right angle there, as she knew but too well, along the water.

"It's as much as I can do to keep her head straight," said Otto, almost in a whisper. "Another minute, and it will be too late ! Ursula, can you help hold the reins for a moment without risk of falling out ?"

"Yes !" she cried, vehemently, angry that he had not asked her five minutes sooner. For so the time seemed to her.

"It's only for a moment," he continued, " we've got beyond the side ditches now." She saw that he was using the one hand he had freed to draw something from his trousers-pocket. Her grasp closed, near his other hand, on the reins : she thought that her arms were being drawn from their sockets, but she bit her white lips and held on. He knelt, as well as he could, on the carriage mat, bending over the broken splash-board, and she saw that he held a heavy revolver in his bleeding right hand. The glove was torn to ribbons.

"The instant I fire, drop the reins," he said, quietly, " and hold on to the cart for dear life. It's our only chance. God help me; we can't—are you ready?"

" Yes," she said, with staring eyes.

He had spoken the last question abruptly. In the still evening the line of the embankment already stood out. They were whirling towards it.

Again he bent forward, and fired. The shot missed, and as the report thundered around her and the reins fell loose on her sides, the mare seemed to rise into the air with the fierceness of her flight.

Immediately a second flash followed the first; the horse leaped up with a strain that snapped the shafts like two twigs, then fell, struck behind the right ear, a dead weight in the middle of the road.

Ursula, in dropping the reins as commanded, had flung her full weight on the back-rest behind her. For a moment the dog-cart, crashing forward, tossed her wildly to and fro. She saw Otto ejected, arms foremost, clean away over the dead mare's head.

Another moment and she was kneeling beside him. Horse and cart lay a confused mass of harness and broken wood.

She had nothing at hand to help him. She could do nothing. She looked round wildly, vainly. Not being a hysterical maiden, she did not make up her mind he must be dead. But she knew he was insensible, and the extent of his injuries she was quite unable to determine.

She looked down at his resolute face, bronzed beneath its heavy mustache, and realized, quite newly, how good he was, how strong; this silent man who had seen so much of the world; this simple man, whom her noble-hearted father so greatly praised. The thought of Gerard flashed across her, Gerard, the beau ideal of her girlhood, all glory and glitter, a Stage-Baldur with the footlights out. How she longed for Otto to open those calm, blue eyes. She prayed confusedly, with unmoved stare, looking back along the lonely road for help.

Then she got up and hurried away to the side of the embankment, shudderingly realizing how near it was. She could not help leaving him. She was much shaken, yet she felt quite strong.

There was a barge moored by the little quay; a woman stood on its deck, startled and staring. She called to the woman, who came running up the stone steps.

"Is there no man?" cried Ursula.

"No, the men were gone to the nearest public-house."

The girl waved off the barge-woman's inquiries. She did not want sympathy, but help.

"You must hurry to the Horst," she said, impatiently. "You know it? The large house behind those trees. They will pay you. You must explain that an accident has occurred, not fatal. And bring back assistance at once."

She returned hastily to Otto. His eyes were open, and they smiled to welcome her. A terrible anxiety suddenly died out of them.

"Are you not hurt?" he said, faintly. "I'm not. I shall get up presently."

She could not answer except by a shake of the head. A lump had risen in her throat which she was resolved to keep down.

"How sorry Gerald will be!" continued Otto.

She nodded again, and for a few minutes they were both quite silent. Then the Jonker raised himself on one arm.

"I am only dizzy," he said. "I shall be all right in no time, I assure you. I'm sorry I frightened you. Why, there are some people coming along, are there not?"

It was true; the men from the cottages could be seen running towards them. Otto hesitated, as he sank back, gazing up into Ursula's bent face.

"Ursula," he said at last, calling her by her name for the second time in the course of that evening, "we very nearly went to our death together — and you wouldn't even go to Java!"

There was a ripple in his voice and in his eyes. She held out her hand, and he pressed it to his lips.

"You have saved my life," she said.

Presently the foremost runner reached them, breathing heavily. Otto staggered to his feet, and, as the others came up, began giving orders about the wreck and the poor dead beast.

CHAPTER XIV

" Ursula," began the Dominé, with shaking voice. He went back to the door and pressed his hand against it to make sure that it was properly closed. "My dear child, I have Otto van Helmont with me in the study. I am utterly amazed; I don't know what to say. You will be more astonished even than I am. The Jonker has come to ask my permission— God bless my soul, Ursula, he wants to have you for his wife!" .

Ursula bent over her needle-work; she was sewing buttons on her father's shirts.

The Dominé sat down opposite her and gasped. "It takes my breath away," he explained, apologetically. "He calls it love at first sight. I should think so. I should call it love at single sight, and so I told him."

Ursula looked up quickly. "Oh no," she said, "we have met quite a number of times."

"Why, you hussy, do you want me to accept him?"

"Oh, I did not say that, papa. Please don't say I said anything of the kind. I only meant—"

"I know what you meant. Why, you hussy, do you want me to refuse him?"

"You know best, papa," said Ursula, demurely.

"Then, of course, I shall send him about his business. Imagine the thing. The future Baroness van Helmont, and my child Ursula!"

"I am not such a child," replied Ursula, blushing and drawing herself up.

"Consider, my dear, the match would be an ill-assorted one.

8

Personally, I cannot say I look upon it—no, I won't say that,
either. But, dear me, dear me; I am quite taken aback.
Ursula, my dear, what is your attitude?"

"Oh, I haven't got an attitude," cried Ursula, strenuously
threading her needle. "Oh, don't say another word about it,
please. Go away, dear Captain, do, and leave me in peace."

"But, Ursula, this is childish. Otto—"

Suddenly, while he was speaking, the Dominé's brow cleared;
he thought he understood the situation. It turned upon his
selfishness and his daughter's self-denial.

"Ursula," he said, "you must forgive your poor old father.
I am selfish, and of course there are difficulties. But I see that
Otto van Helmont has somehow already succeeded in gaining
your heart, so I suppose I must go back and tell him so. Or
would you prefer to do it yourself?"

"Don't, father," cried Ursula. "Nobody has ever possessed
my heart but you. I hate all men, as I said the other day. See
how I liked and admired Gerard—for years, ever since I could
think—and now! I could almost have cut off the fingers his
touch had soiled! I don't want to marry any one."

"How beautiful," thought the Dominé, not without a twinge
of self-condolence, "are the unconscious workings of a maiden's
heart. The dear child lays bare her love and doesn't know she
possessed it! It is my duty to prevent a most fatal mistake.
Poor motherless one; I must take a mother's place to-day!"
Like many old-fashioned people, the Dominé believed that when
"a good woman" says she doesn't love a man, this *always* means
she does. So he abstained from useless questions.

"Ursula," he said, heroically, "Otto van Helmont is not one
of these men you dread. Dear child, I know him well. He is
a good and upright gentleman. I should be glad to think, my
dear"—the Dominé flung himself headlong upon the altar—
"glad to think that when I am gone my daughter will have
such a strong defender. The world is evil, dear, and I am old.
At any moment I may leave you unprotected."

She laid down her needle-work, and sat looking out of the
window.

"I don't think I quite love him," she said, slowly. "Not like you." Something in her solemn face filled him with sudden misgiving, although the last three words were reassuring.

"But, my dear," he suggested, gently, "you admire him very much—do you not? You think he is a splendid man?"

"Yes," she answered, still with that far-away look, "I admire him very much. I think he is a splendid man. I—I like to see him, father, and to hear him talk."

"Trust me, my dear child, you are very much in love with him," said the Dominé, sententiously, "as much as any maiden ought to be. Go in and tell him so."

She was willing to believe him; still, she hesitated. Uppermost in her heart, all these days, was a passion of pure scorn. It cast over Otto's honest figure the glory of an aureole.

"Father," she began again, "do you—would you really be happy to know I had accepted him?"

"You could not easily find a better husband," replied the Dominé, evasively.

She knitted her brows, as was her wont in moments such as this.

"It would not make you sad, but happy," she insisted.

"Sad—no, no," cried the Dominé, eagerly. "To think of it —sad!"

"But—Java?" she said, faintly.

"My dear, you will *not* go to Java," exclaimed the Dominé, very loud. "That you must tell him at once. You will stay in Holland. I may be very selfish, but I don't care."

He suddenly felt there were limits.

Ursula rose.

"Yes," she said, softly, "I must go to him myself. "It is a very terrible resolve."

The Dominé smiled, with a tear in his eye.

"'It is ever from the greatest hazards,'" he quoted, "'that the greatest honors are gained.' Pericles said that. It is a good motto for this day."

Ursula went straight to the study, where Otto was tramping up and down. His face brightened as he saw her enter.

"Are you bringing me the answer yourself?" he asked, coming forward with outstretched hands.

"You saved my life," she replied, simply. "It is yours."

"Josine," said the Dominé, "are you well enough to listen to me for a moment?" He spoke with unmistakable impatience, eying the limp bundle on the sofa.

"Roderigue, how can you be so unkind?" came the plaintive answer. "After the terrible escape our dear Ursula has had, my weak nerves are still naturally unstrung. I cannot bear to think of it. All night I seemed rushing through space with her and—him. What must *he* not have suffered?"

"Well, it's over now," replied the Dominé, "and he's thinking of other things. In fact, that's what I came in about. He has just been asking me to consent to his engagement."

"I knew it," said Miss Mopius, and sank back on the sofa-cushion.

The Dominé started. "What!" he cried. "Did he speak to you first?"

"Roderigue," replied the lady, with spirit, "I am old enough —I mean I am not so young that his speaking to me could be considered improper."

"No, indeed," began the puzzled Dominé.

"I gave him the answer of my heart, as I doubt not he told you. You will give us your blessing, my brother?"

The Dominé rose to his feet.

"Hearing you talk," he said, testily, "one might conclude it was you had made the match."

At this monstrous accusation the poor creature burst into tears. "To think," she sobbed, "that my poor Mary's husband should say such a thing of me. Roderigue, I wonder that dear saint . did not teach you what a woman's feelings are!"

Of all means by which Josine unconsciously tormented the pastor there was none like her allusions to his departed wife. Moments could be produced in the widower's calm day when that brave soldier might have felt it in him to strike a woman.

Only to slap her.

"Well, I can't help it," he said, still in the same irritated tone. He was disappointed in his future son-in-law. "Ursula and Otto must just settle it between them."

"Ursula is a child," replied the spinster. "She will be pleased to get so charming an uncle."

"Hey?" said the pastor, stopping very short. Then it all dawned upon him as when a curtain is drawn away.

"Otto has asked Ursula to marry him, and she has consented," he said, gruffly. For some forms of human weakness the man had not an atom of pity. Poor Miss Mopius received the blow straight in her face. She "never forgave" her brother afterwards for striking out. Striking a woman, after all.

She rose to the occasion, sitting up at once, tremulous but dignified.

"There is some mistake," she said. "You have misunderstood or I have been duped. In one case the man is a fool; in the other he is a villain. No gentleman makes love to two women at a time. I will thank you to leave me alone for the present, Roderigue."

"So be it, Josine," answered the Dominé, "but, remember, it was Will-be-Will made darkness in the town of Mansoul." Then his heart smote him for too great severity. "My dear," he said, in a kindly voice, "it is the old story with us all. Still Prince Emmanuel answers Mr. Loth-to-Stoop: 'I will not grant your master, no, not the least corner to dwell in. I will have all to myself.'"

When the last uncertainty had faded from Miss Mopius's soul, she merely said to Ursula, "He might be your father. I don't think it's nice for a young girl to marry an old man."

Ursula did not reply "For an old woman to marry a young man is worse." She only thought it. We can all be magnanimous in victory. But Ursula could even have been so, if required, in defeat. Her faults were never little ones.

To her confidential spinster friends Miss Mopius remarked, "She is very plain. I can't imagine what he sees in her. So brown! But, then, of course, he is past the heyday of youth,

and a little *usé*.   Well, some women like to get their lovers
second-hand.

   " I shouldn't," remarked one mittened crony.

   "No, indeed," replied Miss Mopius.

CHAPTER XV

On the Saturday following the Van Trossarts' garden-party—
two days, therefore, previously to the events just narrated—
Gerard van Helmont called in the early morning at the house
of his betrothed. He could hardly realize, as he impatiently
awaited her, that not twenty-four hours had elapsed since this
new brightness had come into his life. Already he felt accustomed to the new rôle of a very wealthy man with a very
charming wife. How happy his mother would be after the first
shock of the unexpected! They must find another match for
Otto. Sprightly, sportive Helena would never have married
Otto, anyway. He glanced at the clock. Half-past ten. As
long as clocks stood in front of mirrors Gerard never saw only
the time.

The door opened; a servant entered slowly.

"The Freule was not ready, as yet, to receive him." Had
she sent him no message! "No." The fiery lover went off to
the barracks and worried everybody.

In the afternoon he called again. The sounds of a piano
came pouring down upon him from up-stairs during his brief
wait on the steps. How brilliantly she played! A little too
wildly—like a musical tornado.

He was again shown into the front drawing-room. It was
again empty. Again he paced restlessly to and fro, but this
time he twisted his mustache.

He heard a footfall in the adjoining apartment; the music,
however, had not yet stopped. He was longing for it, now, to
do so.

The Baroness van Trossart came bustling in, hot and flurried.

"My dear boy," she began—"my dear boy, sit down." She
caught hold of his hand and drew him down on a low settee by
her side. "My dear boy, you and Helena have had a quarrel.
The worst quarrels always come first. Now tell me what it is
all about."

Gerard opened his light, innocent eyes. "There has been no
quarrel that I know of, Mevrouw," he answered. "What does
Helena say?"

The Baroness's substantial chaps fell. "Helena says nothing
at all. That is the worst of it. She has locked herself in, and
she won't speak to any one. She has been playing the piano
for hours—you hear her now—and her uncle trying all the time
to learn his speech for next Monday! I've been screaming to
make her stop, but I can't, and I got some dust in my eye, as
it is, through the key-hole." She sighed. Gerard, with heightened color, looked down at his spurs.

"Then you don't know what's wrong?" the Baroness repeated, helplessly.

"No, indeed, I don't."

"The excitement must have got on her nerves; but I wish,
at least, she would see Papotier."

They went out slowly into the hall. "Never mind, Gerard,"
said the Baroness, still in that ill-used tone, "it 'll be all right
soon. Come back this evening and settle about going to the
Horst to-morrow. Oh, will that music never stop!"

It followed him down the street in a reckless jingle and crash
of feverish discord, as if all the notes of the instrument together were dancing a devil's saraband.

He went to the club, and, from sheer nervous vexation, bois-
terously got together a game of *vingt-et-un*. He won nearly a
thousand florins in a couple of hours. As a rule, however,
gambling was not one of his weaknesses. He had plenty of
others.

Then he treated the whole mess to champagne, declaring it
was his birthday, and when somebody denied that, he turned
almost fiercely on the caviller. "My death-day, then!" he said.
"It don't make any difference in the wine."

They were all surprised at his irritability, and concluded that

"'THERE HAS BEEN NO QUARREL THAT I KNOW OF, MEVROUW'"

the extent of his winnings was vexing him. That would be quite like Van Helmont, who was free-handed and free-hearted to a fault. He was the most popular man in the regiment.

It was half-past eight when he again rang at the Van Trossarts' door. He was flushed with excitement and champagne. The piano had ceased; the whole house lay steeped in silence. Almost immediately, as he hesitated under the hall-lamp, the Freule's maid came forward with a note. He took it and glanced through it on the spot. It was very brief:

"Yes, I have read Maupassant; all night I sat up reading him. Go back to the house-maid. Thank Heaven, Jeanne is not married yet."

He went out again into the dusk immediately. Dutch shops are open late, especially on Saturdays. He walked quickly to the High Street, which was full of movement and yellow gas. At a well-known bookseller's he stopped.

"Have you Maupassant's *Une Vie?*" he asked the shopman. Oh yes! half a dozen copies lay on the counter. He carried off the blue paper volume, and locked himself up in his rooms.

Turning the pages hurriedly, he read the painful story. Even as he read, he revolted at the thought of his cousin's having come into contact with such scenes as were there described. He flung the book on to the table. "Filth!" he said, angrily. He felt that a woman's soul may pass pure, if such be her terrible fate, through fact, but not through fiction. And surely he was right. A man can judge of purity, in women.

The work he admiringly despised was like all those of its great author, though by no means equal, of course, in literary value, to his shorter masterpieces. It was a perfectly polished crystal goblet—a splendor of workmanship—full of asafœtida. Few men care for the taste, which might be healthful, but we all enjoy the useless smell.

Somebody whistled outside in the street. He went to the window. Two young officers, attracted by the light of his lamp, stood in the dark with upturned faces. His heart leaped with its impulse of relief.

"Is that you, Troy?" he called back. "Who's with you? Never mind, I'll come down. I say, there's a night-train to Brussels! We've just time to catch it. The chief 'll never know, and we'll have such a burst-up as never was before!"

On the Monday morning in the small hours Gerard returned from his escapade into Belgium. The others, who still valued their commissions, had refused to accompany him. He had left a telegram with Willie for the Horst, to the effect that Helena was unable to come. "The Colonel won't be any wiser," he said. And the Colonel never was.

Whether the excursion had been worth its cost—in every sense—was another matter. Such questions are useless, and Gerard preferred not to decide them. He lay down on his bed for a couple of hours, and then—before breakfast, somewhere near seven o'clock—he paid a visit to a lady of his acquaintance whom he had not seen for many months. He had a bad headache, and he felt deeply injured, but also distinctly inclined to indignation and virtue.

"Adeline," he said, pathetically, "I thought you still loved me."

"What a fool you must be then," said Adeline. She lived in a little out-of-the-way house, with a garden and a back entrance. No one was more accurately acquainted than Gerard with her periods of business or leisure.

"Better fool than knave," replied Gerard, bitterly. "But don't let's go on like this. What I wanted to tell you is that our secret's out. There."

"I know," said Adeline, nodding. She sat in her neat little tight-fitting dress in her neat little (tight-fitting) room, with her breakfast in front of her. It was all dainty and attractive. He had seen her sit thus many a time, while he lounged on the little chintz sofa.

"I told," added Adeline, proudly, biting a stiff crust with her pearly teeth.

"You!" He sprang upright. "You lie!"

"Oh, of course," she answered, "I was to sit and see you enjoy yourself, while I went to my ruin. I was to let *you* write

letters to my advertisements and then bring other men to laugh
at me." Her voice grew suddenly fierce. "I hate you for that,"
she cried, "for that most of all. I could kill you for that."

"Good heavens! was one of those unlucky advertisements
yours? I had nothing to do with answering them, I swear to
you. I was only umpire. Why, surely, you'd have recognized
my hand!"

"Humph," said Adeline. "Well, I told."

"It was a woman's trick, retorted Gerard. "But how did
you find out, you little devil, about the Freule van Trossart, or
about my—my—"

"Your what?" she questioned, sharply. "What's this about
the Freule van Trossart? You're going to make her miserable,
are you, as you did me?" She started up, clapping her hands.
"No, you won't," she cried. "No, you won't. I see. He's
gone and told her all about it. Oh, I love him for that!"

"Who? He!" exclaimed Gerard. "Do you mean to say
you've gone noising our shame about to strangers?"

The words stung her to sudden passion.

"Our shame?" she cried. "Our shame? My shame, you
mean. My shame, as Christian laws go in Christian lands.
And who are you, of all men, to taunt me with it? I told your
brother, if you want to know. And he went and told the girl
you were trying to catch, did he? Oh, I'm glad of that; I'm
glad of that!"

Gerard sat for some moments with bent brows and clinched
fists. His still stare frightened her. She sank into her seat
cowed.

"How did you meet my brother?" he asked, at last. His
voice was hoarse.

"You passed the shop with him one morning," she answered,
humbly. "I recognized him by your description. And when
going to my dinner later on, I met him in the Park alone. I
told him everything in half a dozen minutes. That day I was
desperate. I asked him if he could do nothing to help me to
make you marry me. I had some wild idea your family might.
I had never come across any of them. I probably never should
have such a chance again."

"And what did my brother say?" asked Gerard.

"He said he would do what he could. He didn't think he could do much. I don't think he likes you, Gerard." She spoke quite submissively, and, as she finished, her eyes stole across to the looking-glass to arrange a little bow at her neck.

"Oh no," replied Gerard, furiously. "He's too good to like me. *His* little peccadilloes are far away, and black."

"I'm sure I've always liked you, Gerard," she said, coquettishly. "You've treated me very badly. You know you have."

"I have," acquiesced Gerard, in a low voice. "Did you tell Otto, Adeline, of those three thousand florins I gave you?"

"No," she cried, again reverting to her sudden passion. "Do you fling that fact in my face? Do you call that a compensation?"

"No, no. God knows I didn't mean anything of the kind. I was only thinking—great heavens, I don't know what to think!" He buried his face in his hands.

"Poor Gerard," said the girl, softly, after an interval. "I didn't think you'd take on so. But you've treated me very badly, Gerard; you know you have; yet, somehow, I can't help liking you still. You were very good to me, too, once. And it was very sweet." She bent forward and timidly touched his neck. "Gerard, I'm sorry," she said.

But he only shook his head.

"Oh, Gerard, I was so wretched, so fearfully wretched. I couldn't stand the thought of—of the disgrace. I wanted you to marry me. I would have given my life for you to marry me —only to make an honest woman of me first. Gerard, think of it, there was nothing left for me but marriage, exposure, or death. I tried death once—with my fingers—but—but the water was so very cold." She began to cry softly, resting her hand on her quondam lover's knee.

Then Gerard looked up quickly. His face was quite pale and drawn.

"Adeline," he said, wearily, "it's no use, you and I can't be angry with each other. Not seriously, only in flimsy bursts. It's like our love. We can't hate each other, either. Great love turns to hate, they say. Ours is of the kind that one can always take up again as if one had never left off. You've ruined my life, and, somehow, I can't even reproach you with doing so."

" But you've ruined mine, too, or very nearly," she sobbed.

" Yes, that's true ; I don't want, though, to make you so wretched. You shock me with your horrible talk. Adeline, look here, I don't care; if you feel as bad as that I'll marry you. Yes, I will, so help me God. You're the only woman that ever loved me, besides my mother, and I've treated you like a brute. We men don't always quite understand, but, Adeline, I can't bear to see you wretched, and to know it's all my fault. It *is* all my fault ; I've behaved like a cad. Adeline, I mean it ; I'm awfully sorry and ashamed of myself. I'll tell my father exactly how matters stand, and I'll *make* him let me marry you. You poor little innocent, to think that *they'd* make *me !*"

Adeline, for only answer, laid her head upon his shoulder, softly crying on.

" Don't cry like that, dear," he continued, in the same dreary tone. " It 'll all come right soon. I dare say we shall be fairly happy. We've made such a mess of our separate lives that the best thing we can do is to try and combine them."

" Oh, Gerard," sobbed the girl, " if I'd only known a day or two sooner. It's too late now."

" No, no," he said, dully, stroking her hair. " I forgive you the trick you played me. I drove you to it, I suppose. Men are brutes."

" Oh, Gerard," murmured Adeline again, with closed eyes, " it's not that. I'm engaged."

" What ?" he cried, edging back, so that her head almost slipped.

She started up then, quite briskly. " Well, and what was I to do ?" she said, " with every week bringing me nearer. Other people answered my advertisement besides you, Gerard. And he's a very nice young man, a lawyer's clerk. I was out in the country with him all yesterday, and we settled it coming home."

" Indeed," said Gerard, scornfully. " And he—he—"

She blushed crimson.

"Yes, he knows," she murmured. "He thinks you treated me very badly, Gerard."

"I know."

And he consents, thought the young man, to accept the plaster I placed on the bruise. He got up from the little chintz sofa of many memories.

"I wish you had waited to give Otto the last chapter of the story," he said, very wearily. "Poor little girl, I'm not angry with you. Don't cry. We've had enough of that. Good-bye, Adeline. I suppose we need hardly meet again."

And he held out his hand.

"Gerard," she said, taking it, "I'm so glad you're not angry. I like you very much, but, do you know, I fancy I should be happier with him. He isn't as good-looking as you, Gerard— not anything like—but he looks very nice." She raised the young officer's hand to her lips. "Thank you," she said, "for offering to marry me."

"Oh, no thanks," he replied, taking his hat.

"Gerard!" she called him back, her eyes reverted swiftly from the mirror to his face. "You never said anything about my new dress which I had to make. Don't you think it suits me?"

"Oh, everything suits you," he cried, making his escape. There were tears in his eyes as he turned into the street.

CHAPTER XVI

THE dog gave a yelp.

"Do take care, Otto," cried the Baroness, sharply. Her voice was shrill with irritation. "I wish you would sit down. You have trodden on poor Plush's tail! And there really was no reason for that. Not even if I take in earnest, as I have no intention of doing, the exceedingly poor joke you have just concocted."

"I assure you it is no joke, mother, but very sober earnest."

"I am to believe that you have this morning asked Ursula Rovers to be your wife, and that she has deigned to accept you?"

"She has deigned to accept me, mother."

"Then there are other things you can tread on besides little dogs." She was too angry to continue. An embarrassing silence had thickened between them before she added, looking straight in front of her, "But I shall not afford you the satisfaction of a yelp."

"Mother!" he cried, with a pathetic ring of pain in his virile voice. He held out his arms. The movement was an appeal.

But she waved him back.

"Between mothers and sons," she said, "there is a union of sympathy, of interest, not only of intercourse. Dogs have mothers, Otto, and love them and forget them. And when they meet again, after twelve weeks—mother and son walk side by side, *but the pup doesn't know.*"

She held out her trembling fingers to the little animal beside her.

"The mother does," she said, tremulously. "The mother does."

Otto stood by the Dresden gimcracks of the mantel-piece. His head was bent, but across the level eyebrows lay a bar of resolve.

"If you would only let me explain—" he began.

"Surely I can do that for myself. You are 'in love' with the girl, to use the cant phrase. There is no more beautiful word in the world, and none more insulted. With you it simply means that you have been caught by the charms of a piquant brown face. *You*, who are nearly forty, whose calf period might surely be past. Faugh! you men are all the same, like dogs again! You talk of piety, affection, ambition, but when the moment comes you run after the nearest cur. Otto, I won't say any more. I have said too much already. In truth, there is nothing to say. There is only a curse to bear. Nowadays, it seems, the children curse the parents. It may be less melodramatic, but the results are far more visible to the naked eye."

Then he broke down before her hard, her hopeless misery, and knelt by her side.

"Mother, I love her," he said. "Never mind what the word means to me, it need mean but little to you. I will take her away to some place where you need but rarely see her."

"And the Horst!" she cried, looking at him for the first time. The despair in her eyes cut straight to his soul. "You have not even thought of that! And you hardly know the girl. The old house—the old home—you have not even thought of that!"

"I have thought of it," he answered, sternly, returning to his place on the hearth. "It is not gone yet. I will work and make money. Father may still live twenty years."

But she did not heed him. "Only a good-looking face!" she said. "Only half a dozen glimpses of a good-looking face and —pfst!" She snapped her fingers. "Does your father know?" she asked.

"Not yet," he answered. "I came to you first. I had hoped that you—"

"Would join with the happy pair in imploring his blessing. Did I not say rightly, Otto, that a certain amount of mutual understanding is essential to the preservation of natural ties! That you should succeed in making a philosopher of such a crackbrained creature as I am! I hear your father's step in the entrance-hall. The poor fellow is whistling! Never mind, it can't be helped. Call him in." Otto obeyed.

"Well, what is it, my dear?" asked the Baron, entering. "Are you still enjoying your new-found son?"

"Yes, that is it," replied the old lady. "Exactly. My new-found son still prepares me fresh surprises. Otto, tell your father to-day's."

"I have engaged myself," said Otto, steadying his voice, "to Juffrouw Ursula Rovers."

The Baron's thin cheek flushed. He resumed the tune he had been whistling, and carefully finished it. Then he said, "I suppose that is quite definite?"

"Oh, yes," interposed the Baroness, "a fool's decisions always are."

"Hush, my dear. I mean, Otto, that you have fully considered and weighed the matter, and have made up your mind to go through with it at all costs?" The Baron spoke very quietly.

"Yes," said Otto, and their eyes met.

"So I thought. Your decision will not be altered in any way by my pointing out that, as long as I live (which I hope to do for a quarter of a century longer), you will never receive a penny from me towards supporting Ursula Rovers? You probably understood that before?"

"I did," replied Otto. "I don't want any money. I'm going to work."

"Quite so. More tea, I suppose? Java?"

Otto's face fell.

"No," he said, awkwardly. "Not Java. Ursula doesn't want to go there."

The Baroness, who had been beating a silent tattoo with her foot, broke into an impatient exclamation.

"Really, Otto," said the Baron, with a thin little smile, "you must admit that you are rather provoking. When everybody wants you here, you insist upon living in the tropics, and when —well, the whole thing, therefore, is settled, is it, and practically beyond recall? Mistakes, as your mother just now re-

9

marked, usually are. This, of course, is a huge mistake—
a life mistake. However, perhaps you are aware of that,
too ?"

"Perhaps it is," replied Otto, "in some respects. But it
seems to me worth making."

"Possibly. There are no bounds to human selfishness. Men
have thrown away an empire for a night of dalliance. And the
heritage of the Helmonts is not an empire by any means. I am
sure I wish you a more protracted period of enjoyment. Then,
at least, one person will get satisfaction out of this miserable
business. Yes, as there is no help for it, I may as well wish you
joy. Wish him joy, Cécile."

"No," said the Baroness.

"Anyhow, I suppose it won't make much difference to you,
Otto ? Nor, alas, to us. And now that all the preliminaries are
settled, and you know our mind exactly and we yours—excuse
my putting you last—we had better swallow down the rest of
the unpleasantness as soon as possible. Bring up Ursula at once,
and we will give her our blessing. Bring her before dinner
if you can. I'm sure I wish you had her waiting in the drawing-room. I will say this : she is a good-looking girl, and, I
honestly believe, a good one. But what a reason for marrying
her !"

He threw up his hands with his familiar gesture of comical
dismay, and turning his back on his son and heir, went and sat
down by the Baroness. Otto walked slowly from the room, leaving the old couple together.

The little turret-chamber, all flowered silk and china shep-
herds, looked strangely unreal, like a painting on porcelain.
The light crept in through its rounded window with a curve
that lent to everything a glamour as of glaze. The occupants
themselves, bending near to each other, the toy-dog between
them, their delicate features still touched, as it seemed, with
eighteenth-century powder, had the appearance of Dresden figures seen under a shiny glass case. But their sorrow was very
real, none the less so because the Baron was endeavoring, as it
buzzed around them, to catch and kill it in the folds of a cambric handkerchief.

"Theodore," began the Baroness, twisting her rings, "you are always right. I do not mean to doubt your judgment. But it seems to me that you almost encouraged him to do what you disapproved. You—you told him how bad it was, how *wicked*, and then you wished him joy."

"My dear," replied the Baron, "you cannot push over the precipice a man who has already leaped. His mind was made up, and nothing would have changed it. I know Otto. This is just the kind of idiotic thing he might be expected to do. Some men cannot keep away from any folly which has an appearance of elevation. Their souls positively itch to commit it, whether it be useful or pleasant or not. Otto has always been like that. He is a Don Quixote of foolishness. Had Ursula not existed, he would have been bound to invent her."

"Unfortunately she exists," replied the Baroness. "But you might have argued, protested—"

"My dear, he is thirty-nine. And to argue with Don Quixote is to break a straw against armor. There is no strength like the conviction, 'the thing is so utterly asinine that I'm sure it must be right'; especially when the thing is also pleasant. Modern Quixotes are not above distinguishing that."

"Oh, don't reason it out in that quiet way," cried the Baroness, passionately. "It's too horrible for that. I can't bear it."

Her husband took her hand. "Dearest," he asked, "since when have we left off grinning over the things we could not bear?"

The only answer was Plush's grating bark, which she always started as soon as the Baron grew affectionate to the Baroness.

"As for quarrels, they are always a discomfort, but useless quarrels are a folly as well. And a dispute with Otto would soon develop into a quarrel. He knows what we think without further telling; be sure of that. For Heaven's sake let there not be a row. I have not been present at a row since I was twenty. Gerard ran the thing close the other day. We may just as well treat Ursula civilly. I only hope he will bring her at once. The prospect makes me nervous, and I don't see why my dinner should be spoiled because my eldest son is a fool."

"But Ursula should be made to feel—"

He interrupted her, a thing he was not in the habit of doing. "Be sure that Ursula will be made to feel," he said, "whatever we do. Trust human nature for that."

"Had it only been Gerard," she moaned. "And just as I had arranged about Helena!"

"Ah, had it been Gerard, I should have reasoned with him. Gerard can be made to laugh at follies, and the man who laughs can be made to abandon. Fool! Folly! You see, those are the only words I am able to think of. Answer a fool according to his folly. That is excellent advice. Molière's, is it not? I tried to bring it into practice to-day."

"Deeds like his," she said, "should still be preventable by lettres de cachet. They are worse than crimes. A name such as ours may be scotched by the reprobates who bear it, but it takes a fool, such as you laugh at, to kill it outright."

"Whom would you lock up? Ursula? Do you know, I fancy Ursula is in no way to blame. She is really a good little girl."

But the Baroness shook her head. The Baron rose.

"Well, it can't be helped," he said, yawning. "That is the beginning and the end. I wonder what Louisa will say. At any rate, the house is still ours; après nous le déluge. Otto is such an exemplary Noah; he is sure to be saved when it comes. By-the-bye, I had written to Labary about rehanging the west bedroom, but such experiences as this take away all one's pleasure in things of that kind. What's the use of working for such a son as Otto?"

With which momentous but unanswerable question he strolled out into the grounds.

Louisa, when informed shortly after by her sister of what had happened, took off her spectacles, laid down the book she was reading, and said,

"Otto is, at least, the only member of this family possessed of marked originality."

The Freule van Borck's view of the question was not without

importance, for she had some money to leave where she liked. She was exceedingly stingy, and her savings were presumed to be large.

"Yes," replied the Baroness, tartly, "but all his originality is original sin. However, I am glad, Louisa, if you can find extenuations, which I openly confess myself as yet unable to see."

The thin Freule rested an angular elbow on her knees.

"Ah, but that is because you are so entirely conventional," she said, gravely. "You are altogether hereditary, my dear; you cannot step out of your groove."

"Je ne déraille pas," replied the Baroness. "No. Dieu merci. Must Otto, to be happy?"

The Freule van Borck sighed.

"My dear, it is no use," she said. "We shall never understand each other. It is of the very essence of man's making that he should *not* run on rails. Machines run on rails. All the misery of the world has been caused by our doing so, and generally in batches, after one locomotive. When two of our locomotives met, there was a smash and bloodshed."

"But that," said the Baroness, evidently bored, "is exactly opposed to your favorite theory of hero-worship."

"So it is," replied her sister, cheerfully. "We must all be inconsistent at times, except you people on the rails. I was thinking of the hereditary leaders, not the hero-leaders of men. No hero ever—"

"But, Louisa, don't you understand? I have just told you that Otto—our Otto—is going to marry Ursula Rovers."

"Yes, my dear, and I reply that he makes a distinctly new departure. To judge of its expediency, we must know the result."

"The result can only be misery to all concerned."

"You think that because your heredity tells you so. Now, I shall be an interested and unprejudiced spectator. Everything depends upon Ursula. Is she an entity or a nonentity? *That* is the question. I agree with Carlyle—"

"Carlyle was a ploughboy!" cried the Baroness, still too impatient to be polite. "Of course, he would rejoice to hear of milkmaids marrying marquises! Nothing is more lamentable in these levelling days than that all the geniuses are born without grandfathers. The odds in the fight are unfair."

"Just so," replied the Freule, grimly. "Now, who knows what a genius the son of Otto and Ursula may be! My dear, I have been reading a most interesting volume, entitled *Le Croisement des Races*. I could give you some exceedingly curious details—"

"Spare me even the mention of your horrible reading, Louisa!" exclaimed the Baroness. "It is like passing down the streets where they hang out the *Police News*. Dear me, that is Gerard's voice speaking to his father. How excited he seems! I suppose Theodore has already told him. He must calm down a little, for the happy pair will be here in a minute. I saw the carriage turn into the avenue from the road."

Gerard came rushing in, followed more leisurely by his father. "Mamma!" he gasped. "Mamma, Otto has shot Beauty! It isn't possible; I can't believe it. Shot Beauty! Shot Beauty! Great God, what have I done to him that he should treat me like this?" He clinched his fist to his forehead. "Shot Beauty!" he cried again, in a choking voice. "Oh, I hope I sha'n't see him! I won't see him! I'll go back to Drum. If I see him I shall kill him!"

"Gerard!"

"Don't speak to me, any of you. I hate him! I hate him! I hate him!"

"My dear boy, don't be so absurd," began the Baron. "It really couldn't be helped. Your aunt has most kindly offered to get you another horse."

"In recognition of Otto's prompt and spirited action," said the Freule; "it was very dreadful, Gerard, but unavoidable, and he rose to the occasion. That is what I admire. And though I am not in the habit of giving expensive presents, and haven't the means to do so—"

"I won't have another horse," burst out Gerard. "I mean to say, that's not what I care about. He—he—oh, you don't know what he's done to me. And now he's killed Beauty as well! I hate him! I won't, I daren't meet him at dinner!"

" There's the hall-bell," cried the Baroness. " Shut the door, Theodore. Gerard, you had better go out by the anteroom. Otto is bringing home his betrothed for us to welcome as such !"

" His betrothed !" stammered Gerard, looking from one to the other. " What? Helena? Already ?"

" Helena ? No, indeed. The young lady is Ursula Rovers."

Otto and Ursula, pausing outside the door, heard Gerard's laugh of malevolent contempt, as well as the words that immediately followed it.

" Ursula Rovers !" he cried. " The future Baroness van Helmont ! My Lady Nobody !"

BROTHERLY HATE

The two brothers stood face to face by the stables. Otto, running round for Ursula's carriage, after the brief interview with his parents, had almost knocked up against Gerard. He started back.

" Damn you !" said Gerard. He said the hideous words with deep conviction—almost conscientiously, as if acquitting himself of a painful duty. For the last quarter of an hour, ever since he had fled from the boudoir before the approach of the betrothed pair, Gerard had been striding hither and thither, like one possessed, in the close vicinity of the stables. He was hardly aware what he said or thought. Otto had shot Beauty ; Otto had estranged Helena, actuated not even by sneaking jealousy (as had first seemed probable), but by wanton ill-nature. He hated Otto. He would never look upon his hateful face again. He would hurry back to Drum.

Suddenly his elder brother stood before him, almost jostling him in a hasty recoil. All Gerard's confusion of anger and sorrow cooled into one clear thunder-bolt.

" Damn you !" he said. There could be no doubt in his own heart or any other of his concentrated hate of the intruder. What says Tacitus ? " With more than brotherly hate." Tacitus read the inner souls of men.

From the moment when he fired the fatal shot, Otto had felt that he owed Gerard most humble and affectionate apology. Concerning the episode with Helena he was, of course, serenely ignorant. But his attitude had stiffened just now under the cruelly careless words which had fallen like a shadow across the home-bringing of the betrothed.

"Silence, Gerard," he replied, haughtily. "No one can be more sorry than myself. If you will listen reasonably, I will try to explain—"

"No one more sorry than yourself!" burst in Gerard, his whole frame trembling with passion. "No one more sorry! You loved Beauty, I suppose? You loved Beauty better than anything else except — except—" He bit back the word "mother." "You loved Beauty, and first drove her mad by your insane bungling, and then shot her!—shot her! Oh, my God!" The words choked him. Suddenly he grew white and calm. He advanced upon Otto.

"If only you were not my brother!" he said, in a whisper.

Otto met his anger-troubled gaze, unflinching.

"You are a first-rate shot," continued Gerard, with bitter meaning. "Oh, a first-rate shot! Ursula was right. But I, too, can shoot straight."

Then he broke off short, and struck his forehead, bewildered among the madness of his own conceptions.

"Leave me to myself," he gasped. "Only leave me. Go back to Helena—or Ursula—which is it? Tell Ursula also. Be sure and tell Ursula everything about me. Go and be happy, you and your charming—"

"Not a word more," interrupted Otto, forewarned by the other's tone. "I am very sorry, Gerard, and willing to make every allowance. But I will not hear a word against my future wife."

Gerard rushed away.

"Why not, after all?" he asked himself. Brothers had met before in honorable combat alone beneath the moonlight shadows of Rhenish castle walls. He laughed aloud, and when the coachman's dog ran out, barking, to greet him, he kicked the brute away.

Ursula could not but notice Otto's silence—nay, more, his depression—as they drove back again to the Parsonage. She explained it by the Baroness's reception of the engagement. For not even the most laborious amiability could make the two women misunderstand each other.

"Otto, I hope," stammered the girl, with sudden heart-sinking, as they paused under the little veranda, " oh, I hope you will never repent."

He hesitated, and, with human inconsistency, she resented the momentary delay in his denial.

" No, I shall never repent," he replied, " unless—"

He checked himself; he was going to say she must make up her mind to leave Horstwyk, but he realized the unfairness of too precipitate appeal.

" Unless?" she repeated, looking into his eyes.

" We will talk about it some other day," he answered, hastily. " For the moment you and I are simply happy ; let that suffice us. I am proud of you, my darling, and it seems too good, you caring for an old fellow like me."

He kissed her, and she blushed, half unwilling, under the unwonted familiarity from a man she barely knew. Love and marriage seemed so strange to her—not unpleasant, but so strange.

She watched him down the road, and her eyes grew misty. " Unless?" she softly repeated to herself. Then she went and found her father in his study.

" Papa," she said, " you are sure that Otto loves me ?"

" Why else should he ask you to marry him ?" retorted the Dominé, turning abruptly in his round desk-chair.

" Yes, that is true," replied Ursula, humbly. " But they cannot say the same of me."

" How ? What?" queried the Dominé, with troubled eye-brows.

She turned full to the light.

" Papa," she said, impetuously, " it's not that I want to be Baroness van Helmont. I'm sure, I'm sure it's not."

The Dominé struck his hand on the table before him.

" No, indeed," he cried, in a loud voice. " Who says that ? Who dares to say that ?"

Ursula sighed wearily.

" Oh, no one does," she answered. " Never mind. Life is very complicated. I wish one always knew exactly what was right."

" One always does," said the simple - thoughted Dominé.

"'NO ONE MORE SORRY THAN YOURSELF!' BURST IN GERARD"

"Obey marching orders. Forward. Do the nearest duty at once, and with all your might."

Ursula sighed again, still more wearily, and, going out into the passage, happed upon her aunt. Miss Mopius passed on her way to the store-cupboard, her joined hands overweighted with eggs. At sight of her successful rival she started, and one of the eggs flopped down on the stones in slimy collapse.

"I can understand your exultation, Ursula," said Miss Mopius, all a-quiver, "but don't sneer at me like that. I won't stand it. Some day, perhaps, you also will know the curse of Eve."

Ursula, in the cruelty of her youth and beauty, barely pitied her aunt.

"What was the curse of Eve?" she inquired.

"Adam," retorted Miss Mopius, and dropped another egg.

"I'll wipe up the mess," said Ursula, sweetly.

Miss Mopius beat a hasty retreat. She spent the rest of the afternoon diluting one solitary globule of a patent medicine through a series of thirteen brimming decanters of water. A tumbler from the first decanter was poured into the second, and so on through the lot. The thirteenth solution, said the advertisement, was the most "potent." Miss Mopius believed the advertisement. The magnificent name of the small globule had an ever-recurring charm for her. It was called "Sympathetico Lob." "Lob," especially, struck her as so delightfully mysterious. And it cured dizziness, palpitation, bad taste in the mouth, liver complaint, rheumatism, St. Vitus' dance, stitch in the side, and heartburn, besides being highly recommended for cases of agitation, nervous depression, sudden bereavement, and disappointed love. Miss Mopius found it very helpful. She sat in her darkened room, amid the falling twilight, sipping.

That evening there was consternation in the big drawing-room at the Horst. It spread itself like a great mist between the occupants of the apartment, and prevented their looking into each other's eyes. The oppression had begun round Gerard's vacant chair at the dinner-table; it now deepened about the Baroness, where she sat apart from the rest, straightened

among the soft silks of her *causeuse.* In the lap of her pearl
gray evening-dress lay a crumpled white scrap from Gerard:

"I'm off to Drum. I sha'n't come back as long as you've got
Otto. The house can't hold us both.—G."

Father and elder son stood with downcast lids, watching each
other through inner eyes. The Freule laid down her newspaper.

"He will think twice," she said, sharply. "Gerard is not the
kind of man to desert the fleshpots of Egypt because Moses
has come with a plague or two."

The Baron's gloomy face rippled over with sudden sunshine.

"That's just like you, Louisa," he cried, "to select the most
unfortunate simile in a hundred thousand. The worst of all
Moses's plagues was the removal of the eldest son!" He
laughed, looking for the first time at his heir. "I am speaking
from Gerard's point of view," he added. "Of course, of course,
from Gerard's point of view." And he laughed again, but half-
way the laugh died down into a pathetic little murmur. "It is
exceedingly annoying," he said, plaintively. "And I who detest
unpleasantness! We have never had any unpleasantness before."

"He means it," interposed the Baroness, in a dull tone. "I
know he means it, because of the little hook to the 'G.' When
Gerard makes that, he is in earnest. It corresponds to a jerk in
his voice. None of you understand Gerard. He is so good-
natured; you fancy he is all sunshine and no fire."

"Deplorable!" exclaimed the Baron, stopping, helpless, in the
middle of the room. "And incomprehensible. All about a
horse. We will buy Louisa's present, the sooner the better, and
send it to bring him back."

"Ah! but is it all about a horse?" asked the Freule's high-
pitched voice. Once more she emerged from behind her newspaper, her own particular newspapers, the *Victory!* It would
be difficult to say what the *Victory* wanted to conquer; but
you received a general impression from its pages that in this
world the battle was always to the strong.

"Ah! but is it all about a horse?" asked the Freule, amid a darkening silence. "Or could Otto tell more if he would? You consider me none too sharp-sighted, my dear brother and sister; but it strikes me you are blind not to perceive that you would have had a daughter-in-law Ursula anyway, whether your eldest had come back or not, eh?" She shot out this last interjection at her nephew, rising, meanwhile, all in one piece, with an abrupt sweep back of her stand-up silk.

Otto was horrified by the sudden condensation of the amorphous suspicions afloat in his brain. Could it be possible that he had ousted a rival? Certainly, Gerard's fury seemed in excess of the injury to which he owned. For the first time, in the elder brother's heart also, dislike and distrust joined hands.

"Just so," said the Freule van Borck, across his irritable uncertainty. She nodded to the others provokingly, and walked out upon the terrace. Otto followed her.

"Aunt Louisa," he began, "I think you are mistaken."

"Yes, Otto," she answered. "Of course you do now. But you didn't when I first spoke, you see. Let me give you a bit of advice. Eh?"

"Well?" The young man's voice was not inviting.

"Don't go back to Java with your wife, as I dare say you want to do. Stop here and fight it out. Ursula 'll fight it out. I don't give twopence for a married woman who can't live in the same house with her former lover. Of course they were lovers. I've seen it these half a dozen years. Never mind. She was too good for Gerard. There!" She smiled a complimentary smile to her brawny nephew; she liked his brownness and bigness, and straight, square strength.

Otto crept away.

"To-morrow I shall speak about going away," he said to himself. "To-morrow, not to-night. The Dominé must listen to reason. The shadow of Cain lies between Gerard and me."

CHAPTER XVIII

NEXT morning, so it happened, the Dominé awoke to a moderately disagreeable task. While dressing, he grumbled over the speck in his tranquil sky, as mortals will do when unaware of the storm-cloud fringing their horizon.

The Dominé had a parishioner who caused him more annoyance than the rest. This sheep of the flock was, however, not a black sheep. It was serenely white. It never wandered, for it never even got up. Its name was Klomp, and its nature was unmitigated indolence.

This man Klomp inhabited a little cottage of his own, lost among the woods. He shared it with two daughters, aged respectively twelve and eighteen. Like its owner, the cottage lived on, disgraceful but comfortable. Theoretically, it ought to have been pulled down.

Klomp knew better. All summer he lazed over a hedge which mysteriously bore his weight; all winter he dozed by the stove. If any remnant of useless ornamentation fell away from the cottage, the proprietor never winked an eye, but should a tile drop whose fall let in the rain or wind, Klomp would scramble up on the roof and replace it. He was a philosopher.

He never ill-treated his daughters unless they let the fire go out in winter. To keep it lighted during seven months of the year was their whole earthly duty, for house-keeping had long been reduced to an almost imperceptible minimum. The entire family lived on next to nothing very cheerfully, and was a disgrace to the neighborhood.

Vices the father had none. As has already been hinted, he was negatively virtuous. He drowsed at peace with himself

and with all the world above and below him, except when the
Dominé came to make trouble.

The Dominé was making trouble just now. By a stroke of
unexpected good-fortune an opportunity had occurred of "doing something for those poor girls," whose one desire was that
nothing should be done either for them or by them. Freule
van Borck, it must be known, occasionally took a philanthropic
interest in the village at her brother's castle-gates, an interest
which manifested itself in spasmodic bursts of tidying up
neglected corners. She had suddenly disapproved of that long-
standing eyesore, the Klomps' cottage, and had made a beginning of improvement by getting an energetic person in the
north to accept of Pietje, the elder girl, as a possible servant,
wages five pounds per annum, all found. This good news had
been communicated to Pietje by Hephzibah, the Freule's maid.
Pietje had merely answered, "Let the Freule go herself," but
that retort got modified on its way to Louisa.

So now the Dominé went to try his hand. He especially disliked all intercourse with Klomp, because, during their inter-
views, one of the two invariably lost his temper, and that one
was never the parishioner. That was the worst of Klomp ; he
had no temper to lose.

To-day, however, the parson rejoiced in notable compensa-
tions ; these occupied his thoughts as he swung with large steps
through the woodlands. After the first shock of abandonment
which every parent feels in a daughter's sudden rapture, he had
settled down to complacent contemplation of an eligible son-in-
law. For the Dominé, as we know, had never made a secret of
his attachment to Otto. And he lacked the requisite affectation
to convince himself that the secondary consideration of the
young man's social position was altogether beneath the notice
of a humble clergyman like himself.

His darling Ursula would flit from the nest—that is true—
but only to another close by, where he still could hear her singing. The Dominé smiled gratefully over this linked perfection
of prosperity : wife to the heir of the Horst, and wife to Otto
van Helmont.

"Lord God, I thank Thee," said the Dominé, out aloud,

among the fragrance of the solitary lane. His path wound in sandy whiteness beneath the heat-mist of the fir-trees; there was a buzz on all sides of a myriad nothings, invisibly swelling the morning air.

The cottage lay prone upon the ground, asleep. It had sunk as low as it could, and had pulled the ragged branches of the trees over its ears, comfortably hiding in the cool, long shadows, naked and unashamed.

The owner of the cottage lay prone upon the ground also; he had the advantage of the house in that he was consciously—and conscientiously—drowsing. "I sleep, but my heart waketh." Klomp knew he was not awake. Man has few pleasures here below; has he any to equal that sensation?

"Good-morning, Klomp," said the parson's bright, brisk voice at his ear. Klomp did not start; he merely half opened one eye and answered, "Dominé," which was his abbreviated form of salutation. "Save your breath to spare your life," was one of his axioms.

"Klomp, I've come about Pietje," continued the Dominé, with that loudness which, in him, was nervousness escaping. "I've heard about the place the Freule has found for her. What a splendid opportunity! And so kind of the Freule!"

Klomp nodded assent. Like most country parsons, the Dominé was very sensitive to disrespect. "You might get up, Klomp," he said, sharply.

"Oh, if you wish it, sir, of course," replied the man, shuffling to his feet, with an air of contempt for the other's stupidity. He immediately lounged up against the wall, sinking both hands in his pockets. "Them's my sentiments to a T," he ejaculated, and jerked his head in the direction of a paper nailed against the dilapidated shutter, white on the dirty green.

The parson, advancing curiously, read the following sentences in an illiterate scrawl:

> "Standing is better than walking,
> Sitting is better than standing,
> Lying is better than sitting,
> And sleep is the best of all."
> 1 Corinthians xix., 7.

Klomp nodded again, as the Dominé turned with a jump. " How dare you put a Bible tag under such nonsense as this ?" cried the Dominé, sniffing like a warhorse.

" Yes, yes, the Bible knows," replied Klomp, imperturbably. " It's word of Holy Scripture, Dominé, so you can't say it isn't true."

" Word of holy scribbling !" cried the indignant clergyman. " It's no more in God's Bible, Klomp, than you are in God's fold. And you haven't even got it correct, for it ends ' And death is the best of all.' "

Suddenly a dark cloud seemed to spread across the sunlit landscape. The surrounding larch-trees shivered, with a long-drawn sigh.

" I wish you would move a little on one side, Dominé," said Klomp, querulously, though he had never heard of Diogenes. " Thank you. Well, a peddler-man that came showed it me in a book, and he said it was in the Bible, and if it isn't, it ought to be. Them's my sentiments. Morning, Dominé."

His feet slipped forward under the weariness of this long discourse ; he recovered himself with a shuffle. Broad as the concluding hint had been, the Dominé ignored it.

" You never do anything, Klomp," he said, angrily.

" Then I never do anything wrong, Dominé. I don't drink. I don't even smoke. I'm too poor."

" Poverty is not disgraceful to confess," replied the Dominé, quoting Pericles, " but not to escape it by exertion, that is disgraceful."

Every child in the parish had heard the quotation.

Klomp yawned : " ' Peace and potatoes is better than a pother and a cow.' That's in the Bible, at any rate," he replied, and suddenly he collapsed again upon the grass before the startled parson's backward skip.

" Could I see Pietje and speak to her ? Perhaps *she* will listen to reason," hazarded the Dominé, controlling his wrath. The father pointed to the cottage door ; then, suddenly remembering the vague possibility of future poor-relief, as yet not required, he faintly called his elder daughter's name.

She crept out with a half-pared potato in her hand. She was

a ruddy-faced girl, not uncomely in her slovenliness, like an apple that has fallen from the tree.

"Well, Pietje," began Dominé Rovers, patiently, "so you are going to Groningen to a nice home and useful work. It is very kind, indeed, of the good lady who is willing to teach you."

"Yes, Dominé," said Pietje.

"Ah, that's right," cried the Dominé, with pleased surprise. "I'm glad to see you've come to your senses. So you're going, like a good girl?"

"No, Dominé," said Pietje.

"What do you mean, you impertinent creature?" exclaimed the minister, exceedingly irate. "Not going when you said you were. Not—"

"No, Dominé," repeated Pietje, sitting down on the window-sill.

Dominé Rovers turned upon the recumbent father. Of course he had lost his temper; he had known all along that he would do so the consciousness of losing hold caused him to let go all the faster.

"I appeal to you," he cried—"you, the responsible guardian of this child. Her lot is in your hands to-day for life-long weal or woe. She is incapable of choosing, and unfit to do so. It is only your selfishness, Klomp, that is ruining your daughters' lives. You say you want them with you, I hear. A pretty excuse."

"Yes; I love them," murmured Klomp, sentimentally.

"And what would Mietje do?" interposed Pietje, looking up from vague contemplation of the pendent potato-peel. Mietje was the child of twelve.

This objection not being easy to meet, the Dominé ignored it. "Fine love, indeed," he shouted to the father. "When a parent loves his child, he sacrifices any inclinations of his own to that child's real welfare. The parent who doesn't do that, doesn't love. Do you understand me?"

"Oh yes," said Klomp.

"Then take this to heart. If you don't send Pietje to Groningen, and make her go, you don't love her. There!"

"Would the Dominó send Juffrouw Ursula to Groningen?" asked Pietje, askance.

"Indeed I should," replied the Dominé, triumphantly, thinking of the Horst. "Never should I allow my own interests to influence me. Be sensible, Klomp."

But at this moment a welcome diversion occurred. Mietje, the child, came running round the cottage with pitiful cries.

"Pussy!" she screamed from afar; "oh, father, pussy! The rope broke, and she's dropped into the well!"

She was sobbing and shrieking; nobody scolded her for her mischief-making. Pietje started up with eager words of comfort.

"Father would get the ladder. Father would go down into the water. Father would fish out pussy."

Klomp was already up and away. The two girls hurried after him. The Dominé was left alone.

"Well, I have done my duty," he mused, retracing his steps. "The best of us can do no more." He was a very good man. He had a good man's weakness for consciously doing his duty.

As he turned into a little brown hollow all checkered with sunlit tracery, he saw Otto van Helmont come vaulting over a stile.

"Ah, Dominé, I was looking for you," said Otto. Then they walked on side by side, and gradually an embarrassing silence settled down between them. The Dominé broke it.

"It is a very fine day," said the Dominé.

"Yes, replied Otto. "Dominé, when Ursula and I are married, we must go back to Java."

"Never," said the Dominé, and with a sweep of his walking-stick he knocked down a thistle.

"I—I am aware that perhaps I have hardly acted quite fairly," began Otto, speaking with some agitation. "It has all come so suddenly; I have allowed myself to be overwhelmed. Apart from her general condemnation of India, which I have never treated quite seriously, the subject has not yet been mooted between us. I wished first to speak of it to you. I feel that I am asking—"

The Dominé had stopped in the middle of the narrow path.

"It was the condition," he interrupted, hoarsely. "She made it the condition. Never."

"No, indeed, we have not spoken of it," cried Otto, in distress.

The Dominé stamped his foot. "Women always forget everything," he said.

Otto hurried on. "I want to explain," he continued, eagerly. "I hope you will let me explain. It is a most painful thing for all of us. I cannot stay at the Horst, Dominé; that is quite out of the question. In fact, the sooner I leave it the better."

"Why?" broke in the Dominé, vehemently. "What nonsense! Of course you can stay at the Horst!"

"I cannot bear the idea of earning my living in this country; you yourself have always discouraged it. Besides, I must earn much more than my living. That is imperative. Especially now." He checked himself; he was not going to speak to the Dominé of the Baroness's shattered hopes. But Ursula's father understood.

Involuntarily both men's eyes wandered away across the fields towards the chimneys of the Horst embedded in foliage. Then their glances met.

"Never. Never. Never," repeated the Dominé, passionately.

"In a few years I shall probably want money," declared Otto, decisively. "I shall want a good deal of money, I expect. I must do what I can to earn it. You will say, perhaps, like my father, that till now I have tried and failed. All the more reason to try again."

"No, I don't say that," responded the Dominé, honestly. "You know I don't. But, Otto, I can't let my Ursula go to Java."

Otto did not immediately return to the charge. Presently he began again, in quite a low voice, almost a whisper, under the laughing blue sky,

"More than fifteen years ago a young man came to you, complaining bitterly that he was sick of his empty, meaningless existence. He was tired of life, he said. And you answered, 'Go and work. The people who work have no time to get tired.'"

"But I never said, 'Go and amass money,'" interrupted the old man, lifting a shaky arm.

"You said, 'Spend your own money.' How well I remember your saying that the night I came to you! 'You are a grown man. Don't spend any one's money but your own.' It came to me like a revelation. It was so directly opposed to what I had been taught from my youth. In my world they say, 'Only don't earn money. You may do anything except that.'"

"Well, you have obeyed that precept," replied the Dominé, a little bitterly. Then he repented immediately.

"Otto, you're a good fellow. I can't let my Ursula go away to Java."

"I was wrong, perhaps," said Otto, "to demand so great a sacrifice. I ought to have spoken more plainly of my intentions beforehand—"

"You ought, indeed," interjected the Dominé, glad of every vent. "You have behaved exceedingly badly."

"So be it. Well, I leave the matter in your hands. Personally, of course, I consider I ought to return. I have a fresh offer—a really advantageous opening on a sugar plantation, a large distillery—"

The Dominé looked at him.

"That means rough work," said the Dominé.

"But you must decide," continued Otto, evasively. "If you distinctly prefer it, I shall look for occupation in Holland. Only in no case can I remain at the Horst."

"You can," cried the Dominé, quite angrily.

Otto had stopped. His eyes were following a distant swallow's trackless dips.

"And even if I could," he said, slowly, "my wife could not —Ursula could not."

The Dominé's eyes sought his in long inquiry.

"With Gerard," said Otto at last.

"Ah!"

Then the Dominé cried, "Stuff and nonsense! stuff and nonsense! I don't believe a word of it. Nor do you."

"I leave the decision in your hands," repeated Otto. "Some employment of some kind in some Dutch town, if you so wish."

The Dominó leaned up against a tree; he closed his eyes; his bronzed face was quite white. The wood seemed to hold its breath under the sneering sky.

"When a father loves his child," began the Dominó; then his voice broke. "My Ursula," he said. "God have mercy on me! The Lord gives and the Lord takes away." He stopped.

Otto, thoughtfully wending his way homeward, reached a spot where the Manor-house burst into view all at once through the park. Unconsciously he stood still. The moments passed by; he remained without moving; a yellow butterfly came foolishly hovering among the bushes; he did not see it.

Suddenly a single tear lay heavy on his cheek.

CHAPTER XIX

FOR the next three months Otto worked in a sugar-distillery at Boxlo, a little town among the wilds of Brabant. It was rough work, indeed, as the Dominé had foretold. Night after night the Jonker stood, stripped to the waist, before the blazing furnaces; in the small hours he came home to his lodgings and strove to snatch from the daylight such sleep as he could. Fortunately he was very robust, but that, although an alleviation, can hardly be considered an excuse. Sometimes even he wondered whether such slaving, amid grime and oil-stench and sick throbs, was his natural fate, but his father had truly described him as animated by a passion of self-torture. Out-of-the-way horrors were probably one's duty. Besides, what other career was open to him at the moment? Once in India, with his friend's assistance, he would stand an excellent chance of making a fortune by sugar, as that friend had done before him, in half a dozen years.

So he worked, night after night, month after month, with set lips and still eyes. Occasionally he spent a Sunday at the Manor-house, as if a traveller traversing mountain solitudes had halted from time to time at a Parisian café. His father and mother accepted him without comment, adverse or otherwise; in the smooth design of their lives he was an arabesque run mad. During his stay the Baroness chiefly regretted Gerard.

The only person who stuck to him through it all, stanch and true, was Roderick Rovers. Once having accepted the duty of sacrifice, the Dominé delighted in its pain. He rejoiced in proving to himself how, like the old soldier he was, he could probe his own wound without wincing.

"It is a great thing in Otto to go," he said. "It is a great thing in me to let him take Ursula. Great souls do great things gladly." Then he laughed at himself: "Pshaw," he said, "'Men always imagine the struggle of the moment, while they are engaged in it, to be the greatest that ever was.' You will find that in Thucydides, Ursula. Thucydides was a very wise man."

Ursula acquiesced a little impatiently. She did not want to go to Java. She thought Otto should have made known his intentions in time. Placed between the two, she immediately discarded her brand-new lover for the father on whose affection her whole life had been built up. In the sudden certainty of separation from the Dominé, she discovered, with alarming unexpectedness, that she could very well have continued to exist without Otto. For several days their engagement dangled on a thread.

Her irritated hesitancy filled her lover with dismay, for it strengthened all his doubts of Gerard. An honest maiden's accepted lover does not ask her if she loves another man. Indignantly Otto wiped the momentary film from the pure reflection he bore in his heart. But there are actions we barely commit, yet remember a lifetime.

It was the Dominé, after all, who married Ursula to Otto, with deep commiseration for himself. His dear child's filial loyalty, while it wakened all his pride, showed him his own path the more clearly. "A woman shall leave father and mother and shall cleave unto her husband," he said. "Never shall I allow you •to desert Otto for my sake. You do not know your own heart, child. Your magnanimity leads you astray." Ultimately Ursula almost believed this. But she conditioned for a two years' absence only.

"I, had such been my lofty mission, would have proved myself faithful unto death," said Miss Mopius, to whom came outer echoes of the struggle. "A great love, like blazing sunlight, hides the whole world in its own bright mist. Van Helmont has dropped a diamond to play with a pebble. So like a man." Miss Mopius, since her disappointment, had grown very romantic in her talk. According to the advertisements it was the

Sympathetico Lob; according to her own account it was her mighty sorrow. "Ah, my dear, do not let us speak of it. Every woman's heart is a sanctuary with a crypt."

She snorted at Ursula's heavy eyes. "Every man gets the wife he deserves," she said. "With women that is not the case, their choice being limited." Ursula was incapable of small, spiteful retorts; she made up her mind that she would prove to Aunt Josine and the world how worthily Otto had chosen.

So she set to work on her trousseau, and was very affectionate to her father. There was something exceedingly painful in this latter-day softness between two hitherto undemonstrative characters. When Ursula laid down a neglected needle to look across at the Dominé, the old man would jump up with swift repression, and angrily bid her go on. The days shortened: perhaps that made them seem to pass so swiftly, and the appointed wedding-morn drew near.

Meanwhile another wedding was also announced as imminent, and various members of the Helmont family gnashed their teeth over the prospect. The whole of Drum, however, jabbered fairly good-natured approval, which is surely saying a good deal, and more than most young couples can hope for.

"Yes, Gerard, it is quite true," said Helena van Trossart, stopping, in a crowded ballroom, a white vision among the glitter and hum. "You could have assured yourself it was true without insulting me by the question." Her clear eyes flashed. "I am going to marry Willie van Troyen."

Gerard was very hot — the room was hot. "No," he said, thickly, "I should never have believed it, unless I had heard it from your own lips." He drew a little aside, almost secure, yet not quite, among the restless throng.

"I cannot make you out at all," he went on, in great agitation; "I—I don't want to say anything, but—" He checked himself; his eyebrows twitched; his whole face grew troubled with suppressed meaning.

She understood him perfectly. For a few moments—perhaps half a minute—she remained quite silent, with eyes downcast, her bosom heaving, her graceful figure a-tremble, like her lips. At last, amid the rhythmic flow of gayety around, she lifted her solemn gaze to his, and spoke with slow distinctness. "I know what you would taunt me with," she said. "You think me inconsistent. But in his case it doesn't matter. I do not love him."

And then the room swam round in a whirl, and she was gone.

After that they were more than ever unwilling to meet. Yet, in a little circle like theirs the thing was unavoidable, and Gerard had constantly to face what was almost more painful—the tacit misery of the fat Baroness, Helena's comfortable aunt, who understood, with a woman's insight in all such matters, that everything ought, somehow, to have been different to what it was.

The Baroness van Trossart complained to her husband, but the Baron said that the Van Troyens were as good a family as the Van Helmonts, and he didn't see that it mattered.

"Personally," he added, "I am unable to perceive much difference between the two young men. They are both fair-complexioned and gentlemanly, and ill-mannered, like their companions. I wonder that Nellie should have thought the exchange worth her while."

The lady would have protested.

"My dear, I cannot help it. Had *I* been consulted I should have requested Helena to marry your three nephews Van Asveld. Their mother is pestering me to find the whole three of them places with a start of two hundred a year. The thing is impossible!" He coughed testily, and before his important eyes he held a blue-book upside down.

Equally bootless was the Baroness's attempt to seek refuge in the sympathy of Mademoiselle Papotier. That impenetrable Frenchwoman only replied,

"Mon Dieu, Madame, le mariage n'est pas l'amour!" taking the name of three holy things in vain within one short sentence, after the manner of her race.

But one evening towards dusk, as Gerard was dressing for dinner, he heard some one enter his little front sitting-room, to whom he called out, into the heavy twilight,

"All right, old chap! Wait a minute till I get my shirt on. There's some sherry and bitters on the sideboard."

Presently he went forward with his fingers at his collar-stud. In the shadow stood a shawl-enfolded figure whom he thought he recognized.

"Oh, it's you, is it?" he said; "I told the landlady to send you up. If you don't do the things better I must get some other woman. I believe you purposely wear holes in my under-clothing."

"Indeed, Monsieur," came the reply in French, "I am most anxious to wash your dirty linen, but, Monsieur Gerard, you give your family almost too much of it."

"By Jove!" replied Gerard. "I say, Mademoiselle, wait a minute till I—" He disappeared.

Mademoiselle Papotier smiled a supercilious smile. "Ah, que les hommes sont plaisants," she murmured. "Mauvais plaisants!" she added. But when Gerard returned a few moments later she was boldly agreeable to him, with a smirk round her slightly mustachioed lips.

"To what am I indebted?" began the young officer.

She waved a little deprecatory hand in the neatest of gray gloves.

"A moment!" she said. "Can you not spare me a moment? I am fatigued. May I not repose myself?"

Gerard, ashamed and awkward, hurriedly pushed forward an arm-chair.

"Ah, but sit you down also," she expostulated. "Only the disagreeable says itself standing." Then, as he obeyed, she looked at him with an ogle. "What a handsome man you are!" she said. The words frightened Gerard excessively but unnec-essarily; it was only part of Mademoiselle Papotier's philoso-phy that you could put *every* man on earth into a good-humor by broadly praising his looks. If Red Riding-hood had said to the wolf "What fine teeth you have!" instead of "What big ones!" he would probably have abandoned his intention of eat-ing her.

"No wonder the poor thing loved you," immediately added the little governess, casting down her eyes. She was hung round with black jet indiscriminately, and she picked at it— now here, now there.

Gerard, as we know, was not a diplomatist. "Did *she* ask you to come and tell me that?" he cried, with irritable irony.

"Ah, Monsieur van Helmont," replied the Frenchwoman, softly, and her swarthy face seemed to lose its vigor, "it is always like that; you men, you knock at a woman's heart until it opens, and then you cry out in scorn at the open door!" She hesitated for a moment, still plucking at the jet. "First the beautiful Ursula," she said, "and then my own sweet Helena. Aye, Monsieur, it is not right!"

"Ursula?" cried Gerard, in amazement.

"Yes, do you think no one knows? Oh, that is like you men again. You can always trust the woman you have wronged to keep your secret. You are safe. Not a word has the noble Helena spoken; but trust Papotier to see for herself."

"It is not true," said Gerard, with real fervor. "I have never wronged a hair of Ursula's head."

Mademoiselle Papotier blushed, actually blushed. "The word ' wrongs,' " she said, " is not easily defined; it has a masculine and a feminine gender. Ah, there you behold the former governess! One thing, however, I can tell you, Monsieur van Helmont, it is Mademoiselle Ursula and her wrongs that have lost you your bride. I repeat, Helena has told me nothing ; but Mademoiselle Rovers, and she alone, has broken off your engagement." Then she went on to tell her astounded listener about the interview on the garden seat which she had watched from her staircase window.

"And after that," she concluded, "there was an end of it. My Helena would not have the parson's daughter's leavings. And quite right." She shut up her mouth with a snap.

But she opened it again immediately.

"Nevertheless," she went on, "I consider she exaggerates. Especially because she cared for you, and your previous belle evidently did not. It is for that I am come. The step is absurd, perhaps, but what is that to me? I am come to say the marriage with this little rabbit-eye is a farce. It must be prevented. Go tell my Helena that there is nothing between you and the *fiancée* of your brother. Women are vain; who knows but what this Ursula has lied? You appear sincere. And I say

"HE WENT FORWARD WITH HIS FINGERS AT HIS COLLAR-STUD"

one thing more, though I should not. Mark me. Helena will marry you if she can. She is proud, poor little thing, as she has a right to be, but— Ah, these men, these men ! Then you will bid the little comrade go away home. I do not love you, Monsieur Gerard. I do not say these things for love of you. But they are true."

She had spoken with suppressed vehemence, she now smiled a thin smile, and her lips trembled.

" I do not know what to say or think," replied Gerard, great-ly agitated. " Towards Ursula, at least, I am innocent. What interest can she have had in ruining my chance with Helena? Mademoiselle, you—you must really excuse me. I am going out to dinner. I shall be late as it is !" He started gladly to his feet.

She also rose, with a great rustle of scorn.

"Good - night, Monsieur," she said. " A benevolent fairy— remember there are old fairies—has shown you the hole in the hedge ; will you have the sense to creep through unscratched? Ah, be sure that I should rather have barred your path with my body, but that love cannot bear to see the whole life of the beauty benumbed in the wrong prince's arms. Princes, for-sooth ! She dropped him a courtesy and hurried away.

He had not even time to sit down and think it out. His ex-cuse had been as imperative as it was inane. He flew off to his dinner-party and laughed and flirted, wondering all the time whether Ursula could possibly have had "a weakness" for him. That seemed to be the only possible explanation. Evidently it was Mademoiselle Papotier's. Romance, exaggeration, these were probable ; but he could hardly believe in intentional spite or untruth.

And yet—he was very much out of temper with Ursula for her capture of " that fool, Otto." His rage against his brother, softened by time and a capital new horse, melted still more at the thought that he had wronged Otto regarding Helena. Ursula, then, was at the bottom of the mischief. Ursula, the design-ing intruder ; the nobody who, one day, would rule at the Horst. She had always been a subject to him of kindly indifference. He was angry with himself for the violence of his new passion against her.

On returning home he found a note awaiting him. It contained only these two quotations, evidently from Papotier's favorite seventeenth-century romances :

"Said Marcellino: 'Damaris, my brother is faithless. I can prove it to you. Why, then, should your heart, blinded by useless smoke, still refuse to perceive the flame that is burning in mine—*i.e.*, heart.'"

"Rodelinda replied: 'Adelgunda, I thank you for warning me. The lover that deserted you shall never have an opportunity of trampling upon Rodelinda's affections.'"

"Exactly," said Gerard, sighing heavily. He was very miserable. And then he went to sleep.

Meanwhile Otto plodded on, unconscious of the sins laid to his charge and to Ursula's. The story which Adeline had forced upon him in the public gardens at Drum he had folded away on a shelf in his memory. What else could he do? He was not the man to influence Gerard. We know it was not through him that the tale reached Ursula—or Helena.

His occupations called him away from Boxlo to Bois-le-Duc, the capital of Brabant. There he came into frequent contact with a cousin, of whom he had previously known very little— nothing personally — and regarding whom his parents would hardly have cared to enlighten any one. This was a young Van Helmont, who lived with a widowed mother, and supported himself as a post-office clerk. The Helmonts of the Horst did not object to his poverty, but to his mother. To Otto's enthusiastic eulogies the Baroness listened bored. She was too polite to ask him to change the subject ; besides, perhaps she felt that such a measure would have proved quite useless, for, whatever Otto might select to say, he bored her by his way of saying it. She could only love this son, not live with him. She rejoiced with exceeding joy when Gerard, whose character was incapable of vindictiveness, consented once more to sit opposite to Otto at table. Still, the brothers held aloof.

And the wedding-day drew near, overshadowingly near. One person delighted in that thought. Otto.

CHAPTER XX

MYNHEER JACÓBUS MOPIUS stood on the hearth-rug in his wife's bedroom.

" My dear," he said, " I must admit this—since you have taken to spending the greater part of your day up-stairs, the house has become most insufferably dull."

For Mevrouw Mopius this remark had long ago lost all its novelty ; still, she never grew to like it, even while she meekly answered,

" Yes, my dear, yes. I know. I shall be better soon." And she added, as one of her familiar after-thoughts, " Harriet ought to amuse you."

" Oh, Harriet amuses me fast enough," retorted Mynheer Mopius, with unpleasing alacrity. " But you'd soon be all right if you left off remembering you were ill."

" Yes, my dear, yes," repeated Mevrouw Mopius, closing her faded eyes. Her cheeks were faded, her hair was faded, her flannel dressing-gown was faded. In the fading light, complacent Mynheer Mopius, looking down upon her, thought how excessively faded she was.

" Only yesterday," Mynheer continued, triumphantly, " I purposely asked your doctor what was wrong with you. And what do you think his answer was ? He said he really couldn't tell. There !" Mynheer Mopius stood out, defiant, protruding his portly prosperity. " He—said—he—really—*couldn't—tell.*"

It gave Mevrouw Mopius some comfort to learn how literally the physician fulfilled the promise she had extracted from him.

" And it's absurd to have the whole house made wretched by an illness the doctor don't even put a name to. If you're not down to breakfast to-morrow I shall send for a professor from Amsterdam."

"Don't, Jacóbus," gasped the lady. "I'm feeling better to-day. I really am. I don't want no professors from anywhere."

"But I do. Sarah, I believe you enjoy being ill. Thank goodness I can afford to cure my wife."

"There's another reason, besides," he added, after a moment, "why I want you to hurry up. There's this wedding of Ursula's coming on. They've behaved very badly, I know; but Roderick was never a man to know about manners—never in society, poor fellow. However, I'm not one to take offence. I intend to give a big party here in the 'bride-days.'" *

"Jacóbus!" exclaimed his wife. "Why, we don't even know the Van Helmonts. She hasn't even presented him here!"

"My dear, did I not say that Roderick is a boor? Josine tells me they have paid none of the customary visits on either side. In one word, they behaved as people who don't know how to behave, and I am going to behave as a person who does know."

"But, Jacóbus—"

"Ursula is my own sister Mary's child. My own sainted sister Mary's. And I shouldn't even give a wedding-party to my own sister Mary's only child? Sarah, it is all your increasing indolence. You are prematurely making an old woman of yourself. Look at me. I am two years your junior, but it might be twenty. Aren't you ashamed of yourself?" As he said this he arranged the rose in his button-hole, with a great crackle of his blue-spotted white waistcoat. An oily satisfaction played over the yellow smoothness of his cheeks.

The truth of it was, of course, that the whole man burned with eagerness to leap, at one rush, into the glories of the great world. The opportunity was unique; it offered more than the boldest could have hoped for; we may well forgive his anxiety.

Mevrouw Mopius lay in utter collapse, a crumpled rag, against one corner of her great chintz chair.

"I want Harriet!" she said, faintly. Her husband gave a great snort of contempt as he stalked from the room.

---

* The fortnight preceding the ceremony.

A few minutes later Harriet entered, a novel, as usual, in her dangling hand.

"Harriet, I must have my drops," exclaimed the invalid, sharply. "The doctor said I was to have them every two hours. And in freshly drawn water each time. I told him it couldn't be done. Doctor, I said, I've nobody to fetch me the water."

Harriet busied herself about the side-table, mechanically, and in silence.

"'And your niece?' said the doctor," Mevrouw Mopius continued. "So I had to tell him you were no good."

"Oh, he knows that," replied Harriet. "I'm no nurse. I can't look after sick people."

"There's one person you'll nurse, if ever she's sick," replied Mevrouw, with a grunt, swallowing down her medicine. "Harriet, do you know the date for which Ursula's wedding is fixed?"

"Thursday month," curtly answered Harriet, who just now hated the fortunate bride with unreasoning envy—an envy that wrung tears from the lonely girl at night.

"What day of the month?" persisted Mevrouw, wearily.

"It's the twenty-third."

"Harriet, you must go across to the doctor's for me. I can't have him here again just yet; his coming vexes your uncle so. You must say to him — listen — word for word; you must say, 'Aunt bids me ask: Will uncle be able to go to the wedding-feast on the sixteenth of next month?' Just that. And you must bring back an answer—yes or no. Go along."

"But the wedding is on the twenty-third," protested Harriet, sulkily. "And besides, Uncle Mopius isn't ill."

"Yes he is," replied the invalid, with guilty incisiveness. "You just go and do as you're told, and come back with the answer immediate. Harriet, if you don't say a word about it down-stairs — you'd only make your uncle nervous — I'll give you my Florentine brooch, the mosaic of the two doves drinking. Now hurry away."

Thus incited, Harriet sulked off through the stolid streets. If Mevrouw Mopius did not send a note to the physician, it was not only that she felt physically and autographically inadequate,

11

but also because she confidently believed that Harriet would in any case have broken the seal.

The messenger soon reached her destination. A maid-servant admitted her into the young doctor's private room. He was at luncheon.

" My aunt sends me to you on a fool's errand," she began, abruptly. " This is her literal message : ' There's a wedding-feast on the sixteenth '—which there isn't—' will Uncle Mopius be able to go ?' " She hung her head with affected accentuation of the indifference she was really feeling.

The doctor hesitated and looked curiously at her.

" I'm to bring back an answer—yes or no," she added.

" Yes or no ?" repeated the doctor. " Would you mind say-ing it again, Miss Verveen ?"

" There's a wedding entertainment on the sixteenth," an-swered Harriet, with almost ill-mannered impatience. " Will Uncle Mopius be able to *go?*"

The young doctor studied his boots for a minute. Then he he said, slowly : " No ; I believe, considering the circumstances, I may safely commit myself to a ' No.' As your aunt so ex-pressly wishes it, you must tell her my opinion is ' No.' " He was much annoyed, but he could not help himself. By this time he had got somewhat accustomed to Mevrouw Mopius, the strangest of patients, who treated him like a younger colleague called in for a consultation.

" Very good," said Harriet. " I'll tell her. And now, please, a little questioning on my own account. What's the matter with Uncle Mopius ?"

" Nothing, Juffrouw Harriet," replied the young man, heart-ily, with sudden relief. " I am glad to be able to assure you that your excellent uncle enjoys very fair health." ·

" Don't tell me untruths, if you please," persisted the girl, greatly in earnest. " I have very particular reasons of my own for desiring to know. What's wrong with him ? Why shouldn't he go to a party—if there were a party—on the sixteenth ?"

" Oh, he might be a little out of sorts, you know. You had better give your aunt her message. It must be rather dull for you sometimes, Juffrouw Harriet, eh ?" He cast an admiring glance at her; he had quick, sympathetic eyes, good doctor's eyes.

"By no means," replied Harriet; but her attitude, grown suddenly listless again, belied her words. "So you see what a fool's errand mine was! As for Aunt Sarah, of course I know she's very ill. I which she wasn't. It's very hard on me. I can't nurse invalids, and I hate to seem unkind."

"Oh, I'm sure you couldn't be unkind to any one," said the young man, sweetly. It struck him that his lunch-table looked very forlorn. "You couldn't be, Miss Harriet."

"Oh yes, I could," replied Harriet, quickly. "I am always unkind, for instance, to people who call me Miss Harriet, and forget that my name is Miss Verveen."

The doctor laughed rather awkwardly as she turned to go.

"You are quite right," he answered; "quite right. Either Juffrouw Verveen or—not Juffrouw at all; I envy the privileged few."

"So it's 'No'?" she said, with her hand on the door-knob.

"So it's 'No'?" he repeated, boldly, looking her straight in the face. But he read his answer there, and sobered suddenly, as the physician crushed down the lover in presence of the great tragedy so quietly enacting. "Yes, I'm afraid it must be 'No,'" he said. "The sixteenth, you said? Tell your aunt I am awfully sorry, but as far as I am able to judge, she had better think 'No.'"

Harriet hurried home through the autumn grayness of the sleepy little town. A peculiar smile hung fixed upon her forbidding features, a mixture of anxiety and content. She went straight up to her aunt's bedroom.

"The answer is 'No,'" she said.

Mevrouw Mopius made no reply. She lay back, with closed eyes and sunken jaws, almost as her niece had left her when sent forth upon this hideous errand. Harriet flung herself down on a chair, and resumed her novel. Presently she rose to slip away.

Mevrouw Mopius opened her eyes.

"Harriet, give me my tambour-frame," she said. Harriet obediently drew forth Laban from his cupboard, and removed the sheltering tissue-paper. "I wonder could I do a stitch or two," said Mevrouw Mopius, dolefully. She sat trying to thread a big needle with shaky fingers. Harriet waited a moment, watching her.

"Let me do it," suggested Harriet at last.

But Aunt Sarah resented this interference.

"I wasn't attending," she said, angrily; "I was thinking of something else. Surely you don't imagine I couldn't thread a needle?"

And as she still continued trying, pitifully, tremblingly, her niece turned impatiently away.

"Do you know," continued Mevrouw Mopius, contemplating the gaudy flare of patriarchs and camels, "I have been thinking that I should like to give it, if I can finish it, to Ursula Rovers for a wedding - present. She admired it very much when she was here. She was the only person that ever admired it." Her voice became quite sorrowful.

"Dominé Pock admired it," said Harriet, soothingly.

"Yes, after dining here!" exclaimed the invalid, with a flash of grim humor. "He said Jacob must have had just such a face as that. Now, Harriet, that was flattery. For Jacob couldn't have had *exactly* that sort of face." Indeed, had the countenance of the patriarch blazed in such continuous scarlet, his uncle could never have engaged him to look after cows.

"Besides, Pock doesn't really know about Jacob's face," continued Mevrouw Mopius, with a sick person's insistence, "for I asked him myself if we had an authentic photograph"—she meant "portrait"—"and he said we hadn't. Though we have of Joseph, he said. It seems a very great pity. I should have liked to do it from the life."

Mevrouw Mopius sank into aggrieved consideration of the father's remissness about sitting for his likeness as compared with the foresight shown by the son.

"Yes, I should give it to Ursula for her wedding," she resumed, after another long pause, "unless—"

She broke off.

"Unless what?" prompted Harriet.

"Unless I should like it for a cushion in my coffin. I think that might be rather nice."

"Aunt!" exclaimed Harriet, in real horror, and a sudden film of feeling clouded her passionate eyes.

"Why, my dear, whatever is the matter?" queried the elder lady, calmly. "All of us die some day, do we not? And when my time has come, I should like to carry away with me my last bit of work."

"Ah, but this is not going to be your last, you know," comforted Harriet, with the easy infatuation of the survivor.

"Well, if not, then Ursula shall certainly have it," Mevrouw said, cheerfully. "I wish I were quite sure she would put it, as a fire-screen, in her drawing-room. Imagine *my* work in the drawing-room at the Horst. I should like that." She resumed her tender contemplation of the immovably staring figures. "I am very tired," she whispered; "go down now to your uncle, and tell him the doctor says he can have his party on the sixteenth or after. Don't say anything about my message; your uncle's got a cold, but he doesn't want people to know it. There can be no objection, however, to his asking people here."

Poor woman, she prided herself on her clumsy diplomacy.

"Let him get ready for his party," she reflected. "It will keep him busy—meanwhile."

In the face of Mynheer Mopius's blindly staring selfishness, the stratagem was completely successful. Plunged up to the eyebrows in preparations for a gorgeous entertainment, which was, of course, to excel all similar ones, that gentleman forgot to notice his wife's condition. He would run up to her with long descriptions of his arrangements, to which she listened reposefully for hours. When he went down-stairs again she smiled. He was happy, and he was letting her die in peace.

Soon Mynheer Mopius was obliged to slip over to Horstwyk to consult with the relations who had so suddenly increased in importance. He found the trio gathered in the Parsonage drawing-room to receive him, and he patted their heads all round. He even condescended to chaff Josine about "one wedding begetting another," as they say in Dutch, and proposed that she should be bridesmaid and make up to the best man.

"I should never marry my junior. I disapprove of such matches," replied Josine, hitting out, however unreasonably, at both Ursula and Mopius.

"Well, we can't all marry our twin-sisters, like Abraham," said Mopius, reddening. "Can we, Roderick?"

"Sarah was Abraham's half-sister," answered the Dominé, wistfully gazing out at the placid sky.

"Well, at any rate, *my* Sarah's only six years my senior, and I made it two the day we married. I've done my duty to the old girl. Ursula, I hope that thirty years hence you'll be able to say as much."

"You married for money," retorted Josine. As her niece's wedding-day approached, Miss Mopius's growing disagreeableness became a source of great agitation to herself. She smelled at her vinaigrette.

"Pooh!" replied Mopius. "If so, I quadrupled the sum. Don't be more of a nuisance than you can help, Josine, or I sha'n't invite you to my party."

"There are the Baron and the Baroness coming down the road," interposed Ursula, watching her father's flushed face.

"Where? Show me, Ursula," cried Mopius, bounding to the window.

She laughed. "I do believe they are coming here!" she cried. "You will have to meet them now, Uncle Jacóbus."

"I have no objection to meeting them," replied Jacóbus, red and important. "I was going to ask them, of course, to my party. I have no objection to the aristocracy as such."

A moment later he was bowing and smiling—bowing what he considered an eighteenth-century bow. And the Baron was expressing his delight at making the acquaintance of Ursula's uncle, "of whom he had heard so much." Furthermore, Mynheer van Helmont spoke with admiration of Mynheer Mopius's villa, upon which Mynheer Mopius replied, in the kindest manner possible, that it was very nice, but not as fine as the Horst. He also proffered his invitation on the spot, and the Baroness, smiling elaborately, accepted it, as in duty bound. It was some time before her courteous husband consented to catch her eye, and then she immediately arose. In those few minutes the retired attorney had twice called Mynheer van Helmont " Baron," and several other atrocious things had occurred. " How small she is! She needn't look so bumptious!" thought Mopius, as the little lady shook hands. He was telling her how there would be dancing at his party, and he poked Josine in the ribs. " In my young days out at Batavia," he said, "I used frequently to dance with the Governor-General's lady. I dare say, Baron, you remember Steelenaar, a good Viceroy in his day?" He hoped for the honor of the opening polonaise with her ladyship.

" My dancing days are over, Mynheer," said the Baroness, stiffly. " I doubt whether I should be able to acquit myself properly. Things have changed *so* much in society since my youth."

" Ah, there you are right, Mevrouw," replied Jacóbus Mopius with fervor. " Now, at the Drum Casino, nowadays—I am an old member—you meet people who, in your time, would not have dared to appear at a public performance."

" I do not doubt it," replied the Baroness, taking leave.

Husband and wife proceeded leisurely homeward. Presently the Baron said,

" My dear, I cannot understand your caring so much. Surely Mynheer Mopius is only a continuation of Juffrouw Josine."

" I had said nothing," replied the Baroness, quickly. " But, as you broach the subject, I must confess that I think you might have stayed half the time, and showed a quarter the courtesy."

The Baron laughed. " He is Ursula's single rich relation," said the Baron. " I never forget that. And, besides, I am naturally amiable, Cécile. It is a masculine weakness."

" I hate money," cried the Baroness. " If there were no money in the world there would be no vulgarity."

" How sad that would be for the non-vulgar," replied her consort. " Yes, he is Ursula's single ' prospect.' I was aware of the fact, but, of course, he stated it. I had very good reason to be amiable."

" He may live to be a hundred," said the Baroness, petulantly.
" Not he.   His widow might, if she were healthy, but she
happens to be very ill.   My dear, you put things so roughly ;
you love money more than I do.   But I hope he *will* live to be
a hundred.   If only pour nous encourager, nous autres.   We
all ought to live to be a hundred ; a hundred years isn't much.
As a rule it's the widows who live on forever.   We men die
fast enough."

" No, no !" cried the Baroness, drawing her arm through his.
" Don't talk like that, Theodore ; I should never survive you."

" My dear, if I can, I will give you but little opportunity.   Do
not forget that, when I depart, I must leave my art treasures to
Otto, not to mention the Horst."

They walked on, arm in arm, each silently busy with his own
grave thoughts.

" Somehow, I have occasionally imagined of late that it
wouldn't be for long."   The Baron's voice suddenly changed.
" But that's all nonsense," he said, briskly.   " It seems too cruel
to die and leave it all."

He swept his eyes across his fields and forests.   His wife
pressed his hand.

" My dear," he said, " do you object to my lighting a cigar ?"

When the sixteenth came round there was no dancing.
Mynheer Mopius sat in a darkened room.

Yes, Mevrouw Mopius had provokingly died.   At the last
moment she resolved to take her unfinished patriarchs down
into the grave with her, but she left her collection of samples to
Ursula, because Ursula had shown some appreciation of her
work.

"'IT SEEMS TOO CRUEL TO DIE AND LEAVE IT ALL'"

CHAPTER XXI

So Otto and Ursula were married with all the customary paraphernalia of vulgar exposure—paraphernalia which cause a sensible man to resolve, as he runs the gantlet on his way back from the pillory, that the first time in his case shall certainly be the last. Theirs was as quiet a wedding as unselfish people can get—which means that it was not a quiet wedding.

Their honeymoon trip was but an introduction to the longer journey; at Genoa the big Java steamship would meet them; meanwhile, creeping down the Riviera, they lingered for a fortnight in that Paradise of Snobbery, Cannes. Cannes is a beautiful garden, planted with princes; what more can be desired by the millionaire, or by the numerous curs to whom the far scent of the millionaire is as sausage on the breeze? Other towns contain elements manifold, paltry and noble; exquisite, sun-wrapped Cannes has nothing but the worship of gold by glitter, and the worship of glitter by gold.

The young couple, therefore, passed through it unperceived. It was only natural that they should appear in the " Strangers' List " as Monsieur et Madame de Holmani. They held out their hands to nobody, and nobody held out his hands to them, a kind of negative Ishmaelism, which has its advantages, even outside a honeymoon.

To Ursula, crossing simultaneously the frontiers of Holland, home, and maidenhood, this fortnight never assumed the cool colors of reality. Before it could do that it was over. She was back at Horstwyk again, like an awakened dreamer in the dusk of a troubled morning.

While the trip lasted—on the Paris Boulevards, among the

orange-groves of La Croisette—the farewell peep of home hung
heavy before her eyes. She seemed to see them all photographed on the steps of the Manor-house—the Baroness, firm
set and still, the Baron coughing and sneezing, not from emotion, but from the sudden effects of a violent cold which should
have kept him away from the ceremony. And her father, his
one arm drawn tight across the "Legion" on his breast, his
eyes fixed not on his daughter's last appeal for a farewell ben-
ison, but on some far beyond of sunlight after storm.

The thought of Otto blended with the thought of her father,
and over these, which were her thoughts of love, lay ever the
thought of separation. Sadness is not a good beginning for a
young wife who "respects and admires." The Sabines, under
similar circumstances, actually consented to live with their par-
ents-in-law.

"Yes, it is very beautiful," she said, looking across the bay
to the blue-black of the sunset Esterel. They were on the terrace of their hotel at Californie. "Oh yes, it is very beautiful," she said. She spoke with that admission which is a protest. There are times when we think that nature, like some
women, would be all the better for a little less flamboyant
beauty, and a little more homeliness.

"Java is far more beautiful still," said Otto, encouragingly.
"There is nothing in all Europe to compare with Batavia."

And then, for the twentieth time, Ursula resolutely enjoyed
these anticipated glories of the Indies, for the soreness and the
separation were in her own soul, deep down.

Had Otto been more of a Mopius, he would never have
guessed at their existence. Hearts like Ursula's understand
that a woman weds her husband's life.

Nor can it be denied that the novelty of the prospect, by its
very terror, attracted and pleasantly excited her. Still, unfortunately, by nature she was stay-at-home and cat-like. Besides,
she had not left her father to himself, but to Aunt Josine.

So while she was telling herself how unearthly must be a
scene that was even more beautiful than this stage effect of
palm-trees and white buildings against the blue Mediterranean
flare, even while she was schooling herself to this idea, her

whole life suddenly changed with the fall of a curtain. The play stopped at the very opening, and the audience went home again. All the worry and the expectation and the screwing-up had been superfluous. How many of us discover that, even when the lights go out at the conclusion of the fifth act, instead of in the middle of the first.

"Poor people are not poor in India; that is one great advantage," Otto was saying. "There is always plenty of space about one, in house and garden, and even the mendicant, if a white, drives a trap. But I don't suppose there really are any white beggars. You will see how comfortable we shall be in the great veranda of evenings, with all the pretty things around us, while I sit telling you how sugar prices are going up. Ursula, it will be delightful to think we are working for the dear old place at home, which is yours too now, and must *never* belong to any one but a Helmont." His face grew square as he sat staring at the black ridge of distant mountains, and then, suddenly, with a man's embarrassment, "There's the little steamer," he said, lightly, "coming back from the Lérins."

The hotel concierge was going his round on the terrace, leisurely seeking out an occasional lounger in the still, perfume-laden sunset, and distributing a bundle of letters. They watched him coming towards them, from their seat by the balustrade, between two bowls of geranium.

"C'est tout," he said, holding out one letter.

"It's too bad of them not to write!" exclaimed Ursula, as everybody always does on the useless, idle Riviera.

Otto was looking at the envelope, holding it across his outstretched palm, between middle finger and thumb. It was addressed in his Aunt Louisa's handwriting to "Otto, Baron van Helmont."

"Well?" said Ursula, with the impatience of the non-recipient.

But Otto, Baron van Helmont, sat staring at the superscription. The first bell for the *table d'hôte* broke loose, with a sudden continuous clang. Ursula rose. "I'm going up-stairs for a minute," she began. "If it isn't from home, I suppose it's of no importance."

Otto shook himself.

" Wait," he said, and broke the seal.

The note was brief enough. " Dear Otto,—Your father died this morning at half-past-five, from pneumonia. You know he was ailing when you left, but the lungs were attacked only two days ago. We are expecting you back. Your mother is very unhappy. Aunt Louisa. — P. S. Your mother asked me to telegraph, but I consider it better to write."

Even by the road-side of our selfish daily wanderings we cannot hear the voice of death calling a stranger from his field-work without mentally crossing ourselves, suddenly shocked and sobered. What, then, if he enter the court-yard of our hearts? Although, perhaps, he pause before the inner door, every chamber, in the horror of his presence, becomes to us as the innermost.

Ursula and Otto looked at each other with solemn eyes, speaking little. The Riviera evening fell suddenly, with its wiping-out of warmth, like the transition of a Turkish bath. The whole gray seaboard lay bleak and chill in a shudder of autumnal decay.

"Aunt Louisa," said Otto, presently, "has a prejudice against telegrams, chiefly, I fancy, on account of the expense."

Ursula was angry with the Freule van Borck. "She might have prepared you a little," said Ursula.

" Oh, that is her way. 'Simple and strong,' you know. But you are mistaken. She *did* prepare me." He held out the envelope to his wife.

Ursula blushed scarlet. There seemed to her in this brutal fact something strangely painful and insulting both to them and to the dead. She could not meet her husband's gaze. She shivered. " Let us go in, Otto," she said, softly.

As they walked across the terrace he murmured aloud, "' Your mother is very unhappy.' Ursula," he added, " this alters everything. We must go back to-morrow as early as we can."

" Yes," she answered, unemotionally, " I understand."

He did not say anything more till they had reached their

own room. Then, as he struck a light in the dark, he began,
with averted face, looming large against the shadows:
"You will like that, at least, among all the sorrow—the going
back!"
She tried to answer him, not knowing what, and unexpectedly
burst into tears.

Well, it's a good thing that women can weep. Their feelings
are often too complicated for words. The woman who knows
herself incapable of tears is surely one-third inarticulate. But,
alas, that the act of weeping should be so positively ugly! From
a purely æsthetic point of view there is nothing more regrettable in connection with the Fall of Man.

No further news from home reached the young Baron and
Baroness during their hurried flight northward. They themselves were quite incapable of fathoming, even from the most
materialistic point of view, the magnitude of the change which
had come over their prospects. Otto trembled to think in what
condition he might find his father's affairs. Only, he felt certain that the Indian plan would have to be definitely abandoned
on account of the estates at home.

The Dominé met the pair at the little Horstwyk station, and
as Ursula put her arm round her father's neck, she dimly realized that selfishness is man's sole virtue, as, in fact, it is his
only vice.

She could realize it all the more in the shuttered mansion,
which seemed to lie as a waste round that one locked door of the
widow's boudoir. In the dining-hall, surrounded by candles,
stood the coffin, awaiting the heir. All the house and the
village and their surroundings seemed full of a subdued eagerness to bury the past and welcome the present. The library
table was covered with carefully addressed letters and cards.

Gerard was absent. Only the Freule van Borck came forward, with hushed step, to greet them in the gray loneliness of
the flowerless hall.

"My dears," she said, sententiously, "you might have spared
yourselves the shame of running away."

So the old Baron slept in the church-yard under the shadow
of the "Devil's Doll," which he himself had erected on the grave
of his children. Opposite, outside the chancel-wall, shone dully
the great slab which marked the entrance to the family vault,
heavy with the single name "De Horst." The word suggested
a "dépendance" of the Manor-house; hither came for more
permanent residence the successive sojourners at the larger
hostel. It was the widow who, waking from her lethargy, had
demanded separate sepulture for her dear, dead lord, to Otto's
tacitly disapprobatory regret.

She had summoned her elder son into the dusk of her silenced chamber, and speaking softly from amid the solemn
blankness of her loss, " I want your father to lie in the sunshine," she said, " and I wish them to make the—the—in such a
manner that every possible sunbeam shall fall straight across it."

Then, before Otto's unspoken demur: " He always had a
horror of the vault; he never would enter it once during his
whole lifetime. And, Otto, all his life long he detested cold.
In the end it has killed him." She began to cry. Her children had found her greatly changed, quite broken down and
feeble.

" Cécile cannot even take comfort by contemplating the
beauties of adversity," said Freule van Borck, crossly. " Surely
she might understand, in the midst of her legitimate tears, that
sorrow is a great educator. She perversely persists in eluding
the blessings." The Freule did not understand that her sister's
soul was a plant of God's conservatory, a blossom which could
only drop off before the east wind.

Work had to be done, however, and some one must do it.
Otto soon recognized, with anticipated acquiescence, that his
father's affairs had been left in utter confusion. The confusion,
however, was of the orderly kind. There had been a certain
amount of method in the Baron's madness; only, unfortunately,
there had been a good deal more madness in his method. He
had evidently entertained to the full an honest gentleman's distrust of all commercial and industrial undertakings, and had
added thereto a contempt for all usury and money-lending. To
paper investments he would have nothing to say. Every penny
he possessed he had sunk in land or curios.

Also he had made a will, an unwise thing for any man to do.
In that entanglement of spoliation which we have glorified by
the beautiful name of "jurisprudence," any personal effort
towards equity is only another welcome knot to the lawyer's
hand.

The Baron's will disinherited his younger and favorite son so
far as Dutch law permits parents to disinherit, which means
that Gerard would be entitled to exactly one-third of the property as against two-thirds for Otto. Furthermore, the testator
expressed a hope that his wife would allow all her claims on
his estate to be met by an equivalent transfer of art treasures,
and that she would preserve these unsold.

The dead man's object was plain enough; while unable to
stint himself, he yet desired to achieve the retention, after his
decease, of the *status quo*. That is not an easy thing in Holland, where modern law, following the Napoleonic precedent,
aims at the destruction of hereditary wealth. The Baron openly
avowed his intentions in the last sentence of his brief testament; "I hope," he wrote, "that my children will always retain the Horst intact as I leave it. Otto must do this; I believe
he has it in him. I have ultimately succeeded, after infinite
pains, in restoring the whole property as it was at its largest in
1672. I trust that neither Otto nor Gerard will ever consent to
part with a rood of it. They will rather suffer privation, as I
have done."

The Baron's way of "restoring" had been a simple one.
Whenever opportunity offered, he had bought such alienated

lands as fell open, often paying a fancy price, the money for which he procured by mortgaging other property. Nominally, therefore, his landed estate was a very large one, much of it being encumbered, more depreciated. As for "suffering privation"—he had never bought a Corot.

Evidently he had distrusted Gerard, and felt confidence in intractable Otto. The strangest thing about it all was that he, with his fear of death, should ever have summoned up courage to make a will at all. To Otto this fact, more than anything else, revealed how intensely his seemingly shallow father must have loved the home of his race.

And the discovery brought them nearer now in their separation, the dead lord and the new one. Baron Theodore's ambition was one such as this son could appreciate; the sudden self-reproach of undue contemptuousness caused Otto to veer round to the other extreme of veneration. He resolved, under this first impulse, that, come what may, his father's decree should be to him a holy trust.

"Of course," said the Dowager Baroness, relapsing immediately into her continuous mood of mournful indifference. But Gerard demurred.

"I must have *my* share in money," said Gerard. "I can't help myself. Besides, what did father mean? The property can't be said to remain intact if one man owns two-thirds of it and another man the remaining third. Enough of the land must be sold to give me my share in cash."

"None of the land can be sold," replied Otto. He wore his dogged face. The two brothers were together by the library table. In the distant bay-window of the smoking-room Aunt Louisa had fallen asleep over a book.

"Keep the land, if you like, or know how. I don't mind as long as I get my money. You are executor, Otto; pay me my share."

"Do you wish," asked the young Baron, just a trifle dramatically, "to ignore our dead father's commands?"

"No, indeed. No more than you," replied Gerard, with honest disdain. The tinge of melodrama irritated him. The unfairness of his treatment irritated him. But the inherent absurdity of the testamentary instructions was what tormented him most.

"Father's wish was to let me have as little as possible," he continued. "So be it. But your wish is evidently to let me have nothing at all." Both of them waited a moment, in bitterness.

"And"— Gerard ground his heel energetically. "I'm not going to stand that." Then he said, in quite a different tone, "Simply, to begin with, because I can't."

"Of course you have debts," said Otto, sitting down by the writing-table.

"Of course," repeated Gerard, with a pardonable sneer at his immaculate brother. "But it's not that, all the same—at least, not so much."

He paced half-way down the room and back again. Suddenly both brothers heard the ticking of the clock.

"You wrong me, Otto, as usual," said Girard, in a broken voice. "I am as anxious as you are to do whatever's right. But I can't help myself. I may as well make a clean breast of it. I must have the money. You'll think me an unmitigated fool, but, then, you think that already."

He hesitated a moment; Otto did not move.

"Two years ago," Gerard went on, huskily, "I became surety for a chum of mine—never mind his name; he's dead, poor chap—and I've got to pay."

"Surety! Surety!" stammered Otto. "How? What? What kind of surety?"

"It was a debt of honor, between gentlemen. And I've got to pay."

"Of course—a card debt. I understood as much," said Otto, self-righteously.

"It was not *my* card debt," retorted Gerard, feeling his wrongs more acutely than ever, for, as we are aware, he was not a gambler. "It happened playing with strangers, and quite unexpectedly it grew into an enormous sum. For him, next morning, it meant pay or shoot yourself. He wanted it to mean 'Shoot yourself,' but I stopped that just in time and made it mean 'pay—some day or other.' So pay we must. The responsibility is mine."

12

He stopped, staring with solemn eyes, back through the misty past, into what had been, till now, the most dramatic occurrence of his life. He remembered his awakening, the day after the gambling-bout, to the troubled consciousness that he must hurry at once to his friend. He remembered the room as he burst into it: the table with the despondent figure sitting there, the pistol waiting, ready loaded. These things were sacred; he was not going to speak of them to Otto.

"I cannot understand any human being accepting your security;" the elder brother's tone was sceptical to a degree of provocation. "But, at any rate, the other man and his people must pay."

"He is dead," repeated Gerard, gently. "Had he lived, he would have been perfectly well able to do so; we both knew that, or I don't think he would ever have allowed me to incur the risk. It wasn't much of a risk, as I told him at the time. He was sole heir to a stingy old aunt; he died before her, and all her money's gone to charities. So you see I'm fully liable. It's exceedingly unfortunate, but it can't be helped."

"Even admitting all this," began Otto, feeling his unwilling way, "you are not really liable. The law does not recognize gambling liabilities. They are not recoverable." He stumbled over his sentences, thinking aloud.

"Law!" exclaimed Gerard. "Law! I was thinking of the other extreme—honor."

"And you were a minor at the time, besides. Neither legally, nor should I say morally, responsible. It must been an act of madness." He gazed in front of him, troubled, questioning, full of incertitude.

"I thought you understood," said Gerard, haughtily, "that it was an affair between gentlemen. It has nothing to do with moral or legal responsibility." He stood still. "I bound myself to meet this claim, if able, when called upon. The trust is a sacred one. By accepting it I saved my dead friend's life." Even amid the deep seriousness of his mood he smiled at the Irishism, just as his father would have done. "I am not going to desert him now."

"Gerard, God knows I don't want you to do anything ungentlemanly," cried Otto, despairingly. " I am only thinking. Let me think. You say the sum is an enormous one. What do you call enormous ?" His voice trembled with apprehension.

" It's ninety thousand florins, if you want to know," replied Gerard, in a moody murmur. The sombre room grew very silent. Outside the window nearest them a sparrow was pecking, pertly, at the sill.

" I thought so," said Otto, scornfully, " I thought you had ruined yourself ; it seemed so natural. I understood it at once, and that made me look round for the tiniest loophole of possible escape. Gerard, it seems to me you have but the choice of dishonors. Against the memory of your friend I pit that of your father. You cannot possibly do justice to both."

He was desperate, feeling the hopelessness of compromise.

" The will is absurd !" burst out Gerard—"absurd ! He cannot have meant it absolutely, only as far as was practicable. Do you really want to make out that he intended both of us to starve, in the midst of our acres of corn-fields ? I won't believe it; and if he did, why, poor father must have been under some momentary delusion ! Wills are always taken to be binding so far as circumstances will allow. Our father meant us not to sell more of the land than was absolutely necessary. He meant us—"

Otto faced round. " I understand perfectly what our father meant," he said, and there was a roll of suppressed thunder through his patient words. " To me his aspirations do not seem unreasonable or absurd. They are my own."

" I dare say," cried Gerard. " You are the lord of the Horst, and the larger the property is, the pleasanter for you !"

" Gerard, you may accuse me of the most sordid—"

" I accuse you of nothing. Pray let us have no recriminations; we do not understand each other well enough for anything of that kind. All I say is this, and I shall stick to it—I must have my share in ready money. Can't you see I must ? If I were to go to the other fellow—the fellow that won—and say, ' My father won't have any of the land sold,' he'd think I was shirking, after all these years. Imagine that ! He'd think I

was shirking! The time would have come for *me* to decide between 'paying or shooting.' Otto, if father were alive, he'd understand that better than you do. Oh, I wish I could explain
it to him; he'd want only half a word. He'd be the first to say,
'Settle the matter at once.'" The young man was violently
agitated. He tried vainly to steady his features. He had
loved his father with ready, easy affection. It was a cruel
wound to him to bear the appearance of showing less filial piety
than Otto!

"Ninety thousand florins," repeated the elder brother, as if
not heeding the other's passion. "You were mad. You *never*
could have raised the money till father's death. What a specu-
lation!"

. "Who knows," replied Gerard, stung to the quick. "At
this moment, but for you, the sum might have seemed to me
a trifle. Do not you, of all persons, reproach me with my poverty. I should have been a rich man at this moment but for
you."

"But for me?" exclaimed Otto, in blank amazement.

"Yes, but for you," Gerard continued, wildly. "It was you
who told Ursula about Adeline, as if any man ever betrayed
another, even his enemy, to a woman! But your ideas about
honor and dishonor, which you bring forward so frequently, are
certainly not mine." Gerard stopped, eying his brother curiously. "Is it possible you don't know," he said, "that Ursula
told Helena?"

"As you allude to the disgraceful story yourself," replied
Otto, in a dull voice, "I may as well assure you that I have
never spoken of it to any one. Ursula knows nothing about it.
Nor am *I* to blame if Helena does."

However Gerard might have misunderstood his brother, he
implicitly believed him. All his anger turned against the woman who had ruined his matrimonial prospects, while herself grabbing, by any means, even including advertisement, at the first
husband she could catch.

"Then it was Ursula, and Ursula alone," he said, "who would
not let me marry Helena." He forcibly curbed himself on the
brink of accusation, true to the chivalry he had just enunciated;

but his brow grew dark with meaning. And, seeking sudden relief in permissible insult, " My Lady Nobody !" he cried, with an impudent laugh.

Otto rose. " Our discussion ends here," he said. " Leave the room. I will get you the money somehow."

He sank back a moment later, listening to Gerard's retreating footsteps. Gerard, then, had been about to marry Helena, and Ursula had told Helena something which had prevented the match. It must have been something very serious indeed.

He shook off the thought. How should he meet his brother's claim. It is easy enough to say, " I shall pay."

Why not sell a large part of the land, which, after all, was Gerard's and not his? Let Gerard do what he liked with his own. Theoretically, that was plain enough. But when it came to deciding what to abandon—and a good deal would have to go—common sense began to look strangely impossible in the new Baron's eyes. He *could* not cut up the property. He wished his father had not made him executor.

He judged his young brother not only harshly, but unfairly. He could feel nothing for the generous impulse which had brought down upon itself such magnificent ruin. Most of us imagine we recognize virtue when we see it ; in reality we only recognize our own peculiar form.

" There *is* no money," said Otto, fiercely, and he groaned aloud.

Aunt Louisa came gliding in through the open smoking-room door. Her features were sharper than ever in her smooth black dress.

" That is a very bad story, indeed, about Adeline," she said, speaking in a series of bites. Otto looked up interrogatively.

" Oh, of course I know all about it," continued the Freule, who had known nothing up to this hour. " Adeline is an actress, or singer, or something low. Nevertheless, I think Helena van Trossart has behaved like a fool. A strong woman lives down all her husband's love-stories." She blinked her eyes. " Any woman can manage any man," she said. " *I* never considered the game worth playing "—which was true.

"But it's best to know about these things beforehand," she went on. "That's why I told you about Ursula and Gerard. Afterwards they come as an unpleasant surprise, while, before marriage, one simply laughs at them. Helena ought to have thanked Ursula for frankly confessing to a passing flirtation with Gerard. Instead of that, she goes and breaks off her engagement. Inane! We can't all marry first affections, as your poor mother thinks she did. But Helena van Trossart was always a poor, weak, fanciful creature."

"It is not that," thought Otto. "Women never object to a *prior* flirtation." He looked up again, dumbly, to see whether his aunt would continue to use her gimlet.

"However, there's no help for it now," cried the Freule Louisa, changing her tone. "The marriage would have been the best thing for all parties, and that's why it's not to take place. So don't let's talk of it. But the money must be found at once. So let's talk of that."

"It can't be found," muttered Otto, wishing his aunt wouldn't interfere, and very angry with her for eavesdropping.

"'Can't' is a man's word," replied the Freule van Borck. "Your poor father used to say it whenever he didn't want to do anything. You say it when you want to do anything very much. The symptoms are different, but the disease is the same—masculine incapacity. A woman says, 'I will.'"

"Then I wish some woman would say it," retorted Otto.

His aunt smiled. "You are so literal," she said. "You never can enjoy the plastic beauty of a theory. And, Otto, in one thing I entirely disagree with you. Gerard's action was a great one. However unfortunate for us, it deserves our abstract admiration. Yes, I know what you are going to say; but you are wrong. Few natures in our little world are capable of such splendid recklessness. I, for one, applaud it—from a distance. Imagine, in this nineteenth century, a man who will sacrifice his all for a friend!"

"He hasn't ruined you, Aunt Louisa," said Otto.

"I am not worth ruining," she answered, quickly, meekly. "But, Otto, I was coming to that. I am poor, as you know—very poor." She grew suddenly nervous and sat down, trembling, in a big leathern chair. "But I have this advantage over you rich people, that my money is where I can get at it, in the funds. I'm not going to give it to Gerard," she said, racing off sharp and fast. Her cheeks grew pink. She was exceedingly frightened, as many women are whenever they allude to finance. "I couldn't do that and starve, now could I? But I'll lend it to you on the property, Otto, to pay him off. You'll fasten it on the property and give me a pawn-ticket, won't you? And I'll let you have it on easy terms, because I admire Gerard's action and — and yours also. I'm proud of my nephews." She paused, out of breath, and aimlessly stroked her dress."

"Thank you," said Otto, with his reflective reserve. But the fervor of his tone quite satisfied Aunt Louisa.

"Yes," she went on, preparing to hurry away. "The estate must be kept together. I insist upon that. For I can't have other people intruding upon my Bilberry Walk, and that would be the first to go. But, Otto, you must let me have some interest, or else I shouldn't be able to pay you my 'keep.'" Thereupon the Freule departed, fluttered with the consciousness of a heroic atmosphere all round and but little discomfort to herself. She had, indeed, behaved bravely, for scraping was the sole diversion of her life, and she imagined somehow that a mortgage at four per cent. was a very great sacrifice indeed. In common with many people who greatly admire great deeds, she liked to do her own great deeds small.

At any rate, Otto felt immensely relieved for the moment by the certainty that the money would be forthcoming. He went in search of Ursula, whom he found playing on a sofa with his father's great smooth St. Bernard. Ursula's opening days were long in this new home of which she had become the mistress. Everything was as yet in the listless uncertainty of a not-disorganized transition. The Dowager Baroness had nowise resigned the keys, while occupying herself with nothing in the privacy of her own bereavement.

"Dearest," said Otto, "why did you not tell me about Helena and Gerard?"

Ursula blushed.

" Because it was a secret," she replied, hotly. " I told nobody, Otto."

" Nobody ?"

" Nobody but my father. Has Gerard spoken of it ? How
much has he told you ?"

She looked at him anxiously, scarlet with the soilure of
Gerard's sin.

He misread her distress.

" Oh, very little," he said. " Make yourself easy. I don't
want to know any more."

She sprang forward to him, the great dog entangled in her
skirts.

" Otto," she said, pleadingly, " you'll let by-gones be by-gones,
won't you—now ?"

She was thinking of the reconciliation between the brothers
for which her whole heart yearned.

She frightened him.

" Yes," he cried. " Yes, if Gerard goes away. That is all I
demand. *You* must ask Gerard to go away."

" I ?" She drew herself up. " No, indeed," she said. " You
are lord of the Horst. It is you who must forbid your brother
the house, if you wish him to leave it."

As he turned to go she ran after him, and laid her hand
on his arm.

" Only don't let it be for my sake, dear," she pleaded, re-
calling Gerard's initial insult, and continuous cold hostility,
to herself. " Do not, I entreat you, let me be the cause of
further discord between you. Gerard will forget the past, and
I will ignore it. And even if do not, I am strong now, in
your love, to face the future with confidence. Otto, I implore
you, do not send him away for my sake."

" Oh no, for my own," exclaimed Otto, and broke away from
her.

She came back to the dog, completely unconscious of all
complications except the old quarrel between her husband and
his brother.

It weighed upon her; she regretfully felt that she, in her
innocence, was chiefly to blame for it. Gerard had deeply re-

sented, and still continued to resent, the marriage of the head of the house to the parson's daughter. Compared to this, the quarrel about the horse was only a passing cloud, and even that would not have arisen but for her. Men of the world, she felt bitterly, could desert Adelines, but they could not marry Ursulas. It is true; more than that—only she did not know it—men of the world can offer to marry Adeline, and never forgive their brother for marrying Ursula. We can do all that, we men. It is our privilege, because we are thinking creatures.

Just now, Ursula felt that her only duty in the great house was to comfort the dog. Monk was an institution at the Manor; he had been that ever since the old Baron had brought him back from the desolate monastery which is all sunshine within, and all snow without. By this time surely he had forgotten his native Alpine frosts—if dogs ever forget — among the mists of Holland. He had basked for years in the master's smile, unassuming, as no man would ever have remained, under the dignified repose of his assured position. All the household had honored Monk; many with time-service only. This he had understood; he had loved his master alone. He knew that the Baroness endured him; perhaps there was a little jealousy between the two. And on the day of the old man's death he had wandered about, disconsolate, gradually beginning to realize a change. Ursula found him a forsaken favorite, not mourning his fall—again, how unhuman!—but his friend. She looked into his big soft eyes, and the hunger died out of them. Immediately the two understood each other, forever. "I accept of you in my empty heart," said Monk.

In the old Baroness's boudoir the fat ball of white silk on its crimson cushion opened one eye with lazy discontent and scowled across at its mistress. It was disgusted with the selfish irregularity of its meals. The little old woman in the easy-chair near the autumn fire did not even notice it, in spite of the oft-repeated sighs by which it strove to attract attention. Occasionally slow tears would now roll down the widow's sunken pink-and-white cheeks, and glitter amid the jewels of her folded hands. She had reached that milder stage when

we begin to feel our sorrow.   Oh, God, that in this world of
agony, men should find cause to be thankful for consciousness
of pain !

"Plush" considered the state of affairs most disgracefully
disagreeable.

CHAPTER XXIII

GERARD went back to Drum before his leave had expired. "Your share shall be paid to you," Otto had said, perusing the carpet-pattern. "Mother and Aunt Louisa will combine to make that possible. I think that is all, Gerard. Good-bye."

So, dismissed like a footman, the young fellow turned his back on the home of his youth. He little guessed that the stern, middle-aged man, seated at his father's desk, in possession, was, even at that very moment, inwardly tossed by a passion of prayer to keep back the furious inculpations that were beating at his lips.

So Gerard went back to Drum. He realized, as he drove away, taking Beauty's successor with him, that even though he might visit the Manor-house again, henceforth it would be as a stranger. During all the years of his growth into manhood, ever since he could remember, he had been practically the only son, the "young squire" in the eyes of the peasantry. He felt cheated of his birthright.

The packing-up had been a terrible business. Nothing had been said about retaining his rooms, and his nature was one that shrank back before the shadow of a coming hint. Quietly he had put all his things together, turning from Ursula's silent, terrified gaze. Silence seemed to have fallen upon them all like a paralysis. The servants looked at each other.

All his life had been sheltered too warmly in his father's fostering affection. The luxury of his youth hung about him— the easy generosity which had accounted money only a thing to spend on himself or on others, according to requirement. It is a cruel thing, that flow of parental good-nature, while the fingers of Death are playing with the tap.

And at this supreme moment even his mother's sure prefer-
ence deserted him. The Baroness, whose faculties seemed to
lie dulled beneath the veil of her widowhood, had understood,
clearly enough, without need of any malice on Otto's part, that
Gerard objected to the terms of the will. The discovery had
galvanized her into feverish activity. She had insisted upon
sacrificing whatever her husband's improvidence had left her
still unsacrificed. Half a dozen times in the course of one day
she rang for Otto, to ascertain whether everything was settled.
For the moment, Gerard had become the enemy against whom
the forces of the family must unite. She was very angry with
him for wishing to destroy his father's life-work. " You won't
allow it, Otto," she repeated, excitedly. " You will never allow
it." She clung to her strong eldest, in the weakness of abandonment. Her farewell to the traitor was full of reproach.
Gerard went back into life from his father's funeral, alone.

As soon as the money was in his possession he sought an interview with the creditor at the Hague and discharged his debt,
or rather his departed friend's. But he had plenty of liabilities
of his own incurring, and these now came tumbling about his
ears in the crash of his father's removal. By the time he had
effected a settlement there was very little left of his original
curtailed inheritance. This would hardly have disturbed his
calm fruition of all things needful but for the brusque discovery
that his credit was gone. One afternoon he stepped into a familiar shop to order a new saddle, and the obsequious tradesman
asked prepayment of his standing account. Gerard came away
bewildered. It was the turning-point of his life. He was poor.

Before all this, before the Baron's death, he had made one
attempt to act on Mademoiselle Papotier's suggestion. He had
written a long letter to Helena. It had been returned to him
unopened, and from that moment he felt his case was utterly
hopeless. For a woman hardly ever returns a letter unopened.
She is quite willing to do so, only she must read it first. Some
of them manage to.

Gerard was in the position of many a modern spendthrift.
Steal he could not, to work he was ashamed. Besides, what
was he fit for, excepting parade ? It is one of the saddest con-

fusions of this muddled society of ours that only the ˙poor can beg and only the rich can steal. Nothing was left, therefore, to our young soldier but to return to his simplified avocations in the endeavor to make both ends meet on starvation pay. All the color and cake went out of his existence, which became drab, like rye-bread.

Adeline was married to her lawyer's clerk; Helena's wedding-dress had been ordered. Under these circumstances, in his handsome forlornness, dawdling about dull Drum, Gerard found one motherly bosom on which to rest his curly head. The plump Baroness van Trossart, disgusted by her niece's perversity, but resolved not to fret over anything, immediately set herself to pay the poor boy what she considered a family debt, and, after a little preliminary reconnoitring, backed by an artillery fire of praises and pushes, she successfully manœuvred the rejected suitor into a fresh flirtation with one of the most charming girls in Holland, Antoinette van Rexelaer. The Freule Antoinette was not an heiress, like Helena, but she had lately, and quite unexpectedly, come into a snug little fortune through her godfather, a relation of her mother's, and former Minister of State—a windfall, indeed, to the youngest of five children! " A dispensation !" mysteriously ejaculated the young lady's mother, Mevrouw Elizabeth van Rexelaer, née Borck.

Topsy, as her own circle called her, was a distant connection of Gerard's; but then in Holland we are all that, and it no longer counts. The two mothers were some sort of cousins. From the Hague, where the Rexelaers lived, Antoinette came came to stay with the Baroness van Trossart, and, under that match-maker's auspices, she saw a good deal of Gerard. Now, for Gerard to see a nice girl was to be charming to her; he was charming in the most natural, innocent, and infectious way. The Freule Antoinette understood this perfectly, and they lived together in that happy mutual desire to please which may mean everything or nothing, according to Cupid's caprice. When the guest returned home, Mevrouw van Trossart felt convinced it meant everything, and she had easily persuaded Gerard to think so too, for Gerard had taken a real liking to the frank-faced, bright-witted girl.

"My dear boy," said the good-natured Baroness, intent on
further arrangement, "you are positively too dangerous; I cannot introduce you to any more young ladies. You are irresistible; you have now carried off the heart of my poor little Antoinette!"

"One young lady did not find me irresistible, Mevrouw," replied Gerard, bitterly. He was angry with Helena, but he had
never really cared for her. It was she who now avoided him.

"Ah, dear boy, do not let us speak of that; it is too dreadful. Be thankful that you, at least, did not love your cousin.
No, no." She held up a fat forefinger. "Of course you protest; but an old woman like me sees what she sees. We all
make mistakes. As for poor Helena, hers"— She stopped.
"This time, at any rate," she cried, gayly, "there must be no
blundering. Go at once and propose to Mevrouw Elizabeth.
To know you prosperously settled will be a load off my heart."

"Propose to Mevrouw Elizabeth!" said Gerard, with a grimace.

"Don't be stupid, Gerard. Yes, considering the undoubted
fact that Antoinette Rexelaer is so much richer than you—there's
no use in ignoring what every one knows — I think it would
be in better taste for you to speak first to the father — which
means the mother; especially as in this case I feel sure you
can safely do so."   ·

Accordingly Gerard, by no means indifferent as to the issue,
waited upon Mynheer Frederick van Rexelaer, Topsy's papa, a
Judge, and also a Fool. That gentleman received him very af-
fably, and immediately invented an excuse for withdrawing to
consult with the head of the household.

"No money and a very desirable connection," said Mevrouw
Rexelaer, sitting up. "I wish it were Van Helmont of Horstwyk and the Horst. But *he* has behaved like an idiot. This
seems a very agreeable young man, and Topsy might do worse.
Since her miserable failure with poor deluded René I am often
quite anxious about what is to become of her."

"Oh, she'll marry," said the Judge.

"I'm not so sure, Frederick," replied Mevrouw, who was very
impatient, for various reasons, to get this last daughter off her
hands.

"Antoinette is so strange, so ungirlish; no man, as yet, has ever proposed to her. My cousin Herman's legacy was a merciful dispensation; but, all the same, I should consider it very unwise to let this chance escape."

So Gerard was instructed to make his proposal that night at the Soirée of the Society of Arts, and Topsy was instructed to accept him.

"You may thank your stars," said Mevrouw Elizabeth, frankly, to her daughter. "Judging by the past, I should think it's your only opportunity. Money doesn't go for everything, especially if a girl has no 'charm.' I thank Heaven on my bended knees when I remember what might have been!"

"Yes, mamma," replied Antoinette, meekly, with flushed cheeks and downcast eyes. In her own family Mevrouw Elizabeth's will was law, the immovable incubus of many oppressive years.

"What might have been"—what Mevrouw had once yearned and worked for, in spite of present thanksgiving—was Topsy's marriage with a cousin, who had never understood Mevrouw Elizabeth's plans. This cousin was now dead and mad and altogether forgotten and unmentionable. Hush!

The evening exhibitions of the Arts Society are very brilliant social events. Some first-rate private collection or portfolio forms the welcome excuse for coming together, and the people who go everywhere and see nothing insure, by their presence, artistic success. There was such a crowd in the central room—a chattering crowd, unconcernedly self-obstructive with regard to the pictures—that it took Gerard some time to worm his way to Antoinette. His heart fluttered. How sweet she looked with her provokingly clever little face in the turquoise cloud of her evening-dress!

"Let's go into that little side-room, Freule," he stammered. "I should like to show you a picture there."

"Oh, but I don't want to go into the little side-room, Mynheer van Helmont." Her voice was uncertain, like his. "Please don't," she said, "I'm much happier as I am."

He looked at her without immediate answer, offering his arm. Suddenly she seemed to grasp at some mighty resolve,

and, checking further protest, she allowed him to lead her
away.

The little alcove was empty but for a couple of expectantly
staring portraits, forlorn in the gaslight.

"How stupid they look!" exclaimed Gerard, impatiently;
then, rebelling against the still atmosphere of imminence which
seemed to thicken upon this sudden solitude, "Freule, I want
to say something to you," he murmured, hastily. "I don't
quite know how to begin, but, perhaps—"

"Oh, don't," she interrupted him, releasing her arm. "Don't,
please, Mynheer van Helmont, I know what you are going to
say, and I want you to leave it unsaid. I am so sorry, for I
know it must be all my fault. I never thought of anything of
the kind. I had understood you—I believed your affections
were placed elsewhere. I—I am so sorry." She faltered. "I
shall never marry," she said, and plucked at her fan.

He did not answer, in the silence, with the senseless hum beyond. Opposite him, in a big gilt frame, a woman sat eternally
simpering, a lay figure with black laces and Raglan roses. He
hated that woman.

"Shall I take you back to Mevrouw van Rexelaer?" he said.

The name seemed to arouse her from her dream of unmerited
self-reproach.

"Just one moment," she began, hurriedly. "There is—I
should like— Mynheer van Helmont, I am going to ask you
an immense favor! I know I have no right, but I want you to
tell my parents that it is you who have changed your mind.
You haven't really asked me anything, you know. Well, say
you haven't."

"I don't quite understand." Gerard spoke a little haughtily.

"Perhaps it isn't so much of a favor," the poor girl went on.
"It 'll save you the appearance of having been refused. Forgive me, Mynheer van Helmont; I don't quite know what I'm
saying. But my life will be even more miserable than it is; it will
be unbearable, if my mother knows you asked me to be your wife."

She looked up at him pleadingly. He was amazed. What
had become of the bright creature he knew, with her sparkle of
innocent repartee?

"THERE WAS SUCH A CROWD IN THE CENTRAL ROOM"

"My word is passed to your father," he said, tremulously. "You ask me to disgrace myself in the eyes of every decent man."

"Oh no! not that! not that!" She spoke almost wildly. "But, oh, my God! what am I to do? Mynheer van Helmont, don't think me too much of a coward. I believe I could nerve myself to one great sacrifice; it is the daily bickering and nagging which I cannot endure. Never mind, I am ashamed of myself." She dashed her hand across her eyes—but too late. "Good-bye, and forget me. It doesn't matter."

He bent low over her hand.

"It shall be as you wish," he said, very firm and soldierly.

Once more she looked up at him, her eyes full of far-away tenderness.

"I cannot help myself," she whispered. "I shall never love —again."

Gerard found the Judge in the coffee-room. And with the best face possible—which was a bad one—he confessed that he had reconsidered his proposal of the morning, and must withdraw it. Difficulties had intervened.

"Really?" said the little Judge, coffee-cup in hand. "This is very extraordinary. Of course, if you wish, there is an end of it. But—really, Mynheer van Helmont, you must excuse me —for a moment." He sidled to the entrance, in wild yearning for his better half, who fortunately met him there, having gathered that something was wrong.

"My dear," whispered the Judge, "Mynheer van Helmont has changed his mind about marrying Topsy. He isn't going to."

"Nonsense, Frederick!" ejaculated Mevrouw Elizabeth. "Tell him it's all right. Tell him to go and ask her at once."

The little Judge went back into the desolate refreshment-room. His substantial consort lingered near the door.

"Mynheer van Helmont," said Frederick, "it's all right. You had better go and ask her at once."

"Mynheer van Rexelaer," replied Gerard, scarlet as a poppy, "I thought I had made myself understood. I abandon all further idea of proposing to your daughter."

13

Frederick fell back to the door. In her eagerness Mevrouw
put through her big heliotrope - crowned head. "My dear, he
won't ask her," breathed Frederick.

"What?" cried the lady, casting furious glances towards the
young officer, erect and helpless in the middle of the bare,
blazing room. "Go to him, Frederick, at once! Tell him he's
a coward and no gentleman! Tell him you'll horsewhip him!
No, you can't do that, you're a Judge. Tell him one of her
brothers will horsewhip him! Guy ought to. I'll *make* him
do it! She pushed forward her small husband, who reluctantly
returned to the charge.

"You have behaved very badly, Mynheer," he began. "You
must permit me to say that." He looked round nervously.
Mevrouw Elizabeth, distrusting the atmosphere of calm, had
come forward into the full light, and was unconsciously straining nearer. "That your conduct is"—he raised his voice—
"not such as one has a right to expect from a gentleman.
And here the matter must end." He turned hastily; Mevrouw
Elizabeth stood close behind him.

"Say it is blackguardly," she hissed.

"I won't!" replied Frederick van Rexelaer, in a funk.

"It is blackguardly, Mynheer," cried the matron, pushing
past. "You are a coward, Mynheer, and no gentleman."

Gerard retreated towards the gas-smitten wall, looking, in his
tight-fitting blue-black hussar uniform, like an Apollo in utter
disgrace. He wondered, for a moment, whether the woman
was going to strike him.

"My son shall speak to you, Mynheer, as you deserve,"
shrieked Mevrouw Elizabeth. "My son! I will send you my
son, sir, to settle this matter."

"Oh, do, Mevrouw, do!" eagerly exclaimed Gerard, in a sudden rush of relief.

CHAPTER XXIV

MASKS AND FACES

THE day after his wife's funeral Mynheer Mopius sat in the gilded drawing-room of Villa Blanda. His demeanor was properly, pleasantly chastened, for the cud of the pompous exequies lay sweet upon his tongue.

Harriet, busy with her own thoughts at the evening tea-table, said, " Yes, it had all been very nice."

" But the tea was cold, Harriet," grumbled Mynheer Mopius, for the dozenth weary time. " It's a very bad thing in a woman when she can't make tea."

" Of course," replied Harriet, gazing down at her sable garments, and wondering how soon the cheap material would get rusty.

" My mother could make excellent tea," prosed Mynheer, with a melancholy nod. " She could do everything excellently, could my mother."

" A woman ought to," said Harriet, "and when she's done it, she ought to die."

" She ought. She ought." While Mynheer Mopius spoke, his thoughts were dwelling on Dominé Pock's oration by the grave. How well the reverend gentleman had alluded to the charities of our dear brother afflicted ! " The consolation which a noble heart can always find in wiping other eyes the while its own are streaming !"

Mynheer blew his nose.

" This cheap cloth won't last, uncle," said Harriet, briskly.

He pretended not to hear her. She bored him. She had been all very well while his wife dragged on, but now—! And, why, after all, should he be saddled with this sharp-tongued

girl? She was no relation of his, though she called him
"uncle." Mevrouw Mopius's childless sister had been the first
wife of Harriet's father, Dr. Verveen.

"Yes," he repeated, mechanically, "everything my mother
produced was first-rate of its kind."

"Especially her son," said Harriet, with a sneer that positively fizzled.

Mynheer Mopius's yellow face grew a shade healthier in
color. He accepted his third cup in thoughtful silence; then
he said, "And *now*, my dear young lady, what do you mean
to do?"

She looked at him, across the steaming urn.

"Go to bed," she replied.

"Quite so. And after?"

"Why, sleep, of course. What do you mean, uncle?"
She flushed scarlet.

"My dear Harriet, I fear you are too fond of sleeping.
Surely you understand that you can no longer remain an inmate
of this house, now that—that I am a lonely widower? Much as
I regret—ahem!—you will admit, I feel confident, that you
cannot remain under present circumstances."

"Not under present circumstances," answered Harriet.

She waited for one long second, her black eyes aflame, full on
his face. Then the balance in which her fate hung snapped
suddenly. She sat, self-possessed, amid the collapse of all her
hopes.

"I shall always take an interest in you," said Mynheer Mopius, adjusting his neat white mourning-tie; "and I mean to
act very generously, to begin with. I shall take lodgings for
you for one month, paying your board. I should have added a
little cash for current expenses, but you aunt's legacy has made
that superfluous."

"Aunt Sarah left me a hundred florins and her Bible," said
Harriet.

"Dear woman, she did! She always thought of others. You
are welcome to the money, Harriet; fully, frankly welcome.
But the Bible! That is a memento of her I would fain have
retained."

"Buy it of me?" said Harriet. "How much will you give for it? Ten florins?"

"Harriet, I am shocked," replied Mynheer Mopius, hastily. "The month's board will leave you ample time to look out for a situation."

"To look out for another situation," said Harriet.

"Quite so," exclaimed Mynheer Mopius, delighted at her good sense.

Harriet threw back her arm with a jerk that rattled the tea-equipage.

"And to think," she cried, "that only last week I rejected the doctor."

"More fool you!" replied Mynheer Mopius, coolly. "You'll have to be more careful of the Chinese porcelain in a strange house, Harriet, and it probably won't be anything like as good."

"I rejected the doctor," continued Harriet, roughly, "because I didn't care for him. I couldn't live with a young man I didn't care for. Uncles are different."

"Harriet, I am not really your uncle, you must remember, though I am willing to behave as such. If your father—"

"Yes, I know. Well, I shall try to get something in a month's time, and if I can, I'll repay the board and lodging, dear uncle."

"That is not necessary. You can place an advertisement, Harriet, not mentioning names, of course. You don't know enough for a governess, and, besides, you are too good-looking. You had better try to become a companion. If your father—"

"Quite so. Yes, I shall try to become a companion—to a gentleman."

"Harriet! I do not see that it is a laughing matter. To an invalid lady. Not that you have any experience of invalids; for my dear Sarah enjoyed excellent health till almost the last."

"To a gentleman," persisted Harriet, coolly. "It is no laughing matter, Uncle Jacob. When I leave this house, which at least afforded me some miserable sort of protection, I shall advertise for a husband. I dare say something nice will

turn up. I want a husband I can be really fond of. Somehow
I have faith in his turning up."

She spoke to herself, but she rejoiced in scandalizing the
hateful humbug opposite.

· "Harriet, my dear," said the widower, solemnly, "all this
is very much out of place. You should have more respect for
the holiness of sorrow, Harriet."

"Oh, dear, no, you needn't trouble about that," she interrupted him. "I'm in deadly earnest, I assure you. I've
printed an advertisement before, but it came to nothing. I
mean to look out better this time."

Her accent belied the outer calm of her attitude; she began
washing the cups.

"Printed an advertisement from my house? From Villa
Blanda? If so, I have nourished a—"

"No."

"I am extremely agitated, Harriet. You are my cherished
Sarah's step-niece. I cannot imagine that any member, any
step-member, of my dear wife's family would demean herself in
the manner you describe."

He got up and began to walk about, enjoying his brand-new
mourning. "For any one, of however humble origin — and
Sarah's sister married beneath her—to enter into relations of—
of an amorous description with a stranger! Harriet, I am horrified. We are not in India, Harriet. You are not a black
woman, though you may think and act like one. I appeal to
you to remember that you are connected, however distantly,
with an honorable family. You are not free, Harriet, as you
might have been before your father's first marriage."

He spoke with almost desperate energy, for there were some
things he had learned to discriminate in his intercourse with
Harriet Verveen. He knew when she meant what she said.

"Pooh!" replied Harriet. "Good-night, dear uncle. You
give me a month's board, without wages, and notice to quit.
I am very grateful, dear uncle; but henceforth you must allow
me to fashion my own life as I choose."

They stood facing each other. There was no noise and no
recrimination. Each knew it would be useless.

"I have nourished a serpent in my bosom," said Mynheer Mopius, triumphantly getting out his quotation after all. "I can't keep you here a day longer, Harriet, though you seem to be annoyed about going. It wouldn't be proper, and, besides, I may have other plans. I treat you generously. Whatever you may elect to do I hope you will repay me by henceforth dropping all pretended relationship to myself. That must be an understood thing. Such conduct as you propose—clandestine love affairs, anonymous love affairs—I consider most scandalous. All the world considers it scandalous. I cannot allow a breath of ill-odor to sully the unspotted name of Mopius. Harriet, I hope you fully agree to that suggestion. If not I should consider myself compelled to retract."

"Oh, most willingly," again interrupted Harriet. She steadily sought her uncle's shifty glances. "I break all relation between us as completely as—I crush this cup!" The costly porcelain fell to the ground in shell-like fragments. Mynheer Mopius darted forward with a shriek. Meanwhile Harriet slipped from the room, her right hand bleeding, her mood somewhat relieved.

Next morning she left the house. After the night's consideration of circumstances she was not sorry to go. She believed, with a desperate woman's pertinacity, in the ultimate success of the wide choice she had allowed herself. She would take a husband after her own heart. Already she pictured him to herself, good-looking, with a fair mustache.

In the great city close to Drum—a city which may as well remain nameless—a modest variety may be found of those public entertainments which constitute, to the many, a principal criterion of civilization. In the nineteenth-century march of mind—which, after all, is but the advance of 'Arry—a town with no permanent music-hall troupe is voted "slow." Drum was distinctly "slow." Its big sister aspired, in spasms, to be reckoned "fast."

Occasionally, therefore, when the fit was upon her, the big sister clutched, gasping, at some Parisian form of diversion; a river fête with fireworks, horse-races, or, in winter, a *bal costumé*

et paré. The latter was decidedly a bad spasm, for northern
nations can make nothing of the " Veglione." Still, every season a couple of these picturesque gayeties were organized by
indefatigable *impresarii* (in rose-colored spectacles), the price
of admission being fixed at a florin for gentlemen, ladies free.
No respectable person over thirty was supposed to attend.

One of the least unsuccessful costume-balls the city has ever
seen came off just before Christmas, in the year we are describ-
ing. Willie van Troyen was there as Paris, with another Hel-
en, this being a delicate joke on the part of the woman whose
rule was to end next week. As she accurately pointed out, the
right Helen was, after all, the wrong love.

Only Gerard's deep mourning had prevented his presence.
Somebody had suggested, behind his back, that he might go as
a Mute. The gay band he lived among agreed unanimously
that " it was high time that Gerard got over his parent's demise." He was not a success in the rôle of the impecunious
orphan.

Willie van Troyen on this festal occasion was drunk, and
from his place in a stage-box, between two sirens, he was roar-
ing with laughter at the antics of a goose in the pit. The whole
floor of the small theatre had been cleared for perambulation,
while those who *meant* dancing could retire to the stage. Most
of the masks, however, preferred to walk about and make believe they were funny, in a half-annoyed jostle of ungracious
familiarity, under the critical contemplation of the humbler am-
phitheatre side-tables, and of the champagne-sodden boxes up
above. Every now and then some ambitious buffoon, excited
by the continuous spur of the music, would suddenly leap at facile
applause. There would be a sweep of the crowd in his direction and an outburst of meaningless laughter, every one exclaiming that the joke was good, while thinking it rather tame.

But even the numerous laughers who were only pretending
to amuse themselves agreed in recognizing the very real drollery
of the Goose. He—it was evidently a masculine goose, as distinguished from a gander—he trotted about in the stupidest
manner, a great yellow-beaked ball of white and black feathers
with unreasonably protruding quills. Just now he had got hold

of a stout and solemn gentleman in red velvet, who evidently represented a potent, grave, and reverend Signior. This dignified personage looked exceedingly out of place—not to speak of a false nose through his mask—in so foolish a company of mummers.

The Goose had a nasty talent for cackling with the extravagant clatter of his big wooden beak, and he kept up this deafening music incessantly as he ran round and round the fat gentleman in velvet, who turned helplessly hither and thither amid volleys of merriment. Every now and then the cruel bird, as it ran, would draw the pointed quills from under its feathers and therewith prick the reverend signior in unexpected places, causing him to wriggle and twist. Just then there was a pause in the programme; the whole theatre shook with this unexpected fun.

" Why can't you leave me alone?" hissed the unfortunate senator, in streaming suspense. But the Goose made no reply. Stopping his mad race for a moment, he actually began chalking up ribaldry with one of his quills on the senator's pendent mantle, chattering all the while. In vain the proud aristocrat wrestled and protested. The Goose, holding the mantle firmly, chalked a huge note of interrogation upon it, and wrote under this sign, amid breathless interest, the question, ' What does your Worship here ?" A renewed outburst greeted this sally. Willie van Troyen, unsteadily prominent, pelted the witty bird with hot-house grapes.

"Go along, you hypocrite, I know you," said the Goose in his victim's ear. " I've chalked up your real name behind."

At this the crimson noble, breaking down, began to cry real tears of shame and spite. "You've ruined me, then," he exclaimed. " And I can't for the life of me imagine why !"

" Boh," said the Goose, and resumed his clatter more heartily than ever.

But at this juncture a Goose-girl stepped unexpectedly into the arena. She drove off the Goose with some well-directed blows, and, taking the arm of the red-velvet gentleman, led him disconsolate away.

"It's your own fault for coming," squeaked the Goose-girl. "Let's go and talk it over in a private box."

"No, indeed ; private boxes are very expensive. My dear creature, for Heaven's sake, let me sit down on this settee. I —I—anxious to obliterate"— he began, violently rubbing his back against the cushions of the sofa. "I am quite at a loss to understand," he said ; "but tell me, my dear, you didn't— eh ?"

"Yes, indeed," replied the maiden. "Your style and title, Mynheer the Councillor, were written there in full."

He broke into an oath. "Not my name," he sobbed. "You —you didn't see my name ?"

The Goose-girl sat down beside him. She used a small instrument to disguise her voice. "Why did you come here, you horrid old man ?" she said. "I saw you flirting with Little Red Riding-hood. I saw you dancing with that atrocious Bacchante. ' Clandestine love-affairs,' 'Anonymous engagements.' And your wife not five weeks dead ! Oh, Uncle Jacob—Uncle Jacob!" Harriet dropped into her natural voice, letting fall both her mask and her manner.

"Harriet !" exclaimed Mopius, "this exceeds—"

"Indeed it does," she interrupted, coolly. "Don't speak so loud, dear uncle, or the Goose will be coming back."

Mynheer Mopius started to his feet.

"This is some conspiracy to ruin me," he said, speaking like one dazed. "I'm ruined already. I'm going—"

"Wait a moment," objected his tormentor. "It isn't true that your name was written up ; I prevented that in time. So, you see, you have a good deal to thank me for. But, uncle, that Goose is a writer on the staff of the *Drum Independent ;* he is one of their leading men, and a very great friend of mine. His quills are very real quills. He is anxious to tell—when the by-election comes on next week, which is to render you Right Worshipful—an amusing little story of a highly respectable candidate who, barely a month after his dear wife's death, danced with a charming Bacchante at a charming masked ball."

"What do you want of me, Harriet ?" shrieked the wretched

widower. "Do you want money? I can let you have a little, if you like."

"Hush. Let's talk it over quietly in this quiet corner, Uncle Jacob. I am pitiless. Understand that at once. No compounding. You must surrender absolutely. Better do it with a good grace."

"I know you want to marry me," answered Mopius, sulkily; "and I don't mind so very much, though it's hard to have it forced on one. I'd rather have had a woman with a softer tongue; but I've been looking about me, and one has this fault and another has that; I always said you were good-looking, Harriet. I'll marry you, if you like, though I'd rather have had a lady-born."

"Marry you!" she blazed out at him. "No, indeed, I'm going to marry a man whose boots you daren't lick, unless he let you. A good man, beautiful as good, and clever as he is beautiful—a man who will some day be great, and I—love—him. He is poor, and the whole world is before him, and I *love* him. Marry *you!*"

"Well, you wanted to a month ago," muttered Mopius.

"Let me speak. If you want to hush up this disgraceful story you must give my love "—her voice caressed the delicious word—"two thousand florins. He will be satisfied with that; then he can pay off his debts, and we can start our humble house-keeping."

"Harriet, it's a mean trick. I should never have thought that you with your pride—"

"Silence, you !" she exclaimed under her breath, crushing down her own misgivings with reckless vehemence. "How dare you question his good pleasure, or I? You obey, so do I. Only two thousand florins. He is very moderate. He might have demanded ten. But I told him I didn't want your dirty money. Love can be happy in a garret. Come, let's have done with the whole horrid business. I promised to call him, and then you can go." The Goose-girl put a whistle to her lips, and immediately her obedient bird came clucking up from among the motley crowd. As he came his weary din gradually assumed the shape of "Ja-cob! Ja-cob! Ja-cob!" with terrible, reiterated distinctness.

"Hush, please, darling," pleaded Harriet, her voice full of soft entreaty, "uncle is willing to give the two thousand florins, as I propose."

"To further his candidature," said the Goose, bowing low. "It is clearly understood that the money is paid to further his candidature. I am proud, sir, to make your acquaintance." The Goose saluted, with silly flap.

"And now he had better go," exclaimed Harriet.

"My dear child, what are you thinking of ?" protested the Goose, as Mynheer Mopius hastily rose to render ready obedience. "I have only just had the pleasure of meeting your uncle. I am sure he will do us the favor of being present at a little champagne supper in one of the up-stairs boxes—as host."

"Oh no," began the Goose-girl, and checked herself, meeting the Goose's eye.

"I shall be willing," stammered Mopius, "if necessary, to pay—"

The Goose interposed.

"My dear sir, what are you thinking of ?" he said, loftily. "Is this the way such matters are managed among men of honor ? Harriet, take your uncle's arm !"

Together the trio ascended to the grand tier. Mynheer Mopius's supper, as ordered by the Goose, was exquisite ; the host finished by enjoying it himself, and drinking too much wine. Willie van Troyen insisted on rolling in from the adjoining box to shake the Goose by the hand. He also drank to the health of the recumbent masked gentleman in shabby red velvet who was singing sentimental songs in an undertone, with unpremeditated shrieks—

"Dear love, for thee I would lay down my li-i-fe :
For, without thee, what would that life avail ?"

The Goose informed Willie that the Senator was a retired Indian Viceroy, who had given many such a magnificent entertainment in his day. Willie put his finger to his nose, and immediately invited His Excellency to his wedding six days hence. Upon which His Excellency burst out crying, and said that the word reminded him of the best of departed wives. Harriet sat staring down into the now almost deserted pit.

The cold December dawn had not yet achieved more than the hope of its forthcoming when the Goose took away Mynheer Mopius in a cab to a quiet hotel. Behind them still echoed the loud talk of the young officers. They passed, in the fearsome streets, a troop of roysterers from a gin-shop. " We won't go home till morning !" rang hideous on the patient night. Here and there a window shone out, fully lighted, with its message of suffering or suspense.

Up above—far, far above—stood, silent, God's eternal stars ; watchful, serenely waiting, in the darkness whence we come and whither we return.

Three days after the ball Mynheer Mopius paid up like a man, and three days after he had paid up, Mynheer Mopius was sitting one evening in his accustomed arm-chair, reflecting on his loneliness and the unexpected rarity of charming claimants for his hand. In fact, during this month, with his indecent precipitancy, he had exposed himself to a couple of very painful rebuffs. Of course, he was exceedingly angry with Harriet. But, really, all that he cared for was himself, his own comfort, his own glory, an audience, especially for his evening songs.

In the midst of his reflections Harriet walked in. She cast off her wrap, *sans gêne*, upon the nearest sofa.

" I've come to marry you, after all," she said, quite collectedly.

Mynheer Mopius jumped.

" Harriet," he replied, " this is—go away ! After your conduct of last week, go away !"

" I forgive your conduct," said Harriet, unmoved.

" And the—the Goose you were in love with ?" inquired Mynheer Mopius, not without some satisfaction.

" He was unworthy," replied Harriet, with level eyebrows. " He has thrown me over."

" As soon as he had the money," said Mynheer Mopius, rubbing his palms between his knees.

" Yes, as soon as he had the money," admitted the girl, quite

simply. "It appears there is another woman in the business.
All that is dead and gone. All my money's gone. I haven't
had anything to eat since yesterday morning. Never mind that.
But my decision's taken. I've come back to marry you. And
I mean to."

"You can't against my will, Harriet," said Mynheer Mopius,
beaming. "Go away."

"Look here, Uncle Jacob, you're going to marry me, or—
don't make me say the alternative. I'd rather think you married me without the alternative. It's not very nice, anyway,
but I don't intend to starve. And, as I don't believe in men
any more, it really doesn't matter much. Now ring for the servants, and tell them you're going to marry me."

"Harriet, go away!"

Harriet crossed to the bell-rope and pulled it. "What does
your Worship here?" she said, incoherently. "You asked me a
week ago, and I said no. You don't ask me to-day, and I say
yes. Such is woman. Better than man, at his worst."

The footman answered the bell. 'For a moment Harriet's
courage failed her before his severe expectancy. "Bring some
biscuits," she said.

"Harriet," began Mynheer Mopius, thoroughly cowed, like
the bully he was, "you must allow at least another month to
intervene before the thing can be even mooted. I always admitted, Harriet, you know, that you were a very good-looking
girl. But, before I say another word, I must insist on you going down on your bended knees and humbly begging my pardon for your disgraceful conduct of the other night."

Harriet Verveen understood the antagonist she had van-
quished. The proud girl actually knelt on the carpet, and
slowly repeated the humiliating words.

"Very good!" said Mynheer Mopius, in high good-humor,
"and, Harriet, I won't marry you till you succeed in matching
that cup you broke." He smiled to himself in the glass, the
future Town Councillor! "You are very poor, Harriet," he
continued, "and of humble origin. It is a great thing for you
to become Madame Mopius. I hope you feel that."

"Oh yes," replied Harriet, meekly. She had got up from

the floor. Meanwhile the footman had brought in a tray of biscuit. She fell on them ravenously.

" Well, Harriet, if ever I make you my wife—and I don't say I shall, mind—I hope you will be a good and obedient consort, like the faithful creature I have lost."

" Oh yes," said Harriet again. Soon after she went back to her lodgings, with a little money in her purse. She turned in the hall door of Villa Blanda.

" Won't I pay you out for this !" she said aloud. Never till the day of her death could she look down at her knees without seeing dust upon them. Mopius had cause to remember his triumph, though she made him a good wife on the whole.

That evening, far into the night, the miserable woman lay at the open window of her garret, with her forehead knocking the sill. Her neighbor, a poor, blind seamstress, sat up in bed trembling, awe-struck by the sobs that seemed to shake the flimsy house. It was winter, bitterly, frostily cold. On the window-sill, bent, pressed back again, clammy with kisses, stuck a stupid bit of pasteboard—the smirking photograph of a man.

CHAPTER XXV

MEANWHILE, untouched by the bustle and slush of the market-town, or the still greater turmoil and filth of its more distant metropolis, the little village and wide demesne of Horstwyk lay serene under their mantle of unsullied snow. Surely each additional myriad of inhabitants deepens the vulgarity of their place of abode, as when ink-drops fall measured into a glass of pure water. The country has its full share of vices —every anchorite's cave has that. The country has snobbishness, perhaps, more than the town. But it has not vulgarity.

Snobbishness, be it observed, is by no means a marked characteristic of the Dutch. There was little of that element in the heart-felt and healthy veneration which the surrounding countryside offered as natural tribute to the lord of the manor. The lord was a legitimate and very actual centre of interest for miles around, radiating wisely diversified influence to all parts of the horizon. Can any thoughtful man dispute that God had willed it so? The pursuit of rank is one thing. Of that the Horstwykers knew very little. The perception of proportion is another; it is still existent, though moribund, because the masses confuse it with humility, or, still more blunderingly, with humiliation. The Horstwykers were not humble—the Dutch peasant is not—but they were self-respecting. It is the man who dearly loves a lord, and can't get near enough, that wants to see him hung up on a lantern-post.

To many hundreds of simple souls the reigning Baron van Helmont was the one visible manifestation of human greatness.

The Divine is intangible, and, at any rate, non-comparable. The gleam of the Horst through its ancestral trees was a daily reminder of Rule.

The change, therefore, in the King one feels—whom we all have, even Emperors—convulsed the whole community, at first, with much more than curiosity. The old Baron had lolled on the throne for so many easy years. The old Baron had never lifted his sceptre. All his influence—great as it was—had been automatic.

Everybody liked him, for he had never, by doing anything, given cause for offence. And everybody liked Gerard, destined, by the very *insouciance* of his open-handed condescension, to conquer all simple hearts. The new lord was an unknown quantity. Men lifted their heads, expectant, not decided as yet in what direction to shake them.

Ursula, of course, they all knew from her infancy, but as one more or less of themselves. She had lived rather a sequestered life, keeping much to herself and to her father; yet they had always benignly approved of the parson's daughter, chiefly on account of her absolute freedom from all forms of assumption and self-assertion, such as clerical womankind too often affects. But, as Baroness van Helmont, her character seemed out of drawing. It must readjust itself to their ideas, if such a thing were ever possible. On the whole, the peasantry of the countryside did not approve of Baron Otto's choice; there was something incongruous in this too human link between earth and heaven. Pharaoh should marry his sister, not his kitchenmaid.

Even the Dominé had felt this, though he knew himself to be a gentleman. Perhaps on that account.

Pharaoh, settling himself in his unaccustomed seat, might well have wished for a Joseph. His predecessor's years had been years of fatness, agricultural prosperity, but there had been no storing in granaries to stint the full-bellied kine. There had been plentitude everywhere, and plenteous hunger. The hunger remained. Pharaoh resolved to be his own Joseph, but, face to face with famine, Joseph comes too late.

By the united assistance of the two old ladies Gerard's claim had been met. The Freule van Borck had been very particular about the legal part and the mortgage, holding long consultations with her notary. In all business matters women, starting

14

from the conviction that their defencelessness is sure to be imposed upon, insist on driving bargains of granitic hardness. When four per cent. represents a fair rate of interest, a woman demands six, ultimately resigning herself to accepting five, because a woman, you know, can't hold out against men, as she querulously tells you ever afterwards. The notary was compelled to restrain the Freule's fervor of self-sacrificial money-getting. As the weeks crept on she became more and more resolved to assist her nephew advantageously. And, when everything had at last been arranged, the estate was left saddled with a heavy annual payment it could barely sustain.

"Never mind," said Otto, looking round on the costly treasures he mightn't sell and didn't want. That had become the brave refrain of his resolve. "Never mind," and then he set his teeth hard. It was very different from the *tout s'arrange* of his race.

He steeled himself, doggedly, and a little dogmatically, to "putting things right." That process, of course, annoys the numerous persons who don't care to be told that things were wrong before. Besides, no adjustment is possible—especially not a rectilinear one—without knocks and shoves in all directions.

First and foremost, Otto had to do battle with his mother. The widow resented as an insult the suggestion that anything could need alteration.

"Things have always been like that in your father's time," she said over and over again. "And, Otto, I cannot understand all this talk of yours about income and expenditure. Of course, people have income and expenditure. Surely your father must have had them, too; but he never worried about them as you do."

Otto knew this. It had been a favorite maxim of his father's—not, perhaps, an altogether incorrect one—that only small incomes need balance to a hair. "Rich men," the Baron used to say, "have other resources besides their revenues."

"But your father always told me that you were a bad manager because over-anxious to be a good one," the Dowager would murmur, querulously. "The excellence of management, he al-

ways said, was moderation, and, dear me, Otto, you manage more
in a month than your father in all his lifetime. But you don't
sell the art collections, mind. They belong to me. Your father always said you would sell them."

She even insisted on finishing the costly decoration of the
west room, to Otto's bitter annoyance. "Would you leave it
unfinished?" she asked, with a flash of her old bright spirit.
It was almost fortunate for Otto that she had never completely
recovered from the shock of her husband's death. For hours
she would sit, silent and motionless, in the boudoir she had
filled with his portraits from all parts of the house. And
when the Baron entered, she would quote his father at him.

"I *will* spend less than my income," repeated Otto, grinding
his heel into the carpet. It sounds easy in a big house, but,
in fact, it is easier in a small one. He retrenched, and made
the whole family most increasingly uncomfortable. When, at
last, he extinguished the great, wasteful fire in the hall, there
was a palace revolution. The butler gave notice. "For I'm
too old," he informed Mynheer the Baron, letting him have
a bit of his mind, "to expose my life at my age in them
draughty passages."

"Very well, go," said Otto, fiercely. But he didn't like it.
The man had been with them for years. The Dowager-
Baroness cried at thought of his leaving. All the servants
looked sullen and demonstratively blue-nosed. For weeks the
new master had been causing them successive annoyance.
Some kind of chivalry taught him to screen his young wife.

"Let me do it, dear," pleaded Ursula, when Otto complained
that he must speak to the cook. "Surely that is my depart-
ment."

"Oh yes, it is," he said, looking out of the window. "Oh
yes."

"Well, then, what has she done? She seems to me a nice,
pleasant-spoken person."

"Oh, they are all that," cried Otto, facing round, with
sudden eloquence. "They are all nice, all pleasant-spoken!
My father's people always were. Imagine, Ursula, that this
woman, whom mamma has had in her service for fifteen years,

daily—mind you, daily—writes down a pound of meat more than the butcher brings, and divides the profits with him!"

"How can she?" objected Ursula, who had not yet got accustomed to a household in which such things were possible, and even proper.

"How? Don't ask me how. I suppose she calls it "perquisites." I met an English marquess once, who told me that in his father's time the annual beer-bill had touched two thousand pounds. His was three hundred. It's all a question of authorizing theft by silence. Keep your fingers off the tap. That's all." He laughed.

"I'll weigh the meat to-morrow myself," cried Ursula, rising already to do it. "That will stop them at once. We weigh it at home; that's to say, Aunt Mopius often does. And I've had to scold Oskamp's boy before. I should never have thought it of Oskamp. I suppose, Otto, your mother never weighs the meat?"

Otto smiled.

"So that will be all right. Don't worry, dear, I'll see to it myself."

"No, I think you had better not," reasoned Otto, gravely. "I—I think I had better do it. My mother, you see, Ursula, will take anything of that kind more easily from me."

He hurt her cruelly, for it was by no means the first time she had thus been checked in the well-meant endeavor to assume her legitimate duties. She turned away in silence, and took up some needle-work.

Somehow he realized, helplessly, that things were again uncomfortable. "My dear child," he explained, "it is only because I am anxious to shield you."

But she stopped him.

"I don't want to be shielded," she said, quickly; "at least, not *always*."

And she beat back her emotion, looking away, with trembling lip.

He stood, uncertain, gazing at her, and his eyes grew half-reproachful.

"Oh, of course, you don't understand!" she exclaimed, un-

"'OH, THEY ARE ALL THAT,' CRIED OTTO, FACING ROUND"

willingly reading his thoughts. "You have married a plaything, Otto. You cannot comprehend my wanting to be a wife."
" My dear child "— he began.
He too constantly called her that. She detested the name. She knew well enough how much he was her elder.
" I am not a child," she cried, passionately. " I am a woman, and your wife."
" Yes," he replied, sternly, reading discontent in her pent-up vehemence, and perhaps a little assumption; "you are now the Baroness van Helmont."
" I am not. I am not!" she cried, recklessly, and dropped her work in her agitation. " I mean I am not that only. I am sick of merely being that. I am your wife, Otto. I have a right to be recognized as such."
Otto paced down the large room and up again.
" I am sorry," he said, stiffly, "that you consider yourself slighted by any one, but I cannot ask my mother to leave the house. There are difficulties, of course, in your position. I am the first to admit them. We all have difficulties. Often they are unavoidable. Yours seem so to me."
She looked at him, her brown eyes dilated with horror; then suddenly, very sweetly, her tenderness flowed across them.
" Oh, Otto," she said, softly, " why do we so constantly misunderstand each other? It is you by whom I want to be recognized as your wife—nobody else !"
Then he caught her to his breast, and kissed her seriously, as they kiss who love deeply, but apart.
" I want to take my share of your work," she continued, caressingly, " and, especially, my share of your worry. I am so tired, Otto, of sitting in the big drawing-room. To you, at *least*, I want not to be ' My Lady Nobody.' I didn't marry you for that."
" What did you marry me for," he questioned, playfully.
" Certainly not for that," she replied, gravely, and the answer fell cold on his heart, for all that it left unsaid. A moment afterwards she added, " Of course, because I love you." She thoughtfully spoke her conscientious verity; but love is quicker than thought.

He left her, with a kind little pat. of encouragement, and she sank down beside the dog, hiding her sunny brown head in the softly responsive fur. She could feel Monk's great heart beating gravely. The room was very large and empty, the house was very large.

Yes, though he did not realize it, Otto van Helmont had married his wife for her face—a sweet apparition, bright and fresh among the home-flowers, a suggestion of the dear father-land, a dream of wholesome Dutch girlhood. He had married for that most unsatisfactory of all reasons: "because he had fallen in love." Not even a fortnight—be it remembered—had elapsed between his first sight of Ursula and their engagement. A man must either know his wife before he learns to love her, or else he must never need to love her, or else he will certainly never learn to know her. That last eventuality, the rarest, is surely the most desirable, but only if the love be mutual, and exceedingly great.

Otto, then, had never penetrated into a character whose reserve was so like his own that he could not understand it. He loved his young wife, and kissed her; and he fancied, like so many men, that his consciousness of loving her was sufficient for all her wants. As for her position in the house, in the family, if it was uncomfortable, could he help that? Was not he himself weighed down by his difficulties, his responsibilities, the worry of universal deepening displeasure? What were the pinpricks she complained of compared to his wounds? Her mamma-in-law was inconsiderate; his mother was unkind. Her dependants were not always courteous, his own people hardened their countenances against him. He could not help thinking that much of her petulant soreness—well, she was young—was provoked by mortification because of the scant dignity or authority her sudden elevation had brought her. Had she not said to him, "I will not be My Lady Nobody; at least, let me not be it to you?"

She was annoyed, then, at being it to him, and to all. The combination vexed her. She had hoped, as My Lady, to be Somebody indeed.

He sighed from irritation. It was not his fault. Yet he was

a little disappointed in Ursula. He had thought hers was an essentially gentle nature, unassuming, unaspiring. Even not desiring to meddle and share in her husband's affairs, because that, for a young girl, is impossible. A thoroughly womanly woman, who cried out in horror at thought of men's work, such as sheep-slaughtering, or of men's play, such as a fox-hunt; a woman who could be tacitly brave, on occasion, able to endure though unable to act. Thus had she revealed herself to him in the week of his swift immersion, his model woman, in a word. That is the worst of tumbling into love. You marry your model woman and have to live with your wife. Now, Ursula was far superior to Otto's ideal. There is nothing more hopeless in human relationships.

He turned impatiently from himself and went down to the room where his bailiff was waiting. All that morning he had been weighed down by the prospect of this interview. No, he was not the man, in his gentleness of heart, to "set things right."

"You can do as you like," he cried, starting up from the other's excuses and tergiversations. "You can go or you can stay. But never again, if I live"—his heart throbbed wildly as he bent that cruel, hated look of his on the sullen retainer— "never again, by God, shall you charge one and eight for a laborer's wages while paying him one and five!"

CHAPTER XXVI

IN the gray loneliness of Ursula's married life there was, however, very little solitude. The house contained too many various elements for that. And county society, which was plentiful, took a great interest in her on account of the romance of her courtship. By the coincidence of the old Baron's immediately subsequent death, she had come face to face with her whole circle of acquaintance, during the days of her début at the Manor-house, through the medium of that most trying of social functions, the visit of condolence. All these people knew her from her birth; many of them called her by her Christian name; it seemed to her, and to them, that she was masquerading. She was nobody's cousin.

And the Matres Familias who looked regretfully at Otto— there were many such—could hardly be expected to 'look benignly on Ursula. But they all patronized her most amiably, and patted her on the back, and showed that they were trying to "make her feel quite like one of us." And Ursula, who could not be unnatural, nevertheless strove hard to be natural— if any one fathoms what is meant by that combination of miseries! The whole lot of them studied her attitude, and compared her with what she was before her marriage, and endeavored to accentuate a difference. One dear old lady told her kindly "that she really did very well." Another took her aside: "Do not be self-conscious, dear Ursula," she said. "Just be yourself, my dear, just as you were formerly. We like you best like that." Surely, there was no cause for the historic Lady Burleigh to "take on" so; before her marriage she had not resided in Stamford-town.

The Dowager-Baroness was far too well-bred to mortify her young rival intentionally; she was far too well-bred not to do so daily without intention. The Dominé's daughter must now take precedence? Impossible. Mevrouw van Helmont retained her seat at the head of her table. The servants came to Mevrouw for orders; not that Ursula cared at all about this, or wished in any way to domineer, but her clear nature shrank from the discomfort of hourly confusion. " Oh, what does it matter !" thought Otto, harassed by the real troubles of his own administration. His wife did not complain to him. She retired to the big drawing-room, with empty hands, and found solace for hours at her beloved piano. It was a superb Steinway grand of the old Baron's buying, very different from the little cottage instrument at the Parsonage. For, years it had been the object of Ursula's secret envy, and now it was the one acquisition she heartily rejoiced in among all the grandeurs of the great house which were not even hers.

" Does Ursula always play the piano ?" asked the Dowager, wearily, when her son came in to visit her. " Did she never do *anything* else in her old home ?"

" She is such a first-rate musician, mamma," apologized Otto. " That requires a great deal of constant practice."

" I suppose so. In my day nobody was a first-rate musician, except the professionals."

" So much has changed," said Otto, patiently.

" Perhaps." The Dowager was making a spring-coat for Plush, what the French call a *demi - saison ;* she laid down the sky-blue scrap upon her heavy crape. " Still, Otto, I wish things could be arranged a little differently. Does it not strike you as rather incongruous, with an eye to the servants and the tradespeople, that this house of mourning should resound with dance-music from daybreak to dark ?"

Otto went to his wife. " I like the playing very much indeed," he said. " But a little solemn music would make a delightful change. Do you always prefer dances, Ursula ?"

" This is a scherzo, Otto, out of one of Beethoven's symphonies."

" Is it ? I wish it sounded a little less—gay."

Ursula struck the piano a violent crash, and then ostentatiously dragged, banging through the same composer's " Marche Funèbre." Towards the end she looked up defiantly at her husband standing in the embrasure of a window with folded arms. Suddenly she broke away from the music, and threw herself on his breast.

" I am sorry," she said.

The Freule van Borck was the member of the household—an unimportant member—who took most interest in the new-comer. Otto's fondness seemed devoid of investigation, like his mother's apathy, but Aunt Louisa looked upon the fresh factor in her old maid's life of fuss-filled monotony as a worthy subject of scientific experiment. Was Ursula—or was she not—*quelqu'un?* That, said the Freule van Borck, is the question.

Louisa van Borck had created for herself a peculiar position in her sister's family. Some twenty years ago her tiresome existence with her old father in the Hague had come suddenly to an end through the conclusive collapse of Mynheer van Borck's financial operations. He was about seventy at the time, and she thirty-eight. She had never wanted to marry, nor had she ever had an opportunity of wanting. Her ambition had always been to live with herself, occupying, enlarging, and fully inhabiting her own little entity, as few of us find time to do. That nothing much came of it was hardly her fault. She had a lot of little fads and fancies with which she dressed up her soul for want of better furniture.

" We must go and live with the Van Helmonts," Louisa had said to her protesting parent. " It is unavoidable."

" But, Louisa, your money, your share of your mother's money—"

" Cannot support us both. Besides, I don't intend to die in a workhouse."

So the old gentleman had to turn his back upon the sweets of the " Residency," and die away into the wilderness. Of course, the Van Helmont's made room for their relatives. " So that's settled," said the lord of the Horst. *Tout s'arrange.* But grandpapa's brain soon got clogged, in the still country atmosphere, from inertia and want of winding up. For many years his body vegetated in an upper room, with an attendant and a box full of toys. Nobody objected to him, nor was any one ever unkind. Besides, he had still his pension of four hundred a year, which made a welcome addition to the family revenues. Yet it was he they regretted mildly when he died.

Freule Louisa could not honestly be accused of unthriftiness. " I know nothing about money matters," she was wont to exclaim, with pink - spotted agitation. " You mustn't talk to me about money. I haven't got any to spend." Nobody knew how much of her private fortune was still in her possession, or how much she had possibly lost by investments. " You will see," Baron Theodore had always prophesied, " Louisa will die a pauper." His wife doubted it.

She had insisted upon making an arrangement with her relations which was especially antipathetic to their temperament. She paid a "pension" price for herself and maid of so much per diem, with deduction of one-half for board during absences of at least a week. In addition to this, she paid for the use of the carriage each time she drove out, according to a scale of her own careful concocting. So much per hour, so much per horse, so much if nobody else went with her. The whole thing was just like a hotel bill, and she enjoyed it immensely. " I am not going to sacrifice my independence," she said. The Baron, of course, considered the business "disgusting "; but he never pushed his objections beyond a certain limit of opposing vehemence. He simply refused to have anything to do with the Freule's laborious computations, and the Baroness was obliged to receive and receipt the monthly payments, which would sometimes remain on a side - table for days. Once or twice a dishonest servant took a gold piece without any one being the wiser.

The Freule did not approve of her sister's domestics. Her own maid was perfection : angular (like herself), middle - aged, cross-eyed, cross-grained, and crossed in love (so she sometimes told Louisa), one of those bony asperities whose every word, like their every contact, cuts. The name this person gloried in was Hephzibah, and she belonged to a religious sect which was

supposed to embrace exclusively the elect, although these, in
the opinion of each individual member, were represented by a
minority numbering one.

Nobody in the house knew half as much about himself or
about any other member of the family as Hephzibah. Her
mind was a daily chronicle up to date, with all the back num-
bers neatly filed. Fortunately, her exceeding taciturnity limited
the circulation.

"Hephzibah, I am watching my niece," the Freule remarked
from time to time. "She has an interesting part to play in the
comedy of life."

"Yes, Freule," replied Hephzibah, who thought life was a
tragedy.

"Will she rise to the height of her position? I love my sister and I love Gerard, but I should like to see Otto conquer
them both, and Ursula conquer all three."

"Yes, Freule," said Hephzibah. She hated the young Baroness, for Ursula had attempted to show kindness to Louisa,
whose forlorn inanity called for pity. The Freule's sharp eyes
were far-sighted and weak; she liked being read to for hours
together, and she frequently complained of her maid's incapacity for pronouncing or punctuating anything, even Dutch.

"*I* will read French to you with pleasure, Aunt Louisa," said
Ursula.

"Oh no, my dear, no." The Freule took her aside in great
agitation. "I could not be so inconsiderate to Hephzibah, I
could not. Oh no."

Still, in a hundred small ways, too wearisome to relate, Ursula
filled up her time with attentions to the little old maid. It was
a relief to find some one she could do something for. She
learned a lot of Rossini's opera airs on purpose, because the
Freule had stated that she "adored Rossini."

"Otto," said the Freule one morning, "I should like to speak
to you."

He stopped, with his hand on the door-knob.

"Yes?" he answered, his thoughts intent on the morning's
disagreeable work.

"Otto, I have considered, and"—the Freule fidgeted—

"under present circumstances I should wish to—pay seven florins more per week for my board." The Freule gasped.

"Why?" asked the Dowager, sharply, from the top of the breakfast-table.

"Don't interfere, Cécile. I see in the paper that prices everywhere are being raised."

"Oh, nonsense," said Otto, turning away.

"Well, I intend to do it, so now you know. And, Cécile, you need not make any difference."

"Difference?"

"Yes, in the menus."

"I should think not, indeed," exclaimed the Dowager.

How difficult is the path of virtue made for most of us by our relations. During the whole of the Freule van Borck's terrestrial pilgrimage she never committed another action worthy to rank with this voluntary conquest of her ruling passion. Yet nobody understood it.

"Van Helmont of the Horst," she said to herself, "shall remain Van Helmont of the Horst." And she deducted the thirty pounds from her already meagre charities.

No one at the Manor-house had ever been prodigal in almsgiving. The old Baron had reckoned the poor a public nuisance; the Baroness provided them with systematically indiscriminate pennies; Gerard flung away an occasional hap-hazard shilling. And the new lord was by no means generally generous. He had very definite ideas on the subject. Charitable help must be strictly limited to the "deserving poor," whatever that may mean—only the deserving, and all the deserving. The word was his shibboleth. On paper it looks exceedingly well.

Also, he never gave money where he could give work, and he never gave work where he could give advice as to work elsewhere. He was forty when enabled and called upon to put into practice his carefully elaborated theories regarding pauperism. All the paupers of the neighborhood, to a man, resented a charity which had lost the charm of the happy-go-lucky. But to no one came more bitter disappointment than to Ursula, o'er the sun of whose crescent benevolence her husband's theories spread in tranquil clouds.

How often had she not pictured to her father the wide use
she would make of an expanded scope and increasing opportunities! Shall we venture to say that the constant thought had
been a comfort, or at least an encouragement, through the
months of her love-making? She had always worked fairly
hard, with her limited means, in her father's parish, nothing ex-
aggerating, and setting nobody down in malice.

"And you will find sympathetic support in your husband,"
declared the Dominé. "I know that he suffers greatly under
his father's bright indifference"—the Dominó sighed—"for
instance as regards the Hemel."

The Hemel—so it is still inappropriately called; the word
means "Heaven"—was at that time a small hamlet outside the
Dominé's jurisdiction which had long been notorious in the
whole province for the wild and profligate character of its con-
sanguineous population. The people were mostly Roman Catholics, but, even had this not been the case, their pastor would
hardly have paid them much attention. He was a very different man from Roderick Rovers. "The poor ye have always
with you," he repeated. And to his colleague he would have
said, "Hands off!" Ursula rejoiced to realize her new position
as lady of the Hemel as well as of the Horst. Oh, the cruel disappointment of discovering that the poor of the Hemel were not
deserving. They were everything and anything but that.

"Be just before you are generous," said Otto. "First, we
must pay our way, dear Ursula, and that, in a landed proprietor's life, includes an immense amount of unconscious, and
even unintentional, philanthropy. What we have left we will
gladly give away, but let us be careful to confine ourselves to
worthy recipients of our bounty."

Never mind, there is plenty of good to be done, as Ursula
knew, without almsgiving.

"I wish you would not go to the Hemel," pleaded Otto in
the face of her efforts; "you would do me a great favor,
Ursula. Mother has so many causes of complaint against me
already, and she is dreadfully afraid of infection. Besides, it is
altogether useless. They only make a fool of you. Nothing
good ever came, or can come, from that horrible place."

"'I SHOULD WISH TO—PAY SEVEN FLORINS MORE PER WEEK'"

So life flowed on at the Horst, for its chatelaine, in a narrow little stream, over rocks, amid a vast splendor of scenery. The Baron, her husband, working day and night in the almost hopeless effort to make both ends meet, waxed sombre and careworn beneath the ever-increasing dislike of his numerous dependants. Towards his wife he was always affectionate, closing the door to his heart-chamber of torture and seeking relaxation as from a beautiful plaything. And Gerard, except for the briefest of visits, remained at Drum.

When the Stork, some twelve months after the old Baron's death, tapped at Ursula's window, her life was no longer empty. Suddenly the Baby filled it to overflowing. Every one manifested an absorbing interest in the Baby, as was his due, even the Freule Louisa, for babies, surely, are vast potentialities. Miss Mopius forgot her slumbering grievances and rubbed the Baby's back with fluid electricity. The Dominé christened his grandchild, wearing his Legion of Honor, as he had done at Ursula's wedding. But the Dowager Baroness very nearly refused to be present at the ceremony, for the heir of the house received the single name of Otto.

CHAPTER XXVII

" How cross he looks !" said the Dominé, benignly, dangling his grandson on one awkward knee. " I believe he disapproves of existence. Do you know, children, it has struck me from the first, I can't understand why your son should have been born with such a look of chronic discontent. What do you mean, Ottochen ?" He shook the morsel of pink-spotted apathy, and laughed innocently at its unconscious sneer.

Involuntarily the parents' eyes met. Otto walked to the window.

" Life is good, Ottochen," continued the Dominé, his eagle face alight with tenderness. " Life is very beautiful. People love each other, and the love falls like a rainbow across every background of cloud. Everything is beautiful, especially the storms." The baby puckered up its face into one of those sudden, apparently causeless fretfulnesses which the masculine mind resents. " Thou wilt grow up," said its grandfather, "into a brave soldier of the Cross "—the Baby overflowed in slobbery, but agonizing, sorrow. Ursula hastily took it from the Dominé's clumsy deprecations.

" It is strange," protested the Dominé, " that we weep most without a reason. When the reason comes we often forget to weep."

This time the elder Otto's eyes remained resolutely fixed on the snow-girt landscape.

" He was frightened," explained the young mother, reproachfully, as she hushed her screaming charge.

" Frightened ! Ah, just so !" The Dominé rose, a warm flush on his face. " That is the cause of most of our sorrow.

Frightened! If men were less afraid of trouble, they would see how little there is of it. Good-bye, children, I am going back to Aunt Josine." And the Dominé marched off, his armless sleeve swinging limp beside his elastic figure.

Otto turned round into the darkened room. It was true the whole atmosphere of the house had long been one of latent worry. He rested his hand silently on Ursula's shoulder, and a great feeling of assuagement spread over both their hearts. The Baby's shrieks were dying down into an exhausted gurgle. Both parents gazed deeply at the child.

"Ursula," said the Baron, presently, "if you feel strong enough, I should like to have one or two people here for Christmas. I should like to invite the Van Helmonts who were so kind to me during my period of hard work at Bois-le-Duc. Theodore van Helmont and his mother. They are our only relations of the name. And I think they have been kept too much out of the family."

"Are they really the only other Van Helmonts besides us?" questioned Ursula.

"Yes," he answered, recoiling hastily, as she had done, from the proximity of his brother's name; "but there is a brand-new Van Helmont now—the heir!" He placed a soft finger against little Otto's bulgy cheek.

"True. How funny! Do you know, I had never thought of it." She colored. "I never think," she added, "of what is so far away as that." She rose and kissed her husband, and held up the child to him.

"Otto," she added, "supposing—if—if there had been no baby, and "— she stopped.

"The Horst would have been sold by auction," he burst in, violently, "two months after my death. Do you think I have ever lost sight of that? All through this anxious year, Ursula, the thought has never let me rest."

The words frightened her. Could anything have brought home more clearly the separation of their lives?

"Theodore van Helmont is a good fellow," Otto went on, "hard-working and honest. I thoroughly respect him. I should like you to know him. But he isn't much to look at."

15

"Why have they never been here before? I don't remember hearing of them till you went to Bois-le-Duc."

"Well, as I tell you, young Theodore isn't much to look at. And my father greatly objected to his cousin's marriage at the time; he never would see him after."

"Whom did he marry?" asked Ursula, looking down into the cradle and readjusting its coverlet. "I mean—*what?*"

"She was a farmer's daughter from the other side of Drum. He picked her up when staying here, some thirty years ago. I remember it quite well. My father was furiously angry."

"And he never forgave the son," mused Ursula, with one finger in her little Otto's clammy clasp. "Not even the son. I thought people always forgave *the son.*"

"I assure you she is quite a nice, motherly person, and so unpretentious. That is what I like in her. It will be a pleasure to have her here, if only mamma consents to put up with her presence. Poor woman, she told me she had never even visited her own relations. I suppose she didn't dare."

"Her own relations," repeated Ursula. "Isn't that a difficulty?"

"I don't see why, if people would only take things simply! She can go to them from here. No one believes more firmly than I do in true nobility, but it is not dependent on surroundings."

She smiled up at him; "Ah, Otto, you say that on account of—me?"

But the suggestion annoyed him with the pain of its voluntary abasement. "The two cases have nothing in common," he said, almost angrily. "If there is a possibility that you or any one else might draw absurd comparisons, I had better give up the idea at once."

"No, no. I shall be glad to have them. Baby must learn to know and be good to all his relations."

"Next year might do for that. But, Ursula, talking of Baby's relations, we might ask your Uncle Mopius and his wife."

"I consider Harriet has behaved disgracefully"— began Ursula.

"Just so; and your uncle enjoys the idea of our being angry

about the money. That's why I want to ask him," he added, proudly.

" Then, Otto, if it is to be a family reunion, should we not "— her voice dropped to a whisper; she fingered a button of his waistcoat—" ask Gerard too ?"

" Yes, we will ask Gerard," he answered, hurriedly, annoyed that she should utter what he had been making up his mind to say. And then he left the room without another word.

Ursula smiled to herself, and immediately began to apostrophize the helpless infant: " And we will have a Christmas-tree, Baby," she said, "and a lot of beautiful lights, Baby. And warm socks and shoes for the babies that haven't got any, Baby. And you shall give blankets and coals to all the old women, Baby."

But even this appalling prospect did not move little Otto. He lay staring steadily, and that constant frown, which his grandfather said he had been born with, wrinkled the raw beefsteak of his unfinished little face.

Meanwhile Otto had gone to tell his mother of the coming festivities. The old Baroness did not seem to pay much attention, immersed as she was in a sort of memoir which she had been recently concocting to the glorification of her departed lord.

" What did you say young Helmont's name was ?" she asked, suddenly, peering over her heavy gold eye-glasses.

" A family name, mamma—Theodore."

" It is an insult," said the Dowager, and her gaze once more fell on the page in front of her.

A fortnight later the various guests had all arrived ; the Dominé greatly approved of their coming. " Let others less favored share your happiness," he said to his daughter. The good Dominé, while constantly eloquent of the battles of life, rejoiced at the peace which he dreamed round about him. Yet he still had " Tante Josine." The light of his life had flitted away to the Manor-house.

Nobody could see Theodore van Helmont and contest the accuracy of Otto's statement that the young post-office clerk

wasn't much to look at. One thing showed very plainly, and
that was his peasant blood. But he made no attempt to hide
it; he had a quiet and unassuming manner, like his lumbersome
mother, and would hardly have attracted attention but for his
peach-like coloring, which made him almost an Albino. He
was awkward in the unaccustomed vicinity of ladies, and spoke
little, dropping away into the shade, unless somebody touched
on his hobby. This no one ever did, except indirectly, for that
hobby was "social science," a number of " ologies " unconnected
with life. His mother often wondered that so good a man could
also be so clever; her own philosophy was of the simplest, all
condensed into one unconscious rule : never to remember an injury, while never letting slip an opportunity of doing a kindness. Her only attitude towards the old Baroness van Helmont
was one of respectful sympathy. Of Tante Louisa she felt
afraid, for Tante Louisa had asked her, on the evening of her
arrival, whether she believed in woman suffrage, and she had
not known what " suffrage " was. The Freule Louisa, it need
hardly be noted, believed in no suffrage at all. " If only we
could stop the million asses' braying," she was wont to remark,
" perhaps we should hear the lion's voice at last." This remark
was not her own. She had got it out of the *Victory*.

The quiet clerk, dull, with comparative content, over a merciful volume of engravings, had pricked up his ears when he
heard the Freule start "a sensible subject." It was small talk
that did for him, reducing his brain to chaos. " The principle
of government by majority," he said, " being once universally
accepted, there appears to be no logical reason for leaving that
majority incomplete."

" Government by majority is a pleonasm," said the Freule,
tatting away. She meant " an anachronism," whatever she may
have meant by that. The young man hastily returned to his
engravings.

" The majority is always wrong," interposed the Dowager
Baroness, very decidedly, " and, therefore, the larger it is the
more wrong it must be." She had remained in the drawing-
room chiefly from disgusted curiosity, and now sat listless, her
delicate face like a sea-shell among her heavy weeds.

"But, Mevrouw," began Theodore again, from a sense of duty.

"Hush, it is certainly so, young man; besides, my husband always said it was. I am so sorry to see a Van Helmont a Radical." Her face flushed impatiently, and, in the awkward silence, Ursula said it was a beautiful starlit night.

"The stars are so pleasant in winter-time, are they not?" remarked Theodore's mother, whose fat hands lay foolishly in her substantial lap; but the Freule van Borck was not going to stand such sentiments as these.

"Oh yes," she said, briskly; "Ursula always notices the weather. Some people do, and never talk of anything else. I wish you would tell me, Mynheer van Helmont—we were discussing the subject the other day—would you rather do wrong that right may ensue, or right for the sake of wrong?" The Freule was very fond of propounding these problems of the "Does-your-mother-like-cheese?" order. Some spinster ladies "affection" them just as *their* spinster aunts used to propose *Bouts Rimés*.

"You must leave me a few moments to consider my answer," replied Theodore, gravely.

This was quite a new experience for the Freule, and hugely delighted her.

"A very sensible young man," she thought. "And you, Gerard?" she asked, turning to her nephew meanwhile.

Gerard had arrived at the Manor-house the day before; it was just about a year since he had last slept in the house, and his mother's heart yearned over him.

"I should do what I liked best," said Gerard, promptly, always pleased to exasperate his aunt.

"Gerard, you have no principle. What does your cousin conclude?"

"Right and wrong, as we refer to them, are such very vague terms, Freule," responded the young clerk, thoughtfully. "But, supposing the words to be used in their absolute sense "—the Freule nodded—"I should do the immediate right."

"Bravo," said Otto's deep voice from a distant sofa. "And now, Ursula, will you give us some music?"

"Oh yes, music," assented Theodore's mother. "I love music. The loveliest organ comes past our house on Fridays. I quite long for Fridays to come round."

The last sentence was addressed to the Dowager, who smiled graciously, for she was watching Gerard.

"My daughter-in-law plays a very great deal," said the Dowager.

But the evening was long. Every one hoped for diversion from the Mopiuses, who were expected on the morrow, and a general yawn of relief hung heavy round the bedroom candles.

"Theodore Helmont is straight right down to the bottom," Otto said to his wife as soon as they were alone. "You see how earnest he is, and how wise. If ever you stand in need of a counsellor, Ursula, I hope you will turn to Theodore. He is one of the few men on whom I could fully rely."

"You are my counsellor," replied Ursula, wishing the words were more widely true.

CHAPTER XXVIII

WHEN the Baronial invitation reached Villa Blanda, Uncle Mopius immediately said "No." He wanted so exceedingly to go that he revolted from himself, and then stuck to his assertion of independence. For, most of all, he wanted not to want to accept.

"We have no need of their patronage," he said, pompously, over his morning paper. "Villa Blanda will cook its own modest Christmas dinner. Ha, ha! I have no notion of sitting down to a coroneted dish containing one skinny fowl."

"What did you say?" asked Harriet, with an affectation of indifference. "Were you speaking to me?"

"My dear, I said we should not accept."

Harriet, who had been trying to make up her mind, was glad of this timely assistance.

"And why not?" she questioned, sharply. "Of course we shall go. What excuse would you give?" She did not wait for his answer. "I don't intend to have Ursula saying I'm afraid of her, or ashamed, because of the money and marrying you. No, indeed; we shall certainly go. Johan must hurry round to the dress-maker's immediately." She stroked her pretty morning-gown. Her dress-maker now was the one who had employed Mademoiselle Adeline.

"Dress-maker!" said Mopius, sharply. "Nonsense, Harriet; you have more dresses already than my first wife wore out in all her life."

"I am going to have two new evening-frocks," replied Harriet, ignoring the reference. "I have no good dinner things. They will have to sit up all night to get them ready." She smiled pleasantly at her own importance.

" We're not going," said Mopius, settling his bull neck into
his shiny collar.

She looked across at him quickly, and again she smiled.

" Yes, we are, because I want to," she said, cruelly, without
a shadow of playfulness. Mopius by this time had resolved
that wild horses should not drag him to the Horst.

A simple Dutchwoman, however, is not a wild horse. Alas,
she is more commonly a jade. Occasionally she is a mule.

Harriet sat down, watching her husband's sullen face. Suddenly, from love of ease, she changed her tone.

" Did he want to stay at home with his own wifie ?" she said,
"like two turtles in a nest. Did he want to have a Christmas-
tree all to themselves, and buy her a lot of lovely presents ?
That was good of him, and his wifie will give him a kiss for it."

In the first months of their married life this tone had been
fairly successful ; it had obtained for her the numerous fineries
of which Jacóbus's soul now repented.

" Stop fooling, Harriet," he now said, most unexpectedly.
" I'm going to remain where I am because I hate dancing at-
tendance on lords and beggarly great people. I'm a rich man,
I am. And besides there's a meeting of the Town Council on
Tuesday."

" Did you hear me suggest," continued Harriet, sweetly, " that
it was my intention to go ?"

" Yes, hold your tongue and attend to your house-keeping.
The beef was underdone yesterday. It never used to be in my
dear departed's time."

" Jacóbus, that is your second allusion this morning to your
dead wife. It marks a new departure, for till now you had
wisely kept her in the background. But I must warn you, once
for all, that I won't stand it. Besides, it's quite useless. Didn't
I know the poor fool ? Wasn't I present at her daily sacrifice ?
I am perfectly aware that she loved you in a different way from
mine. She was like a faithful dog, poor creature, and you led
her a dog's life."

A reproachful tear—not self-reproachful—stood in Mynheer
Mopius's yellow eye.

" Mine is a more natural affection. I love you in a reasonable, matrimonial way. Not only for your gray hairs "—Jacóbus winced—" but also for the comforts of our mutual *entente.* So we shall order two nice new dresses and depart on Tuesday morning."

" Your aunt was a better woman than you, Harriet."

" She was not my aunt; don't call her so. Of course she was much better than I. Had she not been, you would have been a better man."

" I don't understand," said Mynheer Mopius, helplessly, " but I am not going to the Horst."

" *Don't* want to see wheels go round," quoted Harriet, whose course of novel-reading in all languages was very extensive, " but you will, though."

She went over to her writing-table and carefully indited a little note. Jacóbus sat watching her nervously. She closed her envelope and got up without speaking.

" Written to Ursula ?" asked her apprehensive lord.

" Oh dear, no; there's time enough for that. It's a note to Madame Javardy," and she rang the bell. " Take this at once," she said to the servant.

Mynheer Mopius rose on his spindle legs, protuberant and goggling.

" I am master of this house," he began, " and I forbid—"

" Leave the room, Johan," broke in Harriet, with suppressed vehemence; and, turning, as the man obeyed, " Jacóbus," she said, " listen to me for one moment. That man knows you ill-treated your first wife. Everybody in the house knows it, but Drum society doesn't, so you needn't mind. Poor thing, she never told; but I shall, mind you, Mynheer the Town Councillor. If you ill-treat me, I shall cry out—cry out as far as—as Mevrouw Pock, for instance, and leave the rest to her !"

" Ill-treat you, Harriet !" spluttered Mynheer Mopius.

" Yes, ill-treat me. Do you know what they call Mevrouw Pock in Drum ? 'Sister Ann,' because she's always on the lookout for tidings. Mind they don't call you ' Bluebeard' at the Club to-night."

" They'll say : What did you marry me for ?" cried Jacóbus.

" Yes, they will—the women will; but the men will pity me,

because I'm young and good looking, and you're—old, Jacóbus. Oh, don't bother," she went on, hastily ; " I'm sure I make you comfortable enough, and you can have everything you want. Only, I'm not going to put up with being teased out of pure whim, as you used to do. If you've a reason for stopping, I'll stop, but as you've no reason, we go."

She swept to the door.

" Harriet," said Mopius, solemnly ; " this is very wrong. You make scenes, Harriet ; a thing I detest—"

She came back to him.

" Scenes," she repeated. " No, indeed. This is merely a conversation. If we were to have a scene " — her dark eyes flashed—" I think I should beat you, and if we were to have a second, I—I should kill you. But we love each other; pray don't let us have scenes."

She left her consort to preen his ruffled feathers.

Said Harriet on the night of her arrival at the Manor-house :

" I want to speak to you for a moment, Ursula, where nobody can hear us. Come into my room."

Ursula followed, wondering.

Harriet stood by her dressing-table in Madame Javardy's wonderful white cashmere, all embroidery, with silken Edelweiss. She seemed uncertain how to begin.

" Ursula," she said at last, " I suppose you were very angry with me, weren't you, for marrying your Uncle Mopius ?"

" I ?" exclaimed Ursula, in amazement. " No, indeed ; why should I—"

Then she reddened, suddenly understanding.

" Oh, of course, I remember," continued Harriet, " you don't care about money, and all that kind of thing. Still you married Baron van Helmont. Yes, I know ; he's not as old as Mopius. Don't interrupt me. All I wanted to tell you was this : When I married, I looked to my marriage settlements. Your uncle has plenty of money, and I secured a handsome jointure, but, unless I should still have children, the bulk of his property goes to you and your heirs. I told him to make that arrangement and saw to his doing it. *I* don't want money for money's sake, nor more than I'm entitled to. Good-night."

"Good-night," echoed Ursula, and drew hesitatingly nearer.

"Don't," said the bride, holding her aloof. "I'm all right, thanks. What a dear little boy you have! Good-night."

THE brothers got on very well at first; they sat silent or talked about things which interested neither. They were as little as possible alone.

Gradually, however, Gerard's persistent lightheartedness produced the opposite effect of a dead weight on the other man. His very laugh, so easy, so frequent, jarred on Otto's hearing.

"Debt is theft," thought Otto. "How can he find it in his heart to laugh with such debts as his?" And the Baron bent once more, with a resolute sigh, over his weary pile of accounts.

Gerard, meanwhile, was manfully making the best of his return to his old home. He rejoiced to be again among the familiar surroundings, and especially he rejoiced in his mother's company. He spent long hours in her boudoir every morning, helping her with the Memoir, and, therefore, talking much about old times. It was a difficult diversion. He did his very best to laugh.

He also did his very best to make things pleasant with Otto. Towards Ursula he could not but feel differently; he avoided her as much as possible, and she, in her eagerness to conciliate, seemed almost to be laying herself out to please him. Their relations were strained, and everybody noticed it.

"And what do you say to the baby, Gerard?" demanded Aunt Louisa.

"Nothing, aunt. One has to say, 'Tiddie, iddie, too-tums, then,' to babies, or something of that kind, and I don't feel equal to it. I never say anything to babies."

"Ah, but this is *the* baby," retorted the old maid, annoyed. "However, I can understand your not caring much about him; he has definitely put your handsome nose out of joint."

Gerard did not answer, in his sudden distress. And then, that none might harbor such horrible thoughts with any show of reason, he set himself to heroically admiring his little nephew, and the forlornness of his affectionate nature soon facilitated the task. Ursula was delighted at this *rapprochement* on neutral ground. She initiated her brother-in-law into many shades of infant development where the careless observer would merely have seen a blank.

They were together by the cradle in the breakfast-room on the morning of Christmas Eve. There was to be a small dinner-party in the evening, the Christmas Tree for the villagers not taking place till the following day. The Van Trossarts were coming, and Helena Van Troyen with her husband. Helena had written to say that she must bring a German friend of Willie's.

" He is beginning to take notice," said Ursula, for the twentieth time. " Don't you see how he opens and shuts his little fingers ?"

" But he always did that," objected Gerard.

" He did it without any reason," exclaimed the young mother, sagely. " He does it now *when he knows there's something near.*"

Gerard laughed, Ursula laughed also; she was happy in the possession of her husband, of her little son, all the warmth of a woman's home.

In another moment Gerard's face had clouded over. " Ursula," he said, with a violent effort, "there's one thing I *must* ask you. I ought to have asked it a year ago. It's wickedness letting these things rankle. Why did you make trouble between Helena and me ?"

A flood of scarlet poured over her drooping face. She tried to speak, but, for only answer, fresh waves came sweeping up across the dusky damask of her cheeks. She sank down beside the cradle, hiding away from him.

" Can you not guess ?" she whispered—into the baby clothes.

No ; he could not guess. He had already sufficiently wronged Otto with regard to the Adeline business ; all through the year he had striven to convince himself that Mademoiselle Papotier

must have been mistaken. Spoiled. darling of many women as
he undoubtedly was, he had not enough of the coxcomb in him
honestly to believe that this woman had acted solely from pique.
Nor could he have uttered that explanation, though it still
hovered round him.

"Gerard, I knew," said Ursula, so low that he had to bend
over her half-hidden head. "I *knew*. Oh, Gerard, if only you
had married the other one."

Then a long silence arose between them, for Gerard had understood. In the strange bluntness of our world-wide morality
it had never entered into this honorable gentleman's head that
any one could deem Adeline's claim on him an obstacle to his
proper settlement. And now that strange "cussedness," partly
chivalric and modest, which always caused him to blow out the
lights on his brighter side, checked the easy vindication that he
had actually offered marriage to the foolish little dress-maker.
He stood silent and ashamed. Ursula did not lift her face
from the sheltering coverlet.

When at last he spoke it was to say: "In one thing I have
long misjudged you, Ursula. I should like to confess that just
now. I didn't believe you about that stupid rendezvous. I have
admitted to myself since then that you went, as you said, for
another's sake." He understood that Ursula had somehow con-
stituted herself Adeline's protectress. "I want to confess that
just now," he repeated, contritely.

She did not thank him for telling her he no longer thought
her a liar, and worse. "So you believe now," she simply said,
lifting her head at last. "You believe in my honest acceptance
of Otto." Then she rose from the floor, flushed and troubled,
but with a proud curve of her neck.

"Ursula," said the young officer, as much troubled as herself, "I thank God for the lesson you have taught me. I—if
more women thought as you do, we men would be better than
we are." His young face was very solemn, he looked straight
towards her. Unconsciously she laid one hand on the breast
of her little sleeping child, and, with an upward flutter of her
strong brave eyes, held out the other. He took it, hesitated,
and then, stooping, touched it with his lips.

"SHE SANK DOWN BESIDE THE CRADLE, HIDING AWAY FROM HIM"

When he dropped it, there stood Otto, in the doorway, watching them.

He came forward into the room, pretending not to have seen.

" Well, Gerard," he said, with forced geniality, "so here is the heir. Some day I hope this young man will sit in my seat and look after the dear old place better than I do."

Gerard resented the palpable aim of the words.

" Who knows?" he replied, lightly. " He may never have money to keep it up. If he has brothers and sisters, the estate goes to pieces anyhow. What's the use of your struggling and wasting your life for an idea? Why not sell a couple of farms and have done?"

" That's what you would do," said Otto, grimly; "sell the whole thing."

" Yes, I should, if I really wanted the money."

" I know you would," shouted Otto, breaking loose, glad of the pretext. "I know you would, you spendthrift! Spendthrift and profligate, you would do anything—for pleasure."

His eye flashed from one to the other, and Ursula read the flash.

She remained standing quite still, her hand on the baby's coverlet. Gerard shrugged his shoulders. " My dear fellow, don't be so angry. I shall sell nothing," he said, and walked into the adjoining room. Otto, already ashamed of himself, went out by the passage-door.

The baby was fast asleep, breathing heavily. Ursula remained standing still.

The room was very silent. Presently a quick spasm of trembling shook her, and with a frightened glance to right and left, she hurried away down the vestibule, out into the wintry morning.

She ran swiftly along the avenue and turned into the high road, taking the longest route to the village because it had lain straight in front of her. The gaunt ice-rimmed trees in the pallid air swam round about her through a mist of her own creating; the desolate plain, stretching white and cold, seemed to mock her with its snow-bound loneliness. She shuddered as she ran.

Near the turnpike she stopped. She would meet a human being there, the turnpike man. He would touch his cap. Not that. She shrank back.

And in the pause she asked herself where she was going. To her father, of course, home to her father's consistent love—the one thing in this world she could forever rely on. Home, to the old home, to weep out her agony upon one faithful breast.

And even as she pictured to herself for a moment what she would do when she reached the comfort of that embrace, she felt that she could not do it. There are valleys of the shadow through which a true - hearted woman must take her way alone.

She stood, a black speck in the surrounding bleakness. The turnpike man, peeping through his little window by his cosey stove, wondered lazily why she did not come on.

At last she turned, and, slowly retracing her steps, branched off into the park. Her one aspiration now was to get away from all possible contact with sympathy. She went stumbling, as fast as she could, over the uneven, snow-laden ground, deeper, only deeper into the silence of the wood. Her foot caught in invisible roots, she hurt herself without perceiving it. Her eyes were dry and hard, despite the cloud behind them.

Gasping for breath, she sank down in the snow and leaned up against a tree. All around and beyond her was the absolute desertion she had longed for, stretching away in an unending sameness of confused black pillars, whose naked tracery bore the pellucid vault of heaven. The dull glitter, all - pervading, lighted up her forest " sanctuary " ; not a sound was heard, except when, once, a snapped twig came rustling to the ground.

Her husband had doubted her honor. Even supposing he had done so for the moment only, during the briefest flash of thought. What did that matter? He had doubted her. Other words and acts now came falling into their places, deepening an impression never before perceived. She brushed them away indignantly; she wanted none of these. It was enough.

She could never go back to him. How could she see him? How speak to him? How could daily contact be possible between a husband and the wife whom, for one instant only, his thought had sullied? He who thinks thus once may at any hour pollute his thoughts anew. Priest and priestess cannot kneel again in the temple one of them has desecrated; no repentance, no forgiveness can wipe away the stain across the marble god. She hung staring in front of her, and the soaking snow crept upwards on her dress.

She had no wish to do anything tragic, to make any scene or scandal. Only she felt that she *could* not go back to her husband's welcoming smile. It was not the insult to herself, although that drenched her cheek with purple; it was the new horror that had arisen between them as if a toad were seated in his heart. Gerard's wickedness of·loose living was not as bad as this. Oh, men were horrible, horrible!

Something moved on the white ground in front of her, so close that she could not but notice it. A red-breast, half frozen, hopped near in a flutter of perky contemplation, wondering, perhaps, if she was alive. She pitied the poor little forsaken creature, and felt in her pocket, with a sudden movement that scared him, for some morsel of bread which she knew could not possibly be there.

And as she sat, hopelessly waiting, she could not tell for what, the distant boom of the village clock came faintly trembling towards her in one long stroke, the half-hour.

Half-past—what? Previous warnings must have reached her unheard. She looked at her watch. Half-past twelve. And at noon little Otto would have cried out for her, dependent upon his mother for the very flow of his life.

She started to her feet, and commenced running as best she could among the trees. Constantly she stumbled in her haste; once she fell prone into a yielding snowdrift. She hurried on breathlessly—a clearing showed her the house; she rejoiced to see it. How long the time still seemed till she had reached the step! In the hall her husband crossed her path. She shrank

16

aside : the wailing of the child, above the nurse's vain attempts at hushing, already fell upon her ear.

Otto remarked with astonishment the condition she was in, but he said nothing. Gerard's voice could be heard in the distance, amid the clash of billiard balls. He was teaching Harriet to play.

"Go," said Ursula, roughly, to the nurse. She flung to the door of the nursery, and, violently, locked it. Then she took the screaming child to her breast. Her teeth were firm set; her whole face was hard and rigid, but her eyes were very tender.

Half an hour later she went down to lunch. Her guests were talking and laughing. Otto came forward immediately to speak about the afternoon's arrangements. The Van Trossarts must be fetched from the station. The Dowager beckoned her aside.

"My dear," said the Dowager, "the butcher has forgotten the cutlets."

THAT evening every one was to help Ursula in the arrangement of her Christmas entertainment; but, as usual, a couple
of willing spirits did the work, and the rest lounged about and
talked. A big tree had to be decorated, and plenty of useful
presents were awaiting assortment and assignment. This Christmas benefaction had been a long source of tranquil enjoyment
to the young wife through the expectant autumn weeks; she
had made many of the presents herself in the pauses from dain-
tier work. She still endeavored to-night to take an interest in it
all.

Helena Van Troyen was among the lookers-on. She frankly
confessed that she had come to enjoy herself, and as an immediate step towards the attainment of her object, she drew the gentlemen away from the tree and around her. To her husband
she said :

" *You* may help," and Willie walked away laughing. But
the poor relations were Ursula's real adjuvants, delighted to be
useful while finding some occupation for their hands. The son
stood on a ladder half the evening, the mother's dumpy fingers
fashioned innumerable little gold-paper chains. Willie started
a conversation with Harriet Mopius, and was getting on very
well till he unfortunately asked where she lived.

" Why, in Drum !" said Harriet, whereupon Willie felt annoyed.

" Yes, Gerard is my cousin," cried Helena ; " I am delighted
to see him again ! He is an old admirer of mine, an accepted
lover before you were born, Herr Graf !"

She was all a-sparkle in palest pink and diamonds and her

own pearly vivacity. The German beside her bowed solemnly. He was a very big German, five foot eleven by two, padded at the shoulders and pinched everywhere else so as to look twice his original size, like an enormous capital T. Mevrouw van Troyen called him her *cavaliere serviente*, and had naturally brought him to the Horst, with her maid, her King Charles, and her husband.

"You think me a child, Meine Gnädigste," said the German. "Well, so be it. Cupid was ever a child, yet Venus played with him."

"What nonsense," laughed Helena; "but you Germans are all so sentimental; to us it is delightful, by way of change. My cousin is not sentimental; he is charmingly opaque. Come here, Gerard, at once; I want you to make friends with Count Frechenfels."

There was an attempted challenge in her words and manner, as if she called upon her quondam lover to determine how completely the old wound was healed.

But Gerard had no intention of making friends with his belated rival. He disliked the man; he would have disliked him in any case, for, generally speaking, every Dutchman hates every German. The feeling is inborn, and very deeply regrettable, but it has little to do with the more recent annexation scare. Even the most ignorant Hollander must be aware that the near oppressors of his country have ever been, not Germans, but French. Racial discrepancies are at the bottom of the antipathy, accentuated by the irritating manner in which the overgrown young Teuton now often pats his dwarf of an elder brother on the head. The Count had been distributing pats all during dinner.

Gerard found it very hard work to be happy at the Horst. Even his mother had turned against him, worrying him about a subject he conscientiously avoided — his debts. And now Helena began bothering him with a sequel to Finis. He felt Ursula's eyes upon him, as he had felt them all day; they were full of a dumb appeal, he could not tell for what. The eyes did not answer his question.

Their hunted look grew all the more alarmed if he apprôached. Did she already want him to leave the house? And if so, why? His thoughts of Ursula were growing more kindly, more like the old feeling of careless approval. That morning had revealed her to him in quite a new, and very beautiful, light.

"Count Frechenfels is most interesting, Gerard," said Helena. "He was in the Franco-German war, and he has been wounded— everywhere! There was room. My cousin also is a soldier— Herr Graf."

"Ah!" said the Count, through his eye-glass. "Is it you that the Baron was telling me of, who had served with the army of Africa?"

Gerard looked uncomfortable.

"But no, my dear Count," said Helena, laughing; "that was my cousin Ursula's father! Gerard has never killed anything but ladies."

"Ah!" said the German again, in a different tone, and dropped the eye-glass. "La campagne des dames. Well, it is that in which the worst wounds are received."

"My cousin does not think so," murmured Helena, cruel in her coquetry. Gerard's eyes blazed with a quick flash of resent-ment. His sister-in-law had drawn near, from a helpless feeling that she must amuse her guests.

"Ah, yours is a splendid army," continued Helena, provok-ingly. "I don't think I should care to be an officer unless I could be a Prussian. Victorious, irresistible, bronzed, scarred, the cross on your breast—that's a soldier! What's the use of a sword that you never can draw?"

"Come, come, you are too hard on your cousin," said Count Frechenfels, with patronizing complacency. "After all, he can-not help himself. We Germans, also, we do not kill men in times of peace."

"At least not officers!" exclaimed Gerard, breaking loose.

The big Prussian replaced his eye-glass, with silently insolent interrogation.

"You know as well as I, Herr Graf," continued the young Dutchman, hotly, maddened by the other's contempt, "how many privates commit suicide in German barracks, driven to

despair by ill-treatment and blows. This year's official state-
ment "—he turned first to Ursula, then to Helena—"gives the
number at nearly three thousand. Half the truth, as Von
Grietz assured me, not counting those who are killed outright."
"That is not true," said the Count, coldly.
" What?"
"Your authorities are wrong. It is what the Liberals and ·
Socialists say, and that kind of people. And, supposing it
were true! Meine Gnädigste, I had not expected to find a
Radical among your friends."
"You are quarrelling," replied Helena, brusquely. "That is
very stupid, and very bad form. Of course you Prussians are
brutal, Count; we all know that, but it is what we like in you—
at least, we women. In our effete civilization you are deli-
ciouly fresh."
"All I ask is to please," said the Count, with an unpleasant
grin. "I will appear in a wolf's skin, at your command."
"Hush, you will make Gerard jealous! But imagine, Ursula,
in the West of Europe, an officer daring to flog his recalcitrant
men! It only bears out what I was maintaining. These are
warriors: what say you?"
"The Frau Baronin's opinion has weight," smirked the
German, bowing low. "She is the daughter of a hero," and,
perhaps unconsciously; his half-closed eyes stole round to
Gerard.
"I suppose if a man is a soldier, he ought to enjoy fighting,"
admitted Ursula, coming forward. "It seems a strange occupation for a Christian, but my father doesn't agree to that.
You know, Gerard, he always declares if he had two arms he
would be off to Acheen."
"Ah, Acheen!" cried Helena. "Just so; ·that's where you
ought to be, Gerard! and every Dutch officer! That's what I
can never understand. The whole lot of you dawdle about
here in cafés and ball-rooms, and the flag over yonder sustains
defeat after defeat."
"Tell Willie to go," retorted Gerard.
"So I do. And he asks, ' What! go and get killed?' And
I say, ' Exactly.' "

"Meanwhile, it is we who are doing our best to defend your flag," interposed Count Frechenfels. "Your colonial army consists very largely of Germans."

"Then why do you not defend it better?" said Gerard.

The Count shrugged his shoulders. "What will you have? It is not our own."

Gerard turned mutely to Ursula. Her eyes were flashing. "There are brave Dutchmen enough over yonder, Herr Graf!" she exclaimed, "and brave Dutchmen enough here at home, willing and eager to go! All cannot exchange into Indian regiments. Helena, why do you speak so of our soldiers? There is not a nation in Europe has been braver than ours!"

"Ah, bah!" said Helena. "Then why doesn't Gerard go? You yourself said your father would, and he is a clergyman!"

Ursula looked at Gerard. Again that strange alarm came into her eyes, which still shone with indignation.

"I shall not go for your ordering, Helena," answered Gerard, in a burst of almost ill-mannered spite. "Honestly, I attach more importance to Ursula's opinion."

Helena laughed.

"Quite right," she said. "So do I. Only, unfortunately, Ursula agrees with me. Ursula, you shouldn't be afraid to say what you think."

"I?" asked Ursula, proudly. "Yes, I agree with you in one point. I am my father's child. I think every Dutch soldier who can"—she looked steadily away from Gerard—"should help to blot out the disgrace in Acheen."

They were standing in a circle; the German twirled his mustache.

"When I go," said Gerard, softly, "you will have to be very good to the one loving heart I leave behind." And he turned on his heel.

"Ursula," exclaimed Helena, "your evening is decidedly dull. Your relations from Bois-le-Duc are estimable people, but your evening is dull. I think I shall go and help the estimable young man on the ladder. Make him take *me* for the top device of his tree, Herr Graf. Challenge him if he says I am not enough of an angel!"

But other challenges had to be seen to first. Gerard waylaid his antagonist ten minutes later.

"Count Frechenfels," he said, "you have twice called me a coward in the course of this evening."

The Prussian drew himself up.

"And once a liar," continued Gerard.

"I said nothing of the kind," began the Count.   •

"And twice a liar," amended Gerard. "And I hope you will give me an opportunity of proving that I am neither."

"I am at your service," said the Count, stiffly. "You are quite unintelligible to me, but I am fully at your service. I shall ask Mynheer van Troyen to act for me."

He was passing on with another bow.

"Oh, no nonsense about seconds," cried Gerard. "That 'll stop the whole business. I'll arrange with you whatever you want arranged."

The Prussian noble's eyebrows rose in undisguised dismay.

"Mynheer," he cried, "must I teach you the alphabet of honor? A duel without seconds? Am I speaking to an officer and a gentleman? It would be murder. Of course I refuse."

Gerard barred his way, white to the lips.

"Count Frechenfels," he said, gently, "allow *me* to call *you* a coward."

The Prussian stopped, suddenly frozen into bronze. The Iron Cross gleamed, alive, on his breast.

"What do you want of me?" he asked, huskily. "I will shoot you with pleasure whenever and wherever you like."

"Come out to-morrow morning at seven," replied Gerard. "It won't be light sooner. I shall expect you outside. What will you have? Pistols? Swords? Rapiers?"

"Swords," said the German, walking off.

He hurriedly hunted up Willie van Troyen.

"Your younger cousin," he said, "he is—peculiar, is he not? There is a suspicion of mental derangement?"

Willie roared with laughter.

"Gerard?" he cried. "No, indeed! Why he very nearly married my wife."

"A—ah!" said the German, suddenly thoughtful.

Gerard went up-stairs immediately, after a specially tender good-night to "the one loving heart" that would care. He threw open his window, and stood looking out into the frosty night. The Christmas bells came pealing through the stillness. True, it was Christmas Eve.

The bells were ringing their message of peace and good-will. Gerard closed the window again. He had never fought a duel before. He had never been present at one. Duels are as rare in the Netherlands as in England. He wondered how many "encounters" the German had had.

He sat down to make a few farewell arrangements, as is best in such cases. He wrote a long letter to his mother and a short one to Otto. That was all. What did it matter? Even supposing—

He was furious with the weight of his dejection. He hoped that he would kill the Prussian.

At her dressing-room window also, late, stood Ursula, listening to the bells. They had long since ceased to ring, yet still she heard them on the starlit air. "Peace and good-will. Peace and good-will."

Through the open door came the slow rhythm of Otto's breathing. She quailed as it fell on her ear. Nothing could change.

"Glory to God in the Highest," she said, tremulously. And she passed into the other room.

CHAPTER XXXI

BEFORE the house next morning, in the dull gray dawn, the two antagonists met. It was bitterly cold and misty, with that wet frost, all shadow and shiver, that precedes the late wintry sun. Gerard drew his cloak around him as he saluted the Count. Under his arm he held a long green baize bag.

" You still wish it to be swords ?" he asked.

Count Frechenfels waved his hand in haughty acknowledgment.

" Permit me to precede you," said Gerard, gravely.

They walked away into the park with quick, ringing steps. Only once Gerard broke the silence. " Excuse me," he began, looking round, " but I think we had better go some distance. The clash, you know." The German repeated his gesture.

In silence, then, they reached the little clearing which Gerard had selected. Here he paused. As it happened, the place was the same where Ursula had fought her battle the day before. It was a natural halting-place for those who wandered in the wood.

The robin lay stiff and stark with upturned legs. Gerard kicked it aside.

Count Frechenfels looked to right and left. " Your doctor?" he said at last. " Where is your doctor? At least you have arranged for a medical man ?"

" No, indeed ; he would have warned the police," replied Gerard. " What do we want a doctor for ?"

The German hesitated. " But it is murder," he said, half to himself. " No one does such things. Supposing one of us is badly wounded. Mynheer van Helmont, you know that not one man in ten would consent to meet you like this ?"

"I don't care about the other nine," replied Gerard, inconse-
quentially. He threw down his bag. "Count Frechenfels," he
said, "you insulted the Dutch army in my person last night.
There is nothing more to be said."

The Count began to get ready. "So be it," he answered.
He took up one of the swords. "It is the Dutch army we fight
on," he said, significantly. "However this mad affair ends,
that is clearly understood ?"

"Of course," replied Gerard, with some slight wonderment.

"Very well. I am ready, 'Mynheer. This is not a duel, but
a fight!"

In another moment they were clashing at each other amid the
surrounding stillness, their swords ringing in the constant con-
cussion of the parry. The morning as yet was almost too dark
for their object, especially here, under the white-rimmed trees ;
but as the metal shone and flashed in the haze, high over the
combatants' heads the intensity of the moment's expectation
seemed to clear away the mist. A sword duel, even when well
ordered, is always disconcerting because of the noise; in this
case, as the German had remarked, the combat, when it deepened, without umpire or timekeeper, was not a duel but a
fight.

"I shall kill him," thought Gerard, but at the same moment
he felt that this would not be an easy thing to accomplish. It required the utmost vigilance on his part to ward off his enemy's
blows; he found but little opportunity for independent attack ;
he began uncomfortably to realize that the Count was the better
swordsman. Also the Count was the taller of the two—a very
great advantage. Gerard set his teeth hard in the continuous
crash of the other's onslaught. The whole wood seemed listening, holding its already bated breath.

Suddenly—in a flash of lightning, quicker than thought—the
young Dutchman realized that his guard was gone, that his
opponent's sword was upon him, bearing straight down upon his
unprotected head, with the certainty of terrible wounding, the
possibility of death ! With unthinkable swiftness he understood it and even found time—in that hundredth of a second—
to await the inevitable end. In that hundredth of a second,

also, he saw his antagonist swerve aside under the very force of
sweeping downwards, swerve with a sudden slip of his footing,
just enough to cause the aim to diverge, while exposing himself in his turn. In that hundredth of a second Gerard knew,
as it passed, that he had the German in his power, that he, not
the German, was become, by a twist of the wheel, the irresistible victor, that his sword, once more curling aloft, could de-
scend where he chose. And he *did* choose—still in that immeasurable atom of existence — and struck his foeman, not
through the skull, but, with a quick revulsion from murder, in
a hideous long gash across the cheek.

It was over. The Count reeled and recovered himself as
Gerard ran forward to support him. Then, his long passion
grown suddenly cool, with his profusely bleeding victim beside
him, Gerard felt there was nothing left but to avow himself
tardily "an idiot." He looked round desperately for the indis-
pensable assistance he had previously scouted. He would have
called out, but what was the use of calling? Even as he told
himself that it would be utterly useless, he became aware that
his sylvan solitude was not deserted. The figure of a woman,
making towards him, became visible through the trees.

He recognized her with immense relief—only Hephzibah, his
Aunt Louisa's maid. Angular in every fold of her dark stuff
gown and shawl, that cross-grained female approached the little
group in the clearing.

" Help the gentleman to sit down, Jonker," she said, without
looking at Gerard. And she began deftly arranging a bandage
with two spotless pocket-handkerchiefs which she produced
from inner recesses. They were her Sunday handkerchiefs
(ready for the morning's devotional exercises). No cry of an-
guish broke from her as she calmly tore them into strips.

Count Frechenfels watched her skill with evident satisfaction.
After all, why should he let himself be comfortably killed in
contradiction to all the correct rules of carving? He was contented with himself : he had behaved with great magnanimity,
like the " grand seigneur " he was.

" I will go fetch a carriage from the stables," said Gerard.

The woman nodded, engrossed in her work ; when she had

finished, she stood waiting, erect by the wounded man, like a soldier on guard.

It seemed a long time before Gerard returned with the brougham which he had got ready unaided. As Hephzibah established the Count in the carriage, the Jonker turned for one last look at the scene of the combat, wondering whether he could account for that sudden slip of his adversary's to which he felt that he owed his life. Something black in the hard snow caught his eye. He stooped quickly and took up a woman's dark glove, half imbedded and trodden down. The Count's foot must have slid on the soft kid. Gerard thrust the glove into his pocket. One of Hephzibah's squint eyes, at any rate, was fixed on the Count.

A few minutes later the little brougham stopped before the doctor's house in the village street. The village street was empty, blinded, and asleep, yet Gerard, on the box, as he sat amid the jingle of the harness, felt that the dead walls were Argus-eyed, and that his secret was become the world's.

"Good gracious!" squeaked the doctor from his window, in a red nightcap. "Good gracious, Jonker, what has occurred?"

"Nothing of importance," replied the Jonker's loudest tones. "Come down, and I'll tell you."

Curiosity accelerated Dr. Lapperpap's enrobing. Soon he was examining the patient by the light of hastily raised blinds.

"And how did this happen?" asked Dr. Lapperpap.

"I did it," replied Gerard, promptly. "Sword exercise."

The doctor cast a quick glance from his twinkly black eyes. "H'm," he said; "an accident. *Of course.*"

His tone rendered further discussion superfluous. It was arranged that, for the present, the Prussian should remain where he was. Gerard drove Hephzibah back to the Manor House; the good woman despised all pomps and vanities, yet she was by no means insensible to the honors of her position. The Count had presented her with one florin.

Near the avenue she applied the carriage-whistle.

"I will get out here, Jonker, please," she cried; and then, standing in the early snow: "On Christmas morning!" she said, while her whole figure grew heavy with reproach.

"Hephzibah, however did you come to be out in the wood?" asked the Jonker, hastily.

"In their affliction they shall seek me early," replied Hephzibah.

The quotation was inappropriate, for her omnifulgent eyes had watched the gentlemen leave the house, but the sacredness of the words staggered Gerard. He held out a gold piece.

"No, Jonker," said the waiting-woman. "Not from you. Not for this. It would be blood-money." And she marched away, gaunt and grim, down the lines of grim, gaunt elms.

As Gerard came up from the stables to the house he caught sight of Ursula walking on the carriage sweep. For one moment a great impulse came over him to go and ask her why she, as well as Helena, seemed so anxious to have him out of the way. He could understand Helena's feelings—or, at any rate, he thought he could. Well, he had spoiled the German's fine countenance for the remainder of his stay. Count Frechenfels would carry away with him a memento of his visit to the Lowlands.

But what would be the use of worrying Ursula? Gerard hated to make a woman uncomfortable. He had done it already, yesterday—after a full year's hesitation. And she had taught him a lesson he would never forget. How greatly he had wronged this purest among women! Generous natures always own an immense debt of gratitude to those they have wronged.

"Gerard," cried Ursula, "I have dropped a glove. I feel sure I came out with a pair." She held up one for him to see. Gerard had a disastrous weakness for blurting out the very thing he wanted to keep back.

"Not unless you have been in the wood already," he said, producing the missing article, which Ursula, of course, had dropped, not now, but the day before. Then he put it back. "I want you to let me keep this," he added.

Her eyes grew troubled. "Oh, no — no," she protested. "Give it back to me at once!"

"But it can have no real value for you. Whereas, for me" —his voice trembled with the memory of his terrible escape— "let me keep it," he said.

"GERARD THRUST THE GLOVE INTO HIS POCKET"

Ursula knew not what to say or think. Slowly she dropped the remaining glove on the ground at her brother-in-law's feet; slowly she raised her faithful eyes to the level of his own. In that moment, quite unexpectedly, as by a revelation, he saw how very beautiful she was. He stood before her dismayed, his heart full of yesterday's conversation, of this morning's experiences. "Ursula," he stammered, "I—I am going to Acheen— at once!"

"I thank God," she said, with solemn bitterness, and left him.

Meanwhile the wretched husband shrank back behind his dressing-room curtains. It was true that he had begun to spy on his wife. He hated himself for doing it. He despised himself for believing the clear testimony of his eyes.

He went down to breakfast; somebody said he was looking ill. "It is the worry at the close of the year," he told his mother; "this time I can certainly not make both ends meet." Mopius had a business-man's suspicion of financial complications. Under the influence of the sacred season and the baronial splendor around him, he offered his "nephew Otto," just before going to church, a considerable loan, free of interest. The Baron courteously declined it. "If Mopius were but a gentleman!" he reflected, with a sigh.

So the Dominé preached his festival sermon to various inattentive ears. Gerard had disappeared, suddenly recalled to Drum; Helena was wondering what had become of Count Frechenfels. Willie would have been fast asleep but for Aunt Louisa's persistent pokes; the Dowager was trying to remember whether it was in '42 or '43 that her husband had broken his arm out shooting three days before Christmas. "Note," said the Dominé, "that the message of peace is brought by the hosts, that is, armies, of heaven. It is always so in the history of the Church, as of each individual Christian. Nowhere is this truth made more consistently manifest: *Si vis pacem, para bellum*." That was what the peasants of Horstwyk admired most in their pastor. He quoted the New Testament at them in the original Hebrew.

When the service was over, Otto remained behind to speak
to his father-in-law. The preacher's last words still hovered
about the deserted pulpit: "Not till the city has surrendered
does Emmanuel issue his proclamation of peace and good-will."
Otto went into the vestry where the Dominé was resting in his
arm-chair, the Cross showing bright on his ample black gown.

"I can't bear it any longer!" exclaimed Otto. "I must
speak of it to some one. I must speak of it to *you*."

"What is your trouble, my son?" said the Dominé, gently.
"If we confess our sins to each other, it often helps us to confess them to God."

Otto started back. "How do you know that it is a sin?" he
asked.

"Our troubles usually are, are they not?" said the Dominé,
simply.

"It is a sin, and it is not a sin. I cannot resist it. It is
stronger than I."

"I will help you all I can." The Dominé's face grew very
pitiful. "In most of our troubles men can help, God in all."

"But I have proof," cried Otto, hastily. "So much proof—
too much proof. Only listen, father."

He began speaking of his doubts, and the old man shrouded
his face with one hand—his only one—white and transparent.

When Otto ceased speaking, a long silence ensued. At last
the Dominé removed his hand, and Otto stared in horrified
amazement. The minister's clear face had become dark purple;
veins stood out on his forehead which Otto had never perceived
before. He began speaking, in a very low voice, but that
voice also was new to the hearer:

"Go," he said, "I have nothing to answer you."

"But, father," cried Otto, "speak to me. Pity me! For
pity's sake, don't let me lose the only friend I have!"

The Dominé rose to his full height, in his long robes, pointing to the door.

"Go," he repeated. "God forgive you. I cannot. Not at
this moment. *My Ursula!* Go!"

And Otto, stalwart and sunburned, crouched to slink away.

CHAPTER XXXII

THE GREAT PEACE

THE Christmas party at the Manor-house broke up not over-pleasantly. Everybody seemed to realize the vague clouds that hung over the dark end of the year. Some particulars regarding the German visitor's sudden indisposition had, of course, oozed forth into the half-light, bewilderingly indistinct. Helena departed in high dudgeon, frequently repeating to her husband that whatever had happened—and she didn't want to know—was undoubtedly Ursula's fault. Mynheer Mopius said that "the higher classes of this country were hopelessly depraved."

Count Frechenfels slipped away to his native land in silence, and the military authorities took no cognizance of the affray. Of his own free will, therefore, Gerard asked to be transferred to a fighting regiment in the Indies, and very quietly and quickly he got ready to embark. He was eager to go, to escape from duns and the narrowness of his present hampered existence. And also to fly from a vague new sensation which, whenever he turned to it, caused his heart to leap up with dismay.

"I cannot understand why," said the poor Dowager, feebly; "but, somehow, I seem not to be able to understand anything any more. It all used to be so different. Gerard, the whole *world* cannot have altered because your father died?" She gazed at him as if half expecting to hear that it had. "And I wanted you to help me with the Memoir," she continued. "*You* remember about the old, bright days. Otto doesn't know. And now you also are going away."

She began to cry, looking so white and fragile, with the snoring dog upon her lap.

"I couldn't sell your father's collections, Gerard, could I?"

17

she complained. "He wanted me not to. Still "—a long
pause; her face lighted up—"if that would keep you from
going to that horrible place, I—I think I could venture. I
think he would understand if I explained, when we meet again."

"No, no, let me go," said the young man, in a choked voice.
"I shall come back to you, mother, with a 'position.' You
will be proud of me."

The Baroness shook her head.

"I am that already," she said. "It is so uncomfortable
here, I do not wonder you have enough of it. Otto is always
'busy' with 'business,' like a shopkeeper, and Ursula doesn't
even love him."

"Mother!" cried Gerard.

"Not as I understand love—not as I loved your father. But,
as I admitted, I no longer know. Sometimes I think I shall
end like poor grandpapa, my head gets so tired; only I am
still so much younger than he was, Gerard. Oh, Gerard, your
father died too soon! God has been very hard on me. I never
say any clever things now, as I used to do."

In the hall, Gerard, still stunned and heart-sore, was waylaid by Tante Louisa.

"I have got a little present for you," began that lady, in her
most nervous falsetto. "It has cost me a great deal of privation, Gerard. What with the increase of expenses everywhere
—I have twice already felt obliged to raise my 'pension,' although Otto pretends to object—I really can hardly afford it.
But, then, it is a farewell gift."

Gerard took the envelope she proffered him, gratefully, wondering whether it contained ten florins or twenty-five.

"And I should like to say, Gerard," subjoined the Freule in a
flutter, "that I highly approve of your conduct in going, and
also of your fighting the German. He was insufferable. Hephzibah has told nobody but me."

"Hephzibah," said the Freule, in her own room. "In my
youth I could have married a Prussian. We met him at
Schlangenbad. But I loved my country."

Gerard, opening his envelope, extracted a bank-note for one
thousand florins.

When the younger son had sailed away, with his strange new uniform, to the land of falling cocoanuts and cannon-balls, the waves of emotion at the Manor-house settled down into a disagreeable ground-swell. Otto had made up his mind to "forgive and forget," a combination foredoomed to failure; Ursula walked straight on by her husband's side, with a gloved hand in his. It was useless to talk about forgetting. She would never do that. Not as long as a proud woman's heart beat under her wifely bosom. With scrupulous tenderness she smoothed the daily deepening furrows upon the Baron's careworn brow.

And the months passed on, exceedingly like each other, excepting that Baron Otto made himself fresh enemies with every fresh act of justice. He was stern, and, necessarily, stingy. It was true that his honest impulse to discuss his suspicions with Ursula's father had cost him the last friend he possessed in Horstwyk. He clung the more tenaciously to his life's object. And he idolized his child.

On this point, at least, there could be sympathy between husband and wife. Little Otto was querulous over his infantine troubles. He disliked teething, and going to sleep, and cold water, and hot water, and eczema. He did not take kindly to existence. It is that class of children which, universally forsaken, hang on, by the nails, to their parents' hearts. There was no danger of Ursula's heart becoming atrophied. In one thing she did not obey her husband; she slipped in and out among the poor a great deal more than Otto knew.

But, having no money, she came with empty hands, and her visits were rarely appreciated, except by the purely imaginary poor person, who thought a glimpse of her bonnie face better than a sixpence any day.

Winter was coming round again when Otto one morning received a letter from a person who signed herself "Adeline Skiff." The person spoke of great wrongs she had suffered from Gerard, of present distress, and of possible assistance. Otto had never heard of Adeline Skiff, but with his usual thoroughness he took the next train to Drum, and unexpectedly called upon the lady. He knew her again when he saw her, although she was very much changed.

Adeline lived in a blind alley, among odds and ends. She was the only inhabitant who wore a fringe, and this fact afforded her daily satisfaction. Otherwise, her reputation was dubious, and her slovenliness undoubted.

She received the Baron in a small front room, filled by a sewing-machine and two children. She hastened to explain that her husband, who was not over-kind to her, had lost his last place in a lawyer's office on account of his stubborn integrity; she got a little dress-making, not much; she had hoped that Mynheer the Baron might be moved to do something for her or her children. She pushed forward two dirty-faced boys; Otto started, involuntarily, at sight of the elder. Adeline smiled knowingly.

"I cannot verify your story," said Otto.

Adeline looked up quickly. "Can't you, really, Mynheer the Baron?" she retorted.

"And my brother, did he not give you money?"

"Yes, he gave me three thousand florins," replied Adeline, frankly, "and my husband spent them."

"I cannot help that," said Otto.

No, he was not willing to assist her. She appealed but little to his sympathy.

He could not believe she belonged to the "deserving poor," and he told her so. How had she got hold of her worthless husband?

"By advertisement," replied Adeline, offended. "The same way your worthy lady tried to get hers."

"What do you mean? You are insolent," said Otto, haughtily.

"Oh, of course, Mynheer the Baron; poor people always are when they speak the truth. But when the Baroness was advertising for a husband she couldn't be sure that she'd get such a good one as you."

"If you mean anything except insult," said Otto, frowning, "tell me the truth, and I will pay you."

Whereupon Adeline told, with slight embellishment. Ursula had answered advertisements, Gerard's among the number. She had "wanted" a husband. So, of course, she had accepted Otto's proffered hand.

" A *mésalliance* is a mistake, after all. There is something in blood," thought Otto, in the train. He went home quite quietly. But that evening, to Ursula's wonderment, he dropped, for the first time, his good-night kiss.

That year's winter opened dully. Otto had let the shooting; it was a sacrifice of which he could not trust himself to speak. No one came to the house in the absence of battues. Gerard wrote home regular letters to his mother, bright letters, but the Baroness, bored to death, was growing somnolent and slow.

Bad accounts of Gerard—mostly false—occasionally reached the Manor-house. People said he was exceedingly wild and devil-may-care. Rumor told, moreover, that he had got himself entangled, on the journey out, with the governess of an English family.

" Thank God, we have the boy," said Otto.

One evening, late in October, the father came into the nursery, where Ursula was trying to make " Ottochen " balance himself against a chair.

" Ursula," began the Baron, hurriedly, " where have you been this afternoon ?"

Ursula slowly lifted her eyes to his excited face.

" At the ' Hemel,' " she said, firmly. " Vrouw Zaniksen was ill again. And her baby, too. They were absolutely destitute. So I went."

" The baby is dead," burst out Otto. " It is a case of malignant diphtheria. I met the doctor just now. He warned me." The father sprang forward, placing himself between wife and child. " Leave the room !" he cried. " Don't come back to-day. Leave the child to me !" He caught the boy so violently to his breast that Ottochen began to cry. Ursula hurried away, unresisting, with that wail in her ears.

A few hours later, when they were alone together, she said, very meekly, " Forgive me, Otto."

He looked up wearily.

" I forgive you this," he answered. Then, with an effort as of one who breaks through a hedge, " But not," he added, " the having married me when you did not love me."

She was a very proud woman, yet in this moment of his misery she knelt down by his side. "Dear husband," she said, "if I wronged you it was in innocence. How, except by loving, can a woman's heart learn love?"

Otto sighed, crushing down the accusation that she had learned the lesson since, but from another teacher.

"Ursula," he said, "there is a foreboding in my heart to-night of coming trouble. God grant it prove only a foolish fancy. But, if not, then let us at least lighten each other's load. Ursula, look into my eyes. Tell me, dearest, that it is not true, this story of your hunting for a husband, of your marrying me because others had drawn back!"

"It is not true," she said, bitterly, still kneeling, but with scornfully averted glance.

"Tell me it is not true that you have ever loved any one else."

This time she faced him fully. "It is not true," she repeated.

"Ursula, God knows I have never wronged you by a word."

"I have never wronged you by a thought," she answered, rising to her feet, and he felt that, whatever time might alter, one shadow must remain.

"I love you," he said. "I have loved you from the first. I shall always love you through all my weakness and all my wrong."

She put her arm round his neck and kissed him.

Twice during the night Ursula slipped away from her room to listen at the nursery door. She crept back gratefully amid the perfect silence. The slight irritation in her own throat was what people always feel, she told herself, at the bare mention of diphtheria. Yet all next day she kept away from little Otto.

She was sitting at the piano, when her husband came in to her, with a white scare on his bronzed face.

"The child is not well," he said, hoarsely. "I have sent for the doctor."

Ursula started up. "Oh, Otto," she cried, "is it the throat?" Otto nodded. "Then I can go to him," she said, "now," and ran from the room.

The white spots were there; she saw them despite the little creature's struggles, and her heart sank. But she also had a few white spots. There was so much false diphtheria.

The doctor, however, looked grave, and muttered, "Angina pellicularis." He was angry with Ursula. "I shall stay," he said, and she cowered down by the little bed.

Then followed an evening of unbroken anxiety. The child grew rapidly worse, and the parents could do nothing but watch its gaspings. Towards midnight the doctor performed the horrible, unavoidable operation which gave it a little more air.

In the lull of suspense Ursula's gaze fell upon Otto. "And you!" she said, suddenly, "you are ill! You, too! Doctor!"

Otto sank back in responsive collapse.

"It's no use holding out any longer," he panted. "Doctor, I'm afraid there's something wrong with me too."

"Let me look at your throat," said the Doctor, harshly. "Here's a pretty bit of business," he added, turning to Ursula.

Very shortly after there were two sick-rooms opening out of each other, and the whole household trod softly under the near terror of Death. All through the silent morning Ursula passed from bed to bed, her own pain gone, feeling nothing but the dull agony of useless nursing. Hephzibah had quietly installed herself as an assistant. The child's usual attendant was too full of personal alarm. Tante Louisa came to the door with persistent whisper. Miss Mopius left a bottle of fluid electricity and ten globules of *Sympathetico Lob.*

The doctor, who had been away for his rounds, came back in the afternoon and inserted a tube in the father's throat also. Ursula did not dare to question his solemnly sullen face.

One thought seemed chiefly to occupy Otto as he lay choking. He had written on a piece of paper — finding no rest till they gave it to him—the following words : " I must die before the child. Tell the doctor to *make* him live so long. Or kill me. Never Gerard, Ursula. Never, never. You first. For another Helmont !"

She had read the message in her deep distress, and understood it. Dutch law no longer admits entail. If Otto died childless, his mother and brother were his legal heirs. But Ursula would be heir to her *fatherless* son.

She clasped her husband's hand in response to the hunger of his eyes, and when the doctor came she put the question which was straining through them.

" Doctor, he wants me to ask it. If—if this were to be fatal" —she went on bravely—" which do you think—first ?"

" How do I know?" replied Dr. Lapperpap, roughly. " Pray to God for both. Both of them need your prayers."

Once again Otto signified his wish to write, in the short-lived winter day.

" Never Gerard," he scrawled. " You will help. By every means. Only not Gerard. Promise."

She bowed her head, but he pressed his finger on the final word. In his dying eyes there was a passion of eagerness she could not resist. Promise! promise!

" I promise," she said. And it grew slowly dark.

Presently Ursula came through the intervening door into the nursery. Hephzibah looked up.

" Mevrouw," she said, " it's no use trying to deceive you. The baby is dying. It can't last many minutes. It's the Lord's doing. Blessed be the terrible name of the Lord !"

Ursula knelt down and calmly kissed the little congested forehead. What did the danger matter? Perhaps she was courting death.

Then she went back to her husband, and gazed deeply upon his terrible struggle. She could do nothing to help him. But she felt that this agony, also, was approaching its end.

Hephzibah knocked gently. " Mevrouw," she whispered, " Mevrouw, it is over. The poor little thing is at rest."

Some moments elapsed before Ursula appeared. Then her face stood out, in the dusk, hard and set.

" Go down-stairs," she said. " Go away, and leave me alone with my dead." She pushed forth the waiting-woman, and locked the nursery door behind her. For a moment she waited by the cot; then she returned to the inner room. It was now

quite dark. A quick shuffling made itself heard in the passage.
Somebody tried the lock. Ursula took no notice.

Half an hour later she opened the door and passed out into
the hall. An oil-lamp was burning there. She shaded her
eyes from its glare.

On the staircase she met Aunt Louisa. "Come into the
dining-room, aunt," she said. "There is something I must tell
you." She sank down on the nearest chair, by the glitter of
the untouched dinner-table. "Dearest Aunt Louisa," she said,
"you mustn't mind too much. God has taken Otto to Himself.
And—and He has taken baby also."

Aunt Louisa began to cry.

"Don't cry," said Ursula, almost impatiently; "*I* don't cry."

"Otto and baby!" sobbed the Freule—"oh, Ursula, Otto and
baby!"

"Yes, doesn't it seem strange?" said Ursula, staring in front
of her.

After a moment's pause she added, "Aunt Louisa, somebody
must go at once, I suppose, for the doctor, and also for the
notary. Mustn't they?" She went across and rang the bell.

"Anton," she said, "two messengers must be off instantly,
one to the doctor, one to the notary. No time must be lost.
Anton, your master is dead. And the Jonker is dead also."

The man's face grew white, and his eyes overflowed. Ursula
turned hastily away.

The notary was the first to arrive. The widow received him
alone. After the usual preliminaries of condolence he told her
that Otto had left no will.

"I am sure of it," said the notary, "for he talked the matter
over with me. Before the child's birth he was anxious to disinherit the old Baroness, his mother. When I told him that
this would be quite impossible, he said there was no use in his
making a will."

"The Baroness has no claim on the property now," said Ursula. "She is very nearly childish, as you are aware." The
Baroness would mean Gerard.

"If Mynheer the Baron died after your little boy," said the

notary, as gently as he could, "then his mother and brother are his heirs. But, Mevrouw, if the Baron died first, then your little boy inherited the property *at that moment,* and you, being a widow, are the only person entitled to any estate left by your child."

"My husband died first," said Ursula.

Notary Noks rose in his agitation. "Then, madame," he said, "you are the owner of the Manor - house. Henceforth you are the Lady of Horstwyk and the Horst."

Ursula looked into the lawyer's face. "It is an inheritance of debt," she said.

INTRIGUE

"Ursula van Helmont is better," announced Willie, daw-
dling into his wife's boudoir; "they say she will live."
Helena glanced up from her book, not without a slight shade
of impatience.
"Who told you?" she asked. "Will you have some tea?
It's quite cold."
"Much obliged. Oh, everybody told me—they were talking
it over at the Club."
"And supposing she had died," continued Helena, carelessly,
"of this diphtheria or brain fever, or whatever she had, then I
suppose Dominé Rovers would have reigned at the Horst?"
"I suppose so," replied Willie, eating a great hunch of plum-
cake; "but you mustn't ask me, because I don't understand.
However, it's so idiotic that I dare say it's law."
Helena smiled.
"Really, Willie," she said, "you are growing quite intelli-
gent."
"Oh, it's not me," confessed honest Willie. "Everybody
was saying it."
A tinge of disappointment stole over Helena's mobile face.
"And doesn't it seem utterly ridiculous and unjust that if
Ursula Rovers marries again all the Helmont property will go
to that Smith or Jones, or whatever his name may be? It's
shamefully hard on Gerard."
"Of course Ursula will marry again," said Helena. "People
who have been married like that always do."
"Like what?"
"Willie, you are insufferable. Surely, 'le secret d'ennuyer,

c'est de tout demander.' Like that. Neither happily nor un-
happily. They have had a glimpse of possibilities. It is like
gambling without a decisive turn of luck either way ; one goes
on. *I* should marry again."

"If I give you a chance," grinned Willie, who understood
that.

"Which you are not gallant enough to do. Unless you
seriously object, Willie, I should like to go on with my
book."

He walked across and took it out of her hand.
"*La Terre!*" he said. "Really, Nellie, your tastes are cath-
olic."

"Have you read it?" she asked, with a faint blush.

"Yes. Somebody told me it was Zola's dirtiest, so I looked
at it once in a way."

"Ah, there, you see, lies the difference. You read it for the
dirt. Yes, undeniably, Zola is dirty, but he is not immoral.
However, I think he is dull. He photographs caricatures, and
that is in itself absurd. One photographs realities ; caricatures
should be drawn. No, I am not speaking to you, Willie ; I am
speaking to somebody as an audience : one has to sometimes.
I'll throw away this book, if you like." She looked up at her
husband almost entreatingly.

Willie hesitated, standing in the middle of the room.
"Oh no," he said. "After all, it's your business, not mine."

"All right. Don't eat too much cake."

Helena returned to her volume, but not to her reading. Between
her eyes and the printed page there settled, immovable, a vision
of a handsome, animated, angry face, and once more she saw a
blue-paper novel flying into a corner of the room. "No man
that really loves a woman would like to think of her as reading
such a book as that."

She turned away, on her couch, and stared hard at the pink-
embroidered rosebuds on the wall.

"What! Crying?" exclaimed Willie, in great distress, coming round from the window. "Why, Nellie, what's the matter?
Is your toothache bad again?"

"Yes, very bad," she sobbed, breaking down. "Do go, Willie,

and send me Mademoiselle Papotier with the little bottle of laud-
anum."

Mademoiselle Papotier had remained at the Van Trossarts',
but she frequently came to spend a few days with Helena. She
now duly appeared, summoned by loud cries from her host.

"Papotier," said Helena, thoughtfully, "if ever I have a
daughter, I shall not educate her as you educated me."

"That is a reproach, my dear," replied the French governess,
serenely, knitting on steadily with mittened hands.

"No, it is a compliment. You developed the heart. You
did right. But I should kill it."

"My child, I could not have killed your heart; it was too
large." The little old doll laid down her work, to gaze affectionately at her former pupil.

"Why has God sold us to men that we must live with
them?" cried Helena, passionately. "He should have given us
to angels or to brutes. We could have been happy with either
of those."

"Fi, donc, ma chérie," said Mademoiselle. "The good God
knows his business better than you."

"Ah, my dear Papotier, you are an orthodox Christian. You
enjoy all the consolations of religion and neglect all its duties.
It is a very advantageous arrangement to be an orthodox Christian."

"It is," replied the Frenchwoman, with a quick gleam of
malice. "For we Christians, although we do wrong like other
people, at least occasionally have the grace to leave off." She
dropped her eyelids, and her needles clicked.

"Yes, when you are tired of it," retorted Helena, who perfectly understood the allusion to her penchant for her cousin.
"And then your priest gives you absolution. I would not buy
off the flames of hell at the rate of a florin per fagot." She
paused, meditatively. "And feel them burning just the same,"
she added. Then she laughed. "Papot," she said, "you do
not know that I have got a new admirer? No, I do not mean
Willie, though he certainly is more considerate than he used to
be. My admirer is old, and fat, and yellow; his name is Mopius, and he is uncle to the Queen of the Horst. I met him

there the Christmas before last. Him and his — charming young wife."

" Yes ?" assented Mademoiselle, listlessly. " My dear, you have many admirers. Fortunately they are platonic " — she sighed a little sigh—" as were mine."

" This one is obstreperous," persisted Helena, glancing at the clock. " He presented me with a big bouquet last night at the Casino ball, making a fool of me before everybody. And he asked permission to call without his wife. Such things should be done without asking. I am expecting him even now."

" My dear, what will you do with him ?"

" I don't know. Be revenged on him, some time, for last night's *Jocrissiade*."

Mevrouw van Troyen shut down her teapot with a vigorous snap.

" There he is," she said, as the bell rang.

" My dear, your tea is not drinkable."

" What does that matter ? Is it not for an admirer ?"

Mynheer Mopius entered, looking as smart as a blue-speckled yellow waistcoat could make him. His thin hair was observably neat; he bowed off the retreating Papotier with a grace which bespoke his familiarity with the saloons of the aristocracy.

" I am come, Mevrouw," he said to the mistress of the mansion, " to express my condolence. I assure you I felt for you last night."

" Really ? You surprise me," said Helena, meaningly. " Certainly, I deserved your pity. And every one else's. But these mixed entertainments are always a bore."

" I was alluding," replied Mynheer Mopius, solemnly, " to the tragic death of our cousin Otto."

" Oh, were you ? But that's several weeks ago. I don't think I can claim much sympathy on account of the death of my cousins. Please don't, Mynheer Mopius. Besides, he was your nephew—wasn't he ?—so you can condole with yourself."

" He was." Mynheer Mopius thoughtfully stroked his hat. " We are a—kind of connection, Mevrouw."

" Ursula and you ? So I understood," retorted Helena, hastily.

" I hope Mevrouw Mopius is well? It was very kind of her to send me those flowers last night."

" How delicate! How high-bred!" reflected Mopius. " Oh, Mevrouw," he stammered, "it was nothing. The merest trifle—"

" But she must never do it, or anything like it, again."

Mynheer Mopius was doubly charmed. Whenever he made a fool of himself, he was tempted thereto by the belief that ladies found him irresistible. Some few men develop that fancy. Surely, in Mynheer Mopius's case, his first wife was more to blame than he himself.

"The unfading roses are yours," he said, simpering and bowing.

" Have another cup of tea," interrupted Helena, sharply. The old Indian, as we know, was a great connoisseur; he had gulped down two bowls of hot water already, imagining that it would not be proper to refuse. He meekly accepted a third, but its tepid unsavoriness aroused his native assumption.

" If I may make so free," he said, " I should like to ask where you get—ahem!—*this*, Mevrouw "—he tapped his cup— " and what you pay for it?"

" Two and ninepence, I believe," replied the lady, sweetly. " If you wish, I'll ring and ask the cook. I'm glad you like it. There's plenty more."

" Only two and ninepence!" exclaimed Mopius, horror-stricken. " That's the worst of it; you Europeans fancy you can get things without paying for them. I was in the East myself for twenty years; *I* know what good tea is—nobody better. I was famous for my tea at Batavia, Mevrouw, as Mevrouw Steelenaar told me, the Viceroy's wife. ' Mynheer Mopius,' she said to me, ' where do you get this delicious mixture?' But I wouldn't tell her. However, I'll send you some. 'Pon my soul I shall. You shall know what tea is. I'll send you a pound to-morrow. I'll send you ten pounds."

Helena bent forward from her listless couch; a lily of the valley dropped away among the laces of her gown, and Mynheer Mopius caught at it with eager, fat fingers.

" Mynheer, you will send me nothing," said Helena, gravely.

"Did I not make my meaning plain enough just now?" Then, not wishing to go too far, "I cannot receive presents, thank you." And, unconsciously, the twinkle in her angry eyes wandered away to a big portrait of her florid Willie.

"Ah!" said Mopius, and put the lily in his button-hole. He did it fondly, lingeringly. He understood that young husbands are jealous, however unreasonably, of experienced, intelligent men of the world. His manner exasperated her. "I am sorry," he said, flicking the flower. "I should have been only too glad, had there been *anything* I could have done for Mevrouw van Troyen."

Mevrouw van Troyen burst out laughing. "Really?" she cried, "even leaving me when I must go and dress for dinner? Mynheer van Trossart dines with us to-night; he is going to take me to the theatre." She rose.

Mopius rose also, but hung back. "Ah, the Baron van Trossart," he said. "Just so! I am very anxious to make his acquaintance. Some day, perhaps, I hope—" He hesitated, looking wistfully at Helena.

Suddenly his manner, his tone, his expression explained the whole thing to her. It was not her young beauty that had attracted this poor creature. She remembered having heard some one speak of the town-councillor's ambition. There was a vacancy in Parliament—

"You can stay and meet him now, if you like," she said, ungraciously, but grasping at vengeance swift and sure. "Oh yes, he is well enough, thanks; only rather worried about this approaching election for Horstwyk. They can't find, I am told, a desirable candidate."

She paused by the door. One look at Mopius's face was sufficient. "I don't take much interest in politics," she continued; "but, of course, my godfather does. He has so much influence. And he tells me that at Horstwyk they want a moderate man, one that would go down with many of the Clericals—a Conservative, in fact. Such people are so difficult to find nowadays. Everybody is extreme."

"But—but—excuse me," stammered Mopius. "One mo-

ment, I beg. I had always understood that the Baron van
Trossart was a Liberal—"
"A Liberal? Oh, dear, no. He would be a Conservative if
there were any Conservatives left. As it is, he would never
espouse the cause of an extremist. He sympathizes with the
Clericals in many things. And now I must really go up-stairs.
I will send my husband in to amuse you. Don't talk politics to
him, Mynheer Mopius. He knows no more about them than I."*

Mynheer Mopius, left alone, wiped his blotchy, perspiring
forehead. It was a master-stroke to have insinuated himself
thus into the graces of this great lady whom he had been lucky
enough to meet at the Horst. He felt very friendly towards
Ursula.

"Ah, Jacóbus," he said to himself in the glass, " you will be
'high and mighty'† yet." And he smiled at the vanity of
women.

Willie came lounging in obediently, and carried off the worshipful town-councillor to the smoking-room.

"A fine house, Mynheer van Troyen," said the conciliatory
Mopius. " Exceedingly tasteful."

" Oh, it's well enough," assented loose-tongued Willie. " But
the money's my wife's, you know. And, by Jove! don't she
keep it under lock and key !"

Having reached the tether of his conversation, the young officer fell a-yawning, and soon suggested a little quiet écarté.

" There's half an hour more, at least," he said.

Did Mynheer Mopius know the game ? Yes, Mynheer Mopius
had played it twenty years ago in India. Ah, indeed ; they
play for high stakes there ! Willie suggested fifty florins. He
played better than Mynheer Mopius. Twenty years is a long
time. When Baron van Trossart joined the two gentlemen,
Mynheer Mopius had lost five hundred florins, but he found
himself on quite familiar terms with Willie, and in the same

---

* There are three political parties in the Dutch Parliament—the Roman
Catholics, the permanent Liberal majority (who are aggressively anti-relig-
ious), and a small, much-persecuted Protestant remnant. All issues of any
interest are religious. There is no longer a Conservative party.

† Title of Dutch Members of Parliament.

18

room with Baron van Trossart. He bowed pompously, patronizing the man who had just plucked him. " His wife would
have accompanied him," he said, " but that interesting circumstances—" and he smiled knowingly to the great noble before
him, on whose haughty features the look of chronic moroseness
sat so well.

A little preliminary awkwardness was deepened by his praising, all astray, the amiability of the Baron's " charming daughter," but presently the tide flowed swiftly into its preconcert-
ed channel, Helena herself having entered, resplendent with a
couple of diamond stars, to direct its course.

" No, Mynheer van Trossart," said Mopius, nervously hurried,
" I should never feel in sympathy with extremists. What we
need nowadays, as I take it, is moderation, pacification—the old
Conservative spirit, in fact."

" Ah, yes, ah !" said the Baron. He was rather interested in
Mopius, having heard of him as one of those men who are willing and able to spend money in a good cause, if thereby they
can further their own. " Just the person, perhaps, for a candidate," he said to himself.

" Only," continued Mopius, ingenuously, " such people are so
difficult to find. Everybody is extreme, and that frightens off
the undecided voters. Now, I cannot help sympathizing with
the Clericals in many points. We have wronged them. Undoubtedly, we have wronged them. Each man, Mynheer van
Trossart, ought to be permitted to serve God in his own
way."

" Oh, undoubtedly," said the Baron, a little uneasily, nevertheless.

" Personally, for instance, I take a great interest in the movement on behalf of confessional schools. I am speaking, of
course, of private initiative." He hesitated ; Helena nodded encouragement across the Baron's meditative study of his cigar.
" I would go even a little further. I consider that some well-
proportioned concessions — The development of Atheism,
Mynheer van Trossart, is not one that I contemplate with satisfaction."

The Government functionary turned in dismay. " Why,

Mynheer," he exclaimed, "I had been quite given to understand you were a Liberal?"

Helena's voice broke the ensuing silence. "We really must go in to dinner, papa. We shall be late for the theatre. Good-bye, Mr. Mopius; my compliments to Mevrouw!" She took the Baron's arm and drew him away. "I like a fat fool," she said on the stairs; "your lean fool is only half a fool. He can't look the part."

CHAPTER XXXIV

URSULA awoke from a long dream of suffering. The world was very dark all around her, and she strove to lie still. But even while she did so she knew by the steady pulse once more swelling in her brain that the endeavor would prove fruitless. Alive again, she must live.

Her husband and her child were dead. It was she who, despising Otto's fears of infection, had brought death into the house. Something told her that Otto, had he survived, would tacitly have laid the loss of the child at her door. And yet it was impossible to say for certain. Death changes all our perspectives. Ursula's was not a nature to sink away into maudlin self-disparagement. She did not dash the tears from her cheek, but she resolutely lifted her head.

Nothing, however, makes us so tender towards those who loved us as the thought that we have done them irreparable wrong. When Ursula arose from her sick-bed, it was with the firm resolve to honor her husband's memory by the daily sacrifice of her whole self to that which, but for her, might still have been his own life-task. She took up his cross exactly where he had laid it down. That was all she thought of—neither right nor wrong; neither God's providence nor her own unfitness — only to do exactly as Otto would have wished.

"I understand perfectly," she said, sitting, cold, with the blackness of her mourning about her. "I told you at the time, Notary, exactly how it was. There is no ready money—not even enough to pay the death duties. There is nothing except mortgages, the interest on which only hard work can meet."

"'GOOD-BYE, MR. MOPIUS; MY COMPLIMENTS TO MEVROUW!'"

"You will have to sell some of the land," replied the lawyer, hopelessly. "You had better sell the whole place. You can't keep it up, anyhow. Not that present prices will ever pay off the mortgage."

The widow remained silent for a moment; there was little of the "nut-brown" color left in the stately face against the oaken chair. "I shall never sell an inch," she said, at last. "Never, as long as I live."

"That is a long time," retorted the matter-of-fact man of business. "A great deal may happen" — he glanced at his beautiful, beautified client; "meanwhile, everything of value in the house belongs, I understand, to the Dowager Baroness?"

"It does."

"The Dowager Baroness, it appears to me, if I may venture to say so, is lapsing into second childhood."

No answer. The room was very lofty and empty. The far stretch of naked country was very chill and bleak. The Notary got up to go.

"If I were you," he said, "I should rid myself of the whole thing. I should decline to inherit. It's a hopeless thing from the outset. Gerard will have his mother's fortune to himself now, some day. He is all the better off for having missed the dead weight which has fallen on to your shoulders. It was a narrow squeak."

She came up to him—quite suddenly, close. "You think that," she said, with thick utterance. "You understand that. Always remember it. Do you hear?" A clear passion had overflowed the dull dark of her eyes. Violently she mastered the trembling which shook her from head to foot.

"Of course, my dear lady; it is evident. Your brother-in-law could hardly have sold the property as you will. Yes, yes, as you will. Never mind; take your time. It is an experiment."

"No," she said, "it is not an experiment. Good-day."

Notary Noks considered himself a very shrewd man. He perfectly comprehended the young Baroness's resolution to play the fine lady as long as she was able. "She's been dem lucky," reflected the lawyer as he drove away; " but she'll have to marry again, and marry money if she wants to keep on. It's a queer end of the Van Helmonts." He had known the pastor's girl ever since she was a baby ; his opinion of the proud, pale woman from whom he had just come away was distinctly unfavorable.

Ursula passed through the long, gray library, and, drawing a curtain, softly entered the old Baroness's rose-garlanded sanctum.

Through the south turret window the sunlight lay in an amber bar. And, incased in the clear gold, like a fly, sat the little black Dowager, surrounded by her papers, writing with the serene concentration of a well-defined literary task. She looked up across her glasses, pen in hand.

" I am busy," she said, her tone full of mild annoyance. She was always busy, the more so when Ursula disturbed her—endlessly busy with the " Memoir," noting down the same trifles over and over again.

" I know," replied Ursula, meekly ; " but I thought you would like to have this, so I brought it you out of the hall."

It was a letter from Gerard, away in Acheen, the first response to the more explicit account of their common bereavement, coming back to them across the wide void of five months' illness and solitude.

The Dowager tore open the envelope. Ursula waited, uncertain how to give least offence.

" There is a message for you," said the Dowager when she had finished reading; " but I shall not give it you. It is an absurd message. It is an absurd letter in many ways. Poor Gerard, his sorrows have turned his brain. Like mine. Like mine. Like mine."

She gathered together her papers, aimlessly, scattering them as she took them up.

" Stay with me, Ursula," she said, querulously. " I have nobody to help me with these important documents. There must be a letter somewhere dated August the 5th, 1854. Or is it April —April, '45 ? It is a letter from a friend of your father-in-law;

I forget his name. I had it a moment ago. Or was it yester-day I had it? I was reading it to cook. *She* remembers things. She has been with me a long time. She remembers my dear husband quite well."

"I will look for it," said Ursula, taking care not to disturb Plush, who always made a bed for herself in the very midst of the crackly confusion on the table. "Is this it?"

"No, indeed," replied the Baroness, without glancing up to verify her verdict. "You don't know, Ursula. You are a new-comer. Cook is right, though I told her some things are best left unsaid."

She went on folding and sorting, muttering to herself with a quiet little lady-like laugh.

"Gerard is ridiculous," she presently broke out, with angry energy. "He says he would have had to sell the place as well as you must now, so where's the difference? He is a fool. He would not have had to sell it, no more than Otto. Did Otto want to sell it, Ursula?"

She sat back in her chair, glowering with her light blue eyes at her daughter-in-law.

"No," said Ursula, bending low over the writing-table.

"Aha! I thought you would try to deceive me. I forget a good many things, but I remember this. Do you hear me, daughter-in-law? I have never loved you ; I had little reason to."

Her voice rose shrill with quavery passion ; she tried to steady her feeble little frame with blue-veined hands on the massive arms of her chair.

"But what does Gerard mean when he says—what does he say?—I forget—he says I must be kind to you. What does he mean? I have always been kind to you. But what right had you—better have plain speaking—to come and steal away my house from my son? Eh?" She started to her feet ; the dog, disturbed by her cry, sprang up, barking furiously. "What right?" she repeated. "It is Gerard's—I told him so. I told him to come and take it away from you. He writes back, 'No.' He is a coward—a coward as they all are, for a woman's face."

She sank back, whispering the final sentences, and began to cry, with noiseless, unrestrained tears.

"Dear mamma, we will not sell it," pleaded Ursula, though she knew how uselessly. "You see, Gerard says again he would have done so. Let us be glad, then, that he has not got it yet. Perhaps, some day, when he thinks differently—meanwhile—in—trust—"

She stopped, not daring, nor caring, to proceed. But the Dowager had only caught at one sentence.

"No, we will not sell it," she repeated: "no, indeed. Attempt such a thing and I appeal to the police! *You* sell what belongs to another! You! Listen, Ursula. I am not as strong as I was. I forget things. I dare say you imagine I am growing childish. But be sure of this: that however stupid I may seem to become, I shall always know about the Horst. I shall watch over it for Gerard. I have written to him to come back, and he will come. You alter nothing—do you understand? Nothing. Oh, my God, I am a poor defenceless old woman! Have pity upon me, and make my head keep strong! Oh, if Theodore had only not died—not died! Oh, my God, my God!"

She shrank together, like a lace shawl thrown aside, and the tears trickled down among the trinkets of her watch-chain.

Ursula rose and went out into the deserted corridor. From one of the stands by the distant hall-door a brown-tinged "Maréchal Niel" fell to pieces with a heavy thud on the marble pavement.

"Monk!" cried the mistress of the mansion. "Monk!"

With great yelps of greeting the St. Bernard came bounding towards her.

EVER since Otto's sudden death the Freule Louisa had felt stirred to practical philanthropy. Something about "redeeming the time" had got wedged in one of her ears. With her own fair hand she had concocted during Ursula's long illness uneatable messes for the invalid, and, mindful of the poor thing's former overtures to herself, she had very nearly brought on a recurrence of delirium by insisting on reading Carlyle's *French Revolution* at the bedside. Routed by the doctor, she had extended her uncertain assistance to the village ; but her efforts were much hampered by the steadfast resolution that neither personally, nor through the medium of her maid, would she incur any risk of infection. When the turnpike-woman's little boy went up to the Manor-house for a promised bottle of wine the Freule rolled it across to him, her smelling-bottle held tight to her nostrils, over the broad slab before the open door. And somehow the little boy was awkward or frightened, and the bottle rolled away down the steps in crimson splashes and a puddle. All the village heard the story with a burst of derisive reproach. " Which seeing it was after *confinement*," said the bottle-nosed turnpike-man, " a thing about which the Freule couldn't be expected to know."

" You can never be quite sure with these people, Hephzibah," explained Freule Louisa, anxiously. " There is always a possibility of your catching something they haven't got."

" What you catch soonest is what you can't catch afterwards," replied Hephzibah, who meant fleas. Personally, the handmaid had a weakness for domiciliary visits, which afforded her an agreeable opportunity of telling the people of her own class — her inferiors, as she called them — how entirely they themselves were to blame for any misfortunes they might happen to have had.

On the gusty day which brought Gerard's letter the Freule, accompanied by her faithful attendant, had departed to the Parsonage. Every Wednesday afternoon through the silent winter months the "ladies" of the village met in Josine's drawing-room, and sewed innumerable nondescript garments for tropical converts from nudity to the inspiring strains of long-drawn letters monotonous with sickness and privation. Of this little Horstwyk Society the Freule from the Manor-house was Honorary President. It had taken to itself the appellation "Tryphena, Rom. xvi. 12," and had gloriously fought and conquered the opposition "Tryphosa" which the doctor's wife had rashly started—without Honorary President, but with a mission-field that could boast two genuine murders. Some of the Tryphena people rather regretted the annihilation of Tryphosa. It had formed such a fruitful theme when the missionary letters gave out.

"My dear Josine, I have got a most interesting report," said the Freule, eagerly, taking off her heavy boots in the little Parsonage passage. The President and Secretary hated each other like poison. "The man at Palempilibang has lost two more children from dysentery—isn't it dreadful?—and his wife has been so very bad they will have to take her up to a hill station for change of air."

"I cannot understand it," argued Josine, as they advanced to join the others; "I packed plenty of medicine in the box we sent out last Christmas. I wrote to Leipsic on purpose so as to make sure it should be genuine. And with me, when I have symptoms, Sympathetico—"

"My dear, I should not imagine it of any use in actual disease," replied the Freule, hurriedly taking refuge from her own temerity in the bosom of "Tryphena."

"Ladies, I have a most interesting report for this day's meeting," she began, with the common eagerness to promulgate calamity. "I shall not spoil it by picking out the best bits beforehand, but I must just tell you, because you will be so sorry to hear it, that Jobson, of Palempilibang, has lost two of his remaining seven children from dysentery, and his wife is so exceedingly weak the doctor says she cannot remain at the station. Isn't it very, very sad ? Ah, Juffrouw Pink, I am glad to see your cold is better."

All the ladies looked at each other, and nodded sympathetically. The Freule's news was quite in keeping with the ancient order of things. " Out yonder " was very far away, and people always died there. When they died you had a vague conception that you were getting your money's worth. Juffrouw Pink, the very fat wife of a church-warden, and a recent member, sat helplessly entangling the fateful disease, in her woolly mind, with the crime of Non-conformity. Mevrouw Noks, the notary's angular consort, laid down the little garment she had been engaged on.

"So *that* will no longer be necessary," she said, deliberately. Josine, who liked to be noticeably sentimental, murmured, " Fie !"

Meanwhile, Hephzibah, in the kitchen, was overawing the little Parsonage maid. But the thing was easy, soon effected, oft repeated, and she yearned for bolder game. Presently the drawing-room bell rang, and Hephzibah rose, aware that her weekly deliverance was come.

Every Wednesday afternoon the Freule Louisa would check the Secretary's report-droning to remark, " My dear secretary, I am sure you will excuse me, but might I ring just one moment for my maid ?" Somebody would, of course, hasten to comply with the noble President's request—the interruption was far from unwelcome to the gossip-loving community — and the Freule Louisa would compliment herself on again having invented a pretext to make sure of Hephzibah's obedience to orders. Practically, the pretexts were but three : a handkerchief from the winter mantle, a forgotten letter for the post, and the drying of the Freule's boots. And Hephzibah, having made her cross-grained appearance, immediately sallied out on errands of her own. For the Freule never rang twice — lest she should make the discovery she dreaded.

Hephzibah was not afraid of dirt or disease. Both she knew

to be the outcome of human wickedness, and with human wickedness Hephzibah Botster had little to do. She feared only
one thing in this world, or the other world, the Intangible—con-
solidated and incorporated for her in a great overshadowing
conception—the Devil. Hephzibah believed overwhelmingly in
the Devil. Her existence was full of him. And therefore,
strong-minded saint though she was, she did not like to find
herself alone in the dark.

As a rule, she spent her Wednesday afternoons with Klomp,
the lazy proprietor of the tumble-down cottage in Horstwyk
wood. Klomp was what she chose to call "a sort of a distant
connection of hers," he being disreputable, and a cousin-german.
This disreputable man she had, however, made up her mind to
marry, for her chances were infinitesimal, and she felt that the
tidying him up would be a glory and a joy.

As she now went zigzagging along the road, crooked in feature
and movement, through the sloppy haze of dull-brown bareness,
she came across a shy urchin who was gathering forbidden
firewood. Him she immediately accosted, like the Bumble
she was.

"Do you know, you boy, who comes for children that steal?"

"Jesus," stammered the frightened culprit, giving the invariable answer of all Dutch children to any question that
savors of the Sunday-school.

"The Devil! The Devil! The Devil!" reiterated Hephzibah, with impressive vociferation. "Do you understand me?
The Devil." She attempted, ignoring physical impossibilities,
to fix both her eyes in one soul-searching stare. But the little
boy lifted his own pale-blue orbs in saucer-sized reproach.

"It's very wrong to swear," he said, gravely.

So Hephzibah continued her way, for "Answer not a fool,"
she reflected, "according to his folly." She saw, through the
gaunt glitter of the trees, Klomp's half-detached shutters hanging forlorn. She wondered who had opened them on this usually deserted side. Certainly not Klomp. She smiled grimly.
She would put things to rights, as was her custom, and scold
him.

She heard voices inside the house, an unknown woman's

"'DO YOU KNOW, YOU BOY, WHO COMES FOR CHILDREN THAT STEAL?'"

voice, and laughter—actually laughter from Klomp, whose utmost exertion in her presence hardly attained to a smile. She pushed open the door and entered, indignant. Some chipped crockery was spread over the crippled table, and behind an odorous paraffine-stove and coffee-pot sat a frowzy female of spurious pretensions to elegance—a female with whom Hephzibah was not acquainted, but whose name was Adeline Skiff. The virtuous Abigail immediately wrote down the stranger "a bad lot," and less virtue would have sufficed thus correctly to apprise her.

"Company ! Dearie me !" cried Hephzibah, in a whole gamut of spinsterly suspicion. "And where, pray, are Pietje and Mietje, John ?"

Klomp yawned.

" Wednesday, is it ?" he said. " So much the worse." After which uncourteous allusion he subsided.

" Let me introduce myself to the lady," interposed Adeline, all mince and simper. " I am a cousin of Mynheer Klomp's, and I have come to stay with him for a week or two."

" Cousin !" repeated Hephzibah, in a tone of flat denial. She stalked to the table, and sat down square. " Now, John, I'm a distant connection of yours, and I know all about your family. And what cousin may you be, mum, pray, and on which side ?"

" Oh, I never can remember those genesises !" cried Adeline, with a charming laugh, as she hastened to arrange her fringe.

" Dirty hands !" reflected Hephzibah.

" My name is Botster," she said, aloud, "and one thing I know for certain, madame, that you never were a cousin of mine."

Adeline looked suprised at this open aggression ; but Adeline had never liked disagreeables of any kind.

" Have some coffee ?" she asked. " There is a little—a little taste from the coating of the coffee-pot, whatever it may be, that gives quite a peculiar flavor, as I was just telling Klomp."

She laughed again, and the sluggard smiled contentedly.

" Oh, nobody ever rinses it out," he said. " I boiled some ratsbane in it the other day."

Adeline shrieked.

"Of course, you are a stickler for neatness, Juffrouw—Juffrouw?" cried Hephzibah, furiously, letting one of her eyes travel down the soiled ribbons of the visitor's tawdry dress. "I like people to be tidy, not like you, Cousin John. Cleanliness is a great virtue, Juffrouw. Perhaps you know it is placed next to godliness."

"Yes, I see it is," replied Adeline, with a gesture of sudden malice—"sitting side by side."

To such levity Hephzibah could allow no recognition. She was burning to find out the intruder's name, and, after some futile strategy, which deepened the mystery, she boldly demanded it.

"Why, Klomp," replied Adeline—"Klomp, of course. Isn't it, Cousin John?" She winked at Hephzibah's relation impudently.

"I don't believe it," said Hephzibah.

"Well, if it isn't, I'll make it so. Some day, perhaps, I'll tell you more, and some day, perhaps, I sha'n't. If you were going to have a new white dress, what color would you have it trimmed?"

"If I, or any other decent person of our class, were going to have a white dress, it would be a night-dress," retorted Hephzibah, "and she wouldn't have it trimmed at all."

At this Adeline giggled and Hephzibah glared.

"Any one can see," said Juffrouw Skiff, "that you're a thrifty body and don't waste your money on personal adornment. Married, I dare say, ch?—ah?—and a large family to look after."

Both Klomp and Adeline roared.

"I'm maid at the Manor-house," said honest Hephzibah, proudly ; "own maid to the Freule van Borck."

"You don't say so!" Adeline's manner had grown suddenly serious. "Now that's a remarkable coincidence. I'm very much interested in your Manor-house, Juffrouw Potster. I know your people."

"Really?" replied Hephzibah, politely. "I don't remember seeing you at any of our dinners. Did you come alone, or did you bring your cousin Klomp?"

This time Adeline flushed scarlet, but she was resolved to avoid a quarrel with a servant from the Horst. Deserted, for the time at least, by her husband, she had heard of Ursula's great good-fortune, and had made up her mind to come and find out some means of extorting money from the Helmonts. Her plan of campaign was as yet undetermined; meanwhile she had taken the cheapest of lodgings with Klomp, who was, of course, in no wise a relation. "It will look better to say we are connected," she had suggested, intent upon "keeping dark" at first. "You can have the room for ninepence," had been Klomp's only reply. "No attendance, mind."

She now got up and walked to the window, with a glance at her reflection against the greasy pane. "There are your girls, Klomp," she said, "with the child. The poor darling can never have enough of that dear little porker. Hear him shriek with delight. Are *you* fond of children, Juffrouw Boster?"

Klomp sauntered out to his affectionate Pietje and Mietje, now strapping young women, both. Immediately Hephzibah came up behind the smiling stranger by the open door. She had not much time to lose.

"Look here, you!" she said, hoarsely. "What have you come here for? After no good, I'll be bound. But you leave this man, mind you. Cousin or no cousin, he's my man, not yours." She was desperate at the thought of her lessening only chance.

The other turned tauntingly in the doorway.

"Your man?" she repeated. "What d'ye mean? Can't you take a joke, you fool? You don't imagine, do you, that I want to marry Klomp?"

Hephzibah shivered with horror and spite. Visions of King Solomon's impudent-faced fair ones rose up before her. "Jezebel," she said, inconsistently, but with commendable candor.

"Tut, tut!" answered Adeline, looking away. "Your dress is a shocking bad fit. I'll alter it for you. I had no idea you came here courting, Juffrouw Boster—and in such a dress as that!"

Hephzibah longed to strike the woman, but she only stupidly repeated, "What did you come for?" amid the laughter and

cries of the others close by. Then suddenly she stamped her
foot.

"Go away, or I'll make you."

"You!" retorted Adeline, fairly roused. "What next, you
Poster? Know that you are speaking to your betters. Imagine the insolence of it! I and Klomp! I! The insolence of
it! Klomp and you; yes, that is another matter. Here, Baby!
Baby!" A sudden resolve seemed to seize upon her. Her little
boy of some three or four raw summers came unwillingly towards
the house, diverted from his course by continual grabs at the
porker's wispy tail. "Do you see this child?" asked Adeline,
catching hold of a faded blue mantle, and turning up a pretty
though mealy little face. "This is my child, my only one."
She had shrewdly left the infant at Drum.

Hephzibah started, and vainly pretended to have slipped.
"Well?" she said.

"His name is Gerard."

Slowly the faithful servant lifted her crossed eyes to the
other's better-favored face. "Hussy!" she said, deliberately,
with all an honest woman's slow pressure on the term.

Adeline burned with the immediate umbrage of a girl who
feels her ears boxed. At a leap she resolved to rejoice in the
rôle which had long allured her.

"Menial," she said, loftily, "know your place. You are speaking to Mevrouw van Helmont."

"Well," reflected Hephzibah, pausing for breath on her hurried walk back to the Parsonage, "I am glad that I *told* her she
was a liar. Still—"

Queer stories about the Jonker Gerard had been rife in the
servants' hall. The domestics of the Trossart household had
added their occasional items. It was pretty well known that
Helena would have married her cousin but for some sudden impediment. Judging by appearances and gossip, there was nothing absolutely improbable in Adeline's story. In fact, Adeline
very nearly believed it herself. Hephzibah wished that vigorous denial could prove it untrue.

And then the child! Hephzibah screwed her wrinkled

face up till it looked like an enormous spider. That woman Lady of the Manor! *That* woman! Hephzibah shook her head as she hurried along. "Who is thine handmaid," she said, aloud, "that she should do this thing?"

She was late, and she found the Freule waiting, shawled and gaitered and exceedingly nervous, in the dim drawing-room, amid driblets of unwilling conversation with Juffrouw Josine. Louisa looked vehement reproaches, and longed for courage to speak them; but Hephzibah was too violently excited by her afternoon's adventure to notice such trifles as these. The pair marched off through the damp twilight.

"Red Riding-hood and the Wolf," said Josine.

"Hephzibah," began the Freule presently, in a trembling voice, "I wish you would walk on the other side of the road. One can't tell where you may have been."

Hephzibah obeyed with silent protest.

"Hephzibah," hazarded the Freule a few minutes later, unable to bear any longer the gray atmosphere of disapproval, "what is this terrible secret you said you would tell me the other day? You have alluded to it several times lately, and always declared you dared not mention it in the house. Well, we are alone now, on the road."

"Oh, it's of no account," muttered Hephzibah. "And I couldn't shout it across, besides," she added, in a lower key.

"Well, come a little nearer, if you like, but not nearer, mind you, than the middle."

"It's nothing," said the maid, gruffly.

"Oh, but it is. Coming out, you told me it was most important. Now, Hephzibah, you are in a bad temper because your conscience reproves you."

"My conscience!" exclaimed the immaculate maid. "My conscience reproves me a hundred times a day!"

"So much the better. Then tell me your secret."

A struggle was going on in the handmaid's bosom. She prolonged it for some distance, perhaps unnecessarily; but then she rather enjoyed a moral struggle. At last she said, in a dull, dissembling voice:

19

"I'm sure now, Freule, that Anne Mary steals cook's perquisites.   I can prove it."

"Pooh!   Is that all?" cried the disappointed Freule. "You've talked about that before, and I don't care a brass farthing, Hephzibah.   A nice secret to make secrets of!   Go along to the other side of the road—do!"

Hephzibah obeyed, looking very wise.

"SUPPOSING I had told my secret?" reflected Hephzibah, peeping through the key-hole. "Supposing I had told my secret? If I hadn't met that woman at Klomp's I believe I really should have told the Freule this time. Wonderful are the ways of Providence! Imagine the slatternly creature established here at the Manor-house playing the mistress over—*me!*" Hephzibah peeped down again. "She in there's bad enough, the parson's daughter. But at least she leaves a body alone." Then Hephzibah shuffled away on velvet slippers, the only soft thing about her.

The key-hole which had attracted her was Ursula's. My Lady sat at her nightly task by the lamp. Her forefinger was inked, her earnest forehead was puckered, yet the figures would not add up right. She was learning book-keeping by double entry; twice a week a master came from Drum.

She sighed, and pushed her hand in among her rumpled hair. Romance is romance; alas, that in real life it should so seldom be romantic! There was less money even than in Otto's time. Therefore, things went even worse with everybody than they had gone in Otto's time. She sighed, returning to her distasteful task.

All the villagers disliked her, and she knew it. They considered it a slight upon themselves that their parson's daughter should usurp, by a fluke, the ancient throne of the Van Helmonts.

Ursula would not have minded this, however, had she known how to pay her succession duty and make both ends meet.

As she sat thus, working and worrying, the door was suddenly thrown wide open, and, without any warning, Hephzibah walked in.

Her face shone white; her whole manner and expression were as of one sick with alarm.

"Come up-stairs, Mevrouw," she said, in a shrill whisper; and when Ursula hesitated she caught her by the sleeve. "Come up-stairs," she reiterated, leading the way, but refusing any further explanation. Ursula mechanically followed. Gasping for breath, the woman ran along a dim corridor, and then stopped in the dark of an unused room.

"Hark!" she said, with uplifted finger.

"What?" answered Ursula, impatiently. "I hear nothing. Do you?"

For only answer Hephzibah passed behind her and closed the door, through which a faint glimmer of light had come stealing. They were then in absolute darkness.

"Well, what now? What is the matter?" repeated the young Baroness, with some anxiety in her tone. In the obscurity she yet perceived that Hephzibah had uplifted a finger.

"Hush!" said the maid. "You will hear it presently. There! There it is!" She bent forward, clutching at her companion. "There it is! What do you say now?"

Ursula fell back and tore open the door again, but the light thus admitted only showed looming shapes.

"I hear nothing," she said, faintly, dazed, alone with this mad-woman. She had always had an undefined dread of the crooked-eyed maid.

"Oh, my God, I had an idea that if you came it would stop!" cried Hephzibah. "Oh, never mind the door. Door or no door, it won't stop now. I've heard it before, several times. It's like a man gasping. In there." She pointed to the closed entrance leading to an inner chamber. "Mevrouw, dare you really say you hear nothing at all?"

Ursula shuddered. They were standing in the deserted nursery; the room adjoining was that in which Otto had died. Both were now disused.

"Come, Hephzibah," she said, soothingly. "There is nothing here; you are mistaken. Come down-stairs. You are dis-

"'COME UP-STAIRS,' SHE REITERATED"

tressed, poor thing, by the terrible memory of your nursing in this very room. Do not think of it. I cannot trust my own thoughts to dwell on those days."

But the waiting-woman took no heed. She had fallen on her knees, and remained thus, her face averted towards the closed door of the inner chamber.

"O God, have mercy!" she wailed. "*She* doesn't hear it! What have *I* done? If I have done wrong, my fault is as nothing compared to her sin! She must hear it. Surely she must hear it." She paused a moment, and in a calmer tone, "It isn't fair," she said.

Ursula had clutched her by the shoulder.

"What do you mean? What do you know?" asked Ursula, resolutely.

Still the woman did not seem to hear her.

"Hush!" said Hephzibah, falling, with uplifted finger, into her earlier attitude of intentness. "Listen. A sobbing, choking noise, as of a man gasping for breath. I often hear it there. Not always. If I always heard it it might be fancy."

"What do you know?" repeated Ursula, with persistent stress.

Hephzibah hesitated. Before her rose the image of Adeline, fringe and all, giving orders in the store-room. She turned suddenly.

"Know, Mevrouw?" she said. "What should I know? A great deal less than you, anyway. I'm only a poor servant. I suppose it's some of Satan's doing. Ah, he's mighty strong, is Satan—mighty strong!" She slipped away towards the glimmer from the passage, muttering, "Mighty, mighty strong," and so stole from the room.

Ursula made no effort to retain her. The door fell to, and the black silence seemed to thicken. Ursula stood quite still. Involuntarily she listened, scornful of herself. Something creaked in the next room, or near her—her heart leaped into her throat. With an exclamation of impatience she threw open the intervening door.

She had not entered these two death-chambers since her illness. The inner one was empty and damply chill. Here the shutters were thrown back, and through the gaunt window a bluish grayness fell across the deeper dark. Ursula's figure struck against the dim twilight in a great black bar.

After a moment's hesitation she walked to the window and gazed up into the night. Amid a confusion of tumbled clouds an occasional star lay peeping, like a diamond through black lace. One of them, close above her, seemed to be watching steadily.

"Otto," said Ursula, in a firm whisper, "I am doing my best. I am trying to keep my promise. I don't know how God judges me. I don't know. Otto, I am doing my best."

She stood for some time thinking. Then she shivered, as if suddenly realizing the clammy cold all about her, and hurried away.

In the corridor, just as the cheerful lamplight was broadening to greet her, she met Aunt Louisa, who emerged in a great hurry from her own private sitting-room. Aunt Louisa was evidently in one of her "sinful fits," as Hephzibah called them. (Hephzibah called "sinful" whatever was distasteful to herself.) The Freule's left hand held a letter, and her right hand an envelope. She cried out as soon as she caught sight of Ursula:

"Ursula, I *must* have my interest! I didn't ask you back for the capital—not even when Otto died. But, Ursula, I must have my interest."

Ursula paused. The Freule's whole face quivered with pink excitement. Both her extended hands shook.

"I don't understand, Aunt Louisa!" said Ursula, dizzily. "What is it?"

"Now, Ursula, don't say that. You know how nervous money matters make me. And I'm afraid it was very foolish of me to give my money to Otto, and I didn't ask it back, not even when you got it all."

"It's a good mortgage," interrupted Ursula, "and, besides, you couldn't ask it back."

"Now don't throw those law terms at my head," cried the Freule, in a tremulous screech, "for I don't know what they mean. But I do know that it's very ungrateful of you to speak like that, Ursula, after what I've done for you all. And I left the money in your hands because I think you are strong, and altogether it is a very interesting experiment. But I must have my interest. I can't do without my interest. Here's my man of business writes that Noks has prepared him "—the Freule referred to the paper which crackled between her fingers—"for the possibility of there being some delay in the payment of the next instalment. Now, Ursula, I pay my board and wages punctually, and I can't have that."

"When is the next payment due?" asked Ursula.

"On the first of next month. Now, Ursula, don't look like that. It is you who are to blame, not I. Never have I been twenty-four hours too late, though poor Theodore used to leave the money lying about for days. But your mother-in-law once truly said that, at any rate, you had this of royalty about you— you could do no wrong! Well, *that* is strong, and I have no objection. By-the-bye, your mother-in-law meant it ironically. But strong people should, above all, be honest, Ursula, and it's dishonest to take advantage of the helplessness of a poor ignorant spinster like me."

"You will have your interest," said Ursula, by the stair-head, under the full glare of the lamp. "Noks was wrong." And she went slowly down into the vestibule. She felt that she must get away for the moment from this suffocating house.

She took a hat and passed forth into the night. A cold little wind was curling in and out among the trees. Everywhere spread the grimness, the bare, black hardness of March, shrouded in darkness and indistinctly threatening. Ursula's yearning went out, in this absolute solitude, to the husband whose strong love had lifted her up and placed her thus terribly high. Even a servant still heard his voice in its dying agony. Had she, then, the wife, already forgotten him? No, indeed; more closely than during his lifetime their existences were interwoven in her faithful fulfilment of his charge. She was possessed with a sudden foolish desire to hear that kind voice, that earnest voice again—aye, even the last gasp, as did Hephzibah. She hurried in the direction of the church-yard, of the vault where *he* lay. He had loved her—loved her, lifted her up—the simple village girl— to be my Lady Nobody. She wanted him again. She wanted him.

All at once, as she was hastening on, the memory struck her, like a new thought, of how he had doubted her honor. She stopped, stock-still, in the middle of the road. Then, like a smitten flower from the stem, she dropped by the side of a broad elm-tree, and for the first time since her widowhood gave way to a passion of tears.

"What's this?" said a rough voice, close in front, and a dark lantern flashed out its hideous wide circle. "What are you doing here? Now, then, look sharp!"

The Baroness staggered to her feet.

"It is I," she stammered—"Mevrouw van Helmont;" and then, recognizing the local policeman, "I am not well, Juffers; help me home."

The man escorted her in amazed if deferential silence. He could understand even a Baroness being suddenly taken ill, but he could not understand a Baroness being out there alone at this time of night. It was not difficult for her to read his thoughts as he tramped on, lantern in hand; she gladly dismissed him, with an unwisely large gratuity, as soon as the lights of the house came in sight.

"Well!" he mused, standing, clumsily respectful, with the broad silver piece on his open palm, "she isn't too ill to walk, anyway. Straight as a dart. Blest if I didn't think it was Tipsy Liza! I wish that *she'd* march as easy when I takes her to the lock-up."

Hephzibah came forward as the young Baroness entered the house. With unusual politeness, but with averted eyes, she took that lady's hat. And Ursula, returning to her room, where her copy-books lay patiently, painfully waiting, felt that henceforth she was, more or less, in this silent servant's power.

"I will go on," she said, doggedly, settling down to "debtor" and "creditor," "with God's help or without."

NEXT day, the spring weather being mild and clawless, like a couchant cat, Mynheer Mopius arrived at Horstwyk station. He wore a silk' neckerchief and new galoshes, for Harriet was a careful wife to him in a way. He had not felt in good health of late, and his leathery cheek had deepened to gamboge.

" Be very cautious what you eat, Jacóbus," Harriet had said as he was preparing to depart. " If you partake of anything greasy, you are sure to be ill again."

" I don't care," replied Jacóbus, recklessly. " I'd rather die than not eat. What's the use of living if there's nothing left to live for? I'd rather die at once than vegetate for thirty years on slops. Pass me the pickles. I could wager that you make believe I'm the baby that hasn't come !"

Harriet smiled thinly. The greatest disappointment which can befall a woman lay upon her. Stowed away up-stairs were a pink berceaunette and a quantity of little garments that had never been used.

" There's not much chance of my getting rich food at the Horst," continued Mopius. " Ha! See? I should think they weigh out their butter there."

" Poor Ursula !" said Harriet, softly. After a few moments of silence, she added, " It was such a pretty little boy."

" Huh ?"

" Jacóbus, how late will you want the carriage ?"

" I sha'n't want the carriage."

" Not want the carriage ?" Harriet well knew how he enjoyed driving away from the railway station amid an admiring crowd of acquaintances who walked.

"No, I shall come home on foot. Go you for a drive, Harriet; it's rather a nice day. It 'll put some color in your pale cheeks."

She looked across at him gratefully.

"Law!" he said, "to think how you've gone off of late. Who'd have thought it? You were a deuced fine woman, Harriet, in days gone by."

"Oh, I'm a fine woman yet," she answered. "You must leave me a little time." She got up and walked to the window. "Willem is waiting," she said. "Good-bye. Mind you don't sit in a draught."

Upon arriving at Horstwyk, Mopius went straight to the Parsonage, whence he could most conveniently order a fly for the Horst. The Dominé came out into the garden, and gave his brother-in-law a hearty greeting. Nevertheless, he hastened to cut off any risk of a tête-à-tête.

"Josine will be delighted," he said. "Let us go in to her. We have not seen you for a long time, Jacóbus. Not since—" The Dominé threw open the sitting-room door.

"Not since the funeral," supplemented Jacóbus, standing in the middle of the floor. "Ah, that was a very sad business. Good-morning, Josine." He shook his head mournfully. Jacóbus was of opinion that social events should be made to yield their full meed of emotional enjoyment.

"Ah me!" replied Miss Mopius, heaving an enormous sigh. The whole apartment was littered with varicolored tissue-paper in sheets and strips and snippets. Miss Mopius was fabricating artificial flowers. Her whole face assumed an expression of deeply dejected resignation.

"How do you do, Jacóbus?" she said. "I am glad to see you. I hope you are better. Sad, indeed. Did you say 'sad'?"

"I did," responded her brother, sitting down.

"Some people say 'sad,'" explained Josine, in the same tone of aggrieved acquiescence, "and some people say 'bad.' I say 'bad.'"

The Dominé, who had remained standing near, emitted what sounded like a slight grunt of impatience.

"Yes, Roderigue, you may object," continued Miss Mopius, carefully studying the pink paper frill between her delicate fingers, "but nothing will deter me from doing my duty. And it is my duty to point out distinctly that our dear Ursula has committed what I do not hesitate to qualify as a *crime*. It may be painful to you as a father—"

"Oh no, not any longer," interrupted the Dominé.

"I am inexpressibly grieved to hear you say so. But it is all the more incumbent upon me to show that I, at least, am not blinded by affection—or, let me openly declare, by prejudice. I am devotedly attached to my niece, but, as I regretfully confessed to Mevrouw Noks, and—and one or two other people, with tears—aye, with tears I said it"—Miss Mopius selected a wire and planted it in the heart of her flower—"dear Otto was murdered ; inadvertently, of course, yet none the less wilfully murdered." She shut her thin lips with a snap, and twirled a wisp of green paper round the wire.

"The weather is nice and mild," said Mopius, "and for the time of year I should call it seasonable."

"I notice an occasional crocus," said the Dominé.

"He deserved a better fate," said Josine.

She shook her red ringlets and put up a thin hand to her head. "My heart aches," she said, "to think how easily it might all have been avoided. Ursula was a child. Poor Otto ! he wanted a woman of more experience—not a plaything, but a helpmate. He might have lived forty years longer. Ah, he deserved—"

"You," interrupted Jacóbus, fiercely, with a sneer, his habitual form of humor. She bored him.

Miss Mopius rose to the occasion. Slowly she smoothed out her crimson-figured wrapper. "Yes," she said. "Me, if you like, or any other woman past thirty. Jacóbus, you are unkind. Now you are here, you might as well give me some money for 'Tryphena.' We are sending out a box. I am making these flowers for it."

"Flowers !" growled Mopius. "What—to sell ?"

"No, no—to send. Freule Louisa has knitted seventy-three little tippets for the school-children—that's the useful part, Jacó-

bus. And I make these flowers for their Christmas treat—
that's the ornamental. I must admit," cried Josine, with a simper, "that I *always* prefer the ornamental !"

" Where's your missions?" queried Mopius. "I dare say
they've got flowers enough out there. Better than those." He
contemptuously pointed a fat finger at a whole cluster of bright-
colored balls.

" In Borneo, Jacóbus, among the wild Dajaks, the head-hun-
ters, Jacóbus." She rested her work in her lap. "So you despise my poor flowers? They will have, I feel confident, their
message to those savage hearts."

" Bosh !" said Jacóbus.

" What, do you not believe in the civilizing influences of refinement?" Josine spoke with sudden asperity. "What are
you but a Dajak?"—Jacóbus lifted his big bald head indignantly—"as the President of the Missionary Conference so
beautifully said—"

" I? What does he mean? Who talked about me?" burst
in Jacóbus, furiously. "If my candidature for Parliament ex-
poses me—"

" You, I, everybody. What are we but Dajaks clothed and
in our right minds? I feel confident that when the innocent
children hang up my roses on the rude walls of their dwellings,
their fathers will take down the hideous heads of victims which
now form their only decoration. Jacóbus, could *you* leave a
rosebud lying next to a skull ?"

" Josine, you're a fool," answered Jacóbus. "I wonder how
Roderick can find patience to live with you."

The Dominé sighed, then coughed hastily, blushing.

" What do the city missionaries say?" persisted Miss Mopius,
who was accustomed to having the last word: "'Beautify the
home,' 'Put up a picture in your room.' Mine is the same
principle. Jacóbus, after thus rudely abusing me, you might
give me a contribution."

" Oh, well—there !" replied Jacóbus, fingering out a gold
piece from his waistcoat-pocket. "But I don't believe in missionaries. They're all dashed nonsense and lies."

The Dominé started by the window, like a war-horse that

hears the bugle-call. "Don't say that, Jacóbus," he interposed. "You shouldn't say that."

"Shouldn't? Shouldn't? I know more about missionaries than you do. A set of guzzling do-nothings, living on the money of silly spinsters like her." He pointed to his sister, who immediately put her hand to her head.

"You forget that I also have seen something of heathen countries," replied the Dominé, with somewhat heightened intonation; "and I, who was then a soldier of the sword, I delight to pay my tribute of humblest admiration to the soldiers of the Cross. Theirs is a certain daily sacrifice without possibility of fame or reward; and you, Jacóbus — forgive me that I say it—you people who have gone in search of money, where they go in search of souls, you, on your return, should at least have the grace to be silent about their occasional delinquencies, as they are about your continuous atrocities. Of course I am speaking collectively. I have not the slightest intention to insinuate—"

"Abuse Josine," cried Jacóbus, floundering to his feet; "I see my cab has come. Begad! why don't you pitch into Josine?"

"Josine is a woman," replied the Dominé, shamefacedly, following his retreating brother-in-law down the passage. "I always feel that we are at a great disadvantage with regard to the gentler sex, though I freely admit that Josine—"

"Well, you needn't work your steam off on me, and that when I so seldom come to see you! By Jove! it's too bad. Look here, Rovers, I am going on to Ursula. I wanted to have spoken to you about serious matters, instead of wasting my time on missionaries. You know, I'm the Radical candidate for Horstwyk. Of course you'll support me, and Ursula will take her cue from you."

"I have no politics," replied the Dominé, resting his armless sleeve on the gate-post; "and Ursula will judge for herself."

"You mean to oppose me?" cried Jacóbus, suddenly filling the fly-window with his big orange face.

"No; I never vote—I do not consider it a part of a pastor's work. But I certainly shall not influence Ursula."

"Oh, be hanged to you!" retorted Mopius, immensely put out. "But I'll undertake to manage Ursula without any influence of yours. Drive on, coachman—to the Horst."

The Dominé crept away to his sanctum with slow shakes of the head. He reflected that Mopius might have been right about "letting off the steam." But what can one do? Has Pericles not said that, "He who knows a thing to be right, but does not clearly explain it, is no better than he who does not know." Again the Dominé shook his head, and, with a mechanical glance at the foxed engraving of Havelock, he hurried to his easy-chair and his Bible.

Mopius meanwhile was hastening to his second and far more important interview. Gradually his ruffled feathers smoothed down, and he smiled with a certain complacence. Rovers had always been a wrong-headed fellow, and therefore obstinate. "Head-strong and head-wrong" was a favorite formula with Mopius, who, of course, considered himself to be neither. He had disapproved of Mary's marriage, although not knowing Captain Rovers at the time. Mary was handsome, he said, and might have done better. Besides, some exceptionally important people disapprove of all their relations' marriages on principle.

Mopius was now the official candidate of the Radical party. He had explained that he was uncle to the Baroness van Helmont of the Horst, and everybody had immediately understood his fitness for the post he coveted. For the influence of the Lady of the Manor must be all-decisive. It wanted but a word passed round to the◦ tenants, and the election was secure. Was Mynheer Mopius assured of his niece's support? So many of these high-born ladies had a weakness for religion. It was old-fashioned, of course, and the worse for wear, but they inherited it, like the family jewels, or gout.

Mynheer Mopius shrewdly closed his eyelids. The movement was eloquent of quiet strength. If that was all they wanted, he could set them at rest. He had his little plan.

Well, that was all they wanted. He need only bring them a signed declaration from Ursula, and they would recognize him. So he started for the Horst to fetch it. Meanwhile—

such things leak out — he was practically their candidate already.

Only the Baron van Trossart had been disagreeable and exacting. But he was notoriously an ill-tempered man. He had muttered stupid insinuations about wolves in sheep's clothing. And he had finally insisted upon a written obligation from Mopius—"quite between you and me, of course"—that the latter would always and unconditionally vote with the Liberal party.

"Why, of course, Mynheer the Baron," Jacóbus had said, eagerly. "You must have misunderstood me when we met in Mynheer van Troyen's smoking-room. 'Always and unconditionally vote with the Liberal party.' Where shall I sign it? I have not the slightest objection. You will support me, I hope?"

"Yes, and be damned to you," said the Baron van Trossart.

When Mopius arrived at the Manor-house Ursula was again closeted with the notary. She rose with a swift impulse of relief as soon as her uncle's name reached her ear. She looked harassed. "You must excuse me, Mynheer Noks," she said, going to the door. "We can talk it over again another time."

"When?" said the notary.

"One of these days. To-morrow, perhaps. No, the day after." The notary followed her, inflexible.

"Mevrouw," he said, "we can't put off quarter-day. There is the interest, and there is that bill I spoke of. Three thousand florins are still wanting to make up the sum. In ten days' time you *must* have them."

"Must!" repeated Ursula, haughtily, drawing herself up.

"Yes. Must. It's not my 'must,' but the law's. The law knows nothing of great ladies. High or low, must is must." Ah, thought the irritated notary, Mejuffrouw Rovers, I had you there!

"Mynheer Noks, I cannot keep my uncle waiting."

Mopius was standing in the small drawing-room with the Guicciardi ceiling, his fishy eyes unappreciatively fixed on a Florentine inlaid cabinet full of cameos and signets.

"A lot of money here," he said, by way of greeting, as Ursula entered. "And what rubbish outside a museum! Why, my terra-cottas at Blanda are ten times as effective."

"The things belong to the Dowager Baroness," replied Ursula.

"Why, you're the Dowager Baroness now, ain't you?" objected Mopius. "Harriet said so when we sent our cards. Who'd have thought it of Mary's child? Not that I care a brass farthing for barons or princes of any kind. You couldn't make a greater mistake, Ursula, than to imagine that I felt in any way proud about your elevation; so don't ever come offering to do *me* any service of any kind."

"It is the last thing I should wish to do," replied Ursula. "Won't you sit down?"

"Quite right, though I can't say you put it very prettily. However, in this family, it's I that confer benefits. I've come here with that object now. You're a mighty fine lady, Ursula; but you may be glad of a burgher uncle with a well-filled purse."

Ursula waited, wondering.

"I'm going to offer you money," said her uncle, bluntly.

Ursula dropped her eyes to the floor. "You are doubly mistaken, Uncle Jacóbus," she answered in her coldest manner. "I am not a fine lady, nor am I a beggar."

"Hoity-toity! Not a beggar? H'm. No money wanted? Ha!" Mopius got up, in all the splendor of his well-clothed portliness. "How about that bill which falls due on the first? Ah, you see, I know. How about that, my Lady of the Horst?"

Ursula rose also. She was not too proud to accept assistance. But of some of our friends we know at once that their seeming favors cannot really be to our advantage. It is only a question of finding out.

"Does everybody in Drum know all about my affairs?" asked Ursula, her pale face turning very red.

"Everybody? Fie! am I everybody? Ursula, I can never forget that you are my own sister Mary's only child."

"No," replied Ursula, "I suppose not."

"But a good many people do know, undeniably. And that

must end. It hurts my feelings. I am not a windbag of a noble. I am a simple gentleman, a hater of shams. I like money to ring clear on the counter, full weight." Jacóbus patted his waistcoat-pocket. "So, Ursula, this is what I have to propose : Things can't go on in the present manner, nor can I have my niece sold up. I offer to make you an annual payment of five thousand florins—"

"Uncle Jacóbus !"

Mynheer Mopius smiled with contented deprecation.

"That is your side of the matter. As long as I represent the district of Horstwyk in Parliament. That is mine."

"But you may never represent Horstwyk in Parliament?"

Mynheer Mopius sat down again.

"That depends upon my Lady of the Horst," he said. "So you see it is very simple. You intimate to your tenants that you wish them to vote for Mopius, and I pay in to your bankers the sum I have just named."

Ursula remained silent, thoughtful.

"It is pure generosity on my part," continued her uncle ; "for, anyway, you surely wouldn't have instructed them to vote on the other side. But that's my way. I don't mind. And I'm glad to help my sister Mary's child."

Ursula seemed slowly to have understood the very simple transaction. Her uncle watched her with a trace of anxiety in his unhealthy eyes. Surely there was nothing in his offer dishonest or dishonorable ?

"There is one little objection to the arrangement you propose," said Ursula, at last.

"Of course," replied Mopius ; "women always have one little objection to every arrangement — it is their way of getting the last word."

"I mean one objection which renders all others superfluous. You are the Liberal candidate, and my sympathies are with the Clericals."

Mynheer Mopius sat back, puffing and snorting.

"Nonsense ! " he said—" Ursula, nonsense ! What do women know about politics ? Your father confessed he knew nothing, so he can't have taught you. And Otto, I was given to understand—"

20

"Let us leave Otto out of the question, please," interrupted Ursula, with some asperity. "In this matter, at least, I am my own mistress."

"But the traditions of the Van Helmont family—"

"The traditions of the Van Helmont family are, of course, Conservative, and Conservatism is dead. At this moment I, a woman, have to choose, according to my feeble lights, between State atheism and a persecuted sect."

"And lose," said Mopius, "the five thousand florins."

But that was a stupid move. Ursula's eye kindled in the silence which ensued.

"Ursula," exclaimed Jacóbus in despair, for he saw his chances fading, " you are utterly unreasonable! How dare you suggest that I am an atheist, that I have any objection to religion? I distinctly approve of religion. It is a praiseworthy and highly respectable thing, and I always allow the servants to go to church. Your aunt Josine is right: you are nothing but a foolish child. What do you know about politics ?"

"Very little," replied Ursula, calmly; " but it seems to me that the less one knows about politics, the better one can choose between principles. And I choose the principle of liberty to worship God."

Jacóbus flourished his big hand till he almost touched her face. "Hang your quiet way !" he cried. "There's no talking to a woman like you. So you mean to tell me your mind's made up, you fool? Instead of living here in luxury and splendor, all settled and comfortable, as I suggest, you'll let this over-mortgaged place come under the hammer, and go home to your old father without clothes to your back ?"

Ursula stood, black and tall, by the desolate hearth. "Uncle Mopius, I don't want the money, but I'm very sorry not to be able to do as you wish. This is my sole opportunity, my single bit of influence, so to say, in my new position, and I must use it as I think best."

Tears of spite swan across Mynheer Mopius's vision. "Ursula," he said, "you—you idiot, why didn't you tell me you had political opinions *before* ?"

"I didn't know you cared—but what difference would that have made?" she answered, innocently.

He caught up his hat with an indignant swoop. "Never again," he said, "shall you touch a penny of mine. You are ruining my prospects and your own, from sheer caprice. I shall never, now, be a member of Parliament. But I'll pay you out. And to think that *you* have done this—you, who are my own sister Mary's child."

"Yes," replied Ursula, grimly. "I always was."

" WHAT now ?" exclaimed Ursula, still standing where Mopius had left her, by the great unused fireplace. " I cannot even trust Noks, who chatters. Poor father knows nothing about business. I am quite alone."

Even as she spoke there flashed across her mind a memory of her husband's words : " Not Gerard. Never Gerard. If ever you want a counsellor, turn to Theodore Helmont."

Hardly knowing what she did—certainly not knowing why she did it—she sat down and wrote a telegram, then and there, to this cousin she barely knew.

" Can you come here for two days? I greatly desire it."

As soon as the boy had ridden away she wished she had worded her message quite differently. An hour later she wished she had not sent it at all.

" Mamma," she said at luncheon, speaking very loudly and distinctly, as people had to do nowadays with the old lady, " I have asked Theodore van Helmont to come and stay here for a day or two."

" Whom ?" asked the Baroness.

" Theodore van Helmont."

" The house is yours, Ursula, now, to do what you like with, but "—the Dowager began to cry—" you might have asked somebody with another name."

" It is on business," replied Ursula, curtly.

" Business again," said the old lady, in an aggrieved tone ; " since my poor Theodore died one would think we kept a shop. Oh, ask him, by all means. He is the plebeian young man. I have nothing to say. It is the invasion of the—the—what, Louisa ?"

" I suppose you mean the Goths and Vandals," replied Louisa, very busy with her meal, which she always treated seriously. " Well, the Goths and Vandals were a strong new element; they were just what an effete society wanted. The great misfortune of our modern civilization is that all the Goths and Vandals have been used up."

" Invasion of the Goths and Vandals," repeated the Dowager. " But I don't mind. All I ask is to be allowed to finish my ' Memoir.' Then I shall go and sleep with Theodore and the children. You won't put me in the big vault, will you, Ursula ? Do the graves belong to Ursula, too ?"

" No, no," said Ursula, hastily.

" Who did you say was coming to stay here ?"

" Theodore van Helmont, mamma, from Bois-le-Duc."

" Theodore," repeated the Dowager, reflectively. " That was Henry's son. I'm glad he's coming. He will be able to tell me in what year his father made that ridiculous marriage—the first *mésalliance* in the Helmont family."

" I could have told you that," declared Louisa, brightly. " '54 or '55."

" I want to be exact," replied the Dowager, in her uncertain drawl. " I've got it somewhere among my documents, but I couldn't find it again."

Two days passed without any answer. Ursula's heart burned within her : at the thought of this neglect she turned suddenly hot and cold. In her quietly imperious necessity she had never doubted but that her summons would be obeyed.

Several times during the twenty-four hours the old Baroness would ask when the guest was expected.

" We are in mourning, Ursula," she said. " I hope you will not forget that we are in mourning. I think you went out of it too soon for your father-in-law. But perhaps your customs are different." (This was a standing, oft-repeated grievance.) " However, it is barely nine months since your husband died."

" It is six," replied Ursula; " I shall not forget."

" The young man does not seem too anxious, certainly," interposed Aunt Louisa, over her crochet. "You ask him, and he doesn't reply. I prefer the days of chivalry."

"But you don't remember the age of chivalry, Aunt Louisa," said Ursula, whose patience was distinctly overwrought. She objected to hearing her own innermost thought thus clearly stated by the Freule.

"No; I was born fifty-seven years ago; I am in no way ashamed of it," replied Aunt Louisa, coolly. "But what has that to do with the subject? You must be very unimaginative, Ursula, or have read very little. If you weren't so careless about your books, and didn't let them get dog-eared (as you do), I should lend you Madame de Roncevalles' book on 'The Decline of European Manners.' It is wonderfully interesting. It proves from the fossil remains that the cave-dwellers, at their cannibal banquets, always ate the women first."

"Louisa, it is time I had my piquet," objected the Dowager, who never forgot her game. She had taken the old Baron's place as Louisa's partner, and somehow considered the continuation of this time-honored institution as an almost religious tribute to her lord.

Under the reproachful wonder of her two companions, Ursula began to remember with increasing clearness that her impression of Theodore van Helmont had been decidedly unfavorable. She had not been able to understand her husband's admiration; but then, Otto and she so seldom sympathized. She remembered a grave young man, an awkward man, one of those irritating people who were always judging themselves, and had a logical reason for everything they did. There are people who constantly seem to be standing aside to look themselves down, superciliously, from head to foot. She wished more than ever that she had not sent her telegram. But, unfortunately for most of us, it is easy to say "Come," and impossible to say "Don't."

The only time she had met this cousin was on the occasion of those Christmas festivities, when the house was full of guests. It was a time on which she could not bear to dwell. For it was then that Gerard—

She stopped suddenly when the thought of all this first

rushed back upon her. Since her illness it seemed as if the past had been locked away in a cupboard with many partitions, where its several incidents lay, not forgotten, but unrecalled. One by one, at the touch of Chance, the various doors flew open, and some memory, sweet or painful, would leap forth from a seeming nowhere into the light.

She was out in the wood, on the windy March day, with Monk by her side, and all around her the black tree-trunks streaked the sullen sky. She realized that she was close to the spot where, on that Christmas Eve two years ago, she had sunk to the ground in the snow—the spot where Gerard had afterwards found her glove.

Why had Gerard fought that frantic duel? Otto had said that nobody fought duels but desperadoes. And certainly, as far as Holland was concerned, Otto must be accounted right.

Still, in this matter he had judged his brother harshly. Ursula believed that the duel had been fought in defence of the national flag, and she felt that, had she been a soldier, she would have done the same.

Not in this matter only had Otto wronged a nature he could not understand. Gerard, as their mother had said, was a sunbeam, genially playing from flower to flower. He was a firebrand newly lighted, that fizzes and crackles in its youth, before settling down to a steady glow. Now that he was away in Acheen his good qualities seemed all to stand out against the background of the home that had lost him. She had known him all her life; all during her long childhood, her long girlhood, he had been her playmate, her companion—more than that, the bright Phœbus of her modest horizon, her Prince—in his uniqueness—of Cavaliers. Everything around her, in the Manor-house, in the neighborhood, was connected with memories of joint pastimes and pranks. Ever since she could toddle she had been very fond of Gerard, with the tranquil affection of practised chums. But now he had fairly forgotten her. In his frequent letters to his mother—letters full of tenderness and rose-color—he never even sent a token of remembrance. Stop—there had been that message the Baroness had declined to give in the first letter after their common bereave-

ment. Perhaps there had been more. Ursula did not think so,
for the Dowager gradually communicated her darling's epistles
to every one, repeating and rereading them in scraps. Had she
not immediately let slip the very message in question—" Gerard
says he would have sold the place in any case, so where's the
difference ?"

Ursula sighed. Yes, after all, Otto was right. It couldn't be
helped. Gerard's letters never spoke of danger, but, through
others, news had reached Horstwyk that the Jonker had, on
several occasions, greatly distinguished himself. By-and-by he
would come back, " rangé," and marry—marry a little money,
and then—

Then her task would be done.

Meditating thus, she reached the very spot which she had determined to avoid. A blackbird broke in, almost fiercely, upon
her reverie, and she looked around. In an instant there rose up
before her the meeting by the Manor-house on that Christmas
morning, and again she heard Gerard's voice saying, as he bent
over an old brown glove, " I want you to let me keep this. It
will be the most precious thing I shall ever possess."

The whistling wind struck her hot cheeks; the great dog beside her leaped up, nose foremost, with vague, mute sympathy.
She rushed away from the horrible place, tearing her crape in
unmindful haste, hurrying to the open, the boundless heath,
where the whole air was in a ferment of conflicting currents,
that caught her and buffeted her, and flung her hither and
thither amid a chorus of moans and sobbings, barks, laughter,
and shrieks.

When at last she paused for breath, in a lull, she saw that she
was not far from Klomp's cottage. So she got under cover of
the trees again, and directed her footsteps to the little tumble-
down house. She had a weakness for Klomp. He was so sig-
nally " undeserving."

By the door leaned Adeline, and at a glance each woman
understood that the other had recognized her.

" Klomp, here's the Baroness !" cried Mejuffrouw Skiff, retreating a little before the suddenness of an encounter she had
hitherto vainly sought.

" Wish her Nobleness a very good day for me," replied an uncertain voice from dingy depths unknown.

" Poor man, he's asleep," said Adeline, boldly. " Was it anything particular you wanted with him, Mevrouw ?"

Ursula smiled. " No, indeed," she said. " On no account would I disturb his well-earned rest."

" Well-earned it is," retorted Adeline, pertly. " His younger daughter's ill, and he's been sitting up with her all night."

Ursula's manner changed. " Mietje? I am sorry to hear that. Can I see her ? What is the matter ?"

" Oh, I don't know. Nothing much, I fancy. You needn't know what, I suppose, as long as you send the regulation broth."

Ursula turned away, almost eagerly. That she should meet this woman now ! She had lost sight of her and her story, gladly, for years.

" I suppose you don't remember me, madame," said Adeline, acidly. She had noticed the quick movement of aversion.

" Oh yes, I remember you," replied Ursula, standing still. " But certainly I did not expect to find you here."

" Yet what is more natural, Mevrouw the Baroness van Helmont, than that I should come to have a look at my relations."

" I did not know the Klomps were any relations of yours."

" I did not mean the Klomps."

The two women looked at each other.

" Well," said Ursula, in measured tones, " I hope you are doing better than you were. Good-morning."

But again Adeline stopped her. " I am not doing well at all. As your Nobleness so kindly takes an interest in my career, I should like to explain my position, if your Nobleness would deign to listen."

Suddenly the dog, Monk, who had been suspiciously watching the frowzy stranger, broke into a fury of disparagement which no commands from his mistress could quell. Adeline was horribly frightened. With a very cowed manner she retreated behind the door, but she shrieked from that place of safety that the matter was one of the greatest importance.

Ursula, having compelled the growling dog's obedience, with one firm hand on his collar, called to the poor soul to come forth again.

"Say your say," she decreed, "and have done."

"It's only this," whined Adeline, on the door-step: "I'm destitute, deserted with my child, not knowing where to turn, and I'm Gerard Helmont's wife."

She had calculated her foolish "coup;" she was aware that a wide gulf yawned between Ursula and possible denial from Gerard.

"So it's I," she added, quickly, "who am the Baroness van Helmont, though not of the Horst—*you* know why ; and all I ask is a few hundred florins and to let me go in peace."

"Do you mean to say," queried Ursula, "that you claim to be Gerard van Helmont's legal wife?"

"Yes; and it was you that wanted him to marry me, so, in part, the fault is yours," responded Adeline, who enjoyed lies for the mere telling, even when there was nothing to be gained. "Therefore, give me a generous sum for Gerard's child, and let me go. Why, *everything* ought to be his, the young Baron's—all the wealth and magnificence that you've got hold of, nobody knows how."

And Adeline began to cry real drops. Men cannot yet manufacture genuine diamonds. Women can.

But, notwithstanding her weeping, there was much spite, and even a little menace, in her tone.

"Down, Monk, down!" said Ursula. "I shall not ask you for further proof of your story, simply because I know it is not true. I wish it were. I am fully conscious that you have a claim to be what you say you are and are not. Could I help you to obtain its recognition I would do so ; but otherwise I can do nothing for you. I have no money, and therefore can give you none. In a couple of years perhaps there will be more at my disposal, and then, if things remain unchanged, you may write to me, and I will do what I can for your boy. That is all. Now you had better go away from here. Have you understood me?"

"Give me twenty-five florins," said Adeline.

" ' I SUPPOSE YOU DON'T REMEMBER ME, MADAME ' "

Ursula drew the straining dog towards her, and passed down the narrow path. Half-way she hesitated.

"Oh, keep straight!" she burst out, pleadingly; "keep straight, for the child's sake. I'll send you the twenty-five florins, if you want them. Let me have your address in Drum, and I'll try to find you decent work. Oh, be an honest girl, for the love of God!"

"Send me the twenty-five florins," said Adeline.

Ursula crept back into the wood; her eyes were full of tears.

"Oh, Gerard, Gerard!" she said; "this is *your* work. God forgive you for deserting her. No pure-hearted woman can."

CHAPTER XXXIX

As she emerged into the avenue Ursula noticed a figure in front of her which she immediately recognized. It was walking at a deliberate pace, a valise and an overcoat thrown over one arm. The dog gave the alarm, and the figure looked round.

"Why did you not telegraph for the carriage?" thought Ursula.

The young man waited; his fresh-colored face shone out in the all-pervading gloom.

Ursula wondered, as she drew nearer, what deliverance she expected from this pink-eyed little innocent. He looked like a solemn peach. How could she broach her unusual subject? Visible shyness was not one of her qualities; but she smiled rather foolishly as she walked, thought Theodore Helmont, and, for so recent a widow, improperly.

"You have come up on foot from the station?" she cried. "I wish we had known. Why didn't you telegraph?"

"Telegrams are expensive," replied the young man.

This sounded promising.

"I only got my leave this morning," he continued. "I couldn't let you know, so I simply came."

"Ah, you had to get leave?" said Ursula, her conscience smiting her.

"Yes; government officials always must. Most people must who work for their bread. I am a post-office clerk."

"I know, I know," answered Ursula, hastily. "Of course I know, *Cousin* Helmont. Please put down your bag; it will be quite safe. I will send one of the laborers to fetch it."

"I can easily carry it myself," he said, more courteously; "I always do." And, although this time he said nothing about expenditure, she felt that he considered the tip.

After that the conversation lagged. Presently the young man said, with much timidity:

"There is one thing I should greatly like, if you would be so very kind. My mother is exceedingly anxious about railway travelling of any sort, and she made me promise to let her know at once of my safe arrival. They couldn't telegraph at the station. Would there be a possibility, perhaps, of forwarding a message?"

"Oh, certainly," replied Ursula, demurely. "But—you know—telegrams are expensive."

Theodore's pure eyes grew troubled.

"The matter is altogether different," he said. "Perhaps, if you will allow me to explain—"

Ursula burst out laughing.

"Certainly not," she exclaimed. "What do you take me for? Of course, I perfectly understand. The boy shall get ready at once."

Theodore looked straight in front of him.

"I only wanted to say," he went on, doggedly, "that my mother's anxiety is not irrational. She is quite unaccustomed to travelling herself, and we have never been parted before."

Ursula stood still on the Manor-house steps. "Never been parted before!" she exclaimed. "Woe is me, what have I done?"

Theodore blushed in fresh waves of crimson. "Now you are laughing at me," he said, and his tone was distinctly annoyed. "You mustn't laugh at me. I am not at all accustomed to the society of ladies, and if you laugh at me we shall not be able to get on."

"No—no, I really meant it," Ursula hastened to say. "I honestly fear I have been exceedingly inconsiderate. I wish that your mother had accompanied you." ("Oh dear, no," she reflected; "there the expense comes in again!") "But you must not say you are unaccustomed to the society of ladies—"

"My mother is not a lady like you," he remarked, quickly.

"I am Ursula Rovers," she replied—"the pastor's daughter. I remember Mevrouw van Helmont very well."

In the solitude of her dressing-room she wondered what would be the next development of her devotion to Otto's memory, and chid herself for the ungracious thought. Then she went down to luncheon, expecting to find her guest in a corner of the library turning over picture-books. That was the only pose in which his former visit had left him photographed on her brain.

To her astonishment, she heard him in earnest discussion with Aunt Louisa. "My dear Ursula," cried the latter lady, running forward, "your cousin Van Helmont is a most interesting young man. I have been telling him about European manners, and he most sagaciously remarks that the best of manners is to have none. How delightfully true!"

The subject of this outspoken eulogy did not seem at all abashed by it; probably he was accustomed to his mother's estimation of her only son.

"Pardon me," he calmly protested; "I was saying that I had read that observation somewhere. I am not prepared to maintain that it is absolutely correct."

"Oh, what does it matter whose it is," cried the Freule. "Everything we say must have had its origin with some one, so everything is really original. Now that never struck me before. How new!"

"Yes," replied Ursula. "Will you have a rissole?"

"Thank you, my dear. One more, please. Thank you. Personally, what I most reprobate is the walking in line, like ducks. 'Do as others do.' The Bible says, 'Do as you would be done by'—a very different thing. I hope, Mynheer Helmont, that you are unconventional, as I know your father was."

"I do not remember my father well," answered Theodore, pondering whether he could not get away that night.

"Oh, I never *met* him," said Louisa, just as the old Baroness entered. The poor old lady, who would have said 'J'ai failli attendre' in palmier days, now accorded all precedence to her literary labors.

"My dear," continued the Freule, addressing her, "this young man is exceedingly interesting. I had forgotten him, but now I remember I thought so the last time he was here. The best thing is to have no manners. Now doesn't he put that well?"

"I dare say he finds it convenient," responded the Dowager. "How do you do, Mynheer Helmont? I am very glad to see you. I wish you would tell me when your father died?"

"It is seventeen years ago," replied Helmont, wonderingly.

"Quite impossible. I feel sure you are more than sixteen."

"I am twenty-four, but—"

"Mamma means 'married,' I believe," suggested Ursula, gently.

"'Married,' that was what I said," declared the Dowager, sharply. "Ursula, my soup is cold again. Manners or no manners, young man, you shouldn't make fun of a woman old enough to be your grandmother."

"I disapprove of such early marriages!" exclaimed the Freule. Ursula's eyes and Theodore's met. She burst out laughing, but he looked uncomfortably grave. "After luncheon," she said, "I must take you round, Mynheer Helmont. It is no use showing you the stables; we have only three horses left, and they are of the kind that would better do their work unseen."

He followed her obediently when they rose from table, and she pretended to take an interest in the small sights she had to offer her guest. The same can hardly be asserted of Theodore. He was painfully silent while she "made conversation," wondering all the time in what way she should broach the one subject she cared to speak about.

In this, however, he hastened to her assistance, for his patience came to an end, while hers still hung on a thread. They were standing in the palm-house, when he suddenly looked up at her—he had some little height to look up—and asked,

"What did you want me for, please?"

She had been laughing about some of the gardener's queer names for the roses; her voice suddenly changed, and everything but pain died out of it.

"I believe we are ruined," she said, facing him, "and Otto

made me promise, if ever I wanted advice, I would appeal to you."

He seemed still to listen, plucking at the nearest leaves, for a moment after she had finished. Then he said, as if speaking to himself,

"Well, I'm very glad, at any rate, that I didn't ask a holiday for nothing at all." He glanced up at her anxious face. "Holidays are very rare with us, you know," he added, apologetically. "I couldn't soon get leave again."

"Yet I don't suppose you can help us," continued Ursula, relentlessly. "Nobody can."

"When people get down as low as that," replied the young clerk, frigidly, "they can usually help themselves. I presume that, however much money you may happen to possess, you want more. That, I believe, is what people of your class call 'being ruined.'"

She felt that he wronged her the more by this constant distinction, after what she had said on the Manor-house steps. "I possess no money at all," she said, wroth with herself for the helpless confession. "And in about a week's time I must have three thousand florins."

"In other words," he answered, with an angry wave of his short arm round the greenhouse, "you *must* spend thirty thousand florins with an income of twenty-seven. Other people have an income of one thousand, and spent *that.*"

"No," she replied, "it is not that. We will say no more about it. Come, let us walk on."

"Pardon me. It takes one person to start a subject, but two to drop it. Will you permit me to express myself plainly?"

"Oh, certainly. Dear me, Mynheer van Helmont, I had understood you to say you were shy?"

"Again I beg your pardon. I can understand fun, and I can understand earnest; but which is it to be?"

"I apprehend you. You do not recognize humor outside the comic papers. You are like my father. *I* laugh most at the dentist's. It is to be earnest, please."

"The house is crowded with treasures. Sell one or two."

"I cannot; they belong to my mother-in-law."

"Do away with a carriage you can't pay for, and go on foot."

"I cannot. I keep a sort of boarding-house, and my two boarders pay for the carriage, not I."

"Eat dry bread instead of hot lunch."

"And drive away the boarders! There, you see, I answer plainly, too. Do you really imagine that if I could have solved my difficulties by merely eating dry bread I would have troubled you, a comparative stranger, to come all the way from Bois-le-Duc?"

"I don't know. The women of '93 could be guillotined, and willing, but they couldn't eat dry bread."

However, his tone was gentler, and his manner less assured.

"Now will you let me, as we return to the house, explain how matters really stand?" she said. He nodded silently, and under the bare, sky-piercing oaks she softly told him the long story of her father-in-law's slow purchase and last testament, of Otto's life-work and dying charge, of her struggle to continue what they had begun in expectation of better times. He listened, his boy-face puckered up.

"It is your name, too," she said, in conclusion, "your race, your blood." And she measured the little plebeian beside her.

"Yes," he said.

"There it lies. And each rood that belonged to a Van Helmont four hundred years ago belongs to a Van Helmont now."

"It belongs to *you*," he replied, quickly. "And afterwards?" She faltered.

"It will never pass from my keeping till it passes to a Van Helmont," she said, "so help me God!"

In that moment even he could not press the point.

"You must give me time," he said; "I have three days' leave. Do not let us mention the subject again till the day after to-morrow. Meantime, I will have a look round and try to discover if you can keep on, supposing the three thousand are found."

"Thank you. But do you know about land?" She was just a little bit piqued. "I assure you I am very slowly learning."

21

"Oh, I know. My mother is a farmer's daughter. I have always been about with my uncle. If mother had given me my choice, I should have been a common farmer myself."

" A Van Helmont!"

" Pooh! That's what mother said !"

CHAPTER XL

As ill-luck would have it, Helena wrote to announce her visit for the last evening of Theodore's stay at the Manor - house. She arrived before dinner, bringing the unwilling Willie along with her.

An almost oppressive quiet had reigned in the mansion, only rarely disturbed by the deep voice of Monk. The guest had spent most of his time out-of-doors, returning occasionally to closet himself with great memoranda and account books. Tante Louisa complained bitterly that she got next to nothing of his interesting conversation ; Ursula anxiously fought shy of him ; the Dowager, unexpectedly meeting him in the hall, asked her *confidante*, the cook, who he was.

" I shall stir them all up a bit," said Helena to her husband in the carriage. " I have seen them already once or twice since the event, and you · can't go on looking lugubrious forever. Besides, I don't believe Ursula is inconsolable. I shall ask her."

" No, you won't," said Willie.

" Willie, don't ' put my back up,' or you'll make me do an unlady-like thing."

" You won't ask her, because you can't. I'd bet you a gold piece that you wouldn't dare."

" You wouldn't like me to dare." Helena's eyes strayed away through the carriage window.

" Indeed I should. I like pluck of any kind. In a horse, or a woman, or a dog."

" Only not in a man !" exclaimed Helena, a little bitterly.

" In a man it goes without saying. By-the-bye, what atrocious brutes these horses of Ursula's arc. I've an idea, Nellie, that she's very badly off."

"All the more reason for her to console herself. A poor widow remarries much sooner than a rich one, and with far less opportunity."

"'Tisn't said that she'd better herself. If she marries she ought to marry Gerard. It would be her bounden duty."

"Thank you, for Gerard's sake," retorted Helena, now very bitterly indeed. And they lapsed into silence. Was there really any prospect of Ursula's marrying Gerard? It was this question which had long held Nellie van Troyen's heart as in a vise, pinching it and torturing it, and refusing to let it rest. It was this question which now hunted her to the Horst. She was determined to see with her own eyes how matters stood. "I shall find out," she told herself. "I must, even if I have to *ask* her. To think of Willie's trumpery gold piece! It is horrible, all the suffering. But my life is a beautiful romance." She smiled, and reflectively arranged her dress. "You like me, you know, Willie," she said, "in pink."

"Yes," he replied, "though I don't know why. Blue suits your fair complexion better. But, somehow, I can't bear to see you in blue."

"I know why. Shall I tell you? It is because you have some delightful memories connected with a creature in blue."

"You are wrong," he said, quite coolly. "It is because I have some detestable memories connected with a creature in blue."

"Oh, 'delightful,' 'detestable,' that is all one in such cases. So you see, I was right. Here we are."

"Well, shall we wager?" he asked, as he helped her to alight.

"If you like. But you are pretty sure of your gold piece, for I certainly shall not trouble her unless she drives me to it."

"So much the better. Don't dare, and pay me."

"Willie, I believe you would sell your soul for money," she cried.

He laughed.

"No, no, not his soul," she said to herself, half aloud, as she

climbed the great stone steps. " Only his body—only all he's
got to sell!"

The Dowager came forward to meet her niece, who had
always been a favorite with the old lady, and the only possible successor she could consider with equanimity. " My dear,
I am so glad you are come," she said, with a return of her vanished sprightliness. " Your visits are like those of the angels.
And the house is so dull. Though certainly, at this moment,
we have a guest."

" A guest ?"

" Oh, he is Ursula's guest. One of the—the other Helmonts,
that nobody ever used to see. But these are the days of the
bend sinister. We have fallen on evil times."

Helena stood taking off her wraps, the little old lady helping her. " My dear," began the latter, somewhat tremulously,
" I wish you would do me a kindness. I want you to come and
stay with with us for a few days, and I will read you what I
have written about the good old past. I read it to Ursula, but
she does not know what it is all about. She is not one of us;
it will interest *you*. There is a great deal in it about your
mother."

" Yes ?" said Helena. " Is it ready, aunt ?"

" Ready, my dear ? Oh dear no ; how could it be ready ? But
I can show you what I have done. Do you know, I begin to
fear it will never be ready !"—the Dowager's voice nearly failed
her. " To give me plenty of time to write the memoir, your
uncle ought to have died a great many years ago." Then,
vaguely realizing that she had incorrectly expressed her meaning, she began to cry with unmistakable persistence.

" Hush, hush!" exclaimed Helena, in her most impulsive
tones. " Auntie, I shall be delighted to come; we will talk
over the old days, as you say, and all the fun I used to have
with Gerard. But would you not rather pay us a visit ?" She
drew the little lady's arm through her own. " I am so sorry.
This is very hard for you—and for Gerard—this about Ursula."

" My dear, I thank you, but I cannot."

The Dowager nestled confidentially against the silver-pink

sleeve of the fair creature beside her. They cooed over each other like a pair of high-bred doves. "I dare not leave the house for a single night. I have an idea that something would happen if I did. I am the last of us all, and I am set here to watch. When Gerard comes back— Helena, you do not think, do you, that they will really leave it to her forever?"

"Poor auntie!" said Helena, softly stroking the transparent cheek. "Poor auntie!"

"What I cannot understand is that he' doesn't come and take it away from her!" cried the Dowager, with sudden energy. "I wrote to him to do so. Gerard never was a coward. But I fear that Louisa's explanation is correct."

"What is Freule Louisa's explanation?" questioned Helena, quickly.

"She says that Gerard is in love with Ursula, and always has been. She says that *that* is why he went to India. If what she says is true, then Ursula has robbed me of both my sons." And again the poor, forlorn old woman began gently to whimper.

"Perhaps it is not true," replied Helena, pensively. "Come, auntie, let us sit in the window-seat and talk of Gerard. I suppose he will be coming back before long."

"I don't know. I forget. Oh, Nellie, you don't know how dreadful it is to grow old and forget. I can't find my words sometimes, though I take care that nobody notices it. I feel that it would never do for Ursula to discover that I have not all my wits about me. Who knows what she might not do? *Sell the place, perhaps!*"— her voice dropped to a whisper. "Imagine that! Or sell some of your uncle's dear art treasures that he bade me keep. She doesn't care for them, I know, for she never seems to see them even. I've watched her constantly. Oh, Nellie, I'm set here as sentinel, and—my strength is failing."

Helena felt that, irrational as she knew the feeling to be, she *could* not but think ill of Ursula.

"I forgot one of the poor children's birthdays last week," wailed the Baroness—she alluded to her dead infants that slept beneath "The Devil's Doll"—"and Ursula didn't remind me to take any flowers. I have never forgotten before."

Ursula entered at the moment, tall and straight in her heavy gown. To both the gracefully drooping women, whose soft clothes and figures intermingled against the darkening window, her presence at that moment seemed more than ever an insult.

"Shall we have lights?" she said, in her clear voice.

"Oh, in the drawing-room, pray," replied her mother-in-law, pettishly. "Mynheer van Helmont is gone in there. He was looking for you."

Ursula withdrew into an adjoining apartment. It was very large and lofty, and the figures on its tapestried walls, half hidden under the great masses of shadow now clouding around them, peered forth in vaguely distorted gloom. Theodore was pacing the parqueted floor with moody tramp. He came forward at once.

"I want you," he said, hurriedly. "I must leave to-night. So we may as well have our talk at once."

"I am quite ready," she answered. "I did not wish to press you. Will half an hour suffice?"

"Ten minutes. Everything worth saying in this world by one human being to another can be said in ten minutes. But I should like you to sit down."

"Very well," she said. "No, not an easy-chair. Thanks."

"I have looked into everything, superficially," he began, resuming his march in the dusk. "I must, in the first place, beg your pardon for misjudging you all. I came here with false impressions. When a man grows up, as I have done, in the bourgeois daily fight with poverty, he is apt to form erroneous impressions of the life which his 'grand' relations lead, especially when his impressions are gained by hearsay. I beg your pardon."

He paused for a moment; then, as she did not answer, he continued:

"In the second place I want to express my—my admi—my *recognition* of the way in which you have carried on your husband's work. Few women, I imagine, would have taken up such a load or borne it so bravely. I didn't like your sudden telegram. I thought of the people who jump into the water and then call out to strangers to save them. There! that's off my mind. I am not good at compliments or excuses. I've no manners, as Freule Louisa says. Now to business." His tone, which had been agitated, immediately dropped to the habitual growl that masked his shyness.

"He reminds you," Helena had said, when they met by the Christmas-tree, "of a peach with a wasp inside."

"The truth is as you stated," he resumed; "nothing but hard work can keep the whole thing going. A forced sale would mean ruin. On the other hand, barring such extra expenses as death duties, you ought, with rigid economy, to pay your way." He paused for a moment. "With rigid economy," he repeated.

"I know," said Ursula, softly.

"There is nothing so hopeless as farming without capital— you know that better than I do. But the cherry orchards pay, and so, especially, do the osier plantations. Without these latter you could hardly get on. You have good tenants, on the whole. One of them, however, will have to go."

"I know," said Ursula again, in the same tone, through the darkness; "but he can't."

"He must. I see we understand each other—the home-farm man—your sort of agent. I don't say he is dishonest. Otto seems pretty well to have stopped that—but he is expensive— you can't afford him."

"I cannot make cheese myself," pleaded Ursula, a little helplessly, for her. "I tried once, and nobody could eat it. It—it didn't stiffen."

But her stern adviser vouchsafed no responsive smile.

"It's a matter of life or death," he said; "the work that fellow does must be done by another man."

"But where would you find a better?"

"I can't find a better, but I can find a cheaper."

"Have you got him?"

"Yes; I mean myself. Stop a minute—let me explain. I told you I had always wanted to be a farmer"—his voice grew nervous again. "I'm sick of being a genteel sort of manikin in a pot-hat. I'm especially sick of the post-office. I'm going to take that farm and work it."

"But, Mynheer Helmont, this sudden decision—"

"It isn't a sudden decision. It took twenty-four hours to come to, and its twenty-four hours old already. I've announced it to my mother." He again made a pause, away at the farther, darkest end. "Oh, I dare say you don't like it," he burst out; "I didn't expect you would. But it's going to happen, all the same. To have as my lady Baroness's close neighbor a farmer bearing her name—"

"I was not thinking of that," she interrupted him. "For, of course, a gentleman-farmer—"

But he would not allow her to proceed.

"A gentleman - gammon!" he cried, still out of the distant darkness; "a common, common farmer. Nothing in all the world—not even drink—costs half as much as gentility. But, remember, if it isn't pleasant for you people, it's a hundred times worse for my mother and—" He broke off. "But she'll do it," he lamely concluded the sentence.

Ursula rose and came up the big room to look for him.

"Sit down, please," he said, hastily; "I haven't done. Please sit down till I've done. Women are such bad listeners!" She obeyed, knocking the chair against something which crashed to the floor. "I hope that isn't anything expensive!" exclaimed Theodore, emerging from his corner. His tone chid her as if she had been an awkward child.

"It didn't sound broken," replied Ursula, meekly; "but I suppose you object to my getting a light?"

For only answer he struck a match, revealing a cloisonné vase which lay in a pool of water and a tangle of white anemones upon an Oriental rug. The match flickered out.

"That'll keep," said Theodore, coolly. "I only want half a minute more. There is still one point, the most important. The three thousand florins we require next week will be found."

"But how?" Ursula's voice betrayed her.

"Oh, not picked up on the high-road. When I say 'found,' of course I mean provided and paid for. I shall provide them. You can imagine that, poor as we are, we do not live on my salary only. As a matter of fact, I possess about twenty-seven thousand florins; I have looked so much into your private affairs that I suppose you have a right, if you care, to know some-

thing of mine. Three thousand, therefore, I will advance, if
you can give me sufficient security."

" That is just what I cannot do."

" That remains to be seen. Freule Louisa mentioned that
you still had a valuable diamond brooch."

Ursula was thankful he could not see the hot flare of her resentment.

" And do you think," she said, scornfully, "that I would not
have sold *that?* But it isn't mine to sell. It is an heirloom.
I must keep it, like the rest."

" It is legally yours," he replied, " and therefore you must
not keep it. Besides, I trust that you will be able to redeem it
in the slow course of the years. All ladies like diamonds. I
promise to take good care of yours. Bring the thing down before the carriage starts. And now perhaps I had better ring
for somebody with a cloth."

" Stop!" she cried; he had lighted another match and was
looking for the bell-rope. " Before you do that I want to
say—"

" Don't. I really do not think there is anything more to be
said just now." He had found the bell and pulled it.

" But I do not want to do this. I do not want—"

" I know you don't. Did not I tell you so? However, permit me to say that I have as good a right to interfere in this
matter as you. I am quite as much of a Helmont—even a good
deal more." His voice rolled out like the threat of a recoiling
dog.

A female servant knocked and entered, letting in a flood of
light from the hall. She gazed with decorous astonishment at
the occupants of the room.

" Ursula," said Willie, coming in with the others, " is it true
that you have let the shooting?"

" No; that was not one of my crimes," replied Ursula, with a
petulant laugh. " Otto did it immediately after Gerard's departure." Then her voice softened. " I believe it was the greatest sacrifice he ever made. You know, he was such a splendid
shot."

"He was," assented Willie, with that solemn admiration which no man can suppress.

"But, Ursula, I remember you used to say you hated 'splendid shots'?" suggested Helena, looking back over the arm which still supported the Dowager. They were passing in to dinner. Willie, glancing up, saw mischief in his wife's blue eye.

"They are better than stabs," answered Ursula; and from that moment it might be evident to any one that these two women meant war. It would not, however, be the feminine skirmishing of intrigue and innuendo, for Helena, as we know, was reckless, and Ursula blunt.

"I want to sit next to poor dear auntie," said Helena, as they took their places. "Mynheer van Helmont, I suppose *your* habitual seat is next to the lady of the house? Are you going to stay here long?"

"I have no habitual seat," replied Theodore, awkwardly. "I leave to-night. I am only a three days' guest."

"Yes; no one of your name could be anything else at the Horst now. Not even the head of the house, away in Acheen." She smiled sweetly and turned to the Dowager.

Theodore was mortally afraid of this fine lady, all soft texture and vague perfume, like a rose. But he found conversation hardly easier with Ursula, in spite of the sullen admiration he unwillingly accorded her.

"Your mother will be glad to have you back," said Ursula.

"Yes, indeed," he replied, fervently. "And I to go—back," he added, blushing.

"You know, it was impossible," Helena's voice rang out again. "We are speaking of your uncle Mopius, Ursula. They have had to withdraw his candidature. He is a very good sort of man—oh, very good—but he is not what Freule Louisa calls 'strong.' Papa tells me it is quite impossible, though I'm sure I worked hard for him—didn't I, Willie? Your uncle says it's all *your* doing, Ursula. He was very rude about you to papa. I had to stop him, and remind him you were become my cousin by marriage."

"Indeed," replied Ursula.

"Would you like to hear what he said?"

"I cannot say I care."

"Well, as we are quite among ourselves, perhaps it is better you should know. He said that your elevation had turned your head. You know, Ursula, he is rather, rather—pardon me the word—vulgar!"

She had spoken French. The servant, by the sideboard, rattled his plates.

"And he said your political opinions were deplorable. What are your political opinions, Mynheer van Helmont?"

"Deplorable," replied Theodore, with a ready championship which astonished himself.

"Ah, you two are in close sympathy, I see. So much the better." She dropped her voice. "But is it not a strange thought to you, Mynheer van Helmont, that this old place is now certain to pass, in due time, to Ursula's children, whatever their name may happen to be?"

"No," replied Theodore; "it's no business of mine."

"Ah!" she exclaimed, angrily. "The Baron van Helmont thinks differently, no doubt. Why, if Ursula has some seizure to-night, I suppose we shall soon see a Lord Mopius of Horstwyk! Fie, Mynheer van Helmont, this poor creature at my side has more spirit than you."

Ursula could not avoid hearing enough of this aside to understand its meaning. She felt that everybody had heard it. Passionate as she was, she fixed her eyes on the table-cloth. She remained conscious that Helena, that everybody, even while the talk went on, was watching her. At last she lifted them—those steadfast brown eyes.

"It is six months to - day," she said, "exactly six months. Only six months since Otto and Baby died." And she rose from the table.

"Ursula, you have forgotten the dessert," cried Aunt Louisa, lingering.

Ursula turned back.

"True," she said. "I beg everybody's pardon. Won't you try some of mamma's preserved orange-leaves, Helena? You will find them as good as ever."

In the hall, just as the carriage had driven up which was to
convey the three visitors to the station, Ursula appeared with
a small parcel in her hand; she gave it to Theodore, who but-
toned it out of sight, without even saying " Thanks."

" There is one thing still," she began, hurriedly. " You
heard about the election. I had a letter yesterday from the
Opposition Caucus, asking me if I wished to put forward a
candidate, or would accept one from them. I have none. I
have one. I mean, I had thought, hearing what you said at
dinner, that, if your political opinions were theirs—"

" I have no political opinions," he answered, moving away
from the sheltering pillar to the light where the others stood
grouped.

She put out one hand. " I am sorry," she stammered, trembling from head to foot. " I had thought—it is the one only
thing I could have done to thank you—to express my gratitude—"

" I want no thanks," he replied, literally shaking off her hand.
" Gratitude, pshaw ! I told you a couple of hours ago that I
have as much right to do this as you have. I am not *all*
peasant, Mevrouw. You remind me too frequently of that
side." And he went and took up his own valise. " The servants forget these things," he said to Helena.

When they were all gone, Ursula crossed the cold emptiness
of the hall and encountered Hephzibah. The maid shrank
away. " Hephzibah, I want you to do me a favor," said the
young Baroness. " Would you take this letter, when you go to
the Parsonage to-morrow with the Freule, and give it to a
person who is staying at Klomp's ? Please give it into her own
hands. There is money in it."

" H'm," reflected Hephzibah, watching the tall figure in its
slow ascent. " Money in it. Is there ? And why ? Throw a
barking dog a bone." She shook her head. " If I hear that
noise up-stairs again," she muttered, " I'll write to the Jonker,
wife or not. But I've said that so often before ! And if the
Jonker's got a wife already, what business had he wearing
Mevrouw's glove in his bosom and duelling ? I saw him pick
it up. It's a bad world, a bad world. But I'm a blessed body

to feel how bad it is. I told cook about the groanings, though I didn't explain their reason, so she only said I ought to take medicine."

"Well, Willie, I've lost my wager," declared Helena, as soon as they were rid of the "post-boy."

"I don't know about that, but pay up anyhow. You deserve to, Nellie, for your treatment of Ursula. Poor thing, she behaved very well, I thought. She's quite lost that magnificent rich complexion of hers. She looks sallow."

"Oh, that will come right when she marries little Theodore," replied Helena, with tranquil satisfaction. "The person I am sorry for is auntie. I'm sure I cried with her for nearly an hour."

THE scene changes.

For one moment we look, with clearer eyes than the poor old Dowager's, across the cruel waste of waters into a very real dreamland, and we see Gerard, Baron van Helmont, after two years of weary waiting for glory, wearily waiting for glory still.

Gerard van Helmont stood before his hut in the compound of the little fort under his command on the Acheen River. All round him trembled, with soft persistence, the thousand breathings of the tropic night.

An hour ago it had flung itself, the sudden blackness, down the slopes of the Barissan Mountains, and away across the green islands of the Indian Ocean. It had fallen with the swiftness of a blow, wiping out all the luxuriance of dreamy glories that lay reposefully burning in endless variations of verdure under the moist veil of paludal heat. The wide sea of tropical foliage that laughed down the sides of the valley till within a few yards of the river fort had sunk back from view like a swiftly receding tide, and a living silence now brooded over these jungles a-quiver with hate. The roar of the million frogs in the marshes had at last ceased to beat against never-accustomed ears, and all the other manifold murmurs and flut-terings had died down to one dully penetrative tone, whose ringing music, in its rhythmical rise and fall, swelled upon the ear of the listener like the pulse-beat of the world. Now and then the sudden howlings of distant wild dogs broke out hid-eously, or the clattering shriek of the *tokkèh* resounded from the woods. And throughout the long darkness came the swish of the turbid water among its reeds and overhanging branches, as it went playing around the masses of logs and rotten refuse over which it quarrels day and night in slow pushings with the sea.

Nature under the equator knows not even the semblance of rest. In Northern countries she at least appears to sleep; here she sits through the cooler hours on her couch listening.

Certainly there was no rest for Gerard van Helmont, or for any Dutchman at that time in Acheen; there was only the tension of expectant inactivity amid all-encompassing treachery, hundred-eyed and hundred-handed. Barbaric murder lurked behind every tree and behind every smiling face that bent in allegiance. For if an Achinese stoop low before the Kafir it is with the idea, in rising, of ripping him up.

Gerard in this small "Benting" had fifty men under his orders, European and native fusileers. His nearest neighbors were established about half a mile off in a similar intrenchment, a certain number of these permanent camps having been constructed to keep open the way to the sea, for the invading force had gone up the valley into the interior.

The lanterns along the outer side of the wall had been lighted; their yellow reflection created a circle of vaguely lessening defence. Across this, into the dark tangle beyond the clearing, peered solitary sentinels by their guns. A sergeant tramped past. The night was starless and misty.

"Werda?" cried a sentry.

Something had moved, he thought, behind the glooming bushes. Something always seemed to be moving — creeping forward through the whispers of the forest, in the incessant alarm of guerilla night attack.

"Nonsense, it's too early," said the sergeant. "Besides, we're quite safe now, here in these pacified districts. Keep a good lookout, all the same."

Gerard smiled, overhearing the concluding exhortation. He knew that they were not safe—no, not for one moment. The friendly villagers from the farther side of the marsh who had sold them victuals that morning might even now be meditating a raid, one of those terrible Achinese swoops and withdrawals, the hand-to-hand swarm up the battlements—Allah il Allah!—On!

He lighted a cigarette, and wondered how many he still had left. It was painfully lonely and humdrum and wearing. Danger becomes humdrum; death can become humdrum, they say. Occasionally he met his brother officer from the neighboring fort. Otherwise not a white-faced Christian, except his own garrison, and the commissariat people from the camp, at long intervals, with stores.

He was thinking—no, not of home. Soldiers—thank God! —do not always think of home.

He was thinking of his men. One of them, an Amboinese, had got himself killed that morning through sheer temerity and disobedience. There were a couple of these insubordinates in the Benting, who, wearying of inaction, had broken out once before on the spree—that is to say, on the hunt for a grinning, long-haired devil with a klewang. He had punished them, of course, but at daybreak this morning Adja had slipped away alone, and had fallen into the hands of friendly Achinese. Gerard knew what that meant. Death by the most prolonged of cruelties, a slow chopping away of all parts except such as keep life extant. He sighed as he thought of the poor fellow's fate, and the inevitable reprisals, and all the official bother and blame.

And he reflected on certain instructions issued not long ago. The army, whose women and children were daily exposed to fiendish barbarities, had been reminded that every Achinese was a man and a brother, and must be treated as such. Kindness to prisoners (even if they owned to having boiled your envoy) ; kindness to villagers (even if they potted you as you passed their houses)—these were of the elements of Christian warfare. It was quite true. And, moreover, the good people at home that write, in their slippers, to the newspapers never pardoned an act of cruelty, unless practised by the foe.

" I must speak to the other fellow, I suppose," said Gerard. " I wonder how he takes it ? Sergeant, send Popa along," and he passed into his hut, that the interview might seem more imposing under the yellow glare of the lamp. The hut certainly

22

had nothing impressive about it, with its bamboo walls and uneven furniture. There was a small rug by the bed, a red blot
on the planks which alone distinguished this abode from the
mud-floored homes of the soldiery. And two or three of the
articles scattered about bespoke the refinement of their owner.

Popa presented himself, a lithe little fellow, brown and
fierce. He saluted.

"Popa, you know what has happened to Adja?"

"Tjingtjang, Lieutenant," replied Popa, saluting again.*

"You may be thankful that you didn't accompany him this
time. If you had—" He paused, and looked at the man.

"Perhaps—forgive me that I say it—we should not have
been caught, Lieutenant."

"In that case your punishment would have awaited you here.
You understand that *any* attempt at insubordination will hence-
forth be repressed with the utmost severity. I *will* not have it.
You can go."

Popa saluted again, and tripped off. His heart was hot within him for the loss of his comrade.

"They call us 'tiger-faces,'" he reflected; "they will call us
'tiger-tails.'"

"A splendid fighter," said Gerard, aloud, "like so many of
these Amboinese. And nothing to be gained but death or un-
recorded glory. God forgive the worthies at home, who care
for no man's soul or body as long as consols remain at par! If
some of us didn't love fighting for its own mad sake (which I
certainly don't) where would their Excellencies' consols be?"

Then he lighted another cigarette, and once more told himself that really this time he must count his store. So he would
—to-morrow.

He threw himself in his single rocking-chair and yawned.
What should he do the live-long evening? What had he done
through the creeping weeks and months? What could one do?
It was the emptiness which tormented him — the not doing
anything: he wanted to be with the invaders on ahead. He
groaned over this misfortune for the five-hundredth time.

---

* Achinese torture. The Dutch soldier says, "Lieutenant," etc.

Otherwise, Acheen was not half a bad place—much more spacious and much more *mouvementé* than Holland. Of course it was always horribly hot, and here where he lay, by the marsh, it was even especially unhealthy. Everybody sickened. But then, on the other hand, there were no duns. Gerard looked down at his lean, yellow fingers. Yes, he had altered.

But what matter? Who cared? Only he wished he had had something to show for it. He felt that the Home Government may send you to kill savages, but they ought to provide plenty of savages for you to kill.

In the military club at Kotta Radja he was popular. He would always be popular with brave men anywhere because of his unpretending unselfishness. And many of his comrades liked a fellow who was Baron van Helmont, you know, by George! and he never seems to remember, though, somehow, you never forget.

He devoutly wished himself in the club at this moment. They would be playing, and there would be unlimited tobacco.

"Werda?" He leaped to his feet. A swift brightness swept across the gloom outside. A signal rang clear. At his cabin door a sergeant met him.

"Friends, Lieutenant," said the man.

Under the protection of a suddenly uplifted fire-ball, half a dozen soldiers in dark uniform were seen approaching the Benting, whistling a signal as they came. Gerard recognized a party from the neighboring fort, his companion in exile at their head. Greatly surprised, he went down to the gate.

"You, Streeling!" he cried. "What, in the name of mischief, brings you here? That light of yours will rouse the neighborhood."

"Put it out, somebody," said the new-comer. "I only fired it as we emerged from the wood. I felt no desire to test your sentries, thanks."

"Well, what have you come for?"

"And why shouldn't I take my walks abroad in the cool of the evening? Isn't this the pacified zone?"

Gerard's brother-commander was a facetious little man, melan-

choly by nature, and with a melancholy history, which he kept
to himself.

"Let's go into your hut and I'll tell you," he said. "Have
you anything left to drink?"

"Only brandy."

"Lucky fellow to have plenty of spirits still!" He settled
himself, by right of sodality, in the rocking-chair, the proprietor
of the shanty crouching on the bed.

"It's just this," began Streeling, with suppressed excitement.
"Krayveld's turned up at my place from the ships with important despatches. The steam-launch can't get any farther
to-night, and he says they must be taken on to the front, in
any case, at once. It appears they've big plans for to-morrow
up yonder." He jerked his head in the direction of his hopes.

"Yes," said Gerard, and his downcast eyelids twitched.

"His orders are that one of us is to take them on by road,
and that *he* is to remain in command for the man that goes.
He doesn't know the road, you know — what there is of it,
damn it!"

"Yes," replied Gerard, continuing the close study of his
cigarette-point. "*Which* is to take them on?"

"There's the nuisance. The 'Vice' has left that to us to
settle. Didn't know which had least fever, you know. But
one of us may go."

"Yes," repeated Gerard, with a sigh; "I suppose it must be
you."

"I suppose it must," admitted the little man, echoing the
sigh. "I'm the oldest, you see. It's risky work. You're as
likely as not to get hashed into mince-meat by some of those
klewang brutes. Save us from our friends, say I!"

"True, I hadn't thought of the risk," replied Gerard, with
much alacrity. "I'll go, if you like. In fact, you know, I
think it had better be I."

"Why? Nonsense. You were awfully seedy when I was
over here last week. And it strikes me you're looking pale
to-day. The miasma 'll be murderous at this time of night
round by the second swamp."

"Yes," said Gerard again, endeavoring to improve the lamplight. "How long is it—did you say—since your fever went?"

The other did not answer immediately, and in the silence that ensued Gerard let fall one word from the tips of his lips: "Humbug!"

"Humbug, am I? And what are you? Yah!"

The two men looked at each other.

"Well, then, if it must be, it must be," said Streeling, submissively ; "I don't want to spoil your chances, old man. Let's draw lots."

"You *are* the eldest," admitted Gerard. "Thanks."

"The eldest ought to remain in command," replied Streeling, with a grin. "But I'll tell you what—we'll sit by the doorway, and if the first man that passes is a native, it's yours. That'll give me the odds, for you've got more Europeans."

"Done," said Gerard, and they waited near the dark entry in silence, puffing.

Presently Popa came by.

"Damn my luck!" ejaculated the little officer, with great energy, somewhere deep down in his throat. He got up. "Well, it's fairly earned, and I wish you joy. I hope you'll have a chance to-morrow of getting near the blackguards. Meanwhile I must make myself as comfortable as I can."

"Oh, as likely as not you'll see me back before breakfast to-morrow. However, if there's a fight on, of course I shall ask leave to stay."

"Of course. Well, here are the despatches. And—by Jove! Helmont, I beg your pardon—here are your letters that Krayveld brought up with him. I quite forgot, thinking of other things. Well, I wish you joy, that's all I can say."

"Thanks. I suppose I had better be getting ready."

"How many men will you take? Half a dozen?"

"A sergeant and six fusileers. I shall let the men volunteer. But I want a couple of natives for the sake of their ears and eyes." Gerard went out and set to work at once, selecting the best men from among a swarm of candidates. Half an hour afterwards everything was ready; the eight dark figures filed through the purposely darkened gateway : who could say

what eyes might be watching, alarmed by Streeling's sudden
blaze? Gerard came first, with the sergeant, their loaded re-
volvers in their hands. Popa brought up the rear.

Gerard reflected that he owed his good-fortune to Popa's
opportune appearance. "Well, I'll take you," he said. "You're
in want of something to cheer you up. But none of your
pranks, mind."

Popa saluted.

A clearing, as has been said, surrounded the Benting; immediately beyond that, however, the party plunged into the forest, and were obliged to advance along the narrow path in single
file. They had about two miles to go.

The night hung heavy in the enormous trees and among the
tangled masses of underwood. Stars there were none, and the
air seemed to be full of gray floatings that veiled its usual trans-
parency. So much the better.

It was very silent now. The whole line of them went creeping forward, with eyes to right and left, everywhere alert, every
footstep hushed, as the dim trunks loomed through the darkness in continuous clumps. It was the custom of the Achinese
to lurk by these pathways day and night, waiting with infinite
patience for the rare chance of killing a single foe. At any
moment their shriek might burst forth and their scimitars might
flash. The air all around was full of indistinct movement, soft
and sultry under the palms and waringin-trees.

" 'St! What was that?" They all stood as granite, finger
on trigger. Only some faint breath high above them touching
the never-silent tjimaras.

" Confound them tjimaras, sir!" whispers the sergeant.
" They're every bit as bad, sir, as women's tongues."

" 'St! Forward." Every now and then Gerard halts and
listens; his thoughts are of the precious packet sleeping on
his breast.

In fact, it was madness, this night excursion along the most
uncertain of foot-paths. Why couldn't they send up their despatches earlier?

Krayveld had answered that they couldn't send them before
they got them. Gerard shrugged his shoulders in the dark.

Despatches *from* Government were hardly likely, he thought, to
be worth a single soldier's life.

With a feeling of very real relief he reached the rice-fields
beyond the wood. He stopped and counted his men. Rear-
guard there all right? Forward. Who's that making his
poniard click?

Far in the distance, miles away, lay a couple of sleeping vil-
lages; those nearest had been razed to the ground; some brute
was howling among the ruins. From the fort rang the beat of
the hour, as struck by a sentry on a wooden block, breaking
across the solitude with terrifying distinctness. Eleven.

Beyond the rice-fields, through the tall, still grass, and by the
sickening marshes, with their reeds and sleeping water-fowl,
then up again into the great forest, darkling, dangerous. Into
the depths of the forest, deeper, deeper.

"Hist!" In a moment the men had formed round their
leader, for the noise of crackling branches resounded in every
ear. Again.

The enemy was upon them!

"Kalong. Kalong," said one of the Amboinese.

"It's the big bats, sir, out feeding," echoed the sergeant.

"I know," replied Gerard. "What's all this row about?
Single file. We shall have to be doubly careful." And on
they went, with that occasional breaking of twigs around them
that was infinitely worse than the silence had been. It would
now prove impossible immediately to distinguish an approaching assassin. The darkness seemed to thicken, as with a flood
of ink.

At last they once more stood outside the jungle. Before
them, with an open space intervening, lay the camp, black
against the darkness of the plain. All around stretched the
rapid ruin of a roughly widened clearing; the smell of roots
and rotting plants and freshly-hewn logs was almost insupportable. It would have signalled the camp from afar. Every one
who has slept in these clearings knows the odor. From time
to time a rocket went up in silence, piloting the patrols.

"Halt!" said Gerard. "What's wrong behind?"

"Rear man missing, sir."

He turned sharply. "Impossible!" No one ventured to contradict him, but their silence did not alter the fact that Popa had dropped away.

"We must go back," said Gerard. "He must have fallen. How did you not notice?"

"Please, Lieutenant, it was the crackling. I thought it was the Kalongs."

They retraced their steps in glum anxiety, and searched back into the forest for nearly half a mile. At last Gerard dared go no farther; already his military conscience pricked him. The military conscience almost always pricks.

"I must take on the despatches," he said. "After that we can see. I don't understand at all. He can't have fallen. You, Drok, surely we have gone far enough?"

"We have gone too far, Lieutenant," replied the man in an awe-struck whisper. "I saw him farther on than this."

"Very well; it can't be helped. Forward." In grave procession the little party reached the camp.

Having delivered up his despatches, Helmont·asked first for leave to stay and see to-morrow's operations, and secondly for a search-party to hunt up his missing man. It cannot be said that the Colonel jumped at the latter proposal.

The next day was to be an important one, and he wanted every soul that could to get a decent sleep.

"Depend upon it," he said, "the fellow has been cut down by a marauder. They always cut down the last of the troop."

"Yes, but I should like to find that marauder," replied Gerard, "or the corpse. May I go back with my own men?"

"Oh, certainly," said the commanding officer, a little testily. "You may go back all the way, if you like. Good-night."

So the little troop slipped away from the encampment and back into the jungle again. They all considered it hard lines, but entirely unavoidable. And they peered the more closely into the dark.

Presently one of the native soldiers stopped on a slope and pointed to the bush close behind him. None of the Europeans could distinguish anything.

"Man gone down here," he said; "there's a track." He knelt and began cautiously feeling along the ground. "Lieutenant, there's a man gone down here," he repeated; "gone into the Aleh-Aleh (the long grass); you could see if it wasn't so black."

A path of any kind there certainly was not; still, Gerard consented to reconnoitre a short distance, cautiously following the trail.

It turned abruptly, and after a few steps which rendered them clear of the trees, the little party stood enclosed in tall green spikes on every hand.

" 'Tis along here to the right," persisted the fusileer. Here, at least, the dark sky hung free above them, and the air was fresher than in the wood. Gerard hesitated. "We shall lose ourselves," he said. But even as he spoke a faint purl of human voices reached them, evidently coming from some distance farther on down below. For a moment they crouched, with straining ears. Then "Forward," said their leader, and they slunk through the labyrinth, with constant precaution lest any weapon should catch, pausing to hearken, seeking the sound.

Their pulses quickened as they realized that it was drawing nearer. After a slow descent, which seemed wellnigh endless, they could even distinguish a flow of sound in suppressed but eager torrent. It was impossible to distinguish words, yet suddenly each man's heart asked the self-same, silent question: Why were these Achinese marauders, with whom they were on the point of colliding, conversing in *Malay*? The voice ceased.

The Aleh-Aleh broke off unexpectedly on the ridge of a steep incline. Gerard, slipping forward, sprang back under shelter, not a moment too soon. In the sudden opening he had descried above them, a little to the right, as the fusileer had foretold, a dozen of the enemy grouped on a narrow, bamboo-protected ledge round a tiny, low-burning lamp. Cautiously he now peeped forth, and by the feeble flicker recognized the wretched Popa, bound and stripped to the waist, in the centre of the group.

"There," he said, pointing. "Forward." Slipping and crawling along the edge, so as to keep clear of the swish of the grass, the men followed him up. Under them the abyss fell straight.

On the skirts of the little plateau they stopped. They could now plainly perceive that Popa had a gaping klewang wound across his shoulder. What feeble light there was had been turned full upon the prisoner, the wild forms of his captors sinking away into the darkness. They have been arguing with him, reflected Gerard, trying to induce him, by the usual horrible threats, to desert. Judging by the man's countenance, they had now accorded him time to consider.

Even while his comrades stood watching, waiting—to shoot were to imperil the central figure—the allotted moments must have run themselves out. One of the Achinese sprang to his feet, his big gold button twinkling, and with a hideous flash of his scimitar across the dilating stare of the soldiery, he swept off one of the prisoner's ears. Another started up with a similar movement, but before he could fling himself forward a shrill chorus of shrieks overflowed on all sides. Somehow, he can never tell how, Gerard was up on the ledge, in the midst of them; Popa's assailant had fallen, shot through the breast; a dozen distorted, yelling faces were seething around the drawn sword of the "Wolanda."

Thirty seconds, swift, interminable, an unbroken clash of steel through the smoke and crash of the bullets—thirty seconds intervened before his soldiers, getting up to him, plunged fiercely forward, with bayonet and poniard, into the indistinguishable mass. The little lamp had immediately rolled over; the solemn darkness shook with a turmoil of oaths and outcries rising high above the clang of the fighting and the thud of the fallen. In a moment it was all over. Yet the trembling air still seemed to listen among the sudden silence of the tall tji-mara-trees.

A heavy groan shuddered slowly forth. Then another. And again another in a different voice.

Gerard struck a match and lighted a pocket-lantern. Of his seven men, three, including Popa, still stood upright; a fourth rose, stumbling, from the dark confusion on the ground. Of the three remaining, two were already dead (one decapitated), and the third lay unconscious. Not one of the Achinese was able to continue the fray.

"Hurry up," said Gerard, cutting Popa's bonds. " No, I'm not wounded; it's nothing but a scratch. We're quite near the camp; the least hurt must help the others."

The tomtom, the enemy's well-known alarm, came thumping down the valley, re-echoed on every side from twenty watchful hiding-places.

"Hurry up for your lives!" cried Gerard. In shamefaced silence Popa pointed to an easier track. Slowly and laboriously the two badly wounded were passed down by the others; the trail was followed back again; the foot-path was reached. Near the entrance to the wood a patrol met them, sent out on the report of the firing.

"And you, Popa, speak," said Gerard, after the tension was over.

"It is my crime, Lieutenant; the fault be on my head. I observed the trail as we went by; my thoughts were heavy for the murdered Adja. I wandered down it a few steps in my curiosity, knowing I could soon rejoin you. Suddenly one struck at me from the darkness through the grass."

"And why did they not come after us?" questioned Gerard.

"You were gone on, up above; the grass is high. There were two of them only; I was alone, marauding."

"You shall be shot to-morrow," said Gerard.

"Lieutenant, it is right."

But on the morrow nobody had any time to think of shooting Popa. At a very early hour, in the dewy silence of sunrise, the gates of the fortified camp were thrown back, and the stream of soldiers, solemnly emerging, went curling down into the rice-fields, with a long glitter of guns. All eyes were fixed on the farther frontier of forest, where stretched, half-hidden, the low, sullen line of the enemy's defence. A couple of advance forts, whose small cannon were proving especially troublesome, had been marked out for the morning's attack. Of late these operations had been greatly restricted, and the men now

sent out accepted gratefully a possibility of painless death. For
the shadow of cholera lay lurid upon the camp.

Gerard was indeed in luck, as Streeling had said, after all
these wistfully patient months. He had taken a sick man's
place, and was acting as a (mounted) captain.

In the slow splendor of the burning daybreak, across that
vast expanse of increasing sun, the " right half of the seven-
teenth battalion," separating from the main body, advanced
with half a company of sappers, under cover of artillery, against
the fortifications of Lariboe. They were barely within range
when the enemy opened fire from his lilas or little cannon,
almost immediately backing up the discharge with the flat
bang of numerous blunderbusses and the rarer whistle of the
breech-loader. The roar of his resistance now became continuous, and soon his intrenchments ran like a torrent of flame
under rapidly thickening clouds.

At a distance of some two hundred and fifty paces the troops
halted, momentarily, to send back a volley in reply. Then on
they went again, silently filling up the gaps in their ranks,
while, after the custom of Eastern warfare, a hailstorm of curses
and abusive epithets now mingled with the deadlier missiles
that poured into their midst. At fifty paces the order was
given to charge.

The men, rushing forward to their special point of attack,
found themselves arrested by an outer hedge of thick bamboo
bushes, with a broad border of bamboo spikes. Once close up
against this position they were somewhat more sheltered from
the fire of the central line, and, moreover, protected by the
artillery behind them; but the garrison of the fort did not
leave them one moment unharassed. They were now compelled
to unsheathe their knives, and, with the aid of the sappers, they
began calmly carving a passage through the dense obstruction
of the bamboos.

A few terrible minutes elapsed. Some of the soldiers, cut by
the spikes, flung themselves in furious effort against this living
wall; others recoiled for a moment, disheartened by the groans
of the wounded around them, feeling hopelessly arrested between advance and retreat. Then, as death still continued to

"THEY BEGAN CALMLY CARVING A PASSAGE THROUGH THE DENSE OBSTRUCTION"

blaze down upon them, amid the taunts of the enemy, they
rushed bravely to their task again, cheered by their officers,
who well knew the strain of such an obstinate impediment.
Every moment of delay was calamitous. Through an opening
the fort became visible, lying well back behind a field, its ram-
parts vaguely crowded with brightly turbaned heads. And half-
way between hedge and fort rose insolently the banner of
Acheen's Sultan, with its crescent and klewangs, over a stuffed
doll, intended for a caricature of the idolized Dutch General,
ignominiously hanging by the feet.

Not one man who was there but will remember with what
a fury of reprisal this childish insult filled our breasts. Amid
shouts of execration the attack on the breach was renewed;
but at that moment, above the hacking and swearing, a dark
mass, rushing swiftly from the background, rose mighty in
mid-air, and at one leap — grown historic — Helmont's horse
cleared spikes, soldiers, and bamboos, and landed serenely on
the farther side. Then, galloping up to the derisive effigy,
Helmont rapidly cut it loose, bringing down the enemy's flag
along with it, and, flinging the colors of Acheen across his
revolver, he fired through them five swift barrels at the cluster-
ing turbans which were concentrating their aim on this unexpected target. Then, holding the image superbly aloft, he
began backing his horse—all in one exquisite instant of time—
and fell heavily, horse, rider, and effigy rolling together amid a
sudden rush of blood. Before and behind rose a mingling
yell as of wild beasts wounded. A little brown Amboinese,
his clothes and limbs torn and ensanguined, ran forward, having fought his way first through the aperture, and flung himself as a screen across the prostrate officer. Only a moment
longer and the whole lot of them, with faces distorted and uni-
forms disordered, came pouring over the field under a fierce
increase of projectiles. They swept upward in the madness
of the storm, the brief pandemonium of shouts, shrieks, and
imprecations, the whirlwind of firing and fighting, in a mystery
of dust and smoke. And a cheer, leaping high above that hell,
leaping high with a human note of gladness, announced that
the fort had been carried, that victory was won. Up with our

own orange rag on the summit! Hark to the shrill blare of the
bugle! Hurrah!

They disengaged Helmont from his dying charger and
carried him away to the ambulance. In undressing him, cutting
loose the clothes, the doctor came on his parcel of letters, and,
a moment afterwards, on an old brown glove. The left hand
still firmly clutched the hideously grinning doll. Popa would
permit no one to force the fingers asunder—Popa, who, in spite
of his shoulder-wound, had obtained leave that morning to get
himself killed by the enemy if he could, and who certainly
had done his best. The doctor gently put aside the relic and
the opened letters. Gerard had still read them the night before. There had been one more, which he had read twice
over, and had then burned carefully and ground to dust.

"Helmont," cried the purple Colonel, hurriedly, stooping low
by the young man's unconscious ear. "Can't you understand
what I'm saying? I've only a moment. It's the Military Cross.
Gentlemen, surely that should call him to life again. Helmont,
I swear, by the heavens above us, it's bound to be the Military
Cross!"

The Dowager looked up from her placid embroidery and
smiled to Plush. Beyond the great gray window the sleepy
twilight was softly sinking back into an unbroken veil of mist.
"What a dull drab day it has been!" said the Dowager. "I
wonder—" But she left her sentence unfinished. And the
folds of the curtain hung dense. For an Angel of Mercy has
drawn it across our horizon.

CHAPTER XLII

IT was quite true that the days at the Horst were drab-colored. They seemed to be that even all through the long and brilliant summer, and their darkening could hardly be called perceptible when the northern sun sank from sight for seven slow months. Time appeared to lower over the house with the dumb threat of an approaching thunder-storm. And some people are fretful before a thunder-storm; and some hold their breaths.

The Bois-le-Duc Helmonts were settled at the Home Farm. The tranquil mother had said: Oh yes; she still knew how to milk cows; it would really be rather amusing! And she had spread her fat hands on her ample lap and smiled her good-natured smile. But Theodore had frowned. "Leave the cow-milking," he had said, bitterly, "to the Baroness Ursula." As soon as he got away from Ursula he felt that he hated her.

His temper did not improve during the first year of his new occupation. Work as he would—night and day—he could not make up for initial mistakes, nor could he victoriously combat increasing agricultural depression. The dispossessed farm-steward successfully harassed him on every hand. If Otto, the lord of the manor, had made himself unpopular by putting down abuses, what must be the fate of this stranger, with his perky, boyish face? The whole neighborhood, for miles round, was full of people with grievances, some deep down, of Otto's inflicting, others freshly bleeding under Ursula's hand. And a low tide of resentment was secretly swelling under smooth water against My Lady Nobody.

Ugly stories began to be told about her, diligently propa-

gated by Meerman, the discarded agent. As if all her admin-
istrative sins were not sufficient, accusations had lately cropped
up which appealed far more vividly to the popular imagination.
Substantial housewives whispered behind her back " Fie ! fie !"
and young fellows winked to each other, grinning. No one
knew whence these stories had suddenly sprung, but everybody
had heard them. A patient inquirer might, perhaps, have
traced their origin to Klomp's cottage in the wood.

When they first reached the ear of the village constable
that worthy portentously shook his head. It was in the tavern
parlor of Horstwyk, where the lesser notables sat nightly, pipe
in hand, waiting for each other to speak. The village constable
was a great man, chiefly because he managed to keep clear of
animosities, and his opinion carried weight. Every man present,
leering up at him in the peculiar, deliberate peasant way, felt
that he knew more than he deemed it wise to acknowledge, and
they all approved his prudence. But nothing could more resistlessly have condemned the Lady of the Manor. The Law—
mysterious Weigher of all men in secret balances—*knew*.

" There's something written up against her," they reflected,
awe-struck. Juffers, the constable, merely said :

" The Lady Baroness is a very charitable lady. I wish you
all good-night."

He shook his head to himself all the way home, and in passing a particular spot, by a great elm-tree, on the road near the
Manor-house, he flashed his dark-lantern across the ground, as if
struck by a sudden doubt.

Just then—some two years after Otto's death—there were
plenty of rumors afloat to interest the village cronies. Quite
recently lazy, good-for-nothing Pietje Klomp had come to grief,
"as everybody had always expected she would," in the usual
" good-for-nothing " manner. Strangely enough, her equally lazy
and worthless father had driven her forth from under his roof
with unexpected energy—an abundance of oaths and blows—
when, confident in his oft-proven affection, she ventured to confess her now hopeless disgrace. After half a night of hail and
snow in the wood she had crept back to obtain admittance from
the pitiful Mietje, but next morning her inflexible parent had

"SUBSTANTIAL HOUSEWIVES WHISPERED BEHIND HER BACK, 'FIE! FIE!'"

once more turned her adrift. She had watched for an opportunity while he dozed, and then quietly slipped to her accustomed seat. During several days this singular duel had lasted, and ultimately, of course, the woman's persistence had triumphed. Klomp only ejected the girl when he had to get up, anyhow. As long, therefore, as he remained on his bench by the stove she was safe. And Mietje, tearfully exerting herself, took care to anticipate all her father's few wishes—for coffee, fuel, last week's newspaper, et cetera—and to keep him "immobilized" during a great part of the day. He was not unwilling, provided he could scowl at Pietje in the pauses of his almost continuous snore.

Ursula, of course, heard from Freule Louisa what Freule Louisa had heard from her maid. So Ursula called to see the criminal. She had compromised with the ladies of her household, and only went to visit such patients as the doctor had certified free from any risk of infection. The village, knowing this, wrote her down a coward.

"May I come in?" asked Ursula at Klomp's door.

No answer; for the door was locked, Klomp would not stir to open it, and Pietje dared not pass near her father. She cowered in her corner, stiller than any scratchy mouse.

Ursula rattled the lock in vain. Then she peeped through the window, darkening its dirt, and saw Pietje's woful eyes staring out of the gloom from the floor. With the resolute movement she herself delighted in, she thrust up the low window from outside and stepped over the sill.

"Would you shut it, please, m'm, now you're in?" said Klomp's sleepy voice.

Ursula sat down in the middle of the room, facing Pietje's dark corner.

"I've come to see you," she said, very severely.

She could not help herself. She knew that it was every right-minded woman's duty under these circumstances to be very, very severe.

Pietje moved a little uneasily, but did not rise. So, without delay, Ursula began her lecture. It was very conscientious and rather long, and all quite true and exceedingly severe. After

23

the opening sentences Pietje's head bent low, and about mid-way she began to cry. She had not cried much during the scenes with her father, and tears now seemed to come to her as a pleasurable relief. Entering into the spirit of the thing, she cried so very loud that Ursula's lecture had to come to an abrupt conclusion, tailless, like a Manx cat. In how far Pietje calculated on this result none but she may presume to decide.

"So, of course, you must go to a reformatory," said Ursula, firmly. "I am willing to help you on condition that you take *my* advice."

"Don't want to go to no performatory," sobbed Pietje, with vague perplexities concerning circuses and ballet girls. "Father 'll keep me if I says I'm sorry."

A grunt from the other end of the room.

"Pietje, you have behaved very badly," continued Ursula. "It seems to me that you hardly understand the wickedness of your act. You only regret its unpleasant results. No, Pietje, you are"—she felt it her positive, painful duty to speak plainly—"a very wicked, guilty, evil-hearted girl."

"Dear me, Mevrouw," growled a voice half-choked against a sleeve, "can't you leave the poor creature in peace?"

"No, Klomp," replied Ursula, "'tis my duty to help you both. I understand and appreciate your righteous anger, but, fortunately, *I* can provide Pietje with a home. It is only natural you should not wish her to remain near Mietje."

At this very moment Mietje came down-stairs.

"Father, here's your li—yes, sister's going to stay with me," she said.

"Get you up-stairs again," shouted Klomp, with a big oath, "and don't come down till I call you." He sat up, his listless face full of fire. "Now, Mevrouw," he said, "you just kindly go back to the Manor-house, please. That's where you belong —*now*—and thank your stars for it. And leave poor people like us to settle our troubles between us. Pietje's a poor, ignorant girl, and she 'ain't got the wit to go hunting for a husband —least of all in the papers. She just took the first villain that came fooling her way."

" But, Klomp, I had understood—" began Ursula, rising with dignity.

" No, you hadn't, m'm ; there's just the mistake. You hadn't understood nothing, begging your pardon. Nor, in fact, you needn't. There isn't anything to understand."

He actually got up, and, shuffling across to the door, he opened it. There could be no mistaking his exceptional earnestness now.

" Well," said Ursula, gently, preparing to depart, " when you want me, when Pietje wants me, send up to the Manor-house, and I will do whatever I can."

He bolted the door behind her.

" Father—" began Pietje, timidly.

" Hold your tongue," he broke in. " I don't want to know you're there." And he threw himself down violently on his bench.

Ursula had nearly reached home before the meaning of Klomp's attack recoiled upon her brain. " Looking for a husband in the papers." Suddenly she understood. It was the old story of the trysting-place cropping up again. Not for nothing had Adeline stayed with the Klomps ! Her brow mantled, and with quite unusual *hauteur* she acknowledged the salute of two passing laborers.

The men looked at each other.

" Stuck up, ain't she ?"

" Yes "—with immediate oblivion of all former graciousness —" so she allus was."

The old Baroness received her daughter-in-law in a tremble of pink-spotted excitement. There were letters from Acheen— exceedingly important letters ! Ursula must sit down at once and listen. Gerard had been in action. Gerard had done something wonderfully brave. He had been just a little bit wounded in doing it—oh, nothing, the merest scratch ; but it happened to be the right hand, so a comrade wrote for him. He was going to be rewarded in some magnificent manner—made a colonel ?—and the deed had been so very brave he would probably soon be sent home again. *That* was the Dowager's reward.

"Sent home?" repeated Ursula, motionless in her chair.
"Mamma, did you say he was wounded?"

"Oh, the merest scratch," replied the Dowager, testily. "He
says so himself. Ursula, you always try to make people nervous. Gerard never lied to me. And, you see, he is coming back.
If he were really hurt he would never undertake so long a journey. I remember my poor dear husband"—she always avoided,
if possible, saying "papa" to Ursula—"once cut his hand with
a bread-knife so badly that he couldn't use it for nearly a
month."

"Oh yes," admitted Ursula, hastily. "Yes—yes, I dare say
it is nothing. I am glad, mamma, I am glad. I am proud of
him."

"You!" replied the old Baroness, quite rudely, in a tone altogether strange. "What is he to you? When he comes back,
Ursula, he will take away the Horst."

"I dare him to do it!" said Ursula, fiercely. She drew herself up, looking down on the poor little heap of ruffles by the
writing-table. Some moments elapsed before she spoke again.
"I found the letter you were looking for, mamma," she said,
and her voice had grown quite gentle; "it is one from the late
Prince Henry to papa."

"Thank you, Ursula. I am afraid I was rude to you just
now. I have no wish to be rude to you, nor to any one. It is
not in my nature to be rude. But this news from Acheen has
excited me. I am not as young as I was"—she peered across,
with a quick glance of anxiety, at her daughter-in-law—"yet I
am thankful to reflect that Gerard, when he comes, will find me
but very little changed."

The Freule Louisa came in. "Have you heard?" she asked.
"Now, that's the kind of thing I like, and I never expected it
of Gerard. I always thought Gerard was a bit of a coward, a
curled darling of the drawing-room, like Plush. Didn't you,
Ursula?"

"No, indeed," replied Ursula.

Freule Louisa giggled suddenly. "Well, I dare say you knew
better," she said. "Only I hope he won't come back too
soon."

" Why ? What?" exclaimed the Dowager. Ursula had left the room.

" Because Tryphena has just sent him out a large box of Javanese tracts to get distributed among the enemy. We feel that the Achinese should not be killed, but Christianized. Ursula's father behaved very badly about the tracts. He said that the only way to get them 'sent on' would be for the soldiers to wrap their bullets in them. Scandalous, for a Christian minister, and so I told Josine."

" Louisa—"

" And he says, besides, that the Achinese don't know the language."

" Louisa—"

" As if they couldn't learn. I dare say there isn't much difference."

" Louisa, when Gerard comes he will send Ursula back to her father."

" I doubt it. You know, *I* have always said—"

" Don't say it again; it sounds like—like blasphemy."

The Dowager seemed for the moment to recover all her intellectual force.

" He will take back the Horst—do you hear? They dare not refuse it him after what he has done. And he will marry money. Then nothing will be left me to do after I have seen him except to finish my Memoir before I depart in peace. I should like to tell Theodore that the Memoir was finished."

" If he is going to prove so strong a man," replied Aunt Louisa, " I think I shall leave him what little money I possess. But what is that? A mere drop in the ocean. I am a poor woman, Cécile, as you know."

CHAPTER XLIII

THAT evening some household duty called Ursula into the unused up-stairs corridor, which as a rule she avoided. And as she passed the "Death-rooms" she very nearly came into collision with Hephzibah, issuing from them, eyelids downcast.

Ursula felt that the woman had been watching her, as usual. And although, as a rule, she resisted the feeling, to-day, by a sudden impulse, she turned like a dog at bay.

"If it makes you uncomfortable, why do you come here at all?" she said.

"Why do you?" retorted the woman, adding "Mevrouw."

"I never do; I was only passing," said Ursula.

"Ah, you *daren't*. But I must. I can't help myself. I can't rest down-stairs. I seem to hear it calling to me all the time. Mevrouw, it *drags* me up. There's guilt in this house. It won't sleep."

Ursula leaned up against the wall and closed her eyes.

"Have you anything you wish to say to me, Hephzibah?" she replied. "If so, say it."

The woman hesitated.

"No, I've nothing to say to you," she began, slowly. "I suppose it's true, Mevrouw, that the Jonker is coming home?"

"Of course it's true."

Hephzibah began moving away.

"If you go in there, Mevrouw," she said, "perhaps you'll hear it to-night. It's groaning and gasping worse than ever to-night."

She ran down the long passage.

"O Lord! O Lord, have mercy!" she murmured. "I've

done what I could to make amends. I thought, after what I'd
done, I should never hear it again. O Lord, I'm not a bad
woman! There's those sit in high places is a great deal worse
than me."

"The creature is crazy," said Ursula, aloud, as she pushed
open the door of the antechamber.

In the inner room all was dark and still. Ursula shut herself
in, and sank down by the bed.

"Otto, I have done my best," she said.

An immense weight of guilt lay upon her. Gerard was
grievously wounded, was dying; perhaps already dead. Who
could tell what was happening out yonder, in the fatal sun-
blaze? Before a message could be flashed across the waters
his body would already lie rotting in the red-hot ground. And
his soul, for all she knew, might be standing, even now, by her
side.

"Gerard, I have done it for the best," she whispered.

But the words brought her no relief. She knew that if this
man died his life would be required at her hands. And if he
returned alive, yet broken in health, mutilated, crushed, she
would have to confront him ever after, reading in every furrow
of his forehead the charge against herself.

"I have done right," she gasped. "I could not do otherwise. I have done right."

And her thoughts went back to Otto, dying here, gasping
out with every successive stifle his last, his only appeal. For a
long time she knelt there, her face upon her hands.

"If only some one would answer!" she thought. "If only
one of them would speak!"

The place was very silent. She could hear the dog Monk
sniffing and vaguely whining beyond the outer door.

"If only Otto would answer me! If only he would release
me! What am I that I must bear this weight single-handed?
If only I knew—if only I knew!"

A great agony fell upon her, such as was strange to her
strong and steadfast nature. She wrung her hands, and, prostrate against the oaken, empty bedstead, in impotent protest, she
moaned softly through the darkness.

Suddenly some one — something — struck her through the darkness, heavily ; she fell back, losing consciousness, across the floor.

When she opened her eyes they rested on Hephzibah. The waiting-woman knelt, with a crazed expression on her white face, peering close down upon Ursula, by the faint glimmer of a night-lamp on the floor. Ursula shuddered, and dropped her eyes again.

"Not dead!" exclaimed Hephzibah, in a distinctly disappointed tone.

This touch of involuntary humor restored the invalid. She tried to sit up, and lifted one hand to her hair, which seemed to have grown oppressively warm and unsettled. She brought away her fingers covered with blood.

"I am bleeding still," she said. "What has happened, Hephzibah? Help me, please."

The woman pointed impressively to a clumsy carved ornament lying near her, which had fallen from among several others placed on the rickety canopy of the bed.

"*That* struck you," she said. "I thought it had killed you. 'Judgment is mine,' saith the Lord."

Ursula staggered to her feet. She became conscious of the great dog standing close beside her—attentive, benevolent. His deep eyes met hers ; they were overflowing with sympathy. Steadily gazing, he wagged his tail.

"Help me to my room," commanded Ursula. "There is no necessity for saying anything more. Get me some water." She gave her orders calmly, and the woman obeyed them. "Leave me," said Ursula, at last, lying back on a sofa with a bandage over her brow.

As soon as she was alone she got up, still dizzy, and rang the bell.

"The brougham," she said to the man.

He hesitated, in doubt if he could possibly have heard aright.

"The brougham," she repeated. "Tell Piet to get it ready as soon as possible. I am going far."

"Your nobleness is not hurt?" he stammered.

"No, no. Be quick." She hastily found a hat and mantle—

she had recently laid aside her mourning—and then waited till the carriage was announced.

"To the notary," she said. "Tell Mevrouw that I shall not be back till late."

Mynheer Noks lived some way out, on the farther side of Horstwyk. The coachman, unaccustomed to any sudden orders, whipped up his horse in surly surprise, and reflected on the chances of meeting the steam-tram.

His mistress did not think of the steam-tram to-day, often as she recalled, in passing it, her wild drive with Otto, and Beauty's cruel death. To-day she sat motionless in the little close carriage, watching the lamps go flashing across the road-side trees in a weary monotony of change.

"*If* it had killed me!" that was all her thought. She had never realized till this moment the possibility of immediate death. There would always be time, she had reasoned, for final arrangements, death-bed scenes. People did not die without an illness, however sudden. Besides, when she had risen from the long prostration of her early widowhood, "God has not permitted me to die," she had said. "He knew I had a mission to fulfil."

And now—supposing she had never regained consciousness?

She saw the lights of Horstwyk pass by, and wondered if she should never reach the notary's, and reproached herself for her foolishness.

"The notary is in?" she asked, eagerly, at his door.

Yes, the notary was in. He was entertaining some friends at dinner. Ursula drew back. "Show me into an office, or some such place," she said. The notary, convivial in dress and appearance, came to her in a little chilly back room, full of inkstains and dusty deeds.

"Nothing is wrong, I hope," he began; then, noticing the queer bandage under Ursula's dark-red bonnet, "You have had an accident?"

"No," replied Ursula. "Mynheer Noks, I am sorry to disturb you just now, but I can't wait. If I were to die to-night, who would be my heir?"

"That depends upon whether you have made a will," replied the notary.

"I have not made a will."

"In that case your father is your natural heir."

"So I thought. Then, notary, I must request you—I am very sorry to trouble you—but I must request you to make my will to-night."

"My dear lady, certainly. I presume you have brought your written instructions? Leave them with me, and to-morrow I will bring up a draft which we can talk over together." Ursula stopped him by a gesture.

"I must have the document signed and sealed," she said, "with its full legal value, to-night."

The notary stared at her; then he looked ruefully down at his resplendent, though already much crumpled, dress-shirt.

"I can't help it," continued Ursula, desperately. "It will only take you a moment—"

"Only a moment! Dear madame, documents of such importance—"

"Yes, only a moment. Just two sentences. That is all."

The notary sat down with a sigh, and drew forward a sheet of paper. "You wish to say?" he asked, and shivered—twice. The first shiver was real, the second ostentatious.

The second caused Ursula to disbelieve both.

"Only this: if I die without other arrangements—"

"Pardon me. I must already interrupt you. You cannot die 'with other arrangements'—the expression is exceedingly faulty—if you make a will."

"I can alter it, surely!" exclaimed Ursula.

"Only by another will." The notary sighed and looked at the clock. Quarter-past ten.

"Very well. I wish everything I possess to pass unconditionally to my brother-in-law, the Baron van Helmont."

The notary gave a visible start, and pricked his pen into the great sheet of paper. He nodded his head with complacent approval.

"Should he be dead," continued Ursula, "I wish it to belong to his cousin, the Jonker Theodore. That is all."

"Quite so," said the notary. "Quite right. And now, Mevrouw, I have only one objection."

"No objection," interrupted Ursula, vehemently. "There is none. Surely you have understood me?"

"I have understood you, but the objection remains. The thing can't be done. That is all."

Ursula started up.

"Can't be done!" she cried. "I am the best judge, Mynheer Noks, of what I choose to do with my own. I understand your being vexed at my disturbing your party; but if you refuse to draw up my will as I desire, I shall drive on till the horse drops, in search of another attorney." She trembled from head to foot.

But the lawyer was also exceedingly angry. He had always, since Otto's death, disliked and distrusted "My Lady."

"You may drive to Drum, if you wish to," he replied, "but you won't find a lawyer who can alter the law. No, Mevrouw, nor can I, even though you disturb my party to get it done. Be sure that *I'd* draw up a deed of gift, if you chose, this minute; but the law's stronger than you or I. And as long as your father lives he must come into half of your property."

"My father!" repeated Ursula. "Do you mean that I cannot disinherit him?"

"You cannot. If you happen to die before him, half of your possessions *must* pass to him. That is the law of the land; and, as I remarked, the law is stronger than you or I."

"It is stronger than justice," said Ursula.

The notary shrugged his shoulders.

"The case is altogether exceptional," he answered. Again he shivered, and looked at the clock. "So I suppose we may as well leave the will-making to a more convenient occasion," he added, half rising.

"No," replied Ursula, with an imperious movement; "make it at once, if you please, just as I said. Never mind its being illegal. You will be law, and my father justice."

"It is exceedingly incorrect," said the notary.

"A great race like that of the Van Helmonts cannot let itself be tied down by every paltry police regulation," replied Ursula, proudly. How often had she said so to herself, remembering her first experience of Gerard's *hauteur* at the railway station,

hammering the thought firmly into her "bourgeois" heart: the
high-born are a law unto themselves! So Gerard had understood, so Otto, and so she herself.

" Write it down," she said, " and leave the rest to us."

" Now, at once?"

She clinched her hands to avoid stamping forth her impatience.

" Now, at once," she said.

" But there must be witnesses, Mevrouw."

" Must there? Well, there are the servants, if some one can
hold the horse, and—" She stopped.

" Witnesses," she repeated. " You mean people who must
learn what I have just told you? Oh, but that is infamous!
No, no! Do you hear? I will not have it. I don't care for
your infamous laws. What I have said is between you and me.
As long as I live no ' witnesses ' shall know it."

" You wish to make a secret will," replied the lawyer, coldly.
" Well, there is no objection to that. I will write it out for you,
and you can copy and seal it. Then I draw up a deed of deposit, and the witnesses only witness that deed. But all this
will take time. My guests will be thinking of departing. My
wife—"

" Draw up a form," exclaimed Ursula; " I will copy it to-
night. My father and Gerard will respect my plainly stated
wishes, even if—something were to happen to-night."

Her voice dropped.

The notary glanced sideways, as he wrote, at the tall figure
pacing restlessly to and fro. She was not natural, not herself;
and herself, in his eyes, was strange enough for anything. That
bandage! How had she come by so sudden a wound? What
was the meaning of this unseemly hurry? He wondered uneasily whether this strange woman was minded to make away
with herself. He resolved to do what he could to prevent it—
a Christian duty, if rather an unwilling one.

" Here is the paper," he said, rising. " Nothing more can,
with decency, be done to-night. It has, you will understand,
not the slightest legal value."

" Give it me," she replied; " I shall expect you to-morrow

morning with your clerks. Thank you; I am sorry I was
obliged to disturb you, Mynheer Noks. Can I pass out unob-
served ?"

He unlocked the office entrance for her, holding up the oil-
lamp. Under the little portico she looked back.

"I do believe," she said, "you think I am going to kill myself."

"Mevrouw !" he stammered, horrified, over the wine-stain on
his shirt-front—"Mevrouw !"

"Set your mind at rest, my good notary. Only fools think
they can kill themselves. God has not made life quite so easy
as that."

The carriage-lights came twisting round to the little side gate.
As the footman held open the door there was a glitter of polished glass and a cosey vision of shaded silk.

"Come to-morrow morning early," said Ursula, with her foot
on the step, "and you shall have one of my poor father-in-law's
regalias."

As soon as she knew herself to be out of sight she pulled
the check-string and ordered the coachman to drive to the Parsonage.

"There goes eleven o'clock," said Piet to his companion.
"One would think there was truth in what people say."

"What do people say ?" asked the footman.

"Why, that Mevrouw likes being out by herself of nights.
At the tavern they were calling her 'night-bird.' "

"I know what they *used* to call her," grinned the fresh-faced
young footman. "It used to be Baroness Nobody."

"Oh, every one knows that. But hold your tongue. The
Jonker Gerard never would allow a whisper on the box. He
seemed to hear you in the middle of the night."

"The Jonker Gerard was a real gentleman," replied the footman, crossing his arms.

Ursula, as the carriage neared her old home, looked out anxiously, seeking for the light above the hall-door. It was gone ;
yet she knew her father to be in the habit of sitting up late.
She lifted the carriage-clock to the ray from one of the lanterns:
a quarter-past eleven.

"Let me out," she said; "I will go round to the back."

For a moment she stood, in the chill night, by the study window, listening. She knew perfectly well that she was acting foolishly; but that seemed no reason for leaving off.

"I must do it to-night," she said; "I cannot sleep until it is done."

She knocked at the window, timidly, terrified at the prospect of meeting with no response. The soughing of the trees struck cold upon her heart.

"Father!" she cried, with a sudden note of pain. "Father! Father!"

Somebody moved inside, and soon the heavy shutters, falling back, revealed the Dominé's mildly astonished face against the large French window.

Ursula brushed past him and threw herself into the faded old leather chair. She looked up into his questioning eyes for one long moment; then, as the *home-feel* of it all came over her —the room, the books, the loving countenance—she dropped forward on her hands and broke into convulsive weeping.

"Don't be frightened," she stammered between her sobs. "Nothing has happened. It's only—only—" She wept on silently. Presently she dried her eyes. "It's only—nothing," she said, smiling. "I am stupid. I have come to you for courage, Captain, as when I was a little girl."

The Dominé laid his single hand upon his daughter's head, and under his gaze she found it very difficult to keep to her brave resolve.

"No, no, you must scold me," she said. "That is not the way."

"You do the scolding yourself, child. It is only fair that one of us should attempt the comforting. Have you hurt your forehead?"

"Yes," replied Ursula, quickly. "It is not much, but it has upset me. It has upset me, you see."

"Ursula, Ursula, when a woman like you finds cause for tears, a bodily pain comes almost like a diversion. Dear child, I know your path is far from smooth. Sometimes I wonder whether we did right. It seems to me as if, with you, it would have been 'No crown, no cross.'"

"You ought to be proud of my career," said Ursula, still resolutely smiling.

"And, I know, the home-cross is the worst cross," continued the Dominé, as his eyes involuntarily wandered to a simpering portrait of Josine upon his writing-table. "Attack is not so hard, as all young soldiers soon find out. It is standing patient under fire."

"You pity me. You encourage me," said Ursula, with sudden vehemence. "You think I am not to blame. But if I *were* to blame for my misfortunes? If I were wrong? If I had brought them on myself?" She looked up anxiously.

"I should pity you all the more."

"Father"—Ursula rose—"do you think I could ever become a criminal?"

"Let him that standeth," replied the Dominé, "take heed lest he fall."

"And if he be fallen already?"

"There is no better posture for prayer."

The little room, so warm, so *anheimelnd*, grew very still. At that moment, perhaps, Ursula would have confessed everything.

But before she could utter another word the door was thrown violently open, and Miss Mopius, in a red flannel bedgown and nightcap, rushed over the threshold with a recklessness which entangled her in the Dominé's paper-basket, and precipitated her, a brilliant bundle of color, on the hearthrug.

"I wish you would knock!" cried the Dominé, irrational from sheer annoyance. Ursula had started back into the shade, and her aunt did not at first perceive her.

"Roderigue," gasped Miss Mopius, "there are thieves in the house!"

Burglary was Miss Mopius's most persistent bugbear.

"What? Again?" said the Dominé.

"Hush. Not so loud. This time I distinctly heard them."

"You always do," interrupted the Dominé, who was an angel, but angry.

"At the window just under me, as I awoke from a restless

sleep, I heard them, Roderigue. And I *saw* them. I saw two
figures stealthily creeping. Ah!" · Miss Mopius, who had
hissed out all this from the landing, now clutched her brother-
in-law's arm. " We shall be murdered," she sobbed. " Shut
the door, Roderigue; lock it. I don't know how I ever managed to summon up courage to come down."

She gave a shrill scream as something moved behind her.
Ursula stepped forward.

" Fear sees every danger double," said the Dominé, with a
smile to his daughter. " Go up-stairs again, Josine, and take
some of your Lob."

"Ursula!" cried Miss Mopius, in a fury—"Ursula, if I die,
my blood will be on your head! I was ill enough, Heaven
knows, this evening, and now I shall have a sleepless night."
She put her hand to her side. " Ah!" she said. " Ah!" Her
face was deadly pale. " It is not enough that I devote my
whole life to your poor old father, while you—live in luxury
and pomp."

" I am very sorry," answered Ursula, lamely. " You have
dropped all the Sympathetico on the carpet."

It was too true, and this misfortune annihilated Josine. In
her hand she held the bottle, from which the stopper had escaped as she fell.

" I had forgotten it," she said. " I had to take some before
venturing down. Now I sha'n't get a wink of sleep. But I
shouldn't have got that, anyhow." She shuffled towards the
door. " Roderigue, would you mind watching me up the stairs?
I certainly saw two men. But, of course, it is very dark. Is
Ursula going to stay all night?" Up-stairs, at her bedroom
door, she turned. " Nothing wrong, I suppose, at the Horst?"

" No," called back the Dominé from the hall.

" Of course not — only mad pranks. Ursula's behavior is
criminal."

The Dominé's thoughts lingered over this last word as he returned to his daughter. " She did not even observe your bandage!" he said.

" The room is dark," replied Ursula. " I am going now, but
I just wanted to ask you this. I came to ask it. By-the-bye,

Captain, did you know that if I were to die you would succeed
to the Horst and the Manor of Horstwyk?"

"Yes, 1 knew," replied the Dominé, gravely. "But you are
young, and I am old."

"Captain, dear, if ever you own the Horst, I want you to
give it to Gerard."

"Yes," replied the Dominé, more gravely still.

"You will, won't you?"

"Let me ask you another question: Why don't *you* give it
to Gerard, then?"

She faced him. "Because I can't," she said. "Don't ask
me, father. It isn't mine to give."

"Ursula, that would be exactly my standpoint. Property is
never ours; we are God's stewards. And if I became owner of
this great estate—God forbid, child, God forbid!—I should
hardly deem it right to disannul my responsibilities by aban-
doning them to another man."

"You think the property is better in other hands?" cried
Ursula, eagerly.

"I do not wish to say that of Gerard," replied the Dominé,
gently. "Responsibility changes character; even the reckless
Alcibiades felt as much. Still, I cannot help observing, Ursula,
in what a marvellous, I might well say miraculous, manner the
estate has passed away from Gerard, to fall into your hands.
Surely, if ever man can trace Divine interference, it is here.
No, Ursula, inexplicable as the course of events would be to
me, I see God's action in them too plainly to venture on resistance. Never should I *dare*, child, to return the estate to
Gerard. God, in prolonging your child's frail life for those few
minutes, *God himself took it from him*."

Ursula fell back to the door. "And afterwards?" she stammered. "Afterwards?"

"The afterwards is God's. It is only when every soldier
plays general that God's war goes wrong. But, dear girl, you
are young; I am old; we are all, young and old, in His hands."

"Let me go away, father," gasped Ursula, putting out her
hands as if to keep him from her. "It is near midnight. I
must go home. The servants won't understand."

24

He led her to the carriage, out into the night wind again. "Obey orders," he said, softly. "It's so magnificently simple—like Balaclava. Says the private: The general *may* be wrong, but I, if I obey, *must* be right. And our General cannot be wrong." He leaned over the door of the brougham in closing it. "Be of good courage," he whispered. "I have overcome the world."

She caught at his hand and kissed it in the presence of her sleepily staring footman. Then she sank back among the cushions as the brougham rolled away.

"Divine interference," she murmured—"Divine interference. Oh, my God! my God!"

The Dominé stood watching her away into the darkness.

"Ursula and Gerard!" he reflected. "Had Gerard but acted differently! How I wish it could have been! For to human perceptions the estate seems rightfully his. I trust I have entirely forgiven Otto the wrong he did my child!"

He had done so, fully; but a doubt of the fulness was one of his most constant troubles.

CHAPTER XLIV

AFRAID

"URSULA, you look ghastly," said Tante Louisa at breakfast next morning, "and the whole house is full of your gaddings about."

"Ursula," said the Dowager, spilling her egg, "have I told you that Gerard is coming back?"   .

"Yes, she knows," interposed the Freule, hastily. "I can assure you, Ursula, that the servants disapprove."

"The servants!" echoed Ursula, with such immeasurable scorn of the speaker that the latter could not but feel somewhat ashamed.

"No one can afford to brave his servants' opinion," the Freule rejoined, with asperity. "No, not the bravest. Even Cæsar said he was glad to feel sure that all the servants thought well of Copernica. You will find out your mistake too late, if once the servants are against you."

"Everybody is against me," replied Ursula, bitterly.

"Now, Ursula, how unjust that is! I am sure, not to speak of myself, your dear mother here has always shown you the greatest consideration."

"Oh, certainly, and my father, too!" exclaimed Ursula. "I was not thinking of them. And the villagers. And the people at the Hemel. They all love me, too."

"It is for the Helmonts' sake, then," mumbled the Dowager. "They all love the Helmonts."

"They don't love you, and you know it," said Freule van Borck, incisively. "As for me, of course I admire those who dare to confront popular hate. 'Drive over the dogs!' That would be my theory. I envy the woman who had the opportunity of saying it. All I advise is—take care."

"I do," replied Ursula, "of them all, as much as my limited means allow. And this is the way they repay me."

"Ursula, my dear, your charities are all wrong. To give with as much discrimination as you do, you ought to be able to give much more. Only the very rich can afford to give judiciously."

"Aunt Louisa, I believe that is very true," replied Ursula, gravely.

"Of course it is. There are lessons, child, which only a gradual tradition ultimately develops. I am a Radical, of course. That is to say, I am an Imperialist. I believe in the Napoleons of history. But, genius apart, it takes half a dozen fathers and sons before you produce enough collective wisdom to float a family. And I have always declared you were a remarkable woman, Ursula; but I should hardly say of you, as your father-in-law once said of some celebrated artist: 'Heredity? Nonsense! Why, Genius is a whole genealogy.'"

"Did Theodore say that?" cried the Dowager. "Now, I did not remember. But he was always scattering witty things, in bushels, like pearls before swine."

"Thank you," said Louisa, who had not learned in the least to bear with her sister's infirmity.

"I don't mean— Louisa, you must write that down for me. There is nothing that distresses me more than the thought how incomplete my work will be at the best."

"Mynheer van Helmont is asking to see the young Mevrouw," interposed a servant. Ursula rose hastily.

"Take my warning to heart," Aunt Louisa called after her— "about the servants."

"I am not afraid of servants," replied Ursula, disappearing through the door.

"Again!" said the Baroness. "He comes here constantly, and at all hours. It is not yet half-past nine. Louisa, when he marries Ursula, we can go and live on the farm. Ce sera le comble."

"I tell you," replied Louisa, coolly, "that Gerard is going to marry Ursula, and then all will come right."

"And I tell you," echoed the Dowager, with an old woman's

insistence, "that Gerard is going to marry Helena, sooner or later. I have always known it."

" Helena? Helena? Why, she's married already. Really, Cécile, I believe you are going crazy ?"

" I know, I know," replied the Dowager, in great confusion. " But her husband might die. Otto died."

" Pooh !" said Tante Louisa, departing.

The Dowager also beat a hurried retreat. She sat down in her boudoir, and gathered poor grumpy rheumatic old Plush on to her lap.

" They'll find me out," she reflected. " If only I could hold on till Gerard comes." And her chin shook.

" You are come so early," said Ursula to Theodore, " that I suppose your news is especially disagreeable."

" If so, it meets with a fitting welcome," replied her visitor. " But you have guessed right. Ursula, you remember my telling you that the Hemel cottages by the Mill, the worst on the property, must come down, and you said they couldn't ?"

" You said they couldn't," interrupted Ursula. " Who was to pay for rebuilding them ?"

" Well, whoever said it said wrong. They could. They have come down of themselves."

" What ?"

" One of the middle walls has given way during the night, and the three cottages are a wreck."

" Oh, is any one hurt ?" Ursula clinched her hands.

" Only you," answered Helmont, with a sneer—not at her. " All the whole filthy rabble are encamped outside among their household goods swearing at you."

Ursula sat silent for a moment. " They never paid any rent," she said at last.

" No, of course not."

" That is something to be grateful for. Theodore, I cannot help it. You know I cannot help it. Nor could Otto. How could we make good, in our poverty, the result of half a century's profusion and neglect ?"

" I did not say you could help it. And now we shall have

the inspector, and the hovels will have to be put up again somehow. But how ?"

" How ?" repeated Ursula, vaguely. " Never mind. Wait a
little. We shall see."

" Wait !" exclaimed Theodore. " Twenty-four hours ! Have
you no more diamonds ?"

" No. Theodore, I am beginning to feel that I can fight no
longer. I owe it to you that you should receive the first warning. I am going to give up."

He turned on her hotly. " What, frightened already ?" he
cried.

" Frightened ?" she repeated, growing pale. " Why frightened ?" A sudden light seemed to strike her. . " Oh, you mean
because of what they say against me in the village. What do
they say against me in the village, Theodore ?"

" If you know, I needn't tell you," replied Theodore, pale also
under his ruddy glow, unconsciously wondering how much had
reached her.

" They say that I used dishonorable means to secure my husband. There is not a word of truth in it, Theodore."

" I know that," he answered, much relieved. " If I didn't
know that, I should long ago—" He checked himself, as much
from pride as from any gentler feeling.

" Have given it up," she quietly concluded his sentence.
" You are right. I have been making up my mind. I, too,
give over."

" Mynheer Noks is asking to see Mevrouw," said the man-
servant, once more disturbing her, in the same careless, imper-
sonal voice.

Theodore started at the name. " Do nothing in a hurry," he
pleaded—" nothing to-day. As a personal favor to myself. I
have a right to ask that. The villagers will say you are afraid."

" I promise," she answered, " for to-day. I have no right to
refuse you. But I am not afraid of villagers."

A moment later she stood opposite the notary.

" I have brought the deed of deposit, Mevrouw," said that
functionary. " And my witnesses are waiting in the hall. Have
you the document ready ?"

"No," replied Ursula. "My good Notary, I owe you most ample apology, but I cannot help myself. I have been compelled to abandon the idea of making a will."

The notary stared at her for a moment, too angry to speak. He was a rough man by nature, as she had seen, but not devoid of intelligence. At last he burst out, "Then go and — see 'Rigoletto,' Mevrouw, next time you visit at Drum."

Ursula had never been to the opera in her life, Mynheer Mopius's one attempt to take her having failed.

"I do not understand," she said, "but I see you are angry. It is very natural. All I can say is, that I ask your forgiveness. I did not know, when I came to your house last night, that I could not leave my money away from my father."

"But you knew when you left," said the lawyer, surlily.

"True, but I had not had time to reflect. I see now that I must leave things as they are."

"I, too, have had time to reflect, and I have come exactly to the opposite conclusion. You will probably survive the Dominé; you say that you do not intend to marry again; then the best thing you can do is to draw up a will as you intended."

Ursula looked down at the carpet pattern.

"I am an old friend of the Helmont family," continued Mynheer Noks. "I do not deny, Mevrouw, that I was sorry to see this manor pass out of their hands. I should be still more sorry, and so would every one, to find the Mopius family ruling here." He hesitated; then, with an effort, "Mevrouw," he said, "you are, perhaps, the best judge of your own conduct; but, after your visit last night, you will pardon my calling it strange. I don't know whether you came of your own free choice. I don't know what tragedy is being played here. I don't want to know. But something is happening: I can see that." Almost involuntarily he pointed to Ursula's wounded forehead. "All I say is, be careful. You acquired all this property by the merest accident. If any one could have proved that Mynheer Otto lived half an hour longer—there would be no question of any will of yours."

"What do you mean?" exclaimed Ursula. "Do you dare to accuse me—"

"I accuse nobody. I only say be careful. There are strange stories floating in the air, and your strange conduct can only augment them. It only wants an unscrupulous lawyer—"

"I am not afraid of lawyers," said Ursula, standing calm and queenly. "I have humbly begged your forgiveness, Mynheer Noks; I can do no more. This interview is at an end."

She swept to the window, looking out on the lawn, the near cottages, the far-spreading trees.

"I am afraid of myself," she whispered.

Half an hour later the post brought her a letter from Uncle Mopius.

It was a complaining letter, full of the writer's continual ill-health and all his sufferings and disappointments; but it had an unexpected wind-up.

"This year, once in a way," wrote Jacóbus, "I am going to make you a birthday present, that you may be able to keep up the honor of the family in the face of those beggarly Helmonts, who, I hear, are abusing you everywhere. I hope you will use it for *display*. Show the naked braggarts that a wealthy burgher is a better man than they."

The envelope contained a check for two thousand florins.

Ursula stood holding it contemplatively on the palm of her outstretched hand.

"He is wrong about the date," she said to herself. "My birthday is next month—not that any one except father cares. But I will keep the money; it will do to rebuild the cottages."

She wondered if Harriet knew of the gift; she fancied not. In reality it was entirely due to Harriet's influence.

Ursula stood by the writing-table on which lay her dead aunt's faded bit of bead-work: "No Cross, no Crown." She recalled her father's inversion of the words.

"Uncle Mopius has mistaken the date," she said, aloud; "and to-day, of all days in the year, he sends this money. I accept the omen. I will not confess at this moment; I will not give up. No one shall say that my motive was either fear or despair. I will fight them all."

THE rebuilding of the cottages was undertaken without delay, and, chiefly to comply with Mynheer Mopius's injunction, an entertainment was organized by Ursula in honor of her birth-day. It was a feast of the usual kind, in the village school-room, with dissolving views, and still more rapidly dissolving cakes. The whole village criticised the various good things provided, especially the patently didactic slides, and went home replete and grumbling. Furthermore, last year's potato-crop having failed, the village demanded provisions. These also Ursula dis-tributed, especially in the Hemel, as far as the two thousand florins could possibly be made to stretch. Even elasticity has natural limits, and presently dissatisfaction rumbled forth again.

That spring, however, remains memorable in the annals of the Hemel. In April its oldest inhabitant died. He had been break-ing up all through the winter, and his gradual decline had been watched by every man, woman, and child in the place. For, firstly, he was the only one among them who could be described as "pretty well off;" secondly, he was a childish bachelor; and, thirdly, every household in the hamlet laid claim to some form of connection with "Uncle Methuselah," as they called him, though nobody wished him that patriarch's tale of years.

Uncle Methuselah having died intestate on the seventh day of April, every able-bodied adult in the Hemel, not to mention the children, stood outside Notary Noks's little office-door on the morning of the eighth. There was much jostling and jesting, also some affectation of sorrow by those who considered that laughs should be taken in disproof of relationship.

The raggedest of the ragged troop, fat Vrouw Punter, had

actually concealed an onion under her tattered shawl. Her face
was so resolutely jovial that she fancied the lachrymose vegetable might prove useful in her interview with the man of law ;
for she had heard, and devoutly believed, that if you but held
such a thing in your hand, at an emergency, your eyes were certain to overflow. Most of the others poured forth rivers *ad libi-
tum*, scorning artificial assistance.

But Notary Noks put a stop to that. "Come up in succession," he said, "and those who feel bad take a turn outside."

A list was made out of some seventy claimants, and then a
period of darkest anxiety and suspicion began for the Hemel.
Every day, as it slowly wore itself out, deepened the agonizing
conviction that "the judges" were cutting their slices off the
communal cake. "Humpy Jack," who could fluently read words
of three syllables, gave voice to the general sentiment. "A
legacy in the lawyers' hands," he said, "is just like a lump of
ice on a red-hot stove."

Pessimists shook their heads and expressed an opinion that
"nobody would get nothing."

In a fortnight the excitement reached fever-heat. Meanwhile,
numerous members of the community regularly visited—and
called upon—Ursula.

At last, on a beautiful spring day, full of promise and hope,
all the heirs, or their legal representatives, obeyed a summons
to fetch each man his share. Not a soul but was amazed by
the vagaries of "the judges," and annoyed by their rapacity.
The people who received a couple of hundred florins were almost as angry as those who stared down on half a dozen silver
pieces in a grimy palm. Yet surely the queer fractions and
subdivisions should have convinced the unconvincible.

But after the return of the anxiously expected gold-seekers, a
general appeasement settled upon the whole clan. Then followed a brief period of frizzling and frying, of dancing and
shouting, and the children's cheeks were shiny and the parents'
breath was strong. And the voices of the singer and the
swearer were abundantly heard in the land. Then the flame
burned low, like a dying "Catherine-wheel," and fell away.

Seven days after the visit to "the judges" not a penny of Uncle Methuselah's inheritance was left in the Hemel.

On the eighth day several woe-begone faces appeared at the kitchen entrance of the Horst. Not one of these faces, according to information freely vouchsafed, belonged to "a cousin" of the patriarch.

Horstwyk, as always, pulled up its collective nose. "Can anything good come out of the Hemel?" it asked. Besides, Horstwyk had other matters to interest it. Scandal about Ursula had become more general than ever, and to this was soon added the all-engrossing topic of "the Baron's" return. He came back as soon as the chill Dutch summer could feebly be counted on to cherish this hero-son of the soil; he came back, enfolded in wraps and coverings, with the imprint of wearying pain on his white but unchangeably handsome face.

"Your rooms are quite ready at the Manor-house," said Ursula, having gone with the Dowager to greet him on his arrival in Amsterdam. The Dowager could only sit silent with her hand in his; it had been her intention to ask him if really he had been wounded, but she had got sufficient answer before the question could be put.

"Thank you," said Gerard, "I am going to stay a few days with the Trossarts, and I shall be glad to come and see you from Drum. I am thinking of settling down for the present at the Hague."

Ursula bit her under-lip. The Dowager's pale eyes flashed fire. "For the present." Of course. The best legal advice, she supposed, could be obtained at the Hague.

"Gerard," she said, and her eyes grew soft again as she filled them with his presence, "what is the use of letters that only tell half the truth?"

"It is a fair average," he answered, gayly. "Why, even before the introduction of the penny-post man had discovered that the object of speech is to dissemble. A dumb man with expressive eyes would tell all his secrets. And there has been since the creation of the world no greater multiplier of falsehood than the penny-post."

"A man who daren't answer straight is bound to take

refuge in nonsense," replied the Dowager, feeling quite young
and clever again. "I wasn't speaking of the penny-post.
What you say there is so like your father, Gerard. Don't you
remember how he used to declare that the breeding of centuries,
after having come triumphant out of the French Revolution,
had been killed in fifty years' time by the railway and the
penny-post? I have got that down in the Memoir. You remind me so much of your father, Gerard. I must show you
what I have written since you went away."

And then they began talking of many tender memories, and
Ursula left them alone.

Gerard had resolved from the first to avoid anything that
could have the appearance of a home-coming to Horstwyk. This
sentiment Ursula, of course, understood. But there are no
more powerless creatures in the world than its rulers, big or
little. It was a case of the driver driven. For the population
of the whole neighborhood made up its heavy mind to do honor
to "the Hero," as everybody seemed agreed to call him. It
was an excellent opportunity of protesting against Ursula's
government, of glorifying the *ancien régime*, and of saluting the
national flag; also it gave a great many nonentities a notable
chance of displaying their importance : there would be speeches,
and favors, and, best of all, wide-spread good cheer. Once a
committee had been formed and subscriptions gathered, both
Gerard and Ursula saw that resistance would be vain. So they
gave in, separately and simultaneously, each with the best possible grace, and the Lady of the Manor promised flowers and a
collation, and invited the gentry for several miles round. Also
she drove with the Dowager to inspect the triumphal arches in
course of erection at the distant limit of the Commune, on
Horstwyk village square, at the Manor-house gates.

The appointed day dawned white with early heat, rippling
over as the sun rose higher into the color-glories of triumphant
June. The splendor of the cloudless morning lay almost like
an oppression upon the drowsy pastures and the dusty roads.
The washed and smartened crowds by the park gates and near
the church shone visibly with heat and happiness. As always

at the beginning of every public holiday, "the temper of the crowd was excellent:" the local reporter of the *Drum Gazette* remembered that stereotyped phrase without requiring to make a note of it.

The Manor-house carriage with Ursula inside met the train at the market-town station, and, by an irony of fate, she had to drive along the highway seated next to her brother-in-law. It was still stranger, perhaps, that this should be the single occasion on which she appeared since her widowhood, before all the country-side, in the rôle of Lady of the Manor. The "county families"—her cousins by marriage—gathered around her with abundance of malevolent curiosity.

Gerard was very silent and reserved; she saw how distasteful the whole ceremony was to him. He still looked ill, in dark clothing, with his military cross on his breast.

At the first triumphal arch, where a white stone marked the extreme limit of Horstwyk, the simple reception commenced. It had been distinctly arranged that only the returning soldier was to be honored as such. The Burgomaster's welcoming speech, therefore, was all glory and gunpowder, and could hurt no one, not even Ursula, though she might have drawn her own conclusions, had that been necessary, from the silence which had attended her solitary drive to the station. Loud cries of "Long live the Baron!" now resounded on all sides; they broke out afresh as the carriage halted by the church, where the school-children sang a couple of patriotic anthems, and the Dominé, wearing his Cross of the Legion of Honor, held a second discourse. The village band having played a military march, the carriage drove off to the Horst. It was unattended, a sore point with the tenantry, whose proposal to get up a mounted guard of honor had been met by Gerard's unhesitating rebuff.

Everybody he cared about (and a good many other people) had assembled to welcome him on the Manor-house lawn. The Van Trossarts were there, and the Van Troyens; and Helena, a fond though fitful mother, had brought her baby girl. A big luncheon was served in the house for the guests, and another outside for the members of the committee and the numerous village notables. Ursula sat calculating the cost all through her father's toast, which was necessarily rather a repetition of his speech, a glorification of bravery, secular and religious. Nobody could doubt that Gerard was utterly miserable.

Nor could any one ignore the delight of the Dowager. She stood by her son's side, bowed yet beaming, all through the sweltry afternoon. It was her feast-day. She drank in with eagerly upturned countenance the unceasing flow of banal compliments, seeming to derive some personal satisfaction from the clumsy praises of the peasantry. For, after luncheon, while the children's sports were in progress, the returned warrior endured a congratulatory levee. Farmer after farmer came up, red-hot with clumsy good feeling; farmer after farmer remarked:

"Now, Jonker, you've kept up the honor of Horstwyk, say."

Gerard, rousing himself, found a kind word of recognition and interest for each. Ursula, as she watched him from afar, saw on the altered features the old smile.

Once she drew near to him suddenly. "How much you must have suffered!" she said. "I had no idea—I—"

He looked at her gravely.

"Not as much as you," he answered. "I would not have exchanged my fight for yours."

"Gerard, you do not mean that," she said, quickly, avoiding his gaze. "Now that you see the old place again, after all these months, you are glad it is still there, still—ours. You would not willingly now have lost a rood of it. Say so—say so, *now.*"

Her voice grew desperately pleading.

Gerard waited long before he answered. "I am glad it is yours," he said at last, "as you seem to care. I should not care for it to be mine."

She sprang back as if he had stung her. For the rest of the time she remained with Theodore, trying to believe that she did not observe the "county people's" impertinences. She felt Helena's eyes upon her constantly, and was surprised by their benignity. That woman must be a worse woman than Helena Van Troyen who can receive, immutable, a little child from God.

All through the sultry splendor of that long-drawn summer

"THE CARRIAGE HALTED BY THE CHURCH"

day the peasantry enjoyed themselves in their own peculiar manner. Towards five o'clock a slate-colored bank of cloud began slowly to border the far horizon, as if rising to meet the yet lofty sun. One carriage after another emerged from the stables, and the local grandees drove away. Then the people gathered for a final cheer, before melting in groups towards their respective neighborhoods to finish the evening, many of them, alas, in drink.

"Hurrah," cried the Burgomaster, "for the hero of Acheen! Hurrah!"

"And now," said Gerard's clear tones in the ensuing silence, "a cheer for the giver of this whole entertaiment, the Lady of the Manor! Hurrah!"

It was a mistake, but Gerard knew nothing of Ursula's unpopularity. His chivalrous impulse met with but feeble response. A strident voice—one of those voices you hear above the crowd—even cried out, though hesitatingly, "Down with all thieves!" A murmur of approbation from the immediate surrounders saluted the words. Ursula overheard them, and, looking up, saw a pair of villanous eyes fixed evilly on hers. "Who is that man? Do you know?" she said, turning to Theodore.

"That man," he answered, with studied carelessness. "Oh, nobody. A writer that the notary has lately taken on. His name is Skiff."

"Stay to dinner," said Ursula. "We shall be quite a small party. Immediately afterwards Gerard goes back to Drum with the Van Trossarts. I want you to see them to the station."

"Very well. There is a thunder-storm coming up."

"Is there? I don't mind thunder-storms. But this one is several hours off. You will be able to get back in time."

It was about ten o'clock. The great curtain of deepening blue had crept steadily upward, sweeping its broad rim like a mass of cotton-wool across sun and sky, and gradually mingling with night in one unbroken heaviness. The black weight now lay low on the thick, expectant air. The summer evening was pitchy dark and threatening.

Inside the Manor-house everything was once more quiet, with

the numbness that follows on a long day's fatigue. A light glimmered here and there in the big, dim building. In the basement the servants were busy washing up. From time to time a distant yell of drunken merrymaking or sheer animal excitement came faintly ringing through the solemn denseness of the trees.

Ursula sat alone in her room, thinking of many things, especially of Gerard's reply to her question regarding the Horst. On her side that question had assumed the importance of a supreme appeal. How coldly he had pushed it aside!

"I know not what to do," she reflected. "I cannot advance or retreat. Merciful Heaven, how he has suffered! And the suffering has taught him nothing."

The noise from the village beat vaguely against her ear. It was growing louder, coming nearer, but she did not remark it. She looked up as from a trance, when Hephzibah broke, unannounced, into the room.

"Mevrouw, they are coming!" shrieked the waiting-woman, her white face still whiter from terror. "Save yourself! Escape by the terrace!"

"Silence! Keep calm," answered Ursula, long ago accustomed to recognize the poor creature's insanity. "If you can calm yourself, tell me what is wrong."

"There's no time," burst out Hephzibah, "for calmness. They are coming — the people, up the avenue! They swear they will murder you, or burn down the castle! Save yourself! Save yourself! Down by the stables."

Ursula, hearkening, distinguished indeed the fierce roar of an approaching mob.

"Hush!" she said, white to the lips. "Go up-stairs to Freule Louisa. Tell her to reassure the Baroness. . Nothing will happen—do you hear me?—if you all keep calm." She spoke slowly and impressively. "But if there is to be shrieking and screaming, I cannot answer for the consequences."

Then, brushing past the momentarily paralyzed servant, she went out into the entrance hall. Its white pillars shone dimly in the insufficient lamplight, half hidden behind gay patches of flowers. The house had not been decorated for the occasion,

but the stands had been refilled and freshened up, and a floral
" Hail to the Hero!" of the head-gardener's fabrication, still
hung unfaded over the great dining-room door.

The loud menace of the swiftly approaching danger rolled up
with increasing distinctness under the lowering heavens. Ursula could plainly distinguish enthusiasm for the rightful Van
Helmont and denunciation of the usurper. " After all, they are
right," she thought, bitterly ; " they little know how right."
Somehow the reflection seemed to bring her assurance. She
now remembered, without bitterness, all the manifold charities
which the usurper, unlike the rightful lords, had constantly dis-
pensed, as bread from her own mouth, to both deserving and
undeserving poor.

She went out on to the wide steps and stood waiting ; the hot
air struck her pallid face, and the clouds seemed to sink yet
lower.

In another moment the cries all around her struck a yet
crueler blow. A dark mass, yelling and drunken, was surging
vaguely across the blackness of the lawn—the lowest rabble of
the purlieus of Horstwyk, and all the aristocracy of the Hemel.

" Down with the usurper !" " Down with the tyrant !" " We
won't have any thieves in Horstwyk !" " Long live the hero of
Acheen !" " Down with the parson's daughter !" And, cruel-
est of all, " Down with the light o' love !"

For one instant, as those mad words reached her, Ursula
shrank back, and a torrent of crimson swept over her cheeks.
Juffers, the constable, had supplemented Adeline's stories, telling how, even in her early widowhood, Mevrouw had despised
all decorum.

At sight of the single light-robed figure standing there in the
dull radiance from the hall, the shrieking, struggling conglomeration swerved back. There came a lull ; then the wild shouts
went up anew.

" As no Helmont's to have it, let's burn down the house !"
cried a dominating twang, which Ursula recognized. A yell of
approval swelled high around the words. The logic of this
tribute to the family immediately enchanted every one ; and all
the half-grown boys and raw youths in the horde howled with
25

delight at the prospect of so grand a conflagration. The tumult for some time, however, rendered action of any kind impossible. Then followed the inevitable ebb.

"There is no necessity for burning anything," said Ursula, in far-reaching tones; "the house is full of defenceless women. I am here. What do you want?"

Another roar answered her, and, with re-echoing cries of "Burn it!" the mob swayed forward to the steps.

Suddenly the fierce note of fury changed to a shrill surprise. Ursula felt a hand upon her arm. Removing her eyes for the first time from the turmoil in front of her, she saw the little Dowager standing by her side.

"Go in, mamma—go in," she whispered, hurriedly. But the little Dowager did not remove the hand.

"Hurrah for the old Baroness?" screamed a drink-sodden voice. The response was lost in an uproar of terror, as the darkness momentarily vanished, and the whole scene—the massive building, the soaring beeches, the upturned distorted faces, the two figures on the threshold—all stood out white for one brilliant instant before the opening heavens crashed down the full weight of their pent-up derision in torrents of mingling rain and thunder on the wasps' nest beneath them which men call the world.

Mechanically the two women fell back under shelter. The rush of water poured past them like a falling curtain amid the tumult of the elements. The startled and blinded crowd, as flash followed flash, sought an insecure refuge under the great trees of the park, still restrained by that pair of locked and steadfast women from roughly invading "the House." The whole place was wrapped as in a whirlpool of contending fire and water. Vaguely the half-sobered drunkard realized that the young Baroness stood inviolable, girdled by God.

House and park were black and still in a widespread drip and shine of water, when Theodore van Helmont, drenched to the skin, sprang from his flecked and foaming steed and rang softly at a side-door. He ran to the corridor, where Ursula met him, lamp in hand.

"That I should have been too late!" he gasped. "O God! Forgive me, Ursula, that I should have been too late!" The tears sprang forward as he looked at her, and rained down his cheeks.

"Don't," she said. "You hurt me." She had never seen a man shed tears before. "Of course you were too late. How could you help it?"

He mastered himself with an effort. "How pale you are!" he said.

"Well, of course, it is hardly a pleasant experience. It was my own fault for encouraging conviviality. It is over now, Theodore. Be comforted; you could have done nothing had you been here."

"I could at least have died first," he muttered. And he went away without saying good-night.

When Hephzibah had carried the alarm to Freule Louisa, the latter had run screaming to the Dowager.

"And where is Ursula?" the old lady had asked, gasping and trembling.

"Ursula has gone out to meet them, like the mad creature she is. Dear Heaven, we shall all be murdered! Come away with me, Cécile—come away! We can get out at the back and take refuge at the gardener's. Come immediately—come away!"

The Dowager rose, tottering, from her easy-chair.

"I am going to Ursula," she said.

"To Ursula? Oh, mercy! Cécile, have you turned crazy, too? Let her get herself killed if she wants to; what business is it of yours? Oh, Heaven, I'm so frightened, I daren't stay a second longer. Come with me! You surely don't care so remarkably for Ursula?"

"That may be," replied the Dowager, with one foot already on the stair; "but I am going to her now."

CHAPTER XLVI

THE FATAL KNIFE

MYNHEER MOPIUS was slowly dying. He amused himself with playing the part and schooling Harriet, little realizing that her willingness to accept the fiction found its source in her certitude of the fact.

"Harriet has become quite docile," reflected Jacóbus; "she will make an excellent wife for my old age. I had always a gift for managing women. Look at Sarah, my first, whose character was fundamentally selfish. Love, based upon obedience, that is the secret of wedded bliss. But it would never do to let the women know it. When a woman knows a secret there's no secret left to know."

Mynheer Mopius spent much of his time in bed, especially the daytime. At night he would gasp for breath and have to be helped to an easy-chair, and Harriet nursed him, carefully balancing her strength.

"Two invalids are no use to any one," she said, when stipulating for repose in an adjoining apartment.

"My first wife—" began Mopius, but Harriet stopped him.

"That subject's tabooed," she said. "Why, Jacóbus, it is months since you mentioned her. Your first wife died. What would you do if, at this moment, I were to die?"

"Marry again," replied Jacóbus, coughing against his pillows, and looking exceedingly yellow and bilious and unwholesome.

"It takes two to do that," said Harriet, coloring, as she spoke, under the reproach of her own acceptance.

"Does it?" answered Mopius, clinking his medicine-bottles.

"Jacóbus, we have never quarrelled. Don't let us begin now.

There is only one question I should like to ask you without requiring an answer. How many people did you propose to
when left a widower before you got down to me?" She left
the room abruptly, and in the passage she struck her white
hand across her face.

Not very hard.

Jacóbus sat up and adjusted his nightcap. "Ah, you see,
she ran away," he said. "A year ago she'd have braved it out.
I shall still make something of Harriet."

She came back presently with a bundle of papers. It was
part of her daily task to read aloud all the official documents
connected with the government of Drum, which were sent to
the caged Town Councillor. Jacóbus fretted incessantly at the
thought how everything was going wrong.

"The people in the streets look just as usual," said Harriet;
but that consideration afforded her husband no comfort. She
yawned patiently over endless statistics regarding gas and
drains. It was her ignorance which caused her to wonder
whether the town would not have been governed far better without a council, and especially without an official printing-press.

"It is time for my medicine," said Mopius, who, by saying
this five minutes too early, constantly succeeded in suggesting
an omission on Harriet's part. "Well, what says the Burgomaster concerning the market dues? He is a fool, that Burgomaster. And so are the aldermen. Heigho! I wonder what
will become of this poor town when I am gone! It is strange
how greatly I have attached myself to it. Almost as much as
if it had been my birthplace. But I had always 'une nature
attachante.' It is a great mistake."

"Not necessarily," said Harriet.

"Yes, yes. Life is too short: here to-day, gone to-morrow.
Ah, well! Is that idiot going to lower the rent for market
stands?"

"I don't know," said Harriet, wearily, turning over her pile
of documents; "I'll read you the whole lot; you can see for
yourself." And she did read, monotonously, for an hour and a
half, Mopius following everything with eager interest, interrupting, gesticulating, nodding approval or, more frequently, dissent

"Right, right," said Jacóbus, in high good-humor over somebody's opposition to the powers that be in Drum. "Give it
them well. I never approved of knuckling under to grandees.
You gain nothing but kicks by bowing to 'My Lord.' Ah,
they'll miss me when I'm dead, Harriet, and so will you."

"Yes, I shall miss you," replied his wife. "Dear me, Jacóbus,
what shall I do with my time all day?"

"First you will cry," said Jacóbus, with ghastly enjoyment of
a far-off possibility; "and then you will get tired of crying."
He waited a little ruefully for a disclaimer. "And then you
will begin to enjoy your money."

"By-the-bye, that is a subject we have never spoken about
since the marriage settlement," said Harriet, holding one of
the stiff yellow papers against her cheek. "At least, *I* have
never spoken about it. Of course, you tell me twenty times
in a week that you will leave me a lot of money; but that
counts for nothing. I believe you used to say the same
thing to Ursula. Seriously, Jacóbus, have you ever made a
will?"

"I have," said Jacóbus, enjoying his importance.

"I thought people who had been notaries always died intestate. If you had died intestate, Jacóbus, I suppose Ursula
would have had all your money?"

"Ursula and that foolish Josine. Ursula, Baroness van Helmont, of Horstwyk and the Horst. This conversation appears
to me unpleasing, Harriet."

"Unavoidable conversations almost always are." Harriet's
face was entirely hid by the "Report on Sewage." "Has this
will of yours really appointed me your heir?"

Mynheer Mopius fell back and gasped. "Can you not wait a
little longer?" he said—"a very little longer?"

"Jacóbus, I am only repeating what you have told me over
and over again. I want to know, if you please, whether you
have really left your whole fortune to me."

She drew near to the bed.

Mynheer Mopius sat up again, and looked askance at his wife
anxiously. "I'm getting better," he said. "I feel a great deal
better to-day."

" I'm so glad. You look better. And now, Jacóbus, answer my question, on your honor."

" Harriet, I do believe you want me to die. I don't think I shall last much longer; still, don't reckon too much on my speedy demise. I heard the other day of a man who was buried and resuscitated, and lived forty years afterwards."

" Nonsense," replied Harriet, unsympathetically. " If you were buried, I should hardly be asking about your will. Now tell me."

. " What if I don't ?"

Harriet shrugged her handsome shoulders. " I suppose the truth is you have left me nothing," she said, walking away, " and you don't want to avow your life-long lies. One can never trust your boastings. Perhaps there isn't so much to leave."

" You will be a rich woman, Harriet," answered Mynheer Mopius, solemnly, " a very rich woman. Yes, I have left you all, on condition that you never marry again."

" A foolish condition," said Harriet, once more applying the · " Report." " Should the question present itself, I would certainly not be influenced by considerations of that kind."

" Hum !" said Jacóbus. " Well, now I have told you. So let's talk of something else. I wish you would give me my jelly."

She got it for him. " And if I marry, everything goes to Ursula, I suppose," she persisted. " Well, so much the better for Ursula."

A sudden jealousy flashed into his orange-green eyes. " I believe, if I died, you would marry the doctor," he said.

Her face flushed protest ; her heart thumped assent. " You have no right to say that, or anything like it," she cried. " I have been a faithful wife to you, Jacóbus. Keep your dirty money."

Her rising violence always cowed him. " Tut, tut," he, said ; " so I shall. For many a long year, perhaps, and after that you may have it."

" Not on those conditions." She turned away from him altogether. " Make your will over again," she said. " Do you hear me ? And leave your money to Ursula, whose, in fact, it is by right. I am content with my settlement, as I told you at the time. You will remember that I told you to leave your money to Ursula. Money, with me, is not the one thing worth living for and talking about. But I wanted, in honesty, to warn you. You had better send for the lawyer to-night."

"What nonsense!" he cried, angrily. "To hear you talk, one would think I hadn't a week left to live. Is that what the doctor thinks, pray? The wish is father to the thought."

Harriet controlled herself forcibly. She came close to the bed. "You needn't make it to-night," she said, softly. "But you had better make it soon."

About a fortnight later Mynheer Jacóbus Mopius was buried with all the pomp he had himself prescribed. All his virtues and dignities were engraved upon his tombstone, so that his first wife's adjoining one looked very bare by comparison. His last words had been, in a tremulous, squeaky sing-song:

> "If thy dear hand but lift the fatal kni-i-ife,
> I smile, I faint, and bid sweet death 'All hail!'"

CHAPTER XLVII

THE day after the attack on the Manor-house Ursula came down to breakfast as usual.

"Has Monk not been found yet?" she asked.

In the servant's face she read disaster. She had not missed any of the menials in the hour of danger, presuming them to be hidden away under bedsteads up-stairs, but she had been astonished by the prolonged absence of the dog.

"Yes, Monk had been found," said the servant, uneasily.

She cast a quick glance at his shifty eyes; then, without further question, she went down to the basement, straight to the mat where the St. Bernard slept. Monk was lying there, in a great huddled mass of brown and white wool, motionless. Before she had come near she knew he was dead. She stood for a moment by his side. Already the limbs were stiffened, the eyes rolled back. She understood that he had been decoyed the day before, and poisoned.

She knelt down and kissed the soft, white head.

"I used to think I was alone," she said, as she rose.

A maid came towards her.

"Yes, it's a pity, Mevrouw, is it not?" said the maid. "The old Mevrouw sent me to ask you to go to her in her boudoir."

Ursula obeyed the summons. As she entered, the Dowager rose to meet her.

"My dear," said the old lady, trembling very much, "you saved the house last night. I'm afraid I have not always been fair to you. I am old, Ursula; you must forgive an old woman's prejudices. But you are worthy to be a Van Helmont. Your father-in-law would have appreciated your conduct, my dear."

Henceforth there was one recent event on which the Dowager's mind remained perfectly clear. Its fierce terror seemed to have burned it in. Much that had happened since the old Baron's death was a blank or a muddle, but she was always ready to talk of the attack. And she spoke, therefore, with far greater kindness of the heroine.

"Yes, Ursula is strong," assented Tante Louisa.

Presently came the tidings of Uncle Mopius's death, and very soon after that a letter from Harriet. She told Ursula quite frankly that she intended to marry again, as soon as her period of mourning was over, so that there would be no use in first .pretending to ignore the fact. "Therefore," she wrote, "I can only lay claim to the ten thousand * a year of my marriage settlements, and, barring a handsome legacy to Josine, you are your uncle's heiress."

Ursula dropped the letter on her writing-table and sat thinking, till disturbed by one of Theodore's frequent business calls. These unavoidable discussions were rarely agreeable.

"First, I can tell you," he began, "that Juffers has been dismissed."

"Good," replied Ursula. "That is only right. It would be foolish to pity him."

"Secondly, nothing will result, I fear, from the judicial inquiry as regards either the attack on the house or the murder of the dog."

"That, too, is natural. It was a drunken outburst. Still, somebody must have been the deliberate instigator, or the dog would not have lost his life. I am sorry they can't find out who did that."

"I think I know. That new clerk of Noks's has some grudge against you. Would you like Monk's murderer punished, Ursula?"

A responsive flame shot into her eyes. They met Theodore's.

"Oh no," she said, quickly. "No, no. Leave the man alone, Theodore."

"Thirdly — the usual worries. The old refrain, 'Money!

* $4100.

money !' Money wanted for the expenses of Gerard's reception. Money wanted for the completion of the cottages. Money wanted for a new roof on the Red-dyke Farm. If only we had more money, Ursula, all would be well. As it is—"

She interrupted him. " There is money," she said. " I am a rich woman, Theodore."

He smiled an annoyed little smile. " Very funny," he said, " if only—"

" It is quite true."

" Oh," he exclaimed, suddenly understanding. " Has that precious uncle of yours disinherited his wife ?"

She colored angrily. " My uncle's wife is quite able to manage her own affairs," she said. " Be thankful, you, that henceforth there will be money enough and to spare."

" How much do you think ?" he questioned, with a man's curiosity to know the figure.

" Some twenty-five to thirty thousand florins a year, Theodore. We shall be able to carry out all your improvements—all Otto's improvements—all that he used to say he would do if he could —all he could have done if he had married his cousin Helena. And I shall have a chance of trying my charity schemes. We must build an Institute. You must help me, Theodore ; there will be heaps to do. We must do it all—all !" She spoke hurriedly, feverishly, as one who crushes down a tumult in her heart.

Theodore stood looking at her, his face puckered and puzzled. " All the fun of the thing is gone," he said.

" The fun ?"

" Yes, the fun. Can't you understand ? I can't explain. There's nothing more for to-day. Good-morning."

" Theodore, I wonder whether thirty thousand florins will suffice to purchase their affection ?" She paused. " Their armed neutrality," she slowly said.

But when left alone her manner changed. She sank down by the window—looking out, looking out. The other day in her supreme appeal she would have abandoned everything to Gerard on his coming home ; she had hoped against hope.

And what had been his reply? "I am glad you have it, if you like it. I would not have exchanged my struggle for yours." The words came to her now with superficial meaning; long afterwards she learned to fathom their sorrowful compassion.

"It is God's doing," she pleaded, still gazing away upon the landscape, "God's answer. He confided these hundreds of human beings to my care, and now gives me the means to help them. I dare not abandon them to Gerard—to ruin. Right is an abstract idea. It were wrong to do right."

The next two days brought Ursula a strange medley of emotions. Gerard had telegraphed immediately after the riot, offering his services; but she begged him not to come over just yet. She dreaded all contact with him. She dreaded his pale face.

He, on his part, gladly held aloof. He was looking for a small house at the Hague, where he expected his mother to come and live with him. The Dowager meanwhile waited patiently. Gerard had only been back a fortnight. To her it seemed one brief yesterday.

Meanwhile the news of Ursula's accession to wealth filled the province. In one moment the tide turned completely, and the waters of adulation came running from all sides to her feet. Tenants and tradespeople vied with each other in denouncing those who had wronged her. Demands for improvements and repairs poured in hourly; petitioners of all kinds jostled accredited beggars on the Manor-house steps. A rumor had gone forth that the young Baroness really intended to spend her wealth on the property, and when early requests received a hearing, and vague projects got bruited, then enthusiasm knew no bounds. Not more than a week after the attack on the Manor-house Ursula was compelled to exert herself, amid a storm of delation, to prevent both a criminal trial and a lynching of scape-goats by lesser offenders. She would have extended small mercy to the poisoner of her dog had not a story recently reached her ears, after going the round of the neighborhood, to the effect that the notary's new clerk had been found one evening, not far from his home, lying in the road unconscious, with the coat thrashed off his back.

Ursula, a little dazed amid this sudden revulsion, could even
smile at the faces that beamed upon her and serenely decline
the honors of a swift counter-demonstration after the manner of
Gerard's reception. She could make every excuse for the fawn-
ing of those whose daily bread lies in a master's hand, but what
hurt her to the quick was the sudden melting of the " cousins,"
who poured down upon her like icicles suddenly struck by the
beams of a belated sun. They could not understand her shiver-
ing in the bath of their congratulatory condolence. Ursula
pushed the Barons and Baronesses aside.

But the rush of popularity was pleasing, even when correctly
estimated ; the importance was pleasing ; and the possibility of
fulfilment—the sudden nearness of life-long ideals—was most
pleasing of all. It was all so sudden, so unexpected. Ursula,
triumphant, gasped for breath.

One morning, three days after the news reached her, Ursula
rang the bell and sent for Tante Louisa's maid.

" Hephzibah," she said, " if you are so wretched in this house
—and your face proves it—why do you remain ?"

Hephzibah began to whimper.

" Klomp won't have me," she said ; " not unless I bring him
enough money to support me. He can't but just support himself, he says. And Pietje and her child would have to be
boarded out."

" You shall have the money. You can go and tell him so—
that is settled."

But Hephzibah lingered with her apron to her face.

" Forgive me, Mevrouw," she said ; " I never meant no harm
to you—but we're all poor, guilty sinners ; and that woman
Skiff, the insolent liar, pretending to be wife to honest folks,
and then bringing along another husband of her own !"

" You have done me no wrong that I know of," replied
Ursula, calmly ; " but I see you are uncomfortable here, and
I am willing to help you. Do you hear your foolish voices
still ?"

Hephzibah shuddered ; then she said, enigmatically,

" No, I don't. Not *after*— Nevertheless, repentance comes

too late. I'm not as bad as other people, but I'm doomed to
be unhappy; privileged, I should say."

"You can go," said Ursula.

Hephzibah turned by the door.

"Why don't you marry the Jonker?" she began, suddenly;
"I know he loves you. He loved you when he didn't ought to,
and I know he loves you still."

"Peace, woman!" exclaimed Ursula, rising fiercely. "The
Jonker does not love me, nor I him. Go you, and marry your
clod."

A few hours later, as Ursula was sitting alone, thinking—
"Why," asks Freule Louisa, "does Ursula always sit thinking,
since her inheritance came? Is she counting up her money?
Oh, fie!"—as Ursula sat alone thinking, a stone flew suddenly
through her open window, alighting almost at her feet. It had
a paper attached to it, and the paper bore these words:

"Beware of Adeline Skiff and her husband. They will work
your downfall, if they can."

She turned the paper over and over. She had no doubt that
it came from Hephzibah, whom she—and the world generally—
believed to be mildly crazy. She knew that Hephzibah had
suspicions regarding many things, but she also had always
known these to be harmless. Nobody would attach any importance to Hephzibah's mutterings.

Ursula smiled sadly.

The paper lay in her lap. And now, unexpectedly, as she
gazed down, a great fear fell upon her, she could not have told
whence. For the first time she was frightened, afraid of a secret enemy, afraid of discovery, exposure. Who was this man
Skiff, the notary's clerk? What did he know? What could he
do? She started up.

To be forced, against her own will, to surrender! To be compelled to do what she would so gladly have done of her own ac-
cord, if she had but known how! She set her teeth tight.

An hour later, in the early fall of the slow August evening,
Ursula knocked at Skiff's humble door. Adeline opened it, and
immediately tossed her head. "And what may you please to
want of me?" she asked.

"I wish to speak to your husband," replied Ursula.

"Find him, then," said Adeline, and banged the door.

The insult did Ursula good in this hour of universal adulation. It braced her.

She took a few steps down the lonely lane, reflectively, and then remembered the public-house at the end. She wondered she had not thought of it before. She called to a child at play, gave it a penny, and bade it tell Skiff he was wanted at home immediately.

"Wanted at home, you hear!" she cried after it, as she hastily retreated.

The urchin scampered off and burst into the bar-room. "My lady Baroness wants Mynheer Skiff!" he screamed. "She's waiting in the middle of the road."

This bomb-shell, at least, had its desired effect, which a quieter summons from Adeline might easily have missed. Amid general but silent astonishment, and much arching of eyebrows, Skiff started up and stumbled out.

"I wonder he ain't afraid of another beating," said one of the topers.

"He gets drunk so as not to be afraid," replied another.

Ursula's heart almost failed her when she saw the miserable little creature come lurching down the lane. Oh, the humiliation of condescending to such a low hound as this! At this moment, standing awaiting his approach, she touched the lowest depth in all her long descent of suffering.

She had not made up her mind what to do. She had no plan. Only she was resolved, in accordance with her character, immediately to face uncertainty.

He slouched up and jerked his hat, "And what can I do for you, ma'am?" he said.

She sickened at his manner, feeling as if a snail were creeping across her hand. "Answer a simple question," she replied. "What do you want of me?"

He swayed to and fro, passing his hand across his eyes. "I'm a poor man," he said, "a very poor man. A little money never comes amiss."

"Money?" she echoed. "What should I give you money

for? Drink? You will get no black-mail out of me!" Her
gorge rose; she felt her pulse grow steady again.

"Now, ma'am, best be civil," remonstrated Skiff, with tipsy
ferocity. "Black-mail isn't the word, yet there's stories enough
about you to make a little hush-money worth your while. You'd
better pay up, my lady; you'd better pay up!"

"Threats! And to me!" exclaimed Ursula, scornfully. But
at this moment the cottage door was thrown open and Adeline
came running out.

"Don't let her off too easy!" cried Adeline. "Skiff, you
fool, how much did you say? It shall be five thousand florins
if it's a penny, my lady. Or we'll show you up, Baroness Helmont of the Horst!"

With Gerard's return Adeline had grown utterly reckless in
her fierce hatred of Ursula.

"I am glad you speak so plainly," said Ursula, coldly. "In
this manner you will certainly never get a penny out of *me*."

For only answer Adeline poured out a flood of accusation,
sprinkled with foul language, from which Ursula gathered for
the first time what tales had been circulated against her in the
village.

She stood frozen to marble—to marble splashed with mud
that no current of years would ever again remove. "That is
all?" she said at length, when Adeline paused for breath.

"All!" shrieked the woman. "Skiff, d'ye hear my lady?
She don't think it's enough! I wonder what your two lovers
'll say, madam, Theodore and Gerard!"

"Hold your tongue," growled the man, shamefacedly, "or
I'll make you. She has such a temper, my lady, she goes off
her head at times. I hope your nobleness 'll forgive her and
remember I'm a poor man."

Ursula had understood, as the torrent swept down upon her,
that these people knew nothing—absolutely nothing. They
could not hurt her, except by such vague slander as any man
may speak. Her secret was still her own, entirely her own,
shared by none but a half-crazy creature, whose tardy story, if
told, would never carry conviction. And now her set face grew
gentle, and the floodgates of her charity opened.

"'IT SHALL BE FIVE THOUSAND FLORINS IF IT'S A PENNY, MY LADY.'"

"I will arrange for your emigrating to Canada," she said, "if you promise to sign the pledge."

"Oh, I'll sign it, and willingly," answered Skiff. "If I may make so bold, how much would you make it, my lady?"

"That will depend on many things," replied Ursula, and turned to go. "I will have no money wasted."

Adeline stood in the path, looking as if she would fain have struck her successful rival.

Ursula paused.

"You poor thing," she said, "I cannot understand what you have against me. I am in no way responsible for your ruin. Believe me, I did all in my power to persuade Baron van Helmont to make you his wife."

No other words the Baroness could have uttered would have enraged Adeline more than these. The woman stood foaming at the mouth with the hysterical passion of her class.

"You! You!" she sobbed out. "*He* asked me to marry him, do you hear, like the true-hearted gentleman he was! And I threw him over for Skiff! What I said later was a lie, as you know; but I'd have kept up the game if the child hadn't died, as it did last year, more's the pity! And I *could* have been Baroness van Helmont, if I'd chosen. So there! You can take my leavings, madame."

Ursula came a step closer; her face seemed to alter suddenly. "Answer before God," she said; "did Gerard van Helmont offer you marriage before your child was born?"

"Yes, I tell you—yes!" laughed back Adeline, impudently. "There; you didn't expect that, did you? There's pleasant news for my lady so proud! Take Miss Adeline's leavings, do!"

The man, who had stood watching them, stumbled forward.

"Go in, d'ye hear?" he said, roughly, "or I'll give you another taste of yesterday's dinner." He turned to Ursula with a leer he intended for a smile. "You must forgive her, Mevrouw," he said, bowing. "She's a bit fantastical, as I said, but I know how to manage her. I hope that Mevrouw will kindly remember the arrangement she has just made with myself."

CHAPTER XLVIII

A WIFE FOR GERARD

Ursula walked back through the darkening fields. She knew herself now to be safe, yet she hung as one trembling in the recoil from the flash across a sudden abyss. *Supposing* she had discovered that these horrible creatures held her in their power? Would she have flung herself down into degradation unspeakable? She hoped not; she trusted not. Yet the oppression of wrong-doing was upon her, the fatal closing of successive links, the terror of the "might have been."

Then every other reflection died away, and one thought only spread large in falling shadows across the clear blue sky.

How greatly had she wronged Gerard through all the silent years! It was but a single point—this question of Adeline's ruin; it was "no business of Ursula's"—oh, pure sisters of the impure!—yet how deeply had it influenced her womanly heart in all her thoughts of him! She could understand, in her own pride, his haughty shrinking from self-assertion before the bar of her complacency. How many err as he! How few make good their error! She saw things more calmly now than in that ignorant girlhood which seemed to lie so far behind her. Her thoughts dwelt sweetly on the companion of her childhood; his happy, noisy youth, his early manhood, now so steadfast in its slow endurance. And her strong eyes grew dim beneath the dying day.

On the steps of the Manor-house a gay party were assembled, laughing and talking, in a bouquet of bright dresses. Helena van Troyen ran forward to meet her.

"We have been waiting to see you," she cried. "I have brought Toddlums — the baby — and also some one I knew would interest you all—Gerard's Colonel from Acheen."

"How delighted mamma will have been!" said Ursula, a little hypocritically, as she advanced to be introduced to a tall gentleman, all brick-dust and mustache.

"Colonel Vuurmont's descriptions of Gerard's bravery are too charmingly thrilling," said Helena. "Dear Gerard! And so romantic! Tell Mevrouw van Helmont, Colonel, about that bit of brown glove."

"Mevrouw, Mevrouw, that is a kind of a sort of a secret," expostulated the Colonel, looking slightly bored.

"A secret! when half a dozen men saw it produced, and all Kotta Radja knew and teased him about it afterwards! Nonsense! Ursula, you must know that when Gerard was so terribly wounded—terribly wounded, it appears, and in four different places—they found an old brown kid glove on his breast. Isn't that delicious? I had *hoped* the glove was mine, but Gerard says it wasn't. There, nurse has let Toddlums upset herself again. Come, Ursula; I can't bear to hear the child scream like that."

The two men remained on the steps. "You must know, Van Troyen," said the Colonel, "that Helmont maintains there is no love-story connected with that glove at all; only it would be a pity to spoil your wife's amusement. He says that the glove saved his life in a duel, through his adversary slipping on it, and that he wore it as a kind of talisman."

"I certainly remember about a duel," replied Willie, "with a foreign officer, who had said, I believe, that Dutch soldiers were wanting in courage."

"Helmont was just the right man to say that to," remarked the Colonel, quietly.

"Ursula, I have got a wife for Gerard at last," said Helena, fondling her baby. "On the whole, I think, she is suitable, though it has cost me a lot of trouble to admit it. But I am growing old, and have a baby, and one learns to see things differently. I have talked to him about it all, and I think he understands."

"Really!" replied Ursula, much interested in Toddlums.

"But men are so contrary! He pretends that he is going to live in the Hague with his mother, and never marry. Gerard

never marry! 'Ah, quel dommage d'un si bel homme!' I
have explained all about it to aunt. She is rather exacting, but,
on the whole, I believe she agrees with me."

" Has this young lady means of her own ?" asked Ursula.

" Fie! what a question! The very last I should have expected from you! Yes, the lady has means of her own. She
has recently come into a fortune. They will be able to live in
some style, as the Baron and Baroness van Helmont should."

" And you think Gerard consents ?"

" Oh yes, I feel sure he will. To begin with, he says he
won't, which is always a very good sign. And then there are
others. I suppose you have no idea who the lady is ?"

Helena looked up sharply, with petulant good-will, into
Ursula's grave face.

" I ? No ; how should I tell ? Do I know her ?"

" Oh yes, better than I ever did. But, really, we must be
going ; we have missed our train as it is. I was so anxious to
tell you about this coming marriage of Gerard's, and to express
my admiration of your bravery last week, that, for the first time
since her birth, I have neglected Toddlums. Colonel Vuurmont
admires you awfully, Ursula. He says he wishes he had had
you out in Acheen."

" He had Gerard," replied Ursula, simply.

That evening the young Baroness's " family circle " gathered,
as usual, round the shaded lamp. Ursula tried hard to bestow
due attention on Tante Louisa's prattle ; the Dowager had sunk
to sleep over a bundle of letters which she had been laboriously
sorting, first according to their writers, and then, all over again,
according to their dates.

The month's *Victory* lay spread out before Tante Louisa, who
was holding forth in Batavo-Carlylese.

" Napoleon was the world's ruler by right of power," said
Louisa. " Kings are they who can rule. An hereditary king is
a puppet."

" But the other day you sang the praises of heredity," suggested Ursula, politely.

" Did I ? Well, that also was consistent. We praise things

for the good in them; we blame for the bad. There is nothing so consistent as inconsistency."

A tap at the terrace-window awoke the Dowager. The Dominé stood outside with Josine. Ursula started up in delight, for her father's visits were of the rarest.

The Freule immediately took possession of the pastor, while Josine considerately settled down by the Dowager to tell her of recent successes gained by Sympathetico in arresting mental decline.

"I disagree utterly," broke out the Dominé, as soon as he had heard a few words of Louisa's jargon. "The world is not ruled by human strength, forsooth! but by the power of God. In big things and little, it is we who make trouble by not marching straight. If only we would do the moment's duty, leaving the responsibility to the Commander-in chief! To do a great right, do a little wrong!" exclaimed the Dominé, spluttering in his energy. "It is the worst lie ever invented! It is the curse of a little evil conscientiously done that wrong must breed wrong forever. Satan himself is nearer than a Jesuit to the kingdom of God!"

Suddenly Ursula looked up from her work. "Is that not putting it rather strongly, papa?" she said.

"It is the simplest of Christ's teachings," cried the excited Dominé. "It is the deepest conviction of my heart. Never was good got out of a false start! To deny that is the confusion of all distinctions—the death of all discipline. Ursula, would you make of the Lord's army a company of free-shooters? Right is right; wrong is wrong; shout it out upon the house-tops! If you don't know, for the moment, *what* is right, ask God to help you. *When* you know, do it. That is all philosophy and all religion. Sufficient for the day is the duty thereof!"

He had got up, pacing the room with rapid stride, and waving his empty sleeve.

"I'm excited, ladies," he said, wiping his forehead. "This afternoon I heard the dying confession of a man who has ruined his whole life and his brother's by a generous lie told in his youth. It is not to remain a secret; I will tell the story to you some day. Well, Mevrouw, that is a pretty child of Helena van Troyen's!"

"Captain, listen." Ursula followed her father out on to the terrace after he had taken leave. "Do you really mean it all?"

He did not ask what she alluded to, but answered straight: "From the bottom of my heart. You know I mean it. Remember our talk about Gerard. And you, too, mean it. Did you not go down last week, like a soldier's daughter, to face the mob!"

"Papa—" began Ursula.

"Why are the Helmonts going away?" asked Josine's voice behind her. "I shall miss Theodore's mother very much. She is a good, plain, sensible body, and not above taking judicious advice."

"Going away? How do you mean?" asked Ursula.

"Yes, going away. Don't you know? How odd! She told me that Theodore had come in this afternoon, after having met the Van Troyens, and had said in his disagreeable way (though she didn't call it that, but I think him very disagreeable), 'Mother, our work here is done; we are going back to Bois-le-Duc.' She couldn't get anything more out of him. He went away and banged the door. So selfish."

"Josine!" called the Dominé on ahead.

"Coming! coming, Roderigue. How odd, Ursula, that you didn't know that!"

Ursula stood looking after her father's vanished figure. "To-morrow I shall tell him," she said.

CHAPTER XLIX

SHE stood on the terrace, amid the gloom of the placid, moonless night. The great house gleamed dully white behind her, and the wealth of foliage that embowered it stretched in black masses beyond.

"It is the end," she said, clutching at the flimsy folds about her throat. "What a pitiful little end it is!"

Fronting the facts calmly, as was her manner, she knew everything she had striven for to be now fully in her power. At last every enemy was silenced, every danger averted; with the money just inherited she could begin her great work of regenerative charity; in fulfilling her dead husband's ideals she could accomplish her own.

Had she desired greatness for herself, now was the moment to grasp it firmly as it lay in her hand. "No, I have not desired it for myself," she said aloud.

She had done her evil deed for Otto's sake, for the sake of all these Helmonts. She had done it with the desperate self-persuasion that the wrong she was committing was better than all right. She had taught herself fiercely to believe it so, strengthened again and again in the teeth of growing conviction, by Gerard's recklessness, by Otto's dying entreaty, by her own invigorating failures, dangers, sudden deliverances. She had struggled to believe that God Himself was helping her in this self-appointed mission—the saving of Horstwyk and all its dependencies under her righteous rule.

She knew now that the truth was otherwise. She had known it long, with a gathering clearness that broke in sunlight through the fogs of her own calling up; but now, in the sudden hush of the contest, the falling away of all adverse winds to dead calm, she saw God's reality of right as she had not beheld it before. Right is right. Little wrongs do not bring forth great blessings. Her father, in his simplicity, spoke true.

She herself—what had she called up in the hearts of these people around her, by the sense of the great wrong done to Gerard, but a foolish, fruitless hate, to be bought off now by the vilest of all persuaders—gold? She loathed—suddenly—this filthy popularity she had thought pleasant for the moment. Better, a thousand times better, the frank rebellion against her stern and sterile righteousness, better than *this*. And for her own heart—she knew that her sin had brought her own heart no profit. Far from it. With loathing she remembered Hephzibah and Adeline and Skiff, and all the possibilities of shame. Oh, her father was right, a thousand times. The outcome of evil is evil, the outcome of sin is sin.

She had been resolved ever since the day of Gerard's return to Horstwyk, though she was not aware of her own resolve, to give up the Manor to its rightful lord. Resolved to do it, come what may, leaving the further development of events to Him whose the end will most certainly be if only the beginning be His.

She would have done it at all costs, but now God, in His mercy, made the duty yet plainer. The moment was come to which she had ever looked forward, when the Manor would be safe in Gerard's hands. He was about to unite himself in marriage to some wealthy woman. He would be able, as Helena had unwittingly pointed out, to fulfil the duties of his position.

So far, so good. She could reason calmly; she could even face the shame of her confession. She could see herself pointed at, hooted by all. She would be punished, she supposed, when the crime got abroad. Even if the Van Helmonts were merciful—as why should they be?—Government punished such criminals as she. She would be sentenced, in open court, to a long period of solitary confinement or of penal servitude—she did not know which—as a common convict. That was inevitable. She stopped for one moment in her rapid walk along the terrace. Pooh, she had judged that issue so many times already!

When a citizen commits a crime, the State must attempt to check him. The State punishes crime, and God punishes sin. The two have but little in common. So far, so good.

But now! now! She pressed both hands to her forehead, staring out wildly into the darkness. She loved Gerard. She knew that she loved him. She loved him since his return ; but Adeline's confession had opened the floodgates of her heart's admiration for the man she had wronged. She was one of those women who fancy there can be no love without respect; she had taught her own soul that early lesson. But now she knew that she loved him. She had honored Otto and dutifully admired him, but this—now at last she recognized it—was love. She loved his manliness, his uprightness, his chivalry ; the pale face she herself had discolored, the form she had wounded, the glory her guilt had called forth. Aye, she even loved the memory of youthful errors courageously atoned for.

God punishes sin. Perhaps, if she had let all things take their natural course, Gerard might in due time have made her his wife. However that be, now, at any rate, nothing need have kept them apart. For she knew that Gerard also loved her, in spite of this unwilling marriage to which his womankind were pressing him. And between her and him arose up, for all eternity, the shadow of her crime. She herself must speak the word, crushing down his righteous love into a pool of scorn.

She sank by the parapet, with her face on the stone, and then nothing disturbed the breathless silence but one sudden, suddenly arrested moan.

When Ursula came down next morning there were circles under her eyes. Yet she had slept peacefully enough towards dawn. It must have been the merest accident that Aunt Louisa noticed—for the first time, she declared—some faint suggestion of gray about her niece's brown ripple of hair.

"I am going to town on business," said Ursula, "so I shall want the carriage, if you please."

"Dear me, how annoying!" exclaimed Tante Louisa. "I had been wanting to drive across to Mevrouw Noks, and arrange about Tryphena. You're sure you couldn't select another day?"

"Quite sure," answered Ursula, cutting bread. "It is business which can't be put off."

"Well, that's very provoking. But if you're going to town you must bring me some floss-silk from the Berlin-wool shop."

"I am going to the Hague," answered Ursula.

"The Hague? Oh, you're sure to be able to match it there. I must give you a bit to take with you." Tante Louisa felt aggrieved, for did she not pay her "pension"?

Ursula, alone in her compartment between Horstwyk and Drum, could not but reflect on her first railway journey with Gerard. "The great of this earth are above the common law." She smiled bitterly at the thought of the error. There may be two social laws for high and humble; there may be even two civic laws for rich and poor—there are no two laws of right and wrong with the Judge of all the Earth.

But at Drum acquaintances got in, and she had to talk of the weather. She said it was very fine, though a little too warm. It was a pity, she said, that the days were growing so short already.

Arrived at the Hague, she thought she had better begin by hunting for Aunt Louisa's silk. She tried several shops without success. At last she found herself compelled regretfully to desist.

She hailed a passing tram-car, which took her to Gerard's lodgings. As she lifted an unfaltering hand to the bell the door was suddenly drawn back, and Gerard himself appeared, coming out. Both of them started aside for the moment.

"You here?" exclaimed the Baron. "We very nearly missed each other. I had no idea you were coming."

"Nor had I," she replied, "till I came. I want to speak to you, Gerard."

"Yes," he assented, without inviting her to enter. "Can I walk on with you? I am due at the Ministry in half an hour. You have connections, if I remember right, in the Hague?"

"I was coming to you," she answered. "Let me go into your room for a moment. I shall not keep you."

Reluctantly he led the way.

The thud of the closing door crashed down upon her heart; in the sudden stillness and shutting-out she realized that the crisis was come: her courage sank. And while leaning against some unnoticed support she was angry with the pride within her which could not as much as ask for a glass of water. The room swam past her eyes in a swift recognition of many familiar objects — mementos of her child-life with the owner— among a recent glitter of gaudy trophies and gleaming swords. As he threw back his coat she noticed, with dull indifference, that he was dressed for some Ministerial mid-day reception. Somehow she connected this fact with his life in society, his search for a suitable wife. She sank into a large arm-chair, shielding her brow for one instant with both hands.

Gerard waited, standing by his writing-table. The room seemed very subdued after the glare of the noisy street.

Presently she lifted her still white face—as a vessel might right herself, suddenly becalmed.   •

"Gerard," she said, "I have come to tell you something I have long been wanting to tell you; but I didn't tell you, and that makes it all the worse. I have wronged you very cruelly."

She rose and remained standing before his stern attitude, grown suddenly rigid, his crossed arms, and relentlessly downcast gaze.

"I am not come to ask forgiveness," she went on, hurriedly. "I am come to make confession and then to leave you. There is nothing to be done but to confess. Gerard, when Otto died, and Baby, it all depended, you remember, upon the question who died first. I said that it was Otto who died, and I inherited the property from Baby."

She paused with a gasp. He neither spoke nor moved.

"It was Baby who died before Otto, Gerard, and you were Otto's heir."

A faint flush crept over Gerard's firm-set cheeks. It was the only proof that he had understood.

"That is all I have to say," she went on, in the silence closing round her. "But I wanted to say it to you first before repeating it to strangers."

Then, suddenly, amid that deepening stillness, she felt that she must get away, must escape, and she hurried towards the door.

"Ursula!" said Gerard's voice behind her, quite gently.

She turned; he had lifted his eyes, and his steadfast gaze met hers.

"Have you really nothing to say?" he continued. "No explanation? No extenuation of such conduct? *No* excuse?"

She drew herself up. "What would be the use of all that?" she answered, coldly. "Who listens to a criminal's perversions? I have told you now, and you know."

"I knew before," he said.

When the words had struck her ear, an instant of expectation intervened. Then she caught at the wall beside her, saw him, as she did so, check a futile impulse to spring forward, and once more stood outwardly calm.

"I learned the news some weeks ago," he continued. "On the night before the battle, as it happened. I got a letter from —some one who knew."

"From Hephzibah," said Ursula. "But then — when you came back—why—"

"When I came back I told her to await my good pleasure. I myself was waiting for this moment, Ursula. God only knows *how* I have waited for it, hoped for it—" He broke off.

"Then be thankful it has come," she answered, in the bitterness of her righteous abandonment.

"Yes, it has come. And now there is nothing else to say?"

"No, there is nothing else to say."

She fancied she caught a strange flicker in his firmly fixed eyes.

"And of what use will the Manor-house be to a poor beggar like myself?" he went on. "You had much better have kept it—you, who are rich."

She flushed scarlet under the taunt.

"May I go?" she asked, almost meekly, under the pain at her heart. "You will do what you like with the Manor. Perhaps you will sell it. Though Helena van Troyen tells me you are going to marry a rich wife of her choosing—and your own."

"Did Helena van Troyen tell you that?" he asked, uncrossing

" ' I AM COME TO MAKE CONFESSION AND THEN TO LEAVE YOU ' "

his arms, and the brightness of his nature seemed to come flowing back from all sides.

"Yes; but do not be afraid. She mentioned no names. Besides, it is no business of mine. I do not know whom she means."

"I am sorry it is no business of yours," replied Gerard, coming boldly forward, "for, Ursula, she means yourself."

"She—she—" stammered Ursula.

"And so do I." Very quietly he put his arm around her, and drew down the tired head upon his breast. "We have both of us suffered quite enough," he said.

The tears came swelling across her eyes.

"Through my fault," she whispered—"my fault."

"Let *me* find the criminal's extenuations, Ursula. Do you really think, you poor, noble creature, that I do not understand?"

"I must confess to my father," she continued, in the same tremulous whisper. "To my father and the world."

"To your father, if you will. But the world has not been injured by anything you have done, and you owe it no reparation. It is not our function to supply the world with the empty scandals it delights in. Suffering is a holy but a very awful thing. We will have no more superfluous suffering, Ursula."

"It shall all be as you wish," she humbly answered, her head at rest upon his shoulder. She closed her eyes. "Gerard, I am not afraid of them. I was never afraid of them. But from the very first, I think, I was afraid of God."

"God be thanked for it!" said Gerard, softly. And a flood of sunlight, falling leisurely around them, lighted into sudden brilliance the cross upon his breast.

THE END